EUROPE

ASIA

Ainu

Vasilika

AFRICA

Ifugao

Ibo

Nuer

le

Ashanti

Tiv

Azande

Banyoro

Kapauku

Manu

Yoruba

Arapesh

Mbuti

Alorese

Tiwi

Trobriand

Yir Yoront

Barotse

INDIAN

Bushman

Swazi

OCEAN

Arunta

AUSTRALIA

Cultural anthropology

Holt, Rinehart and Winston, Inc.

New York
Chicago • San Francisco
Atlanta • Dallas
Montreal • Toronto

Cultural anthropology

William A. Haviland
University of Vermont

A Leogryph Book

Design: **Ladislav Svatos/Graphicon, Ltd.**
Line art: **Vantage Art, Inc.**
Photo editing: **Robert Morton**
Cover photos: **Claudia Andujar/Rapho Guillumette**
              Roland and Sabrina Michaud/Rapho Guillumette

Contents

Contents

Chapter 5   Personality and culture   108

Contents

Contents

Contents   xvii

Contents   xix

Preface

Purpose of the book

This text is designed for introductory anthropology courses at the college level. It focuses primarily on cultural anthropology, presenting the key concepts and terminology of that branch of the discipline, but also includes chapters on physical anthropology and linguistics.

The aim of the text is to give the student a thorough introduction to the principles and processes of cultural anthropology. Because there are many ways to teach anthropology effectively and because anthropologists in general are a pragmatic group, willing to draw on any theoretical approach that offers insights into human behavior, the text draws from the research and ideas of a number of schools of anthropological thought. Therefore, the student will be exposed to a mix of such approaches as evolutionism, historical particularism, diffusionism, functionalism, French structuralism, structural functionalism, and others.

Each author has his own ideas about the way a textbook should be written and how the material should be presented. Some prefer to present only the most basic information about the subject with a minimum of graphic material and student aids. Such a design, it is felt, allows the teacher great latitude in the classroom: it is up to him to fill in the details and enrich the text with examples and other explanatory materials. Other authors think the best texts are those that attract the student's attention with extensive, lavish photographs and other graphics, study questions, projects, sample tests, and the like. Each of these methods has its merits. However, this text takes an eclectic approach, choosing the best from both methods. The book attempts to evoke a maximum of student understanding by presenting anthropology as interestingly as possible: clarity of expression in defining ideas and concepts; an orderly presentation of material; abundant colorful examples to illustrate concepts; numerous photographs and other graphic material including six full-color portfolios;

suggested annotated reading lists and up-to-date original studies at the end of each chapter; a glossary; and a comprehensive bibliography with 500 entries.

Advantages

In addition to thoroughly covering the basics of cultural anthropology, the text also recognizes the fact that anthropology is the most human of the social sciences, examining through participant observation the intimate details of the daily lives of people in small-scale societies. To give the student some of the flavor of the close relationship that prevails between the anthropologist and the people he studies, the text includes at the end of each chapter an Original Study excerpted from the fieldwork of some eminent practicing anthropologist. Moreover, the study presents the most interesting part of the work from which it was drawn, thus functioning as a stimulus to learning, indirectly inducing the student to consult the original work for further reading. For example, at the end of Chapter 1 is an Original Study extracted from *The Mountain People* by Colin Turnbull, who explains what it is like to be an anthropologist by discussing in vivid detail some of the unique experiences encountered by him in the field.

Another advantage of this text is that each chapter has been developed as a self-contained unit of study. This method of organization facilitates student comprehension and gives the teacher greater freedom, enabling him to assign readings from the text in accordance with his own particular pedagogical method and sequence of presenting the material. Finally, each chapter itself has been organized into easily digestible segments by the liberal use of sub-heads, numbered entries, and other dividing techniques.

Organization of the book

The book has been divided into five parts.

Part 1 **The study of culture,** introduces the concept of culture, discusses its role in anthropology, and its history. Chapter 1 defines culture, its characteristics, and processes; Chapter 2 is a history of the development of the discipline; and Chapter 3 describes the role of culture in human evolution.

Part 2 **Culture and man,** covers the way man communicates, behaves, and lives in groups. Chapter 4 examines language, the vehicle by which culture is transmitted, and thus introduces linguistics as a sub-division of anthropology; Chapter 5 raises the question of the relationship between culture and personality, thus introducing the student to psychological anthropology; and Chapter 6 discusses patterns of subsistence, analyzing the ways small-scale societies successfully adapt to the environment through culture.

Part 3   **The formation of groups,** deals with the ways culture brings about the organization of groups, which themselves are necessary for the cooperative behavior on which human life depends. Chapter 7 describes marriage and the family, Chapter 8 looks at kinship and descent, and Chapter 9 analyzes other forms of social organization necessary for group living.

Part 4   **Social integration,** deals with the things groups do, and the ways different groups are integrated into larger social units. Chapters 10 through 12 describe economics, politics, and other kinds of social controls. Other chapters examine the integrative roles of religion and art.

Part 5   **Change and the future,** treats the ways cultures change, and how change may affect future social life. Chapter 15 looks at the dynamics of culture change, and Chapter 16 concludes the text with some speculations on the future of man from an anthropological viewpoint.

Outstanding features of the book

1. Readability

The purpose of a textbook is to transmit and register ideas and information, to induce the readers to see old things in new ways and to think about what they see. A book may be the most elegantly written, most handsomely designed, most lavishly illustrated text available on the subject, but if it is not interesting, clear, and comprehensible to the student, it is valueless as a teaching tool.

To aid readability, this text is carefully structured, each section within the book and each chapter within each section organized so that the material is presented to the student in segments, each clearly separated from the other. It is easier for the student to grasp and retain the material if it is presented as a series of discrete "quanta," rather than as a continuous flow of information.

The readability of the text is also enhanced by the writing style. The book is designed to present even the most difficult concepts in prose that is alive, energetic, and easy to retain. Where technical terms have been necessary, they are always italicized, carefully defined in the text, and defined again in the glossary in simple, clear language.

Because much learning is based on analogy, numerous and colorful examples have been utilized to illustrate, emphasize, and clarify anthropological concepts. Wherever possible, there is a cross-cultural perspective, comparing cultural practices in other societies with those of the student's own culture. Many educators feel that this practice makes ideas easier to grasp because it renders them more familiar. For example, in the chapter on sex and marriage, the marriage system and sex roles practiced in our own country are compared with those practiced by non-Western peoples. Additionally, the text points out how the communes organized by the disenchanted young of this country are really attempts to recreate the kinship networks found in small-scale societies. Thus, from such examples, the student can perceive the nature of a cultural entity, such as marriage; he can also see its varieties, its processes, and the way it relates to his own culture and existence.

2. Original studies

A special feature of this text is the Original Study that follows each chapter. These studies, which consist of selections from case studies and other original works of anthropologists, are the actual writings of men and women working in anthropology today. Each study is integrally related to the material in the chapter it follows, and often sheds additional light on some important anthropological concept or subject area found in the chapter.

The idea behind this feature grew from an appreciation of the fact that anthropology does not operate in a vacuum: it is a fast-developing discipline that studies new societies and examines old ones from new points of view. Consequently, new ideas and models of social interaction are generated each year by practicing anthropologists. The studies represent an attempt to keep the student abreast of current research in the field, and enable him to experience almost first-hand some of the excitement generated by new anthropological ideas and discoveries.

Moreover, the new feature is most suitable for anthropology because it is difficult for the student to learn and develop an interest in the subject without some feel for what a real small-scale society is like, and how anthropologists actually go about studying it. Thus, at the end of Chapter 10, which covers economic systems, there is an Original Study by Robert and Evelyn Rohner which describes the events that take place during a Kwakiutl potlatch. Other Original Studies include details of the Nambikwara family life by Claude Levi-Strauss, following Chapter 7; an examination of Peublo kinship by Edward Dozier, following Chapter 8; and an analysis of the role of the shaman among the reindeer herders and fishermen of northeast Asia by William Howells, following Chapter 13.

3. Illustrations

Sociologists, anthropologists, and other social scientists have discovered that, under the influence of television, visual material is gaining increased importance as a teaching tool in today's classroom. Accordingly, this text uses numerous illustrations and other graphic materials. The illustrations have been chosen to supplement and emphasize the text and to clarify for the student concepts that are not easily rendered into words. A number of the illustrations are unusual in that they are not the "standard" anthropological textbook photographs; each has been chosen because it complements the text in some distinctive way. For example, the photos on pages 250–251 depict several market scenes that display various cultures' approaches to trade. The line drawings, maps, charts, and tables were selected especially for their usefulness in illustrating, emphasizing, or clarifying certain anthropological concepts and should prove valuable teaching aids.

The six full-color portfolios, designed to stimulate the student's eye and mind, encompass the prehistoric megaliths of Europe, ancient art of the old world, art of the Precolumbian New World, the culture of the Persian Nomads, the world of the Eskimo hunter-gatherer, and the American Indian. Each portfolio has a definite theme and includes a text that explains the illustrations and makes some important anthropological point. For example, the portfolio on the American Indian contains, in paintings by European and American artists and in the words of a Seneca Indian chief, a capsule history of the cultural contact between the Indians and the white man.

4. Summaries and Suggested readings

At the end of each chapter is a summary containing the kernels of the most important ideas presented in the chapter. The summaries, which are numbered and so broken down into easy-to-cope-with units, provide handy reviews for the student. Also following each chapter is a list of suggested readings which will supply the inquisitive student with further information about specific anthropological points which may interest him. Each reading is fully annotated and provides information as to the content, value, and readability of the book. The books suggested are oriented either toward the general reader or toward the interested student who wishes to explore further the more technical aspects of some material.

5. Glossary and Bibliography

An extensive glossary at the end of the book provides the student with a complete anthropological dictionary in miniature. The glossary defines all the important terms used in the text, in clear, understandable language. The bibliography at the end of the book is a complete reference tool in itself; it contains a listing of 500 books, monographs, and articles from scholarly journals and popular magazines.

6. Supplement

Teachers will find the accompanying Instructor's Manual helpful in arranging their curricula. The Manual contains suggestions on topics for class discussions, subjects for student term papers, and sample questions for objective and essay-type examinations.

Acknowledgments

So far as acknowledgments are concerned, I owe a large debt to those anthropologists under whom I was privileged to study at the University of Pennsylvania: Robbins Burling, William R. Coe, Carleton S. Coon, Loren Eiseley, Robert Ehrich, J. Louis Giddings, Ward H. Goodenough, A. Irving Hallowell, Alfred V. Kidder II, Wilton M. Krogman, Froelich Rainey, Ruben Reina, and Linton Saterthwaite. They may not always recognize the final product, but they all contributed to it in important ways.

I also owe a debt to a number of anthropologists with whom I have worked, discussed research interests, or the field in general. Particularly influential here have been Warren W. Caldwell, Ann Chowning, Lucian and Jane Hanks, Frederica de Laguna, Evon Z. Vogt, and Gordon R. Willey.

And I owe a debt to my colleagues at the University of Vermont: Louise Basa, Paul J. Magnarella, William E. Mitchell, Stephen and Carroll Pastner, and A. Peter Woolfson. They all, at one time or another, helped me with specific problems connected with this book. Neither they, nor any of the other anthropologists mentioned here, should be held responsible for any defects in this book.

I also wish to acknowledge my debt to a number of nonanthropologists who helped with this book. To begin, David Boynton of Holt, Rinehart and Winston talked me into this project, and I have valued his friendly advice on a number of matters. I have also profited from his broad knowledge of anthropology and anthropologists. Caroline Latham, and all the people at Latham Publishing Enterprises, helped immensely with research, writing, and selection of illustrations.

The greatest debt of all is owed my wife and children, for having put up with my preoccupation with this book for the past several months.

Cultural
anthropology

portfolio one

Art as cultural anthropology

Cultural anthropology studies the social and cultural beliefs and practices of peoples of diverse ethnic backgrounds, particularly small-scale or non-Western societies. The anthropologist analyzes the social institutions that underlie various societies, noting the similarities and the differences, and attempts to arrive at generalizations about human society as a whole. Thus, he studies the ways the family and kinship systems operate, as well as the political, economic, and religious systems of different cultures. One of the most significant aspects of a culture is its art, the way its members shape and interpret their natural environment through architecture, sculpture, painting, jewelry, pottery, music, dance, and folk tales. Often the artistic expressions of a small-scale people tell the investigator much more about the culture than do the people themselves, because artistic artifacts and acts embody important religious and social ideals.

Archeologists have been able to reconstruct the cultures of the various high civilizations of the New World partly by examining their art, which was produced in Pre-Columbian America from Northern Mexico to the high Andes of Peru. Some examples of this magnificent art are illustrated here. Archeologists have discovered in these artifacts a native art of high cultivation, great craftsmanship, and deep emotive power that had flourished for over three thousand years.

Tragically, much Pre-Columbian art was destroyed because it was made of gold, turquoise, or jade. Countless thousands of beautiful objects were melted down to replenish the dwindling treasury of Charles V, or broken up to decorate the jewelry of the court.

Head of warrior wearing jaguar headdress; Las Remojadas Style.
From the American Museum of Natural History.

Wooden mask with jade; Olmec Style.
From the American Museum of Natural History.
Jade effigy axe (the "Kunz" axe); Olmec Style.
From the American Museum of Natural History.

The cache of La Venta; Olmec Style.
From the National Museum of Anthropology, Mexico City.

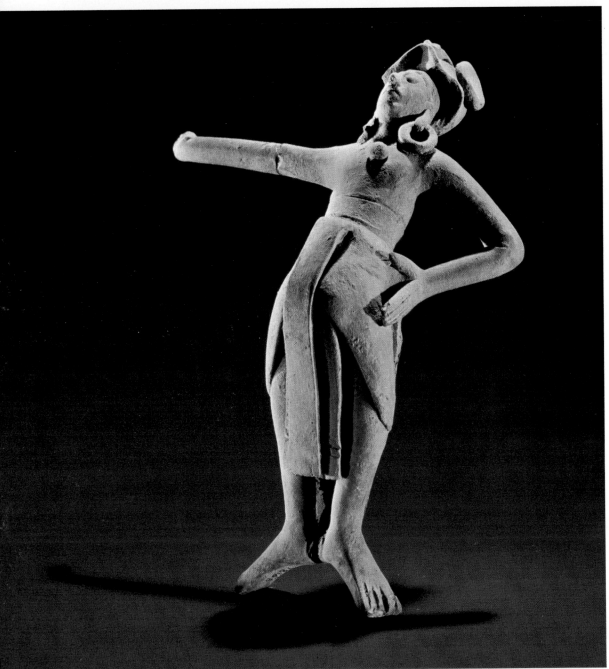

Nobleman; Jaina Style.
From the National Museum of Anthropology, Mexico City.

The photographs on the preceding pages represent art from Mexico only. It was there that one of the two great generic civilizations flourished, the Meso-American; the second was the Peruvian, which built its own distinctive style. On the center-spread is a photograph of one of the great "finds" in recent New World archaeology—a ritual group of sculptures from La Venta, the important Olmec temple-city, shown exactly as they were excavated. The meaning of the group is as yet unknown, but clearly the figures express a purpose. Whether it is ritual and religious, whether this may be a trial of some kind, or perhaps simply an entertainment or contest remains to be discovered. But the images are compelling; with their down-turned "crying baby" mouths, flaring jaguarlike lips, and flexed leg stances they are uncompromising and imposing. The other objects on the same pages are also in the Olmec style, the earliest coherent period of high civilization in Mexico. The "Kunz" axe, weighing some 15 pounds, is one of the largest jade objects known in prehistoric art.

Along with jade and other stone carvings, Pre-Columbian art represents a peak of achievement in ceramics. From tiny figures, some made as whistles and some wheeled to serve as toys, to large effigy vessels and incense burners, the range of subject and style is great. On the first page of this portfolio is a ceramic figure of awesome power—a man's head encased in a jaguar mask with fierce jaws agape. Done in the Las Remojadas style, the sculpture is from central Vera Cruz, near Mexico's Gulf Coast. The elegant figure opposite is from the island of Jaina, off the Campeche coast of the Yucatan Peninsula. One of the temple-cities of the Classic Maya period, Jaina is separated from the mainland only by a narrow stretch of water and apparently served as a ritual burial ground. The figures found there, of fine clay and brilliantly glazed, are small in size but monumental in conception; they represent a peak in Pre-Columbian art.

Photographs by Lee Boltin

part 1

The study
of culture

Anthropology
studies culture

For as long as man has been on earth, he has wondered about who he is, where he came from, and why he acts the way he does. It would seem that much of human history has resulted from man's efforts to answer these basic questions. Because of the limits of his knowledge and technology, man, throughout most of his history, has been unable to accumulate an extensive and reliable body of data concerning his own behavior and background. Hence, he has relied on bodies of myth and folklore to answer these questions. Anthropology, as it has emerged over the last two hundred years, is the scientific approach to answering man's questions about himself.

Simply stated, anthropology is the study of man and his cultures. The anthropologist, unlike the botanist or the zoologist, is concerned primarily with a single species—*Homo sapiens,* or man, his ancestors, and near relatives. Because the anthropologist is himself a member of the species which he studies, it is sometimes difficult for him to achieve the same level of objectivity with which, for example, the botanist might pursue his work. Nevertheless, the anthropologist endeavors to study man from an objective and scientific viewpoint. His goal is to arrive at a realistic and unbiased understanding of human diversity.

Development of anthropology

The discipline of anthropology is, in its modern form, a relatively new one. If men have always wondered about themselves and their origins, why then did it take such a long time for a systematic discipline of anthropology to appear?

The answer to this is as complex as man's history. In part, the question of anthropology's slow growth may be answered by reference to the limits of man's technology. Throughout most of his history, man has been highly restricted in his geographical wanderings. Without the means of traveling to distant parts of the world, man's observation of cultures and peoples far from his own was a difficult—if not impossible—venture. Extensive travel was usually the exclusive prerogative of a few; the study of foreign cultures was not likely to flourish until adequate modes of transportation and communication could be developed.

A significant element that contributed to the slow growth of anthropology was the failure of European man to recognize the common humanity that he shares with people everywhere. Those societies which did not subscribe to the fundamental cultural values of the European were regarded as "savage" or "barbarian." It was not until the late eighteenth century that a significant number of Europeans considered the odd behavior of foreigners to be at all relevant to an understanding of themselves. This awareness of human diversity cast doubts on the traditional biblical mythology, which no longer adequately "explained" things. From the reexamination that followed came the awareness that the study of "savages" is a study of mankind.

Cultural anthropology

The discipline of anthropology may be divided into two fundamental areas. **Physical anthropology** is that aspect of anthropology which is primarily concerned with man as a biological organism. The physical anthropologist applies his knowledge of genetics and biochemistry to achieve a fuller understanding of human variation and evolution. His work lays the foundation for the study of man as the animal of culture. This study is referred to as **cultural anthropology.**

Cultural anthropology may be broken down into the areas of archeology, linguistics, and ethnology. Although each of these areas has its own special interests, all are dealing with cultural data. The archeologist, the linguist, and the ethnologist may take different approaches to the subject, but each is primarily concerned with gathering data that may be useful in explaining the various cultures of man, and the way that these cultures have developed and adapted.

Archeology. Due to the intangible nature of ideas, much of man's past survives only in the form of things which he once made. The area of anthropology concerned with finding and studying the material remains of earlier cultures is called archeology. The archeologist studies the tools, pottery, and other enduring relics that remain as the legacy of long-extinct cultures.

The archeologist serves in many ways as the

Figure 1-1. *Dr. Malcolm McKenna studies this fossil under a laboratory light. Precision instruments aid the study of fossils, which is at the heart of physical anthropology.*

historian of anthropology, reconstructing the events of man's past. However, unlike the historian, who is concerned only with the past 5000 years during which men have left written records of their accomplishments, the archeologist is also concerned with the millions of years in which man developed culture without the benefit of the written word. By studying what ancient man left us, the archeologist gathers evidence of the ways in which cultures grow, change, and interact with one another. Scientists cannot experiment with humans, as they can with other animals, to see what may happen in certain circumstances. But they can formulate hypotheses—for example, about cultural change in given conditions—and then test these archeologically by investigating situations where those conditions actually occurred. Although the destructive forces of time

Figure 1-2. *Material remains of early cultures include artifacts such as pottery, and settlement and ceremonial sites. Archaeologists use many techniques to discover material remains, one of the most recent of which is aerial photography. Shown below is an aerial photograph of the Great Serpent Mound in Ohio. The mound itself, over a quarter of a mile long, was built around 600 B.C. by Indians of the mound-building Adena Culture. The center of the mound served as a burial place for members of the tribe; other parts were used for religious ceremonies. Similar ritual and ceremonial mounds are found in many parts of North America, sometimes in the shape of animals, birds or giant human figures. Such mounds are known as "effigy mounds."*

have obliterated much of the valuable evidence of man's prehistory, archeologists continue the search for the earliest roots of man's culture.

Linguistics. Perhaps the most distinctive feature of man is his ability to speak. Man is not alone in his use of symbolic communication. Studies have shown that the sounds made by some other animals—especially by apes—may serve functions comparable to that of speech in men; yet, no other animal has developed so complex a system of symbolic communication as has man. Ultimately, it is man's languages that allow him to preserve and transmit his culture from generation to generation.

The branch of cultural anthropology that stud-

Figure 1-3. *Anthropologist Napoleon Chagnon spent much time among the Yanomamo of South America as he studied their culture. The photo at upper left shows the site of a village, surrounded by cleared land that has been planted with a crop of plantains. Other photos show the plantains being gathered and stored. On special occasions plantain soup is drunk from a gourd.*

ies man's languages is called linguistics. Linguistics may deal with the description of a language (the way it forms a sentence or conjugates a verb) or with the history of languages (the way languages develop and influence each other with the passage of time). Both approaches shed valuable information, not only about the ways in which people communicate, but about the ways in which they understand the external world as well. The colloquial language of Americans, for example, includes a number of slang words, such as "dough," "greenback," "dust," "loot," and "bread," to identify what a Papuan would recognize only as "money." Such situations help identify things which are considered of special importance to a culture. Through the study of linguistics, the anthropologist is better able to understand how people perceive themselves and the world around them. In his analysis of language, the anthropological linguist makes a significant contribution to our understanding of man and his prehistory.

Ethnology. As the archeologist studies cultures of the past, so the ethnologist studies culture of the present. While the archeologist must count on the mercy of time in his pursuit of data, the ethnologist is able to study cultures from firsthand experience. It has been observed with some validity that "the ethnographer is an archeologist who catches his archeology alive."[1]

The heart of the ethnologist's approach is field work. Whenever possible, the ethnologist lives among the people whom he is studying. By eating their food, speaking their language, and personally observing their habits and customs, the ethnologist is able to understand a society's way of life to a far greater extent than any "armchair anthropologist" ever could; he learns a culture by learning how to behave acceptably himself in the society in which he is doing field work. The ethnologist does not rely upon research; rather, he is a dynamic investigator. He tries to become a participant-observer in the culture which he is studying. This does not mean that he must eat human flesh to study cannibals. By living among cannibals, the ethnologist may understand the role of cannibalism in the overall cultural scheme. He must be a meticulous observer in order to be able to get a broad overview of a culture without placing undue stress on any of its component parts. Only by discovering how all social institutions—political, economic, religious—fit together can he begin to understand the cultural system.

Every society is a complex system of interrelated elements, and often the ethnologist will be more interested in one aspect of a culture than another. For example, he may be especially interested in the religious practices of a particular group of people. As a trained anthropologist, however, he almost invariably discovers that each aspect of a culture is tied in with nearly every other aspect. That is, he discovers that the culture's religious beliefs are reflected not only in people's overt religious rituals, but in the food they eat, the games they play, the structure of their families, and the ways in which they go about fulfilling their daily needs as well. Christians celebrating Lent, for example, may follow certain dietary restrictions, may observe certain religious holidays by going to church and attending mass, and may refrain from playing music or dancing. The ethnologist may stress certain aspects of a people's behavior, but the complex nature of culture makes it almost impossible to isolate any single feature for exclusive study. By cross-cultural comparisons of cultures which survive today, the ethnologist is able to arrive at valid conclusions concerning the nature of culture everywhere.

The concept of culture

In order to understand the work of the cultural anthropologist, it is first necessary to clarify what we mean when we refer to culture. In ordinary usage, we might refer to an individual as being "cultured" if he is well mannered, well read, skilled in several languages, and able to chat

[1] Clyde Kluckhohn, *Mirror for Man: A Survey of Human Behavior and Social Attitudes* (Greenwich, Conn.: Fawcett Publications, 1970).

knowledgeably about art and music. While these abilities certainly reflect upon the individual's knowledge of his culture, they do not confer upon him the exclusive right to "culture" as that term is employed by the anthropologist. When we speak of culture, we refer to man's learned behavior, passed on from generation to generation by nonhereditary means. Culture is the way of life of an entire people. The manifestations of culture may vary in complexity from place to place, but no man has more culture in the anthropological sense than any other.

The first important definition of culture was proposed by the British anthropologist, Sir Edward Tylor. Writing in 1871, he defined culture as "that complex whole which includes knowledge, belief, art, law, morals, custom and any other capabilities and habits acquired by man as a member of society." This definition effectively suggests the complex nature of culture, but, as our knowledge of culture has increased, Tylor's definition has proven somewhat limited.

By the mid-twentieth century, human knowledge had so far advanced, and so many previously unknown peoples had been studied, that numerous definitions of culture were suggested at one time or another. In the 1950s, Alfred L. Kroeber and Clyde Kluckhohn examined over two hundred definitions of culture proposed by anthropologists and social scientists, in an effort to arrive at a consensus of what culture is.

They concluded that culture consists of patterns of behavior acquired and transmitted by means of symbols and artifacts—for example, through language and art. Such patterns of behavior are based on traditional ideas and values and are characteristic of a specific human group. More recent definitions of culture tend to emphasize the abstract elements that lie behind man's observable behavior. A people's attitude toward war would be more important to an anthropologist studying culture than the material out of which these people construct their weapons. Culture, then, is not the actual observable behavior of a group of people, but an abstraction derived from it. Culture is a set of rules or stand-

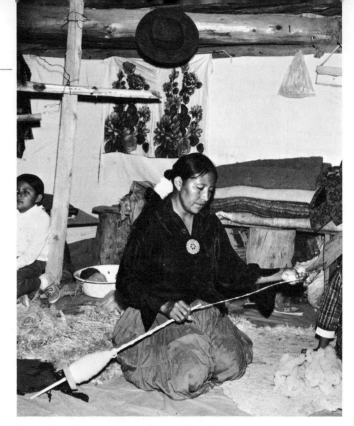

Figure 1-4. *The top photo shows a Navajo woman spinning wool inside her hogan; at bottom her kinswoman is weaving the wool in a traditionally patterned rug.*

Figure 1-5. *A group of Amish children walks briskly in the near-zero weather to the schoolhouse several miles away. Because of a religious prohibition against mechanized vehicles, they do not ride a school bus. The clothes the children wear also reflect the difference between the values held by the Amish and those of the dominant culture.*

ards which, when acted upon by the members of a society, produces behavior that falls within a range of variance the members consider proper and acceptable.

Culture as consensus

Culture can be seen from two closely related viewpoints. On the one hand, it may be studied strictly as that which anthropologists can observe, that is, on the **phenomenal order.** For example, an anthropologist might travel to the Southwest to watch the Navajo Indians weaving rugs. The tools they use, the designs they choose, the way the work is allocated, are all observable phenomena of the Navajo culture, or system of behavior shared by all members of a society. The Navajo culture could also be studied in another way, by trying to determine the beliefs, values, and principles of the rug makers. The anthropologist might observe that the rug serves a purpose beyond that of the purely utilitarian. It might be used in conjunction with a religious ceremony, or its designs might possess some magical significance. In trying to determine what these symbols mean to the Navajo, the anthropologist is studying the **ideational order.** It is the ideational order that is most relevant to a definition of culture, because notions of "proper" and "acceptable" behavior stem from values, and it is the abstract values that make the behavior acceptable.

Not all individuals within a culture think and behave in exactly the same way. One may find a group of individuals who, because of age, sex, occupation, or beliefs, share somewhat different standards. Such a group functioning within the confines of a larger culture is called a **subculture.** The degree to which subcultures are tolerated varies greatly from culture to culture.

An example of a subculture in the United States can be seen in the Amish.[2] The Old Order Amish originated in Austria and Moravia during the Reformation; today members of this order number

[2] John Hostetler and Gertrude Huntington, *Children in Amish Society* (New York: Holt Rinehart and Winston, 1971).

about 60,000 and live mainly in Pennsylvania, Ohio, and Indiana. They are pacifistic, agrarian people whose lives focus on their religious beliefs. They value simplicity, hard work, and a high degree of neighborly cooperation. They dress in a distinctive, plain garb, and even today rely on the horse for transportation as well as agricultural work. They rarely mingle with non-Amish.

The goal of Amish education is to teach reading, writing, and arithmetic, and to instill Amish values in the children. They reject "worldly" knowledge and the idea of schools producing good citizens for the state. The Amish insist that their children attend school near home and that teachers be committed to Amish values. Their nonconformity to the standards of the larger culture has caused the Amish frequent conflict with state authorities, as well as legal and personal harassment. They have resisted all attempts to force their children to attend regular public schools. Some compromise has been necessary, and "vocational training" has been introduced beyond the elementary school level to fulfill state requirements. The Amish have succeeded in gaining control of their schools and maintaining their way of life. In return, they are a beleaguered, defensive culture, more distrustful than ever of the larger culture around them.

The experience of the Amish is one example of the way a subculture is tolerated by the larger culture within which it functions. As different as they are, the Amish actually practice many values that our nation respects in the abstract: thrift, hard work, independence, a close family life. The degree of tolerance accorded to them may also be due in part to the fact that the Amish are white Europeans, of the same race as the dominant culture. The American Indian subcultures were treated differently by the white man. There was a racial difference; the white man came as a conqueror; and Indian values were not as easily understood or sympathized with by the larger culture. The nation was less willing to tolerate the differences of the Indians, with results that are now a matter of history, and very much a current concern.

Anthropological studies of culture

A definition of culture is not an adequate research tool for the anthropologist doing work in the field. Culture itself cannot be directly observed; only outward behavior is actually observable. In order to understand the problems of an anthropologist doing field work in a strange culture, it may be helpful to imagine the unlikely situation in which a native from the interior of New Guinea is brought for the first time into a modern urban hospital, free to explore at will. He would find rooms containing one, two, four or six very odd-looking hammocks occupied by resting or sleeping persons. He would see men and women in white going to and from the hammocks, as well as pausing at little sites in the corridors. There would be strange moving rooms that go from floor to floor. He might find eerily masked figures probing inside an apparently lifeless body. Elsewhere there would be offices, restaurants, shops, kitchens, a laundry, a pharmacy, voices filling the air from nowhere saying "Dr. Wilson, Dr. Jones, Dr. Shapiro, Dr. Anderson." The visitor would have no way of understanding any of this, and would be unable to fit any two parts together. How would he know the main purpose of the place he was in? How would he know which, of all the people he has seen, are the beneficiaries of this main purpose and which its agents? How could he distinguish which rooms and activities are devoted to primary tasks, and which to secondary, supportive tasks? If he were to decide that the cafeteria or the laundry were the center of this place, he would be wrong. If he concluded that there was no relationship between any of the things he saw, he would be wrong again.

The anthropologist is not really in the same position as this imaginary visitor. The anthropologist goes into the field with the most advanced tools and methods of investigation available to him. Nonetheless, he will be confronted by a series of interrelated activities that at first he may not understand. What he sees may be as foreign to him as an urban hospital may be to a New

Figure 1-6. *An elder of the Tiwi tribe stands near the road leading to Darwin, Australia; note the elaborate body painting.*

Guinea tribesman. Moreover, what he sees will in reality be as cohesive and interconnected to the insider as the various departments of a hospital are to an intern. The anthropologist must try to abstract a set of rules from what he observes and hears in order to explain social behavior.

Try as he might to be objective, the anthropologist's own personal and cultural biases are bound to color his conclusions. In order to arrive at a realistic description of a culture, he should approach his subject matter from three different viewpoints. First, he must examine a people's own understanding of the rules by which their culture lives—their notion of the way their society ought to be. Second, he must determine the extent to which the people believe that they are observing those rules—how they think they actually behave. Third, he must describe the behavior he himself observes—an impartial reporter's account of the way they behave.

Anthropologist Bronislaw Malinowski encountered this problem and discovered a difference between what people do and what they say they do. The Trobriand Islanders believe that the rules of exogamy—sexual relations outside one's own group—ought to be observed.

> If you were to inquire into the matter among the Trobrianders, you would find that . . . the natives show horror at the idea of violating the rules of exogamy and that they believe that sores, diseases, even death might follow clan incest. (But) from the viewpoint of the native libertine, *suvasova* (the breach of exogamy) is indeed a specially interesting and spicy form of erotic experience. Most of my informants would not only admit but did actually boast about having committed this offense . . .[3]

Malinowski himself believed that although such breaches did occasionally occur they were much less frequent than gossip would have it. Had Malinowski relied solely on what the Trobrianders told him, his description of their culture would have been inaccurate. There may be a

[3] Bronislaw Malinowski, *Argonauts of the Western Pacific.*

variance between the way a people think they should behave, the way they think they do behave, and the way others see them behave.

Culture and society

Every human being is a member of a culture and of a society, because every human culture exists within a human society. It is within Chinese society that Chinese culture exists. Man possesses the instinct for social organization. A group of people from many cultures stranded over a period of time on a desert island would become a society. The members would have a common interest—survival—and would develop techniques for living and working together. Each of the members of this group, however, would retain his identity and cultural background, and the group would disintegrate without further ado as soon as its members were rescued from the island. The group would have been merely an aggregate in time and not a cultural entity. Society may be defined as a group of people occupying a territory who are dependent on each other for survival. The relationships that hold a society together are known as **social structure** or **social organization.**

British and American anthropologists have debated the relative importance of culture and society for understanding human behavior. A. R. Radcliffe-Brown, a leading exponent of the British viewpoint, was more interested in observable social relationships than in the rules that lay behind them. Essentially the conflict is a difference of emphasis. Culture and society are two closely related concepts, and an anthropologist must study both.

Characteristics of culture

Through the comparative study of many different cultures, anthropologists have arrived at an understanding of the basic characteristics which all cultures share. A careful study of these charac-

Figure 1-7. *Man is not the only primate with culture. Here, two chimpanzees use twigs as tools to extract termites from a nest, a feat which the animals learn and pass on to others.*

teristics may help us see the value and the function of culture itself.

Culture is learned

All culture is learned, not biologically inherited. Every person learns his culture by growing up in it. Ralph Linton referred to culture as man's "social heredity." The process whereby culture is transmitted from one generation to the next is called **enculturation.**

Most animals eat and drink whenever the urge arises. Man, however, eats and drinks at certain culturally prescribed times, and feels hungry as those times approach. These eating times vary from culture to culture. Similarly, an American's idea of a comfortable way to sleep will vary greatly from that of a Japanese or an African. The need to sleep is instinctual; the way it is satisfied is cultural.

Through enculturation one learns the socially appropriate way of satisfying one's instinctual needs. It is important to distinguish between the needs themselves, which are not learned, and the learned ways in which they are satisfied. Man's instinctual needs are the same as those of other animals: food, shelter, companionship, self-defense, and sexual gratification. Each culture determines how these needs will be met.

Not all learned behavior is cultural. A dog may learn tricks, but his behavior is reflexive, the result of conditioning by repeated training, not the product of enculturation. On the other hand, primates other than man are capable of forms of cultural behavior. A chimpanzee, for example, will take a twig and strip it of all leaves in order to make a tool that will extract termites from a hole. Toolmaking, learned through imitation, is unquestionably a form of cultural behavior until recently thought to be exclusively human. The cultural capacity of apes, however, is obviously not nearly as well developed as that of a man. It is man's superior learning ability that makes him distinctive as a cultural animal.

Culture is shared

Culture is a set of shared assumptions; it is the common denominator that makes the actions of individuals intelligible to the group. Because they share a common culture, people can predict each other's actions in a given circumstance and react accordingly. In every culture, there are persons whose idiosyncratic behavior has earned them the terms of "eccentric," "crazy," or "queer." Such persons are looked upon suspiciously by society and are sooner or later excluded from participating in the activities of the group. Such exclusion acts to keep the deviant behavior outside the group. Most societies have mechanisms whereby some forms of deviant behavior are incorporated into the group in an acceptable way. Among the Mohave Indians, for example, transvestitism is accepted so long as the transvestite undergoes an initiation ceremony; the person then assumes for life the role of someone of the opposite sex and is permitted to marry.[4]

Because individuals who share a culture tend to marry within their society and thus to share certain physical characteristics, some people have mistakenly concluded that there is a direct relationship between culture and race. Research has shown that racial characteristics represent biological adaptations to climate and do not imply differences in intelligence or cultural superiority. Some American blacks have concluded that they have more in common with black Africans than they do with their fellow Americans who are light-skinned and straight-haired. Yet if they were suddenly forced to live with Bantu tribesmen, they would find themselves lacking the cultural adaptations to be successful members of this group. The culture they share with white Americans is more significant than the physical traits they share with the Bantu.

Culture is based on symbols

The American anthropologist Leslie White considers that all human behavior originates in the use of symbols. Art, religion, and money involve the use of symbols. We are all familiar with the fervor and devotion that religion can elicit from a believer; a cross, an image, any object of worship may bring to mind centuries of struggle and persecution or may stand for a whole philosophy or creed. The most important symbolic aspect of culture is language—the substitution of words for objects. Stanley Salthe points out, "Symbolic language is the foundation upon which human cultures are built. The institutions of these cultures (political structures, religions, arts, economic organization) could not possibly exist without symbols. . ."[5]

[4] George Devereux, "Institutionalized Homosexuality of the Mohave Indians," in *The Problem of Homosexuality in Modern Society,* Hendrik M. Ruitenbeek, ed. (New York: E.P. Dutton, 1963).
[5] Stanley N. Salthe, *Evolutionary Biology* (New York: Holt, Rinehart and Winston, 1972) p. 402.

Figure 1-8. *A group of young unmarried women takes time out for a chat during the long festivities that attend the killing of a pig among the Kapauku.*

It is through language—defined by Edward Sapir as the "purely human and noninstinctive method of communicating ideas, emotions, and desires by means of a system of voluntarily produced symbols"[6]—that man is able to transmit culture from one generation to another.

Culture is integrated

For purposes of comparison and analysis, anthropologists customarily break a culture down into

many discrete elements, but such distinctions are arbitrary. When an anthropologist examines one aspect of a culture, he invariably finds himself examining others as well. This tendency for all aspects of a culture to function as an interrelated whole is called **integration.**

The integration of the economic, political, and social aspects of a society can be illustrated by the Kapauku Papuans, a mountain people of western New Guinea studied by the American anthropologist Leopold Pospisil.[7] Among the status-oriented Kapauku, wealth comes from the

[6]Edward Sapir, *Language* (New York: Harcourt Brace Jovanovich, 1949) p. 8.

[7]Leopold Pospisil. *The Kapauku Papvans of New Guinea* (New York: Holt, Rinehart and Winston, 1963).

breeding of pigs; and wealth is the key to political and legal leadership. The pigs are fed on sweet potatoes. Hence, agriculture is of prime importance. Since it is the role of women to cultivate sweet potatoes as well as to raise the pigs, there is a direct relation between women and the production of wealth. The Kapauku practice polygyny; one man possesses many wives. This makes possible the cultivation of more land and the breeding of more pigs. The increased wealth thus generated enables a man to buy more wives. Because the bride-price paid for every wife is high, the men exploit their investment to the fullest, providing as much work for the women as possible. Women cannot weed and harvest, however, until the men have cleared and drained the ground. So the more wives a man has, the more he must work.

The sweet potato can be regarded as the origin of wealth in Kapauku culture, since it makes possible the sale of pigs, the main source of income. But because only women can cultivate sweet potatoes or raise pigs, another factor in generating wealth is the possession of many wives. The men with the most wives have the most pigs and the most land under cultivation. They are also the wealthiest.

In a polygynous society, there are usually more adult women than men. The imbalance between the sexes is maintained among the Kapauku through intertribal warfare. The Kapauku will never shoot in battle at an adult female, because they consider it highly immoral. Since a part of the male population is regularly eliminated as a result of wars, the surplus of adult females tends to be maintained.

Were warfare to be eliminated in the New Guinea highlands, it would alter the ratio of males to females, disrupting the sex ratio characteristic of a polygynous society. Were an attempt made to introduce new agricultural methods that would make the labor of women unnecessary, Kapauku society would find itself with a surplus of unemployable women. The different elements of Kapauku culture—the economic, the political, and the social—are compatible with one another.

The raising of sweet potatoes and pigs, the practice of polygyny, and the frequency of intertribal warfare all work together like cogs of a gear system. A culture can be compared to a machine; the parts must all be adjusted to one another or it will not run properly.

Culture and process

Culture has been more powerful than nature in shaping man as we know him today. By manipulating the environment, man can occupy the Arctic, the Sahara, or the moon. The social environment in which man lives is not only very complex but demands a rapid adjustment to unforeseen changes. Man often adapts by changing the world, not himself. Evolutionary changes arising from man's need to cope with change on short notice have favored behavioral plasticity and the ability to learn from experience.

Cultural adaptation

There are at least as many forms of adaptation as there are environments. The Yanomamo people of Brazil studied by the American anthropologist Napoleon A. Chagnon provide a good example of the way man adapts to a sociopolitical environment. The Yanomamo's adaptation to the sociopolitical environment is as important as their adaptation to nature and it illustrates how a people must relate themselves to each other in order to survive. This adjustment affects the way they are distributed over the land, their patterns of migration, and the kind of relationships they maintain with their neighbors.

The Yanomamo are a fiercely aggressive people who inhabit jungle villages numbering 40 to 250 persons. Village life revolves around the cultivation of a plantain garden and warring against other villages. Because peace is so uncertain, a village must be prepared to evacuate, either to a new location or to the parent village, on very short notice. But since the garden is of such economic importance, abandoning it to start a new one elsewhere is seen as a formidable task, and is resisted except in the most extreme situations. Alliances are therefore made with neighboring villages, so that one village joins another's war parties, or takes in the inhabitants of another village during times of need.

Figure 1-9. *Archaeologists reconstruct the material remains of past cultures from artifacts such as pottery. Analysis of pottery composition, design, function, and shape reveal how a culture changes over time, as well as contacts with other cultures.*

The Yanomamo are so aggressive that in a village of 100 people there is bound to be feuding and bloodshed, necessitating a split, with the dissident faction going off to establish a new garden. Although Yanomamo try to avoid the establishment of a new garden because of the labor and uncertainty of the first harvest, their political way of life forces them to this decision frequently. Although they are an agricultural peo-

The study of culture ● part 1

ple, their choice of a garden site is based on political considerations.

It has become apparent in recent years that man's control over the environment can be pushed to a point at which he is endangered, rather than protected, by the effects of cultural evolution. Scientific control over the environment and medical control over the human body can alter, for example, the effects of natural selection. As a result of routine use of antibiotics in medical treatment, many people have become sensitized, running the risk of violent allergic reaction if the drug is administered to them; moreover some virus strains, such as certain types of gonorrhea, have developed a resistance to antibiotics.

Culture and change

All cultures change over a period of time. This might be due to the intrusion of outsiders, or to modification of behavior and values within the culture. Within our culture, clothing fashions change frequently. It has recently become culturally permissible for us to bare more of our bodies both in swimming and in dress. Along with this in recent years has come greater permissiveness about the body in photographs and movies. Finally, the sexual attitudes and practices of Americans have become more permissive in recent years. Obviously these changes are interrelated, reflecting an underlying change in attitudes toward cultural rules regarding sex.

Culture change can bring unexpected and often disastrous results. For the Yir-Yoront people of Australia, the stone ax was the main technological tool as well as one of the most important mythical symbols. The ax was a tribal totem and a symbol of masculinity. As such, it had an important place in the cosmology of the Yir-Yoront. Moreover, ax heads were an important object of trade acquired annually at ceremonial tribal gatherings. Because they were scarce, stone axes were owned only by senior men. Several decades ago, some well-intentioned missionaries provided the Yir-Yoront with steel axes. The steel axes became plentiful, so that even women and children had their own. The steel axes eliminated the need for the more primitive stone ones. As a result, the stone ax as a symbol of masculinity was destroyed; and as the steel ax could not be related to the tribal totem, the whole ideological system of the Yir-Yoront began to disintegrate. The annual tribal gatherings dwindled, as there was no need to obtain stone heads through trade. The introduction of steel axes undermined the whole structure of Yir-Yoront society, and no substitute for the old order has yet been found.

Functions of culture

A culture cannot survive if it does not satisfy certain basic needs of its members. The extent to which a culture achieves the fulfillment of these needs will determine its ultimate success. "Success" is measured by the values of the in-group; the outsider may find the culture "unsuccessful." A culture must provide for the production and distribution of goods and services necessary for life. It must provide for biological continuity through the reproduction of its members. It must socialize new members so that they can become functioning adults. It must maintain order among its members. It must socialize new members so that they can become functioning adults. It must maintain order among its members. It must likewise maintain order between its members and outsiders. It must motivate its members to survive and engage in those activities necessary for survival.

Cultural focus. Every culture tends to emphasize certain cultural activities. In Western civilization, for example, technology occupies a prominent place; ours is a technology oriented culture. This emphasis on an area of cultural activity is known as **cultural focus.** Cultural focus is significant because it determines the things individuals value and want for themselves. To suggest to a Kapauku that his people stop raising pigs would be the equivalent of suggesting to an American engineer that the United States abandon technology and all the research, marketing, transportation, and investment that goes with it.

Evaluation of culture

It is an inextricable aspect of the process of enculturation that we all grow up thinking that our culture is the best there is. In the nineteenth century, Western man had no doubts about the fact that Western civilization (most particularly that of Victorian England) represented the peak of mankind's development. Some inquiring anthropologists, however, realized that all cultures yet studied also saw themselves as the best. This was reflected in the way the members of a society called themselves, which, roughly translated, meant "we the people," as opposed to "you subhumans." The belief that one's own culture is the best is called **ethnocentrism.**

To judge the behavior of others according to ethnocentric standards of the anthropologist's own culture is misleading. When anthropologists began to live among the so-called savages, they discovered that under the seeming strangeness was a recognizable counterpart of their own society. This led anthropologists to examine each culture on its own terms. They questioned whether or not the culture satisfied the needs and expectations of the people themselves. If the people were cannibals, for example, they asked whether or not the eating of human flesh was acceptable according to native values; why it made sense; and what were the alternatives. The idea that a culture must be evaluated according to its own standards is called **cultural relativism.** One could say, for instance, that the eating of other human beings may be acceptable to cannibals, yet it is a custom Americans would not wish to emulate, no matter how functional it may be to some other group of people.

Both cultural relativism and ethnocentrism represent extreme viewpoints. Cultural relativism merely replaces one set of subjective standards (the anthropologist's own) with another (the culture that is studied). To be truly objective, however, the anthropologist needs a criterion for evaluation that is not derived from anyone's cultural values. A culture is essentially a system designed to insure the continued existence of a group of people. Therefore, the ultimate test of a culture is its capability of change in new circumstances. The ability of a culture to survive seems to be the best criterion by which to evaluate the success of a culture.

☐

Original study

THE ANTHROPOLOGIST IN THE FIELD

Any description of another people, another way of life, is to some extent bound to be subjective, especially when, as an anthropologist, one has shared that way of life. This is as it should be; but then the reader is entitled to know something of the aims, expectations, hopes and attitudes that the writer brought to the field with him, for these will surely influence not only how he sees things but even what he sees. At best his story will be only a partial one.

In this case there was all the advantage of an almost completely clean slate. Beyond the most superficial glimmerings, there was no way of knowing anything about the Ik, or the Teuso, as I thought they were called, for even their correct name was unknown. I could not have had a preconceived notion if I tried. I neither knew anything nor, to tell the truth, did I particularly care. The Ik were, at best, a third choice, a last-ditch stand not to lose an opportunity to get into the field. So if I brought any attitudes with me, enthusiasm was not one of them; clinical observation was more like it.

For me this was something new. Until then I had been enthusiastic about almost everything I had done. India was my first enthusiasm, then colonial Africa, and then the Congo Pygmies. Up to this point I had made three field trips to the Pygmies, each with undiminished enthusiasm, but the nature of the work there was such that I was virtually excluded from village society. My major research objective for some time had been to return to the Ituri Forest and work among the villagers to complete the picture. When the opportunity for this time in the field came up, my first thought was of the Ituri, but continued disturbances in the northeastern Congo made it impossible.

A second project offered itself which was in some ways even more promising, and about which I felt no less enthusiastic. That was to return to India and work in the Andaman Islands, particularly the Little Andaman, among the Onge. Far removed from the Central African Pygmies, the Onge resembled them in a remarkable manner, both physically and culturally. They had never been adequately studied, and for years had been isolated on the Little Andaman Island, on which there were no foreign settlements of any kind, and which was accessible only by the sea, and only during two months of the year, due to heavy surf. There were the usual rumors about their cannibalistic tendencies, almost certainly unfounded, and the very isolation that seemed uninviting to others seemed to me to offer ideal and almost unique opportunities for some very special and vital research. The project met with enthusiasm and support everywhere except in India. I should have recognized those vague responses for what they were, attempts to avoid the unpleasantness of having to say "no," but I refused to believe that even the legacy of two centuries of British bureaucracy could defeat such a worthwhile project, and I persisted up to the last moment. I was finally persuaded to leave for India regardless and argue it out there, when the polite correspondence stopped abruptly, and I got the briefest and simplest of notes refusing permission, with no stated reason.

There was little more than a month or two until I was due to leave for the field, so I hurriedly drew up a triple project to be carried out in East Africa, where there was the least likelihood of any offical refusal of permission. One possibility was to investigate the scattered groups of nomadic hunters collectively known as Ndorobo (Wandorobo), still to be found in Kenya, Tanzania, and Uganda. Another possibility was to do some research work among black-smiths and iron forgers. Work in both these areas was badly needed, and either would have justified my time in the field. The third possibility was a more detailed study of a small group of hunters isolated in the mountains separating northern Uganda, Sudan, and Kenya. My attention had been drawn to them by Elizabeth Marshall Thomas, who had run across them while working with the Dodos, in northern Karimoja. Rather like the Onge, this project offered some opportunity for comparison between two very different groups of hunters living in very different environments. One of the objectives of anthropology is to discover basic principles of social organization, and small-scale societies are ideal for this purpose, the more isolated the better. Comparison between different societies is especially instructive, and since I had no means of knowing what to expect of the "Teuso," my attitude remained clinical rather than enthusiastic. But no amount of clinical interest could suppress the disappointment at the failure of the two preferred projects.

If I had known what to expect I would almost certainly not have gone, but as it was I still had a few days of contented optimism left. I had no very clear idea of how I would get up into the mountains, but if the Land Rover failed to make it I was prepared to walk as far as was necessary, and indeed had begun preparing for a strenuous time while I was still in New York, walking to and from work every day, from Twenty-first Street to Seventy-seventh. It proved to be rather inadequate preparation, excessive though it was by New York standards. But I somehow visualized myself appearing up in the mountains and being welcomed by a warm, friendly people. I had never had any experience other than this in Africa, and saw no reason why the Ik should be different. The physical details of how they lived did not bother me at all, as I had survived happily in the arctic as well as the tropics, the desert as well as the forest. Nor did the prospect of high altitude worry me over-much, for I had spent some time up in the Himalayas. Having lived with the Pygmies, who eat almost anything that moves, I didn't give food a second thought. In all, I was just about as unconcerned as if I had been going upstate for a weekend.

As far as academic expectations went, I had neither any specific hopes nor any specific fears, and this was as it should be. It is too easy to go into a field situation expecting or hoping to find this or that, for invariably you come out having found what you wanted. Selectivity can do great things in blinding one to a wider reality. I was interested rather in a very general comparison between two hunting-and-gathering societies (Pygmies and Ik) in totally different environments; it was more of a fact-finding mission than the testing of some theoretical point of view; that could come later. It was unambitious, but practical and of solid worth.

It is a mistake to think of small-scale societies as "primitive" or "simple," however simple they may appear on the surface. Hunters and gatherers, most of all, appear deceptively simple and straightforward in terms of their social organization, yet that appearance is far from being true. What is true, perhaps, is that the result of a typical hunting-and-gathering social organization is a

A field anthropologist studies Navajo Indians.

simple and effective system of human relationships, and this is what so strongly appeals to many of those who have worked with them. If we can learn about the nature of society from a study of small-scale societies, we can also learn about human relationships, and that seems fully as valuable and valid. The smaller the society, the less emphasis there is on the formal system, and the more there is on interpersonal and inter-group relations, to which the system is subordinated. Security is seen in terms of these relationships, and so is survival. The result, which appears so deceptively simple, is that hunters frequently display those characteristics that we find so admirable in man: kindness, generosity, consideration, affection, honesty, hospitality, compassion, charity and others. This sounds like a formidable list of virtues, and so it would be if they *were* virtues, but for the hunter they are not. For the hunter in his tiny, close-knit society, these are necessities for survival; without them society would collapse. It is a far cry from our society, in which anyone possessing even half these qualities would find it hard indeed to survive, yet we are given to thinking that somehow these are virtues inherent in man.

It was not foremost in my mind, I suppose, but, as with the physical conditions, I took it for granted that the Ik would possess these same qualities. It was a shock to find myself wrong on almost all counts. The Teuso were not the Teuso, they were the Ik; they were not hunters, they were farmers, their mountain villages were far from livable, the food was uneatable because there was not any, and the people were as unfriendly, uncharitable, inhospitable and generally mean as any people can be. For those positive qualities we value so highly are no longer functional for the Ik; even more than in our own society they spell ruin and disaster. It seems that, far from being basic human qualities, they are superficial luxuries we can afford in times of plenty, or mere mechanisms for survival and security. Given the situation in which the Ik found themselves as I headed toward them, man has not time for such luxuries, and a much more basic man appears, using much more basic survival tactics. The much vaunted gap between man and the so-called "lesser" animals suddenly shrinks to nothingness, except that in this case most "lesser" animals come off rather well by comparison, displaying many more of those "human" qualities than the Ik did. Yet the relationship between cause and effect is so undeniable that one does not blame or criticize the Ik; if anything, one admires them for surviving in spite of themselves. It is rather like suddenly catching sight of oneself, in middle age, stripped naked in front of the bathroom mirror. One is forced to admit that the paunchy body is no longer as beautiful as it used to be, if indeed it ever was, and one hastens to don one's clothes to restore the illusion, for the greater ease of mind of others as well as one's own. The beautiful human, like the beautiful body, seems to be a myth perpetuated by the game of self-deceit, at which humans are so singularly adept. In fact, after even a few months with the Ik one is tempted to think that if there is such a thing as a basic human quality, self-deception is it.

Source:
From *The Mountain People* by Colin M. Turnbull.
Simon and Schuster, A Touchstone Brook, 1972. pp. 15–17, 30–33.
Copyright 1972 by Colin M. Turnbull.
Reprinted by permission of Simon and Schuster.

Summary

1.

Anthropology is the study of man and his culture. Physical anthropology is concerned with the evolution of man as a biological organism. Cultural anthropology studies man in the context of his culture.

2.

Three disciplines within cultural anthropology are (1) archeology which reconstructs man's cultural past from tools, pottery and other enduring relics of past societies; (2) linguistics which is a study of the languages of men and (3) ethnology which is concerned with the study of extant cultures.

3.

Culture refers to man's learned behavior and beliefs, passed on from generation to generation. Culture is acquired and transmitted by means of symbols and artifacts, for example, language and art. Culture may be studied in terms of its phenomenal order—observable behavior—and in terms of its ideational order—the ideas, beliefs and values of its members. Many societies such as our own, contain subcultures—groups within the larger culture whose members behave according to a set of rules somewhat different from the standard.

4.

The work of the anthropologist is to abstract a set of rules from what he observes and hears in order to explain the social behavior of a people. In order to avoid his own cultural and personal biases, an anthropologist must (1) examine a people's notion of the way they think their society ought to function; (2) determine how the people in the society think they actually behave; and (3) describe the observable behavior in the society.

5.

Society is a concept closely related to culture. A society may be defined as a group of people occupying a territory who are dependent on each other for survival. The way social relationships are organized within a society is known as social structure or social organization.

6.

Culture has the following characteristics: it is learned; and the learning process is called enculturation; it is a set of assumptions shared by the society; it is based on symbols; different facets of a culture are interrelated and function as an integrated whole.

7.

The way in which a group adapts to its environment is an important part of its culture and enables humans to survive in a wide variety of environments. Nevertheless, cultures change over time, sometimes due to influences from other cultures and sometimes brought about within the group.

8.

A culture must satisfy certain basic needs of a group if the group is to survive; economic subsistence; biological continuity; maintenance of order and relationships with outsiders; and motivational system.

Suggested readings

Fried, Morton H. *The Study of Anthropology*. New York: Thomas Y. Crowell Co., 1972.
This is a nuts-and-bolts discussion of anthropology as a way of life and study. A modest, how-to volume addressed to undergraduates and potential graduate students. Fried delineates the character of anthropology in the United States, as well as how to get into the profession.

Goodenough, Ward H. *Description and Comparison in Cultural Anthropology*. Chicago: Aldine, 1970.
The major question to which Goodenough addresses himself is how the anthropologist is to avoid ethnocentric bias when studying culture. His approach relies on models of descriptive linguistics. A large part of the book is concerned with kinship and terminology, with a discussion of the problems of a universal definition of marriage and the family. This is a particularly lucid discussion of culture, its relation to society, and the problem of individual variance.

Keesing, Roger and Felix Keesing *New Perspectives in Cultural Anthropology*. New York: Holt, Rinehart and Winston, 1971.
This book approaches anthropology by pinpointing the basic problems of cultural anthropology, discussing them through ethnographic examples and theoretical considerations. It also gives a very concise historical account of past theories and works.

Kluckholn, Clyde, and Alfred L. Kroeber "Culture: A Critical Review of Concepts and Definitions," in *Papers of the Peabody Museum of Archaeology and Ethnology*, vol. 47, no. 1, 1952. Cambridge, Mass.: Peabody Museum.
This paper presents varying definitions of the concept of culture. There is a semantic history of the word "culture" and its related word, "civilization," analyses of various definitions according to anthropological concepts, and indices of the definitions categorized by author and conceptual components. In addition, Kluckholn presents definitions of "culture" as employed in other countries.

Kroeber, Alfred L. *Anthropology: Culture Processes and Patterns*. New York: Harcourt Brace Jovanovitch, 1963.
This volume consists of chapters dealing specifically with matters of culture patterns and processes. The chapters are selected from Kroeber's major work, *Anthropology*.

Linton, Ralph *The Study of Man: An Introduction*. New York: Appleton-Century-Crofts, 1964.
Linton wrote this book in 1936 with the intention of providing a general survey of the field of anthropology. His study of social structure is illuminating. This book is regarded as a classic and is an important source historically.

Oliver, Douglas Z. *Invitation to Anthropology*. Garden City N.Y.: Natural History Press, 1964.
This guide to the basic concepts of anthropology is seen by the author as an outline of what ideally he would like all high school graduates to know about the anthropological profession. This slim volume is neither a textbook nor a substantive introduction, but a brief overview of the field.

The development
of anthropology

Travelers have always been fascinated by the seeming strangeness in the behavior and beliefs of people in other places. Marco Polo, perhaps the most famous traveler of the thirteenth century, wrote to his Italian relatives of his amazement at the manners and morals of the Chinese court; the Spanish conquistadors were perplexed by the customs of the New World civilizations they eventually destroyed; modern travelers leave their 747 with camera in hand, ready to record on film the landmarks of their destination and the dress of its inhabitants. Underlying this widespread curiosity about the culture of other peoples is an equally widespread desire to understand the meaning and significance of physical and cultural variety. Although people have been asking the same basic questions about the differences between cultures for a very long time, the answers which have been proposed in the past have differed dramatically from those which are now offered. Most of what we now believe to be true of the development of mankind was discovered in the last one hundred years, and much of it only in the last few decades. The history of anthropology's development as a science is closely tied to the changing views of man's cultural history.

Historical background

The story of modern anthropology really begins around the middle of the nineteenth century. Before that time, European thought was dominated by the traditional teachings of the Bible and the Christian Church. According to these authorities, all things in the universe, ranging from the lowly rocks to the heavenly angels, fit into some predetermined niche in the Great Chain of Being. Furthermore, according to this view, the entire world and every species of plant and animal in it were created by God in one masterful stroke some six thousand years previously. Challenging these long entrenched ideas was no small task, and it was not until the close of the eighteenth century that a number of courageous men dared to take up the questions of human progress and the perfection of man's condition on earth.

The eighteenth and early nineteenth centuries

The eighteenth century was an era of many exciting discoveries for European man. Extensive sea voyages were uncovering a great deal of information which seemed to challenge the traditional views concerning the origins and diversity of plant and animal life forms. As the age of discovery made the global survey of man a reality, major advances in science, philosophy, and technology rapidly altered the European's perception of the world. The concept of a world in equilibrium was giving way to the concept of a world in progress.

As advances in chemistry and physics were beginning to stir public faith in scientific inquiry and analysis, important archeological breakthroughs challenged some of Europe's most established beliefs. In the early nineteenth century, Jacques Boucher de Perthes, a French customs official and amateur archeologist, discovered some flint tools along with the bones of extinct elephants in the Somme Valley. Despite the strong evidence uncovered by him that men had actually lived on earth long before the date provided by the Bible for the Great Flood, Boucher de Perthe's findings were largely ignored for many years. Most scholars were not yet prepared to accept such a radical departure from the traditional view of the Creation.

Even the most determined traditionalists, however, were finding it difficult to ignore the mounting evidence of man's long history on earth. The discovery of stone implements in Danish peat bogs confirmed an earlier theory that man had endured through sequential ages of stone, bronze, and iron. Later excavations uncovered artifacts which predated even the Stone Age. By the time Charles Lyell published his geological evidence that the earth was considerably older than the Bible stated, it was difficult for any but the most stubborn to be contented with the biblical version of the Creation. Before the nineteenth century, there was little reason to believe that the orderly appearance of new living types had taken any more time than the duration of the recorded history of mankind. By the middle of the century, the principle of geological succession had made it nearly impossible for any educated person not to believe otherwise.

As the geologists and archeologists increasingly turned toward an evolutionary view of man, po-

litical and economic theorists too began to discuss man's behavior in less static terms. Men of such different visions as Karl Marx and John Stuart Mill were analyzing man's institutions in terms of his development from the primitive to the modern. At the same time, evolution was the dominant theme of such early anthropologists as J. F. McLennan and J. J. Bachofen. As far back as the eighteenth century, the notion of human progress was becoming the guiding light for anthropological thought.

The first half of the nineteenth century represented, for the most part, less a departure from the beliefs of the previous century than a culmination of those beliefs. It was at this time, for example, that the theory of racial determinism was proposed to account for the differences between various cultures. According to this theory formulated before the development of modern genetic science, the differences between people were attributable mainly to their varying "racial" backgrounds. The Hottentots, for example, were considered to be one step above the apes, but that step was judged to be a very small one. Although the influence of the environment on human culture was conceded, racial determinism was based on the premise that heredity is the main factor in determining a culture's potential for achievement. Meanwhile, theories of psychic unity were formulated in order to explain the many similarities between cultures. These theories held that the human mind was essentially the same all over the world and that all people began to develop their cultures with the same psychological potential. In keeping with the eighteenth century belief in the doctrine of progress, both the racial determinism and psychic unity theories assumed that man and his cultures changed and developed with the passage of time.

Evolutionism

The concept of evolutionism was already an important aspect of anthropology before the appearance of Charles Darwin's theory. Europe of the early nineteenth century was in a state of

| Charles Darwin | Herbert Spencer | Edward Tylor |

Figure 2-1. *Three nineteenth-century Englishmen, Charles Darwin, Herbert Spencer, and Edward Tylor, helped further the theory of evolutionism in anthropology. Darwin was a biologist, Spencer a philosopher, and Tylor an anthropologist.*

dynamic change. As science and industry developed and the continent continued to be torn by war, class struggles, and technological changes, interest was focused more than ever before on the human condition. The time was right for a science of man.

Charles Darwin.   Among the most important events in the history of modern science was the appearance, in 1859, of Charles Darwin's *The Origin of Species*. Darwin's work represents the first formal statement of the theory of evolution. Although Darwin himself was concerned primarily with the way in which various species develop through biological evolution, his ideas gave new impetus to the concepts of cultural evolution which had been roughly developed by earlier anthropologists. Although Darwin commented only briefly on the evolution of man himself, the implication of his theory was obvious and far-reaching.

Anthropological evolutionism

The anthropological evolutionists believed that society and culture developed in a regular sequence of predictable stages. By studying social evolution, they hoped to develop a science of culture that could formulate universal laws of human behavior and cultural development. In looking for such laws, the evolutionists tended to emphasize the similarities among cultures rather than the differences. Although they did not completely deny the importance of the exchanging of cultural traits between societies, they believed that isolated societies tend to develop similar tools and institutions independently in the

Figures 2-2, 3, and 4. *Stratigraphy is now a valuable aid to anthropologists. Archeological sites are dug slowly with concern for the location of fossils and artifacts. Upon the opening of an archeological site, such as the one in Figure 2-2 at High Lodge, trenches are dug to establish strata. Determinations are made as to how the site relates to previous geological data and age calculations. At a site where humans have lived, such as the one in Figure 2-3 at Nippur, stratigraphy reveals floor levels. At Nippur, 12 floor levels have been unearthed, with artifacts sticking out at each level. Archeological sites are broken down into square meter segments. Measurements are taken to establish the position of each fossil and artifact relative to the position of each other object. The cubic meter in Figure 2-4 contains hand tools, animal bone, and the remains of a hearth. Such graphic representation helps piece a site together.*

In the figure labels on the cube:
39 inches 1 meter

1
2
3
4
5

39 inches 1 meter

39 inches 1 meter

course of time. The process whereby cultures develop similar features without cultural exchange is called **independent invention.**

Because they believed that all societies passed through the same stages of evolution in a fixed sequence, the evolutionists held that contemporary primitive cultures closely resembled an early stage through which their own culture had once evolved. Victorian society was imagined to be the highest stage of the sequence through which less "civilized" societies were still evolving. Therefore, the evolutionists believed that the behavior of the "savages" could be compared to that of the early Europeans, and their method is referred to as the **comparative method.** An important feature of this method was the belief that the behavior of people within a culture can be explained by reference to conditions earlier in their history which no longer prevail. The rule requiring marriage to outsiders, for example, was thought of as being left over from a hypothetical stage of cultural evolution in which women were kidnapped from outside groups to provide wives for the men of the tribe. Although the kidnapping is no longer practiced, the rules requiring marriage to outsiders may remain.

Among those individuals most important in formulating the evolutionist position were Lewis Henry Morgan, Sir Edward Tylor, and Herbert Spencer.

Lewis H. Morgan. In *Ancient Society* (1877), Lewis H. Morgan defined savagery, barbarism, and civilization as the three basic stages of social evolution. By associating certain specific attributes to each of these stages, Morgan intended to create a complete scheme of characteristics that would define the various evolutionary stages. He associated the use of bows and arrows and the gathering mode of subsistence, for example, with savagery; whereas the domestication of animals he viewed as a feature of barbarism.

Sir Edward B. Tylor. The English anthropologist Sir Edward B. Tylor also attempted to describe the evolution of culture in his work, *Primitive Culture*

(1871), but his focus was primarily on the development of religion and not on technology. According to Tylor, religion generally evolves from animism (the belief in spirits, ghosts, and souls) to polytheism (the belief in numerous deities) to monotheism (the belief in a single God). At its most advanced stage, Tylor claimed, religion is associated with morality; questions of right and wrong are related to the idea of God. Tylor concluded that these progressive stages of development were the result of increasing rationality on the part of man.

Herbert Spencer. Tylor's approach was closely paralleled in the writing of Herbert Spencer, although Spencer's emphasis was considerably different. In *Principles of Sociology* (1896), Spencer traced the supposed evolution of marriage from polygamy through monogamy, stressing the evolution of society towards increased specialization and complexity. Like Morgan and Tylor, Spencer envisioned the evolution of culture as taking place in distinct and definable stages.

What the nineteenth century evolutionists were attempting to establish was a scheme for the historical progression of cultural forms. In seeking out universal cultural laws, the evolutionists hoped to explain the similarities and differences between cultures. Although the work of the evolutionists was an important step toward finding natural causes for cultural developments, their basic belief that all cultures pass through identical stages of development often led them to excessively generalized and overly simplified conclusions.

Reactions to evolutionism

As the nineteenth century drew to a close, many anthropologists were beginning to voice their objections to the methods and findings of the evolutionists. Until that time, little actual ethnological data had been available, and the conclusions reached by such men as Tylor and Morgan were generally based not on first-hand experience but rather on the frequently unreliable accounts given by travelers, missionaries, and colonial officials. Furthermore, the evolutionists were frequently guilty of forcing their essentially unreliable data to fit certain preconceived schemes.

Franz Boas.   Among the first to voice his objection to the "arm-chair" school of anthropology was a German-born anthropologist named Franz Boas. Boas maintained that it was necessary to gather as much data as possible about individual cultures before any general laws of cultural development could be stated. He suggested that the anthropologist should study each culture thoroughly, both in its present and historical forms, while carefully recording his findings in detail. By placing great emphasis on fieldwork, Boas was attempting to set higher standards of research for anthropology. Boas demonstrated his approach by directing his attention to the fading American Indian cultures before they were lost to study and analysis forever.

In gathering data on Indians of the United States and Canada, Boas discovered many facts which did not seem to correspond to the generalized schemes of cultural behavior described by the evolutionists. He found, for example, that clans among the Northwest Indians resulted from village fission, whereas among the Navajo they resulted from the fusion of separate groups. Simple geometric designs did not necessarily represent the degeneration of what once had begun as a naturalistic design. Masks were used by different tribes for quite varied religious purposes. Boas upheld that the same factors could hardly account for similar developments among different cultures. He formulated the thesis that each culture is unique and that similarities between cultures are best explained by the assumption that cultural exchange has taken place. In this thesis—known as **historical particularism**—Boas was voicing his objection to the evolutionists' attempts to formulate one grand scheme of cultural development without adequately considering the diversity of human cultures.

Boas objected not only to the methods of the

Figure 2-5. *Franz Boas was a prominent cultural anthropologist. He led the opposition against predetermined evolutionism. Boas stressed that an individual cultural trait must be studied in the context of its society.*

evolutionists, but also the manner in which their findings were evaluated. Generally speaking, the evolutionists thought of non-Western people as savages and freely made value judgments based on European cultural standards. Tylor, for example, although among the most liberal of his contemporaries, wrote of the "stupidity and unpractical conservatism and dogged superstition" of certain contemporary "primitive" societies. Boas denied that any society was any more rational, logical, or civilized than any other. His thesis that a culture must be judged according to its own standards and values rather than those of the investigator is known as **cultural relativism.** Relativism, as opposed to the belief that one's own culture is inherently superior to any other, represented a tremendously liberating philosophy at that time.

Boas' work represents a major step forward for the field of anthropology. As developed by Boas' students, ethnography, a detailed description of a society's culture, concerned itself with the exact recording of all the characteristics of each individual culture, interpreted as closely as possible according to the viewpoint of the native. This approach gave long overdue recognition to the validity of the world's various cultures, but it failed to stress the discovery of general laws of cultural behavior and development. Although Boas recognized the search for universals as a valid ideal, the collection of data became the primary function of the anthropologist, and the search for the laws of culture was temporarily abandoned.

The diffusionists

While the students of Boas pursued their work in America, several related movements were gathering strength in Europe. In opposition to the evolutionists, some European anthropologists argued that all culture began in one or more specific areas, from which it then spread throughout the world. The belief that all cultures share a common origin is known as **diffusionism.**

The most extreme form of diffusionism was proposed by a small group of British anthropologists that included Grafton Elliot Smith and W. J. Perry. These men argued that all cultural traits were originally developed in Egypt and subsequently spread throughout the world in waves of emigration. "Primitive" cultural forms, therefore, were thought of as being no more than degenerate forms of the original Egyptian civilization. The emphasis of these British diffusionists was on the inherent uninventiveness of mankind. They believed that all cultures on earth were merely a reflection of the one great original civilization that flourished thousands of years ago. In stressing the degenerate nature of all "primitive" non-western societies, the extreme diffusionists proved themselves to be nearly as biased as the evolutionists.

Most advocates of diffusionism, however, did not assume such an extreme position. The largest faction of diffusionists included such German anthropologists as Fritz Graebner, Father Wilhelm Schmidt, and Martin Gusinde. These men believed that culture originally arose in several areas, called culture circles, from which it gradually spread out. Similarities between cultures were believed to be the result of the overlapping of culture circles; accordingly, the more ways in which cultures resembled each other, the greater were the chances of an historical relationship. These German diffusionists are known as the *Kulturkreise* (culture circle) school.

Meanwhile, similar schools of thought, based largely on the theories of Boas and his students, were developing in America. Rather than asserting that cultural traits diffused from a few select areas, members of these schools associated various traits with certain geographical environments which they referred to as **culture areas.** After mapping out and classifying the tribal groups of North and South America, they proposed a law of diffusion stating that cultural traits tend to spread out in all directions from their center of origin; therefore, the relative age of cultural traits could be determined by their geographical distribution. Those traits which have spread farthest from their center of origin were assumed to be the oldest. The larger the area, the older the trait. Taking tepees as an example, we can infer that they represented quite an old trait, for by the time the white man had penetrated the American continent, the American Indian tepee was a widespread form of housing, adapted to a number of varied environments. In the Far West, tepees were made of cedar bark; the Plains Indians made theirs of hides; and the Indians of the Northeast made theirs of birchbark. By the time a trait has reached its marginal area of diffusion, it will probably have been replaced at its point of origin, wherever this may be, by another trait. Taking an analogy from zoology, we find, for example, that marsupials, which once occupied the ecological niche today filled by placental mammals, are to be found nowadays only in certain geographical fringe areas of the world, such as in Australia and Oceania.

The main problem with the culture area concept and the related age-area hypothesis, however, was that they tended to be no more than simplified versions of environmental determinism, or the belief that the form of a culture can be explained entirely in terms of its general environment. Such a belief by itself became increasingly unacceptable to twentieth century anthropologists.

Diffusionism, then, did not prove to be a satisfactory framework for anthropology. None of the

Figures 2-6, 7, 8, 9, and 10. *Masks are an important part of many people's culture. The double face mask in Figure 2-7 is from an African tribe on the Ivory Coast; the other masks are from North American Indian tribes. Masks serve a variety of functions. They have been used in birth, marriage, and death ceremonies, in governing, and to symbolize power. The mask is strongly associated with social control.*

diffusionist approaches could adequately account for the primary origin of cultural traits. How, for example, did the original culture of Egypt develop? By maintaining that the development of culture happened only once and then spread outward, the extreme British diffusionists still retained much of the faulty cultural scheme proposed by the evolutionists. Diffusionism, like evolutionism, ultimately failed to provide all the answers.

The functionalists

An important school of anthropology which arose in opposition to the extreme evolutionist and diffusionist positions was known as **functionalism.** Although the functionalists shared Boas' emphasis on intensive field work and the detailed collection of data, their approach differed from that of Boas and the diffusionists in one very significant respect: the functionalists were not concerned with the historical approach to the study of culture. Dissatisfied with the far-fetched reconstructions of the past offered by both the evolutionists and the diffusionists, members of the functionalist school reacted by abandoning all such efforts. Rather, they emphasized the study of contemporary cultures without drawing any analogies to the past.

The functionalists maintain that each of the traits within a culture has a specific function which serves to hold the social system together and that the structure of a society is determined by the way in which it fulfills those functions. The work of the anthropologist, as envisioned by members of this school, was to study the ways in which various cultural institutions function to solve the problem of maintaining the system. Although the evolutionists had also recognized the interrelationship between culture traits, they focused primarily on tracing the origin and development of those traits. The functionalists denied the importance of historical background and limited themselves to the study of twentieth century cultures.

North America:
1. Plains Area
2. Plateau Area
3. California Area
4. North Pacific Coast Area
5. Eskimo Area
6. Mackenzie Area
7. Eastern Woodland Area
8. Southeastern Area
9. Southwestern Area
10. Mesoamerica

South America:
11. Chibcha Area
12. The Inca Area
13. Guanaco Area
14. Amazon Area
15. The Antilles

Figure 2-11. *This map shows various culture areas of North and South America; within each numbered area the tribes share many adaptive culture traits.*

The study of culture ● part **1**

A. R. Radcliffe-Brown. One of the major theoreticians of the functionalist school was A. R. Radcliffe-Brown. He interpreted ceremonies, myths, and legends as expressions of a society's collective emotions, an idea which he borrowed from the French sociologist Émile Durkheim. To Radcliffe-Brown, ceremonies served to regulate individual conduct and promote a feeling of solidarity among the members of a group. According to this functionalist view, the significance of a revivalist meeting, for example, lies in the fact that it serves to bring people together; its religious value is secondary. He viewed societies as composed of a system of customs, and he discussed customs in terms of their relation to other customs. But the question remains: why did a particular custom arise in a society in the first place? In his study of the Andaman Islanders, an island people living off the Indian subcontinent, Radcliffe-Brown voiced his objection to the search for cultural origins, arguing that it is possible to discover natural laws of society by analyzing the interrelation of customs within contemporary societies. Although he invoked the idea of "psychic unity" so dear to nineteenth century evolutionists (he spoke of "universal psychological processes"), Radcliffe-Brown ultimately declared that anthropology should limit itself to the description of existing societies.

Bronislaw Malinowski. Another major theoretician of the functionalist school was the Polish-born anthropologist Bronislaw Malinowski. Malinowski argued that people everywhere share certain biological and psychological needs and that the ultimate function of all cultural institutions is to fulfill those needs. Everyone, for example, needs to feel secure in his relationship to the physical universe. Therefore, when his science and technology are inadequate to explain certain natural phenomena—such as eclipses or earthquakes—man develops religion and magic to account for those phenomena and to restore his feeling of security. The nature of the institution, according to Malinowski, is determined by its function.

Unlike Radcliffe-Brown, Malinowski did not entirely reject the question of cultural origins; rather, he argued that the origin of cultural traits could be discovered by the analysis of the trait's function within a given society. Malinowski outlined three fundamental levels of needs which he claimed had to be resolved by all cultures.

1) A culture must provide for biological needs, such as the need for food and procreation.

2) A culture must provide for instrumental needs, such as the need for law and education.

3) A culture must provide for integrative needs, such as religion and art.

If the anthropologist could analyze the ways in which a culture fills these needs for its members, Malinowski believed that he could also deduce the origin of cultural traits.

The functionalist approach represented another step forward for anthropology. It was functionalism which finally emphasized the analysis of relationships within cultures and the ways in which cultures function to fill the needs of its members. Yet the functionalists failed to account adequately for the origin of cultural phenomena. Despite Malinowski's claim, the relationship between traits and their functions does not seem to be a directly causal one. Cultural traits and functions affect each other, but they do not seem to have a strict cause and effect relationship. Furthermore, the functionalist approach fails to adequately explain the similarities and differences between cultures. Why does a culture choose one institution to fill a function when a different institution might fill that same function? The functionalists, for example, tried to explain kinship systems in terms of a cohesive function. This explanation begs the issue; ultimately, every aspect of a society can be explained in terms of function. Yet such questions as why a kinship system arose remain unanswered. It is like explaining the function of an organ of the human body without ever asking what part of the body it helps to maintain. Although the functionalists served an important role in pointing out many of the oversimplifications proposed by the evolutionists and diffusionists, they did not offer acceptable alternatives to historical analysis.

Recent trends

Just as the schools of Boas, the diffusionists, and the functionalists appeared in response to the inherent weaknesses in the theories of the evolutionists, later anthropologists have searched extensively for suitable alternatives to the weaker theories of their predecessors. Whereas the general tendency of the counter-evolutionists was either to abandon or postpone the search for universal laws of culture, later theorists have tended to resume interest in that search. At the same time, they have been attempting to develop more precise means of studying and measuring cultural phenomena.

Structuralism

One important theory of culture is that of the French structuralists. Led by Claude Lévi-Strauss, the structuralists think of culture as an expression of the underlying structure of the human mind. This approach is another step away from that of the evolutionists, in that it is concerned primarily in analyzing societies through the observations of the members of the society.

Claude Lévi-Strauss.   In his writings, Claude Lévi-Strauss has argued that human behavior within a cultural framework is a surface representation of an individual's underlying mental structures, or ideas. The structuralists analyze the psychological structure of a society by examining the beliefs and ideas of its members. Lévi-Strauss' studies have centered around the concept of polarity, explaining cultures in terms of a complex system of oppositions. The spatial arrangement of a Trobriand village, for example, presents a series of concentric rings which are said to reflect a series of symbolic polarities. Moreover, the village

Figure 2-12. *Claude Lévi-Strauss is the most prominent advocate of French structuralism, an approach to analyzing cultures. He concentrates on the origins of societal systems, and looks to a culture for its underlying rules of thought.*

is divided into central and peripheral, sacred and profane areas. The central area may be inhabited only by bachelors, whereas married couples must dwell in the periphery.

Ethnosemantics

Ethnosemantics—sometimes referred to as cognitive anthropology or the "new ethnography"—takes the approach of Lévi-Strauss a step further. The goal of the ethnosemanticists is to arrive at a description of a culture as a member of that culture would see it, free from the biases of the outsider. An Englishman describing American football to a fellow countryman would probably do so in terms familiar to themselves; most likely he would describe the game in terms of rugby, a somewhat similar game widely played in England. The description, however, would fall short of conveying to an Englishman exactly what the American game consists of, since it would be described in terms of another game. Football would probably emerge as a caricature of rugby.

The way languages categorize colors has been a subject investigated by the ethnosemanticists. They have grouped societies in terms of the number of colors they perceive. Some societies, for instance, think only in terms of black and white, whereas others think in terms of upward to eleven color categories. If one knows the number of color terms in the language, one can predict with a fair amount of certainty what those colors will be. All languages have terms to describe black and white; the other colors to be added, listed in order, are red, yellow, green, blue, brown, gray, orange, pink, and purple. Most technologically simple societies have very few terms for colors; the number of terms increases with the complexity of a society because color naming is apparently of relatively little use to societies living close to nature. The inference is that such societies reflect the first stages of abstract color naming.

The approach of the ethnosemanticists clearly has its roots in the cultural relativism of Boas and his students. Because they rely on data obtained from a small number of individuals, however, the ethnosemanticists sometimes limit the validity of their work. The data they obtain is based on ideal situations as the ideal is perceived by a small percentage of the population.

Taken alone, both structuralism and ethnosemanticism display significant limitations as approaches to the study of culture. In conjunction with other approaches, however, these schools represent a valuable contribution to anthropology.

Neo-evolutionism

The main thrust of anthropology during the first half of the twentieth century had been a reaction against the generalizations proposed by the nineteenth century evolutionists. In the late 1940s, however, several anthropologists—most notably Leslie White and J. H. Steward—called for a revival of the search for universal laws of culture and cultural development. This school of modern anthropology is referred to as **neo-evolutionism.**

Leslie White. According to Leslie White's system of analysis, all culture consists of three essential components. He refers to these components as the techno-economic, the social, and the ideological. White defines the techno-economic aspect of a culture as the way in which the members of the culture deal with their environment, and it is this aspect which then determines the social and ideological aspects of the culture. In effect, White combines the principles of economic and environmental determinism. Because White considers the manner in which a culture adapts to its environment to be the most significant factor in its development, his approach has been labeled the **cultural materialist** approach. In *The Evolution of Culture* (1959), White stated his basic law of evolution, that culture evolves in proportion to the increased output of energy on the part of each individual, or to the increased efficiency with which that energy is put to work. In other words, culture develops in direct response to technological progress. Unlike the historical particularists, White concentrates primarily on the similarities between cultures in an attempt to arrive at universal cultural laws. White's position is weakened, however, by his failure to account for the fact that technological "progress" may occur in response to purely cultural stimuli. In this respect, his theories are heavily influenced by eighteenth century notions of human progress.

Julian H. Steward. Because Julian H. Steward too is concerned primarily with the response of a culture to its environment, he might also be labeled a neo-evolutionist. Unlike White, however, Steward is concerned with the evolution of specific cultures rather than with the examination of culture in general. Whereas White is concerned with the general categories of culture, Steward is concerned with the comparison of specific historical sequences. His approach, a blending of evolutionism and historical particularism, involves the identification of recurrent developments which can be used as the basis of valid cultural laws.

Because it views evolution as a sequence of steps generally applicable to all cultures, White's theory has been referred to as general evolution. Steward's theory that each culture adapts differently in response to unique environmental pressures, on the other hand, has been labeled specific evolution. Steward himself referred to his approach as **cultural ecology**—that is, the interaction of specific cultures with their environments. Initially, Steward was struck by a number of similarities in the development of urban civilizations in both Peru and Mesoamerica and noted that certain developments were paralleled in the urban civilizations of the Old World. He identified the constants and abstracted from them his laws of cultural development. Steward proposed three fundamental procedures for cultural ecology:

1) The interrelationship of a culture's technology and its environment must be analyzed. How effectively does the culture exploit available resources to provide food and housing for its members?

2) The pattern of behavior associated with a culture's technology must be analyzed. How do members of the culture go about performing the work that must be performed for their survival?

3) The relationship between those behavior patterns and the rest of the cultural system must be determined. How does the work they do to survive affect the people's attitudes and outlooks? How is their survival behavior linked to their social activities and their personal relationships?

Steward's method incorporates the best features of the functionalist approach and calls for scientific observation of the ways in which environmental and cultural phenomena are related, stressing cultural systems as wholes rather than individuals within the culture. In cultural ecology, the first concern is the culture's adaptation, and other aspects of the cultural system are determined from that basis. Like White, Steward argues that the environment is the chief determining factor of culture.

The future

It should not be concluded from our discussion of the foregoing approaches that the field of anthropology is split into a number of warring factions. With few exceptions, anthropologists have shown a great willingness to draw on any theoretical tool, no matter which theoretical "school" gave birth to that particular tool. The primary concern of modern anthropology is that of cultural evolution and the search for general laws that govern the way cultures form, develop, and adapt to changes in the physical and social environment, but this search is being carefully conducted within the context of rigorous field research and sound data. At the same time, there is a wide-spread interest in the interrelationship between culture and environment, tying anthropology to the natural as well as to the social sciences. This combination of concerns holds great promise for the continued growth of our understanding of human behavior.

□

Original study

TRAVELERS
AND
ENCYCLOPEDISTS

It is customary to credit Herodotus (c. 484-c. 425 B.C.) as fathering history and anthropology, and I do not dispute either of these claims. He begins by stating, "What Herodotus the Halicarnassian has learnt by inquiry is here set forth; in order that so the memory of the past may not be blotted out from among men by time . . ." In the era of Herodotus "history" meant inquiry or research and by extension information resulting from inquiry; by the second century B.C., however, the word had come to mean the particular kinds of descriptions recorded by Herodotus. *Histories* by Herodotus is primarily an account of the Greco-Persian War, with the additional presentation of related and unrelated information ranging topically from anthropology to zoology; about one-ninth of this work is devoted to ethnographic data. Herodotus personally visted Egypt and much of the Near East and the quality of his description of Egyptian homelife speaks for itself.

But concerning Egypt I will now speak at length, because nowhere are there so many marvellous things, nor in the whole world beside are there to be seen so many works of unspeakable greatness; therefore I shall say the more concerning Egypt.

As the Egyptians have a climate peculiar to themselves, and their river is different in its nature from all other rivers, so have they made themselves customs and laws of a kind contrary to those of all other men. Among them, the women buy and sell, the men abide at home and weave; and whereas in weaving all others push the woof upwards, the Egyptians push it downwards. Men carry burdens on their heads, women on their shoulders. Women make water standing, men sitting. They relieve nature indoors, and eat out of doors in the streets, giving the reason, that things unseemly but necessary should be done in secret, things not unseemly should be done openly. No woman is dedicated to the service of any god or goddess; men are dedicated to all deities male or female. Sons are not compelled against their will to support their parents, but daughters must do so though they be unwilling.

Everywhere else, priests of the gods wear their hair long; in Egypt they are shaven. With all other men, in mourning for the dead those most nearly concerned have their heads shaven; Egyptians are shaven at other times, but after a death they let their hair and beard grow. The Egyptians are the only people who keep their animals with them in the house. Whereas all others live on wheat and barley, it is the greatest disgrace for an Egyptian so to live; they make food from a coarse grain which some call spelt. They knead dough with their feet, and gather mud and dung with their hands. The Egyptians and those who have learnt it from them are the only people who practise circumcision. Every man has two garments, every woman only one. The rings and sheets of sails are made fast elsewhere outside the boat, but inside it in Egypt. The Greeks write and calculate by moving the hand from left to right; the Egyptians do contrariwise; yet they say that their way of writing is towards the right, and the Greek way towards the left. They use two kinds of writing; one is called sacred, the other common.

The brevity, clarity, and scope of this passage is striking. Admittedly we would prefer to know more about each topic discussed, but what is more important in the present context is that this description has a calm and studied objectivity. To Herodotus the Egyptians were different from the Greeks, but they were not quaint or bizarre. In his accounts of them he usually described what he had seen or heard. His record of the esoteric Egyptian embalming practices, for example, could only have been obtained through lengthy and systematic interviews, and the same is true of his discussion of their religion, to which he gives an ethnological perspective by comparisons with Greek ideas. On the basis of this Egyptian material, Herodotus should be credited with fathering ethnography.

The 1492 voyage of Christopher Columbus is not only a watershed in the history of exploration, but an ethnographic landmark as well. The original letter in which Columbus reported the results of his first adventure is not known to exist, but an approximation of the primary text is available from copies. Two of the eight printed pages of text are devoted to Indians of the Caribbean, and those met on the island of Haiti are described in the following words.

The people of this island, and of all the other islands which I have found and of which I have information, all go naked, men and women, as their mother bore them, although some women cover a single place with the leaf of a plant or with a net of cotton which they make for the purpose. They have no iron or steel or weapons, nor are they fitted to use them, not because they are not well built men and of handsome stature, but because they are very marvellously timorous. They have no other arms than weapons made of canes, cut in seeding time, to the ends of which they fix a small sharpened stick. And they do not dare to make use of these, for many times it has happened that I have sent ashore two or three men to some town to have speech, and countless people have come out to them, and as soon as they have seen my men approaching they have fled, even a father not waiting for his son. And this, not because ill has been done to anyone; on the contrary, at every point where I have been and have been able to have speech, I have given to them of all that I had, such as cloth and many other things, without receiving anything for it; but so they are, incurably timid. It is true that, after they have been reassured and have lost their fear, they are so guileless and so generous with all they possess, that no one would believe it who has not seen it. They never refuse anything which they possess, if it be asked of them; on the contrary, they invite anyone to share it, and display as much love as if they would give their hearts, and whether the thing be of value or whether it be of small price, at one with whatever trifle of whatever kind it may be that is given to them, with that they are content. I forbade that they should be given things so worthless as fragments of broken crockery and scraps of broken glass, and ends of straps, although when they were able to get them, they fancied that they possessed the best jewel in the world. . . . And I gave a thousand handsome good things, which I had brought, in order that they might conceive affection, and more than that, might become Christians and be inclined to the love and service of their highnesses and of the whole Castilian nation, and strive to aid us and to give us of the things which they have in abundance and which are necessary to us. And they do not know any creed and are not idolators; only they all believe that power and good are in the heavens, and they are very firmly convinced that I, with these ships and men, came from the heavens, and in this belief they everywhere received me, after they had overcome their fear. And this does not come because they are ignorant; on the contrary, they are of a very acute intelligence and are men who navigate all those seas, so that it is amazing how good an account they give of everything, but it is because they have never seen people clothed or ships of such a kind.

What is most significant about this ethnographic sketch is the author's attitude of objectivity, which resulted in a report unadorned with embellishments and exaggeration. At the same time we miss details and note that most of the account deals with cultural dimensions which need only have been seen to be described. One would gather that Columbus had an attitude toward the people which would have led to a competent account if he had been interested enough to compile it.

Source:
From *Other Peoples, Other Customs: World Ethnography and its History* by Wendell H. Oswalt. Copyright © 1972 by Holt, Rinehart and Winston, Inc. Reprinted by permission of Holt, Rinehart and Winston, Inc.

Figure 2-13. *Indians depicted as cannibals.*

Summary

1.

Evolutionism grew out of a period of important advances in science, philosophy, and industrial technology during the first half of the nineteenth century. Darwin's *On the Origin of Species* was the first formal statement of the theory of biological evolution and provided the first model for anthropology. The evolutionists of nineteenth century anthropology employed the concepts of adaptation and natural selection from biological evolution and conceived of society as developing in a regular sequence of predictable stages. Lewis H. Morgan defined three basic stages of cultural evolution: savagery, barbarism, and civilization, all characterized by specific technological attributes. Sir Edward Tylor focused upon the development of religion, postulating three basic stages: animism, polytheism, and monotheism, each resulting from increasing rationality in human concepts. Herbert Spencer's *Principles of Sociology* traced the evolution of marriage forms from polygamy through monogamy. The nineteenth century evolutionists were attempting to discover universal laws of cultural behavior in a single progression of stages through which all cultures passed or must pass.

2.

Franz Boas was the major theoretician of the historical particularist school of the twentieth century. He objected to the general lack of ethnographic data and the ethnocentric values employed by the evolutionists in formulating laws of cultural behavior and development. Boas emphasized the careful study of individual cultures and collection of ethnographic data, and in doing so he observed cultural phenomena which did not correspond to the generalized schemes of the evolutionists. This led him to conclude that each culture was unique in its development and that similarities between cultures were due only to diffusion. The historical particularists abandoned the search for universal cultural laws and stressed the collection of data.

3.

Diffusionism is the belief that all cultural traits spread throughout the world from one or more points of common origin. It was the primary movement in early twentieth century European anthropology. Grafton Elliot Smith and W. J. Perry were major proponents of the extreme diffusionists and argued that all cultural traits originated in Egypt. Fritz Graebner and Father Wilhelm Schmidt were representative of the *Kulturkreise* school in Germany. Less extreme than the English diffusionists, they contended that culture arose in several areas and spread throughout the world from these "culture circles." The culture area school developed contemporaneously in America, arguing that specific cultural traits were found in association with particular types of environment. This school developed the diffusionist theory that cultural traits spread within these culture areas and that the relative age of each trait could be calculated from their distance from their points of origin.

4.

The functionalists, unlike the evolutionists, were interested in the function of specific cultural traits in maintaining a social system rather than in the origin of those traits. A. R. Radcliffe-Brown argued that it was possible to discover universal cultural laws by analyzing the function of specific cultural traits in societies, and proposed the existence of universal psychological processes as responsible for such laws. Bronislaw Malinowski proposed three levels of fundamental human needs which every culture has to fill—

biological, instrumental, and integrative—and argued that the origin of cultural traits could be discovered by the analysis of their function within a given society.

5.
The French structuralists, led by Claude Lévi-Strauss, proposed a model of cultural behavior whereby culture was a surface representation of the underlying structures of the human mind. They approached their analyses through the examination of the conscious beliefs and ideas of individuals within a culture. The ethnosemanticists attempted to analyze cultural phenomena by studying the intentions, goals, and values of individuals within the cultural system according to linguistic models.

6.
The neo-evolutionists revived the search for universal laws of cultural phenomena and development. Leslie White proposed that all culture is composed of three components: the techno-economic, the social, and the ideological. The way a culture utilized its environment is the significant factor in its development. White proposed a model whereby cultures evolved in proportion to increased utilization of energy by the system. Unlike White's approach to the evolution of culture in general stages, labeled general evolution, Julian Steward was interested in specific deviations from those stages, an approach called specific evolution. Steward was the founder of an approach now known as cultural ecology in which cultural phenomena are analyzed in terms of their interaction with the environment.

Suggested readings

Eiseley, Loren *Darwin's Century: Evolution and the Men Who Discovered It*. Garden City, New York: Doubleday, 1958.
Eiseley traces the development of evolutionary ideas in biology from the seventeenth through the nineteenth centuries. Darwin's thought is examined in relation to his predecessors and contemporaries; minor evolutionary theoreticians are also discussed. Footnotes and a bibliography present a wide range of primary, as well as secondary sources.

Harris, Marvin *The Rise of Anthropological Theory: A History of Theories of Culture*. New York: T. Y. Crowell, 1968.
One of the most recent histories of anthropological theory, this book traces the development of the profession as a science. Harris takes a very definite stand in support of the cultural-materialist approach and criticizes his colleagues from this point of view. Because of the opinionated nature of the book, it has been the focus of much controversy in the field, but still stands as one of the most exciting histories of the field ever written.

Hays, H. R. *From Ape to Angel: An Informal History of Social Anthropology*. New York: Putnam, 1964.
The focus of this book is on personalities and anecdotes. It is written in a lively, readable style meant for the general public. It is an informal history of the science. The book is divided into four sections: the Classical Evolutionists, the Critical Reaction, Diffusion and Sociology, and Psychological Insight and Social Responsibility.

Hodgen, Margaret T. *Early Anthropology in the Sixteenth and Seventeenth Centuries*. Philadelphia: University of Pennsylvania Press, 1964.
In an attempt to explore the antecedents of anthropological theory, this book considers the heritage of Renaissance, Medieval, and Classic Grecian social philosophy in anthropology.

Lowie, Robert H. *The History of Ethnological Theory*. New York: Holt, Rinehart and Winston, 1937.
This book is devoted only to that part of anthropology which concerns culture, and indicates the course of theoretical progress from evolutionary precedents to the time of its publication. It is a classic in its field.

Penniman, T. K. *A Hundred Years of Anthropology*. New York: Humanities Press, 1965.
Penniman outlines developments in prehistory and technology in the Old World. Following this is a good survey of physical anthropology by J. S. Weiner and by Beatrice Blackwood. Only the section by Weiner has a bibliography. Penniman's approach is comparative and analytic, with a tolerance for all methods.

Stocking, George W., Jr. *Race, Culture and Evolution: Essays in the History of Anthropology*. New York: Free Press, 1968.
A collection of essays which, unlike most such collections, is intended to be read as one book. Stocking presents a unique approach to the history of anthropological theory. This is not a retrospective justification of present methods but a historical account of the development and progress of a social science. Each idea is presented as reasonable within its own period and not attacked with the hindsight of numerous generations.

The history of culture

Early man, like all creatures in his environment, depended on his physical attributes for survival. His behavior was primarily instinctive rather than learned; and his legacy to each succeeding generation was that of favorable genes rather than accumulated knowledge and skills. In the course of evolution, however, man was to take a significant departure toward a more rapid and more efficient way of adapting to the environment. He learned to manufacture and utilize tools; he organized into social units more proficient at hunting and gathering than any single member of the species had ever been; and eventually he learned to preserve his traditions and knowledge to bridge his past and present, through the use of symbols. In other words, man acquired the ability to produce culture.

This ability has made man the most influential creature on this planet. Man does not merely adapt to the environment; he attempts to mold and manipulate it to suit his needs and desires. Medical technology may eventually enable him to control genetic inheritance and thus the future course of his biological evolution. Space technology may enable him to propagate his species in extraterrestrial environments. And computer technology enables him to correlate and organize an ever-increasing input of knowledge, and thus keep pace with the changes he himself has brought about.

At this stage in his development, however, man is also concerned with the implications of this remarkable culture-creating ability. Survival is no longer threatened by the environment but by man himself. Atomic and hydrogen bombs, pollution, the population explosion—all these products of modern man's civilization have triggered questions concerning the direction of his progress. On the verge of a civilization even more highly organized and automated than our present urban environments, many people are attempting a "return to nature," to a simpler existence in which modern man, like his ancestors, must rely more heavily on his instincts and physical prowess. Others, bewildered and frightened by the complexity and pace of life, have escaped not to nature but into madness. And still others, who feel excluded and uncertain of their roles in our sophisticated culture, have resorted to violence and aggression.

Yet the desire to get back to "simpler" times is a futile one. The simplicity of bygone days is largely an illusion, a sentimental attitude that fails to take into account the harsh realities of a time when survival was every man's primary occupation. And even if a return to the past were desirable, it would still be impossible. Change is inescapable for twentieth-century man, just as it was millions of years ago for his ancestors. There is no going back, but we may be more capable of clarifying and adjusting to present and future cultural transformations by simply *looking* back. Behaviorally and biologically, we are still in many ways similar to prehistoric man. By studying the evolution of the hominid line and the physiological and cultural adjustments our ancestors have made, we may gain greater insight into the problems of adaptation that we face today.

Culture in other primates

One might properly question the value of studying primates other than man when it is man himself, and his distinctive cultural capacities, that concern us. But man did not start out as a cultural being—he did not even start out as man. His roots, like those of the other living primates, lie in ancient times and in less specialized biological creatures; his development was influenced by the same evolutionary processes. It is believed, therefore, that in studying the environment of those times, the anatomical features which evolved in response to that environment, and the rudimentary cultural adaptations of those primates who share in man's ancestral heritage, we will draw closer to an understanding of how and why man developed as he did.

Environment

The early primates emerged during a period when the earth was undergoing radical change. The surface crust was buckling and heaving, forcing huge chunks of sediment to rise from the ocean floors. Retreating seas revealed new land masses that became swamps. Old land surfaces were being eroded, thus altering their vegetational covering. The formation during this period of the great mountain chains—the Rockies, Andes, Alps, and Himalayas—affected the distribution of forests, grasslands, and deserts.

A new, mild climate favored the spread of dense tropical and subtropical forests over much of the earth, including North and South America, Southeast Asia, the Middle East, and most of Africa. This led to an increase in the numbers and spread of grasses, ivies, shrubs, and other flowering plants, such as the trees that are found in forests. Forestation set the stage for the evolutionary advance from a rodentlike ground existence to tree living. Forests also provided our early ancestors with ecological niches, or functional positions in their habitats. The relatively small size of the early primates allowed them to exploit the smaller branches of trees; larger and heavier competitors and predators could not follow. The move to the smaller branches also opened up a more abundant food supply. The primates were able to gather leaves, flowers, fruits, and insects, rather than having to wait for them to fall to the ground.

Figure 3-1. *Man shapes his environment through culture, exemplified by this figure.*

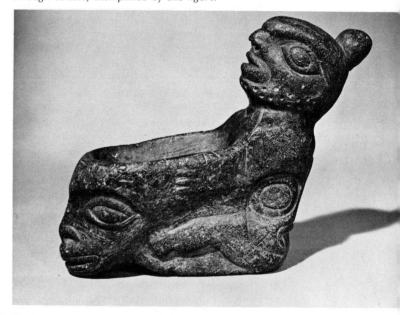

The study of culture • part **1**

The move to an arboreal existence brought a combination of the problems of earthbound existence and those of flight. In their exploitation of space, birds developed a highly stereotyped behavior pattern, keyed to the exigencies of flight. Animals living on the ground developed a slower-paced, more flexible relationship to the environment.

The tree-dwelling primates, however, were obliged to develop both flexible behavior as well as virtually automatic mechanisms for moving through the trees; for if they were no longer limited to roaming along the ground, they also no longer had the certainty of a substantial surface directly beneath their feet. Initial forays into the trees must have included many errors in judgment and coordination, leading to falls that injured or killed those who were poorly adapted to arboreal life. Natural selection favored those who judged depth correctly and gripped the branches tightly. It is possible that the early primates who took to the trees were in some measure preadapted; they had already developed certain rudimentary features useful to tree-dwellers while still living on the ground. In any case, the transition was anything but easy and required important physical adjustments. The way in which early primates anatomically adapted has considerable relevance for man, their close relative.

Anatomical features

The primate order includes the lower primates—tarsiers, lemurs, and tree shrews; and the higher primates—New and Old World monkeys, anthropoid apes, and man. Based on a study of both ancient and living primates, anthropologists have worked out a list of characteristics common to them all.

Primate dentition. The diet available to arboreal primates—shoots, leaves, insects, and soft fruits—required less specialized teeth than those found in other mammals. On the evidence of comparative anatomy and the fossil record, pri-

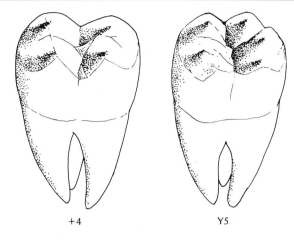

+4   Y5

Figure 3-2. *The Y-5 molar tooth pattern is found, sometimes in modified form, in gibbons, great apes, and men—and in some of their ancestors—but not in Old World monkeys. The "Y" pattern leaves 3 cusps on the cheek side, 2 on the tongue side. The + 4 tooth is a modified form of the Y-5 pattern. Both types evolved from a three cusp pattern.*

matologist W. E. LeGros Clark has postulated the existence of an archetypal primate ancestor that possessed three incisors, one canine, four premolars, and three molars on each side of the jaw, top and bottom, for a total of 44 teeth. The incisors were used for gripping, canines for tearing and shredding, and molars and premolars for grinding and chewing food.

The evolutionary trend for primate dentition has generally been toward economy, with fewer, smaller, more efficient teeth doing more work. In the early stages, one incisor on each side of the upper and lower jaws was lost, further differentiating primates from other mammals. The canines of most of the primates grew longer, forming daggerlike teeth that enabled them to rip open tough husks of fruit and other foods. Over the millennia, the first and second premolars became smaller and eventually disappeared altogether; the third and fourth premolars grew larger and more efficient by adding a second pointed projection, or cusp, thus becoming "bicuspid."

The molars also evolved from a three-cusp to the more efficient four-cusp pattern. Thus the functions of grasping, cutting, and grinding were served by one type of tooth.

Sense organs. The primates' adaptation to life in the trees involved changes in the form and function of their sensory apparatus. The sense of smell declined since primates no longer needed to sniff close to the ground in search of food. On the other hand, the senses of sight and touch became highly developed.

Travelling through trees demands judgments concerning depth, direction, distance, and the relationships of objects hanging in space, such as vines or branches. In tarsiers and higher primates, this is achieved through stereoscopic vision, or the ability to see the world in the three dimensions of height, width, and depth. It requires two eyes set apart from one another on the same plane so that each eye views an object from a slightly different angle. Stereoscopic vision is one of the most important factors in primate evolution, for it is believed to have led to increased brain size in the visual area and a greater complexity at nerve connections.

A more acute sense of touch also characterized the arboreal primates. An effective feeling and grasping mechanism helped prevent them from falling and tumbling while speeding through the trees. The primitive mammals from which primates descended possessed tiny hairs that gave them extremely sensitive tactile capacities. In primates these hairs were replaced by the more informative pads on the tips of the animals' fingers and toes.

The primate brain. By far the most outstanding characteristic of primate evolution has been the constantly increasing growth of the brain. The cerebral hemispheres—the areas of conscious thought—have grown dramatically. In all higher anthropoids, they completely cover the cerebellum, which is the part of the brain that coordinates the muscles and maintains body equilibrium.

One of the main reasons for this change is probably the primates' arboreal existence. An animal living in the trees is constantly acting and reacting to the environment. Messages from the hands and feet, eyes and ears, as well as from the sensors of balance, movement, heat, touch, and pain, are simultaneously relayed to the cortex. Obviously the cortex had to develop considerably in order to receive, analyze, and coordinate these impressions and transmit the appropriate response back down the motor nerves to the proper receptor. The enlarged cortex not only made the primates more efficient in the daily struggle for survival, but also prepared the way for cerebration, or thought—an ability that probably played a decisive role in the primate evolution that led to the emergence of man.

The primate skeleton. The skeleton gives an animal its basic shape or silhouette, supports the soft tissues, and helps protect the vital internal organs. The opening of the skull through which the spinal cord passes and connects to the brain is an important clue to evolutionary relationships. In primates, the trend is for this opening to shift forward, toward the center of the skull's base, so that it faces downward, rather than directly backward as in dogs and other mammals. This shift enables the backbone to articulate at the center of the base of the skull, thereby placing the skull in a more posterior position and imparting to the animal an upright posture. The head is thus balanced on the vertebral column, instead of projecting forward from it.

In most primates, the snout or muzzle portion of the skull has grown smaller as the sense of smell declined. The smaller snout offers less interference with stereoscopic vision and also enables the eyes to be placed in a more frontal position. A solid partition exists in most primate species between the eye and the temple to protect the eyes in their vulnerable forward position.

Below the primate skull and neck is the clavicle or collarbone. It acts as a strut, placing the arms at the side rather than in front of the body and thus permitting them to swing sideways and outwards from the trunk of the body. The forearms of higher primates articulate with the shoulder and can move with great freedom, enabling them to swing and hang among the trees.

The limbs end in hands and feet with five extremely flexible digits. At the tips of these digits are sensitive pads protected by flat nails which provide the animal with an excellent grasping device for use when moving from tree to tree. The thumb and great toe are opposable to varying degrees, so food can easily be handled and branches grasped.

Hindsight indicates that the flexible unspecialized primate hand was to prove a valuable asset to later primates. It was, in part, the generalized grasping hand which enabled hominids to manufacture and utilize tools and thus speed their evolutionary change.

Adaptation through culture

The term **adaptation** refers to the possession of certain anatomical, physiological, and behavioral characteristics that permit organisms to survive in the special environment in which they are generally found. The process of natural selection favors the survival of well-adapted individuals and the propagation of their genetic traits. Although some specimens less suited to the environment may in fact survive, they often do not reproduce; they may be incapable of attracting mates, or they may be sterile, or they may produce offspring that do not survive after birth.

As we have already noted, early primates developed physical mechanisms that helped them to adapt to their environment. With succeeding generations these mechanisms improved and, by a process of natural selection, inessential anatomical features and poorly adapted specimens were slowly weeded out. But even in these early times in primate history, physical adaptation may not have been the only way of coping with the environment.

Studies of two of the higher primates living today—the gorilla and chimpanzee—indicate that learned social behavior may have played a role in adaptation. Admittedly much of this behavior is inextricably woven with instinctual imperatives. Furthermore, modern chimp and gorilla communities have in their own way advanced from earlier times, and undoubtedly certain forms of behavior that they now exhibit were not found among their primate ancestors. But still we may discover fundamental behavior patterns that contributed to primate adaptation and the evolution of human cultural behavior.

Chimpanzee culture. Studies in genetics, biochemistry and anatomy indicate the chimpanzee is man's closest relative. Among chimps, the group social structure is rather loose and considerable independence is tolerated among individuals. There is, however, a group leader (usually a mature male) who signals the group when it is time to move from one foraging area to another. In the absence of the dominant male, or in the case of subgroups that have formed for the day, a senior male becomes the leader.

One of the most notable activities is grooming, the ritual cleaning of another chimp's coat to remove parasites and other matter. This seems to be a gesture of friendliness, submission, appeasement, or closeness. Group sociability, an important behavioral trait probably found among man's precursors, is also expressed in embracing, touching, and the joyous welcoming of chimps from the same or other neighboring groups. Group protection and coordination of group efforts is facilitated by visual and vocal communication. Apparently, there are warning calls, threat calls, and gathering calls.

The sexes intermingle continually and, as with humans, there is apparently no breeding season. However, sexual activity—initiated by either the male or the female—occurs only during the period each month when the female is receptive to impregnation. When chimps are born, they are given much love and protection. The mother-infant bond is especially strong and may last as long as four years. Unlike nonprimates, the chimp baby must be ready at birth to go everywhere with its mother, for its survival depends on the ability to remain close to her. As among the early nomadic groups of man, males wander freely; the females and children provide stability in the group. However, the males are attentive and often share in parental responsibilities. At the least, they provide both mother and infant with protection from other animals. This grouping of adult male, often several adult females, and children may have been the forerunner of human family groupings.

Chimpanzees show a remarkable ability to learn from, and thus adapt to, the environment. Jane Van Lawick-Goodall has seen an infant chimp intently watch its mother building her nest, then build a play nest of its own. One infant watched its mother copulate, and explored with its hands the genitals of the copulating pair. Experimental monkeys raised in captivity often have difficulty in copulating successfully, possibly as a result of limited learning experience in an artificial environment.

Along with the ability to learn, chimpanzees possess the ability to make and use tools, and will often teach toolmaking to the young. Admittedly, the trait is elementary in its exhibited form; but it may reflect one of the preliminary adaptations that led to man's cultural achievements. Chimps have been observed using grass stalks, branches they have stripped of leaves, and sticks up to three feet long, to catch termites. If the end of the stick becomes bent or unusable, the chimp breaks it off and discards it. Chimps are equally deliberate in their nest-building, and will test vines and branches to make sure they are usable.

Termites, plants, and fruits form the usual diet. But occasionally, as Goodall has observed, chimpanzees will kill and eat monkeys and other small animals. For example, one chimp was seen climbing tree A., where it caught the eye of a small monkey sitting opposite in tree B. While the monkey was thus distracted, a second chimpanzee climbed tree B, sprang on the monkey, and broke its neck. Several chimpanzees then ate the monkey. This one "scene" contains several interesting features which may have been signifi-

Figure 3-3. *Whereas a colt can stand within two hours of birth, a primate infant is helpless. Primate infants are dependent upon their mothers for food, transportation and protection. Only in rare cases do primate mothers not care for their young. The young female baboons in the photo below seem to be learning child care from a mother with child.*

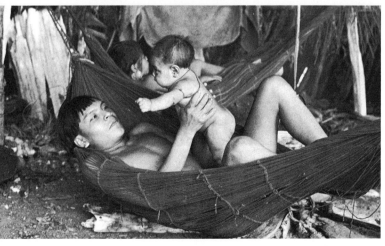

cant in man's evolutionary development: teamwork in order to trap and kill prey; group sharing of the spoils (though this is not always observed among chimps); and meat-eating, an activity which eventually established itself among the hominids and which significantly affected their biological and technological development. Goodall's chimps may be recent meat-eaters; living at the edge of the savanna, they may be just starting to exploit a food source that hominids tapped in similar circumstances millions of years earlier.

Gorilla culture. The gorilla is the largest of the apes, with some adult males weighing over 400 pounds. They live and travel in groups led by a mature, silver-backed male, which include younger, black-backed males, females, and infant gorillas. As among the chimps, there is considerable tolerance of independent behavior. Individual males may join or leave the group for a day, several days, or even months. Large groups may split up for the day and keep in touch by periodic calling (some 20 distinct calls have been recorded for gorillas). But on the whole, gorilla groups are much less transitory than those of the chimps.

Gorillas are gentle and remarkably self-controlled toward the behavior of others, especially their physical inferiors; they may try to intimidate with a chest-beating show of strength but will not actually attack unless protecting their home and food supply. They are aloof and independent, and there is little personal interaction among them. Gestures of friendship between adults are rare, and usually quite restrained. Grooming is mainly a hygienic activity. Furthermore, while one band of gorillas may associate with another, the visiting group is not accorded the excited and joyous welcome shown among bands of chimps.

Sex does not appear to be very significant in the gorilla lifestyle; in almost a year of investigating mountain gorillas, zoologist George Schaller witnessed only two copulations. As with chimps, breeding may occur whenever the female is ready for fertilization, and both menstruation and pregnancy are of nearly the same length as among humans. Gorilla infants and young juveniles share their mother's nests and have been seen sharing nests with mature childless females. Schaller observed such a relationship as well as one in which a gorilla infant went "visiting" another infant its own age and the infant's mother daily for weeks.

Unlike chimps, gorillas do not appear to be even occasional meat-eaters, and neither make nor use tools in any significant way. These facts are not meant to imply a lesser degree of intelligence, but perhaps simply a different temperament and somewhat different way of life. The size and strength of gorillas have enabled them to live comparatively untroubled lives and to develop a rather self-assured stance toward their environment; and they have never had much difficulty in locating adequate quantities of plant food. In other words, their lifestyle has perhaps contributed to a certain "complacency," to use a word which generally describes a human attitude; and thus motivational rather than intelligence factors may account for the absence of certain types of protocultural behavior observed among the chimps.

Man's ancestors

It is believed that apes and man separated from a common evolutionary line about 25 million years ago. But in tracing man's lineage from the earliest hominids through *Homo sapiens,* it is difficult to segregate these physical changes from the cultural changes which irrevocably severed man from the subhuman primates.

A cooler and drier climate, for example, reduced the number of tropical forests that had once provided man's ancestors with a protective home and an abundance of food. In the transition to life in the savannas and woodlands, both physical and cultural changes were necessary in order for man to adapt to new foods, new ways of getting and providing for this food, and new ways

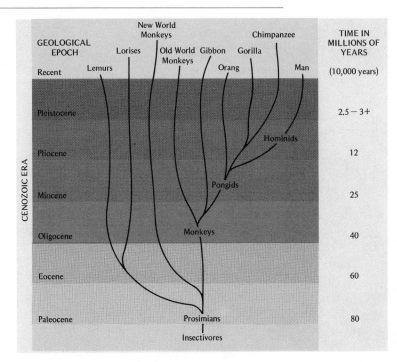

Figure 3-4. *There is still a mystery in man's evolutionary tree: where did man's true earliest ancestors diverge from the line that produced the gorilla, the gibbon, the chimpanzee, and the orangutan?*

of protecting himself in the altered environment.

Current thinking, therefore, tends toward the hypothesis that the entire complex of physical and cultural changes that took place in the early hominids probably developed more or less simultaneously through a process of mutual reinforcement.

Ramapithecus

Ramapithecus unquestionably bore greater physical similarity to anthropoid apes than to anything we willingly regard as human. Furthermore, there is no conclusive evidence that the behavior of *Ramapithecus* was significantly different from that of his pongid relatives. But according to E. L.

Simons and other scientists from Yale University, its jaw structure and dentition earn *Ramapithecus* a place, if a somewhat narrowly circumscribed one, in the family of man.

Ramapithecus, whose fossil remains were first discovered in the Siwalik Hills of India in 1935 and later in east Africa, existed about 12 million years ago. At first he probably lived in, or in proximity to, forested areas where vegetation was available for consumption. This diet is suggested not only by what is known about the environment at that time, but also by the jaw structure and

Figure 3-5. *The skulls shown in following figures were the result of many hours of patient labor. Most fossil remains look more like this when they are found; they are embedded in a matrix of rock. It takes a trained eye to recognize a fossil remain in its original condition, and it takes professional skills to remove the matrix without damage to the valuable fossilized bones.*

dentition of *Ramapithecus.* The canines of this early hominid were noticeably smaller than those of apes and would have been more useful for chewing vegetables; big interlocking canines prevent rotary motion.

It has been postulated that the absence of large canines reflects a behavioral change in which the defensive function of the teeth was replaced by the use of hand weapons. In other words, the defensive use of manufactured tools made large teeth unnecessary for early man's self-protection. But thus far no such weapons have been found with any fossil remains of *Ramapithecus.* It is more probable that the changes in environment led to changes in diet (and therefore dentition) and only later resulted in pronounced cultural and behavioral changes. As the tropical forests diminished because of a shift in climate and rainfall, the early hominids were obliged to supplement their diet first with seeds and later with food readily available in the open savannas. The new diet correlated with a change in dentition which enabled man to masticate a variety of plant (and eventually animal) foods, but which left him defenseless on the open plain against carnivorous predators.

Slowly, however, physical and cultural changes improved man's chances for survival. As a development of primate "threat gestures" which frequently involve shaking branches and throwing things, he learned to use his hands to throw available objects at predators and later learned to use them to manufacture more efficient weapons. The resultant bipedalism further contributed to hominid development by freeing the hands for making such weapons and tools. Although it made man an easier target for keen-eyed predators and thus in itself may have enhanced the need for weaponmaking, it also gave him the advantage of a better long-distance view, so he could spot predators sooner than could his relatives who walked on all fours.

Ramapithecus was not advanced enough in his behavior to manufacture tools and to know how to use them, nor is it likely that he required this more sophisticated method of defense, since the environmental transformation which forced man to roam unforested areas was only in its initial stages. But he is thought to have sometimes walked erect. The first truly biped hominid with erect posture of which we have a record is *Australopithecus*.

Australopithecus

The intermediate stages of development between *Ramapithecus* and *Australopithecus* are open to conjecture, since no fossil remains from the gap separating the appearance of these two hominids have as yet been discovered. The transformation was indeed significant: *Australopithecus* was a primitive hominid, but one that was well within the hominid line, physically and perhaps culturally as well.

It is generally accepted to divide the different "genera" of this hominid under the single heading of *Australopithecus* and to divide the genus into two distinct species: *A. africanus* and *A. robustus*. The latter species differs from the former in superficial respects such as a heavier and more robust physical frame. *A. robustus* had large jaws relative to its brain case; *A. africanus* had a large brain case relative to its jaws. They represent two differing lines of hominid evolution, with *A. robustus* ultimately becoming extinct and *A. africanus* giving rise to more modern hominids.

All these hominids were about the size of pygmies. The structure and size of the teeth bear close similarity to modern man's, and the condition of the molars suggests that food was chewed in hominid fashion. Unlike the apes, no gap exists between the canines and the teeth next to them on the lower jaw. And the large mandible is very similar to the more advanced hominid, *H. erectus*. The brain-body ratio is closer to the hominid than the ape range; and the structure of the skull reveals certain transformations which may have paved the way for the later acquisition of speech.

Australopithecine fossils have also provided anthropology with two striking facts. First, as early as three or four million years ago, this hominid

Figure 3-6. *These early hominid skulls are important clues to man's evolution. The one shown at the top is an* Australopithecus *specimen; the other two, found near Lake Rudolph, Kenya, are thought to be skulls of a variety of* A. robustus. *Debate continues about the members of this hominid genus.*

ancestor of man was bipedal, walking erect. Second, despite traditional emphasis on the importance of the brain in evolutionary development, hominids may have acquired their erect bipedal position before they acquired their highly developed and enlarged brain. Bipedalism was an important adaptive feature in the savanna environment. A biped could travel long distances in search of food without tiring. It could hold objects in the hands while running, rather than abandoning them in an emergency that required a speedy departure. And, standing erect on the open savanna, a biped could see further and spot both prey and predators.

Australopithecus, then, was equipped to be a primitive hunter and gatherer. He no longer had to depend solely on plants and fruits which were becoming scarcer; the dentition of this hominid suggests that, like modern man, he was a meat-eater (although he almost certainly needed sharp cutting tools to butcher the meat). But did he simply steal carrion left behind by wild predators, or did his carnivorous appetite and new physical potential lead him to become a weapon- and tool-using—and therefore *culturally* adapted—predator himself?

Among the remains of *A. africanus* found in South Africa were a number of baboon bones. Most of the baboon skulls were crushed, suggesting they may have been deliberately broken to extract the nutritious brains. Furthermore the majority of the skulls had been struck on the left side, indicating the killers were right-handed, as are most men. It is conceivable, then, that the killers were Australopithecines. At another *A. africanus* fossil site, scientists found a disproportionately large number of antelope thighs and jawbones which could easily have served as clubs, thus further supporting the theory that South African Australopithecines made deliberate use of weapons or tools. Even if these bones were simply found and not actually fashioned by *Australopithecus,* their use would indicate that he had made a cultural adaptation to the environment, and thus opened a new chapter in the evolution of man.

The controversy sparked by this theory was further exacerbated by discoveries in Olduvai Gorge, a fossil-rich area in East Africa. Scientists found a number of crude stone implements made of pebbles (rather than flaked stone) which bear evidence of being shaped by the human hand. Certain tools appear to have been produced by percussion flaking, whereby flakes are removed from a stone core by chopping away at its surface, leaving either a one- or two-faced tool. Such tools could be used for cutting meat, scraping hides, or cracking bones to extract marrow. This represents an important technological advance for early man that not only saved labor and time but also made possible the exploitation of a whole new food source. The existence of these tools predictably led scientists to postulate the existence of a pebble tool culture, which they named "Olduwan." But what people were responsible for this culture?

Fossil remains subsequently discovered at the Olduvai site seemed to be those of an East African variety of *A. robustus* and were eventually designated as *A. boisei.* But it was argued that the tools found with this hominid were not produced by him but rather by a more advanced contemporary—one, in fact, who was capable of victimizing *A. boisei.* The theory of a "Homo habilis"—an "able man" capable of both making and using tools and thereby deserving membership in the genus *Homo*—was tentatively supported by fossils dating from about 1.8 million years ago which were discovered a few feet below the *A. boisei* find.

Many scientists were willing to concede that a relative of *A. robustus* (namely, *A. boisei*) could not make the Olduvai tools. But they questioned the designation "Homo habilis" for those who did make the tools, since the fossils classified under this name (those found below the *A. boisei* remains) bear a close resemblance to *A. africanus.* Present thinking, however, simply postulates a line of evolutionary advance from *A. africanus* to *Homo erectus,* with "Homo habilis" placed in between as either a late form of *Australopithecus* or an early form of *Homo.*

Homo erectus

Although there is still disagreement over whether certain Australopithecines ought to be classified as man or simply forerunners of man, no dispute exists concerning the status of the next figure in human evolution. Scientists concur in their belief that he was a man and have designated him *Homo erectus.*

No previous hominids were as widespread as *Homo erectus,* whose remains have been found in Asia, Europe, and Africa. In spite of this broad distribution, the fossils reveal few significant physical variations. However, as we shall note, the *H. erectus* of the East was in some ways culturally different from that of the West.

The two types of *Homo erectus* found in Asia—Java Man and Peking Man—are the earliest known members of the genus *Homo.* Of the two, Peking Man is regarded as the more advanced, partly on the basis of a larger average cranial capacity, smaller teeth, and short jaw. But the sensory, speech, memory, and motor areas of both varieties indicate a capacity for language and culture. Dating of the remains of Peking and Java fossils shows Peking Man to be the more recent.

Fossils from both Java and Peking populations of *Homo erectus* indicate that he was about five feet tall and bore some resemblance to the Australopithecenes from whom he is probably descended. Unlike his ancestors, however, his average cranial capacity (at least that of Peking Man) was within the lower range of modern man's. The dentition of *Homo erectus* is that found in meat-eating hominids. And anatomical studies of his leg and foot bones indicate that he was able to walk and run like modern man.

Little is known of the culture of Java Man because no implements of any sort have thus far been discovered among his remains. (Chopper tools found in other sites in Java indicate the possibility of a pebble tool tradition similar to that found at Olduvai.) But our knowledge of Peking Man's culture is considerable.

Evidence of human bones scattered among the animal remains at Choukoutien, a fossil site about

Figure 3-7. *These three sets of pictures compare jaw bones and teeth of Java man with those of "Homo habilis" found in Olduvai Gorge. Many anthropologists were surprised by the marked resemblance between the two. It had previously been assumed that geographic regions so widely separated would contain hominid fossils of great diversity. The discovery of such similar specimens suggests that these two hominids have a close evolutionary relationship.*

Figure 3-8. *The excavation site where Peking man was found is carefully marked off in a numbered grid system to locate fossil finds.*

30 miles from Peking, suggests that Peking Man practiced cannibalism. The skulls had been entered through the opening at the base, presumably to extract the brain; and the long arm and leg bones had been split to obtain the marrow. This find is interesting, but it is scarcely as important as another discovery—that Peking Man used fire for protection, warmth, and cooking. Thousands of broken and charred bones of deer, sheep, antelope, roebuck, small hares, camels, bison, and elephants indicate that *Homo erectus* was a mighty hunter who cooked his food.

It is likely that Peking Man used fire that was originally started by lightning or through spontaneous combustion, rather than by instruments he himself had developed. But the use of fire in itself represents a very significant step in the cultural adaptation of man. It may have influenced the forces of natural selection which previously favored individuals with heavy jaws and large sharp teeth (needed for chewing and ripping uncooked meat), thus paving the way for reduction in tooth size as well as supportive facial architecture. Like tools and intelligence, fire gave man more control over his environment. It may have been used, if not by Peking Man then by subsequent hominids, to frighten away cave-dwelling predators so that man might live in the caves himself; and it could then be used to provide warmth and light in these cold and dark habitations. Moreover, because fire could harden wood to produce better spears, it enabled *Homo erectus* to become a more efficient hunter.

The cultural advance represented by Peking Man's use of fire, however, was not complemented by any significant development of stone tools. He did make chopper tools but they reveal a lesser degree of technological skill or concern than those being produced by western *Homo erectus.*

Unlike their eastern counterparts, western members of *Homo erectus* were refining the tradition begun by the pebble toolmakers at Olduvai. While Asians were still making chopper tools, *Homo erectus* in Africa was transforming the Olduwan chopper into the more sophisticated hand ax. (The more primitive pebble tool tradition was still extant in marginal parts of Europe at this time). Later in both Africa and Europe the hand ax appears further refined and developed.

During this time tool cultures also began to diversify, indicating the increased efficiency of *Homo erectus* in exploiting the environment. At first the hand axes—shaped by regular blows that gave them a larger and finer cutting edge than pebble tools—were probably allpurpose tools, useful in food processing, hide scraping, and defense. But *Homo erectus* then developed cleavers (u-shaped chopping tools) which could be used for killing and butchering; several different types of flint-core scrapers which would be used for processing hides for blankets and clothing; and flake tools to cut meat and process certain vegetables. Adaptation to specific regions is also indicated: there is a greater prominence of flake tools in north and east Europe than in the south and west, and cleavers have been found only in Africa.

The superior technological efficiency of *Homo erectus* is also evident in his selection of raw materials. Formerly he had used large pieces of flint in creating heavy-duty tools. Eventually, however, he began to select harder rocks for making smaller but equally durable tools. This not only saved material but increased his mobility, since he could then wander further from known flint deposits.

Later, western *Homo erectus* developed two toolmaking techniques to produce thinner, straighter, and sharper axes. The baton method of percussion manufacture produced shallow flake scars, rather than the crushed edge found on the older axes. The striking platform method created even sharper and thinner axes. The toolmaker would strike off flakes to create flat surfaces (striking platforms) along the edge of the tool and perpendicular to its sides. He could then remove long thin flakes stretching from the edge across each side of the tool.

Advanced toolmaking in the west and knowledge of fire in the east would obviously enable *Homo erectus* to become a better hunter than

Figure 3-9 and 3-10. *The great technological strides made by man over a relatively brief period of time are shown by a comparison of top photo, a hand ax about 400,000 years old, and bottom, a hand ax about 200,000 years old. The methods of manufacture shown at right are: direct percussion with a hammerstone (A and B), indirect percussion (C), baton percussion (D), and pressure flaking (E). The tools were used chiefly for butchering and defense.*

Figure 3-10. *Drawn after figures in Bordes,* The Old Stone Age (*World University Library*) *and Bordaz,* Tools of the Old and New Stone Age (*Natural History Press*)

Australopithecus. However, the sophistication of his hunting techniques suggests more than just greater technological capability; it also reflects an increased organizational ability. For example, excavations in Spain at Torralba and Ambrona indicate group hunting techniques were used to kill a large amount of game; fire was used to drive elephants into a bog, where the trapped creatures could easily be slaughtered.

With *Homo erectus,* then, we find a clearer manifestation of the interplay among the cultural, physical, and environmental factors than ever before. Social organization and advanced technology developed concomitantly with an increase in brain size and complexity. Cultural adaptations such as cooking and more complex tool kits facilitated dental reduction; and dental reduction in turn encouraged an even heavier reliance upon tool development and facilitated the development of language. Improvements in communication and social organization brought about by language undoubtedly contributed to the use of improved hunting methods, a population increase, and territorial expansion. Evidence from tools and fossils indicates that *Homo sapiens*—the subject of our next discussion—was able to live in areas previously uninhabited by his primate ancestors.

Homo sapiens

About three million years ago, our planet experienced an unusual geologic epoch of alternating periods of cold and subtropical warmth. In Europe, the polar ice cap moved south and vast glaciers pushed their way down from the mountains to the lowland regions that had previously enjoyed subtropical climates. The tropical parts of the world, particularly Africa where *Australopithecus* and other hominids developed, underwent rainy and arid climatic changes. It is during a break in the weather, so to speak, that our early sapient ancestors first appear.

Fossil remains which date back 150,000 to 200,000 years leave only a gap of about 100,000 years between these primitive *Homo sapiens* and *Homo erectus*. Their discovery in the 1930s and 1940s surprised the scientific community and created some controversy because it indicated that sapient man had been around much longer than had been previously thought. His most outstanding characteristic was apparently a large brain with a cranial capacity well within the range of modern man's cranial volume. However, he seems to have made little cultural progress over his predecessor, *Homo erectus*. A probable descendant of this *H. sapiens* population is Neanderthal man.

Neanderthal man

The discovery of the remains of Neanderthal man in 1851 was greeted with incredulity and distrust by those who protested that humans were descended from humans—Adam and Eve—and not from primitive primates. Even today some scholars persist in excluding Neanderthals from our ancestry, though for reasons other than biblical transgression. But the sum total of investigations has proven that Neanderthal was truly *Homo sapiens* and not, as had once been thought, a deformed or aberrant specimen unrelated to man.

It is generally acknowledged that there are two types of Neanderthal: Classic (so called because this was the first type to be found), and General. Classic Neanderthal was typically heavier and lived in Europe; the generalized type was lighter and more modern in form and facial features and lived in the Near East. Despite this fundamental classification, it is acknowledged that several varieties of Neanderthal were in existence and that gene exchanges might have occurred between different populations. In 1931, for example, a number of interesting fossils were found in Java, near the Solo River, that suggest a being with features common to *H. erectus,* Neanderthal and modern man (*Homo sapiens sapiens*). It is presently believed that this "Solo man" was a Neanderthaloid and that his singular features probably reflect a retention of characteristics from earlier populations. Rhodesian man, an individual postulated from fossil remains in South Africa, also manifested a combination of Neanderthal and modern traits. Like Solo man, he probably represents a local population.

Adaptations to the environment for the classic and generalized types of Neanderthals were, of course, both physical and cultural. In adapting to the cold, for example, the Classic Neanderthal developed a large nose that made breathing the icy air somewhat easier; and the massiveness of his form, particularly in the shoulders, chest, and skull, may have served to help him retain body heat by reducing the body's surface area in relation to overall body size. Conversely, the smaller physical features of the generalized type who lived in the Middle East, Java, Africa, and Eastern Europe, may have been due to the more temperate, less demanding climate of these areas.

Classic Neanderthal man's capacity for cultural adaptation was predictably superior to his predecessors. Neanderthal man's extensive use of

Figure 3-11. *The colored areas represent land masses of the earth about 60,000 years ago; superimposed is the outline of the continents as they appear today. During the period of glaciation, the ice sheets spread to cover even a larger area than is shown here. It is interesting to note the wide variety of habitats in which Neanderthal man lived and flourished; he seems to have lived in tundra, savanna, desert, tropical forest, and even on the edge of the ice sheets.*

Ice

Tundra

Savanna and open woods

Desert

Tropical forest

1. Spy (Belgium)
2. Dusseldorf (Germany)
3. La Chapelle-aux-Saints (France)
4. Monte Circeo (Italy)
5. Krapina (Yugoslavia)
6. Gibraltar
7. Tabun and Skhul (Israel)
8. Shanidar (Iraq)
9. Teshik Tash (U.S.S.R.)
10. Ma-pa (China)
11. Trinil (Java)
12. Broken Hill (Rhodesia)

fire was essential to his survival in a cold climate. He lived in small bands or single family units both in the open and in caves, and undoubtedly communicated by speech. Evidence of deliberate burials suggest a belief in some kind of afterlife, and other remains indicate ritualistic or religious behavior in the form of animal cults (especially cave bear cults). Moreover, the remains of an amputee discovered in Iraq and an arthritic man unearthed in France imply that Neanderthal man may have cared for the disabled, an unprecedented example of social concern.

Hunting techniques improved with a higher level of social organization and an advanced technology in weapon and toolmaking. The toolmaking tradition of the Neanderthals which dates from 100,000 to 60,000 B.C. characterized this period.

Flake tools are lighter and smaller than those of the previous tradition. Whereas previously only two or three flakes could be obtained from the entire core, Neanderthal toolmakers obtained many more smaller flakes, skillfully retouched and sharpened. Their tool kits also contained a greater variety of tool types than the previous traditions: hand axes, flakes, scrapers, borers, notched flakes for shaving wood, and many types of points that could be attached to shafts of wood to form spears. This variety of tools facilitated a greater exploitation of food resources and improved the quality of clothing and shelter.

The question which continues to perplex scientists is "What happened to Neanderthal man?" In the Near East, fossil remains show transitional forms between Neanderthal and modern man. In Europe, however, there is a 10,000-year gap in the fossil record. What happened in the interim is unknown. Some hold that Neanderthal man disappeared; others suggest that he simply evolved into modern man.

It has been suggested that the small family units of Neanderthals were physically and culturally overspecialized and therefore could not adjust to the warmer and drier environment which developed as the glaciers retreated. This theory implies that modern man is probably descended from the more successful generalized type of Neanderthal who emigrated from the Near East when the European climate improved. A second theory claims that Classic Neanderthaler did not disappear but simply interbred with the modern Cro-Magnon types from whom modern Europeans eventually evolved. It has been argued, however, that there is no conclusive evidence of this interbreeding.

Figure 3-12. *These two views show a skull of the generalized Neanderthal type. This fossil, found in a cave on Mount Carmel in Israel, appears amazingly modern.* Homo sapiens *is thought to have evolved from this form rather than from the Classic form.*

A third theory contends that *Homo sapiens sapiens* did not interbreed with Neanderthals but in fact evolved from *both* Neanderthal types, Classic and Generalized, depending on the local population. Anthropologist Loring Brace believes that European Neanderthalers produced 1200 generations during 35,000 years of existence—a population and time span that he considers adequate for selection pressures to transform Neanderthal man into Cro-Magnon man.

Cro-Magnon man

About 35,000 to 40,000 years ago, the Neanderthal race of Western and Southern Europe were replaced by a people who possessed a body structure, brain, and physical appearance similar to ours. Whether or not there were transitional forms remains uncertain. But our record indicates that the dominant form in existence at the time was a true *Homo sapiens sapiens:* Cro-Magnon man.

Cro-Magnon remains reveal considerable physical variability, as one might expect from any human population. Generally speaking, however, these people had characteristically modern-looking faces. As suggested in our discussion of *Homo erectus,* specialized tools and cooking helped achieve this modernization by gradually assuming the chewing and softening functions once served by large teeth and heavy jaws. The muscles involved in chewing also diminished and consequently the bones to which these muscles were attached became smaller and finer.

At this point in human evolution, culture has become a more potent force than biology. As Cro-Magnon's smaller features suggest, man no longer required physical bulk for survival. Fast technological developments had contributed to the increasing complexity of his brain, and this complexity now enabled him to create an even more sophisticated technology. It also made him capable of conceptual thought and an advanced level of ritualistic behavior, evidence of which is provided by the remains of religio-magical cere-monies. Intelligence henceforth provides the key to man's increased reliance on cultural rather than physical adaptation.

In Paleolithic times, man's intelligence enabled him to manufacture tools that surpassed the physical equipment of predators and to develop a high level of social organization and coopera-tion—all of which made him an extremely proficient hunter. Cultural adaptation also became highly specific and regional, thus increasing man's chances for survival under a variety of environmental conditions. Instead of manufacturing crude allpurpose tools, Paleolithic populations of the savanna, forest, and shore each developed specialized devices which were suited to exploiting the particular environment, and the different seasons, in which they were being used.

This degree of specialization naturally required improved manufacturing techniques. The blade method of manufacture used less raw material than was needed before, and resulted in smaller and lighter tools with a better ratio between weight of flint and length of cutting edge. The pressure-flaking technique—which used bone, antler, or a wooden tool to press off small flakes from a flint core—gave the toolmaker greater control over the shape of the tool than he had had with percussion flaking. The pressure-flaking process was also made easier and more efficient by another innovation, the heat treatment of raw materials.

The invention of the burin—a stone tool with chisel-like edges—provided an excellent means of carving bone and antler, used for such tools as fishhooks and harpoons. Also invented at this time was the atlatl, which consisted of a piece of wood with a groove in it for holding a spear. By using the atlatl, a hunter increased the force behind the spear throw. The bow and arrow worked on the same principle. The bow string increased the force on the arrow, enabling it to travel farther and with greater effectiveness than if it had been thrown by hand.

One important aspect of Cro-Magnon culture is the art of this period. As far as we know, man had not intentionally produced artwork before this time; therefore, the level of his proficiency as an artisan is certainly amazing. He decorated tools and weapons with engravings of animal figures; he created pendants made of bone and ivory; and he sculpted in clay. He is perhaps best remembered, though, for his cave paintings in Spain and France. Made with mineral oxide pigments, these skillfully executed paintings almost exclusively depict animals that were hunted by Upper Paleolithic man. It is not known for certain why other subject matter was not chosen, nor compositional background provided for the animals portrayed. It is also curious that later paintings were found in the darkest recesses of the caves, suggesting that they served other than a decorative function. Some anthropologists suggest that these paintings served a religio-magical function having to do with control over the animals thus represented, or a symbolic function

Figure 3-13. *The skull of Cro-Magnon man, above, differs little from our own. Below, an enterprising French businessman has built a hotel on the site of the excavation in which the first Cro-Magnon man was found. The open door of the garage leads to the excavation; the back wall of the hotel is the cliff that sheltered early hotel-less man.*

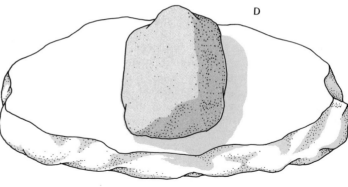

Figure 3-14. *These drawings show some of the tools with which man began to cultivate crops. Most tools were a combination of bone or wood handles and flint or in some cases bone blade. Microliths are commonly found in many agricultural tools of this period.*

having to do with male initiation ceremonies. In any case, they reflect a remarkably developed aesthetic sensibility.

Mesolithic man

Cro-Magnon man was engaged in hunting, fishing, and gathering whatever nature happened to provide. He followed wild herds, moving on to new areas when the old food supply was exhausted. He probably had neither the time nor the technical knowledge required to care for animals or cultivate plants.

But about 12,000 B.C. man was obliged to exchange his nomadic hunting way of life for a more secure sedentary one. The glacial period was ending, thus causing great physical changes in the environment. The sea levels rose; and in Europe the tundras and savannas disappeared and were covered by oceans and hardwood forests. The herd animals also disappeared: some, like the reindeer, moved to colder climates; others, like the mammoths, became extinct. During this period, called the Mesolithic, or Middle Stone Age, man turned toward the more stable food supplies found in the rivers, lakes, and oceans. He developed boats which enabled him to exploit deep water resources as well as the coastal areas. And on the shores of lakes and rivers, he formed small permanent settlements that later developed into rudimentary farming and fishing villages. In short, man began to evolve into the social being he is today.

The changed postglacial environment necessitated new technologies. Ground stone tools, shaped and sharpened by grinding the edges against sandstone, were very effectively used as axes and adzes. They were helpful in clearing forest areas and in fashioning dugout canoes and skin-covered boats. The characteristic tool, however, was the microlith. Microliths were sharp blades that could be made of flint as well as other materials. Their small size (one-half to two inches long) made them easy to mass produce and provided Mesolithic man with an important advantage not found in one-piece tools: composite tools—such as sickles, harpoons, and daggers—could be made by fitting microliths into grooves in wood or bone handles. Microliths were also attached to arrow shafts by using melted resin as a binder. The bow and arrow thus became the Mesolithic culture's deadliest weapon.

Microliths were the most important tools used by the two major Mesolithic cultures which developed in Western Europe: the Azilian (southern France and Spain) and the Tardenoisian (England, Germany, and France). Most of the remains of these cultures are found along the edges of inland waters and swampy areas, indicating a heavy dependence on fishing for subsistence.

In the Near East, the two important cultures were the Capsian and the Natufian, which flourished about 11,000 years ago. The Capsians, centered mostly in various parts of North Africa, developed the microlithic culture later adopted by the Mesolithic hunters of Europe; they probably lived in large village settlements along lakes and rivers. The Natufians lived in what is now Israel and Jordan in caves, rock shelters, and small villages with stone-walled houses. Plastered storage pits beneath the floors of these houses indicate that the Natufians were the earliest known Mesolithic people to have stored crops. Basin-shaped depressions in the rocks outside the homes are also believed to have been used for storage. Mesolithic sickles found among the Natufian remains provide some evidence that they may have cultivated grain (wild grain cannot be harvested by sickles, for its delicate head breaks open and scatters the valuable granules).

Neolithic man

The Neolithic, or New Stone, Age witnessed a major transformation in the subsistence patterns of early man: the transition from nomadism that began in the Mesolithic period now culminated in a truly agricultural economy. Early forms of food production had preceded the actual growing of crops and domestication of animals. Acorns were leached, for example, to clear them of tannin and so render them edible; woods were burned over to improve the berry bushes; pebbles in estuaries were cleared away to improve the size and quality of plants already growing there. Furthermore, cultivation and domestication did not necessarily occur simultaneously—in the New World, horticulture clearly came first.

The consequences of cultivation and domestication are so momentous for the development of civilization that several theories have been proposed to explain the transformation. One of them suggests that after people had familiarized themselves with their environment and settled down in one area, they began to domesticate the plants and animals that were already there in wild abundance. Domestication and cultivation clearly began when man had acquired adequate knowledge and technical skill, but there is evidence that settling down and mastering the environment did not inevitably culminate in domestication. The year-round occupants of a stone-house group in Southwest Asia, for example, were apparently hunters and gatherers and not domesticators. Furthermore, "settling down" may not have always been a prerequisite for domestication—some of the early farming villages were occupied only seasonally.

Dating about 11,000 to 9,000 years ago, the earliest known sites of plant and animal domesti-

Figure 3-15. *An important consequence of Neolithic man's adoption of the agricultural subsistence pattern was house building. Early houses were made of wood, stone, or sun-dried brick (adobe). Shown here is a Neolithic adobe apartment complex located on a cliff in Arizona.*

cation are found in the Near East. Agriculture seems to have spread out from southwest Asia to adjacent areas, eventually reaching eastern Europe by 6000 B.C., central Europe and the Netherlands by the end of the fifth millennium, and England late in the fourth. The Neolithic Age began independently in southeast Asia and the New World and possibly North China and other regions. Some environments were not conducive to the spread of agriculture. For example, the Russian steppes, with their heavy grass cover, were not suitable to farming without a plow, but were ideal for herding.

The Neolithic developed much later in the New World than in the Old. Neolithic agricultural villages like those which developed in the Near East did not appear in the New World until about 3400 B.C., in Mexico. Although the domestication of plants probably occurred around 4000 to 2000 B.C. in west central South America, the people remained nomadic for some time and only gradually became sedentary, depending primarily on hunting for meat. North American Indians apparently never experienced a complete change from a hunting and gathering mode of life, except to a limited degree in the southern regions where climate permitted the cultivation of maize. The crops of most of these New World regions differed from those of Europe and Asia.

The summit of achievement among the prehistoric Americans is represented by the settlements in Mexico and the Andes. These cultures were based on communities whose ancestors had turned from hunting and gathering to cultivation and domestication. But agriculture was only one part of a complex of ideas fundamental to the emergence of civilization, and the New World, like the Old, became an uneven mosaic of cultures.

The technology of the Neolithic predictably reflects the new economy. The tools which were invented and manufactured were suited to agricultural needs. Early harvesting tools were made of wood or bone with inserts for edged flints. Later tools were made by chipping and flaking stone; and stones that were too hard for this technique were ground and polished into shape. Man developed scythes, forks, hoes, and hand plows (later redesigned for use with draft animals) to replace simple digging sticks. Pestles and mortars were used in preparing grain.

Figure 3-16. *Depicted here are successive stages in the manufacture of clay pottery commonly used as containers.*

The manufacture and use of pottery was also characteristic of the Neolithic, though it did not develop in the New World until about 2300 B.C. Although hunters and nomads had usually found baskets and hides easiest to transport, farmers needed heavier vessels for storing grain, seeds, and material possessions. Pottery containers answered this need because they were impervious to insects, rodents, and dampness. Moreover, they were very useful for cooking; food could be boiled directly over the fire rather than by the ancient technique of burying food with hot stones. Engraved and painted decorations on many of the remains suggest that Neolithic man found potterymaking to be a creative as well as practical activity.

Agriculture and the new sedentary lifestyle engendered another technological development—house-building. Nomads lacked the leisure time, technical skill, and presumably the interest to be concerned with anything more than efficient and easy-to-make dwellings. Cave shelters, pits dug in the earth, and primitive lean-tos made of hides and tree limbs served their purpose of keeping the weather out. In the Neolithic, however, dwellings became more complex in design and more diverse in type. Some, like the Swiss Lake Dwellings, were constructed of wood, housed several families per building, had doors, and contained beds, tables, and other furniture. More elaborate shelters were made of stone, sun-dried brick, or branches plastered together with mud or clay. An amazingly advanced architecture developed in the Near East and Mesoamerica.

The new economy of the Neolithic also enabled man, for the first time in history, to make clothing of woven textiles. Flax and cotton came from agriculture, and wool from the domestication of sheep. Neolithic man's inventive and technical capacities provided him with the spindle and loom. It should be noted, however, that textiles continued to be manufactured by primitive manual means in the New World. Evidence of the loom and spindle does not appear in that area until 1000 B.C.

Evidence of all the economic and technological developments listed thus far have enabled archeologists to draw certain inferences concerning the social structure of Neolithic society. The general absence of large buildings in these small settlements may suggest that neither religion nor government was yet a formally established institution able to wield real social power. Although it is conjectured that the markings on some of the artifacts, such as hunting tools, may have had religious or magical meaning, no concrete evidence of a centrally organized and directed religious life has been found. The experiments in irrigation must have required some kind of social organization, since they called for the labor of many men; but again there is no evidence that this control was provided by an organized governmental institution. Many anthropologists believe that kinship groups, such as clans, were the organizing unit for this kind of work.

The general picture that emerges is one of an egalitarian society with little division of labor and probably little development of social roles. Since no early Neolithic graves have been found containing tomb ornaments or burial equipment, it is believed that no person had attained the superior social status that would have required an elaborate funeral. The smallness of the villages suggest that the inhabitants knew each other very well, so that most of their relationships were probably personal and emotionally significant ones.

IS THERE A DIFFERENCE BETWEEN MEN AND GORILLAS?

One hundred years ago the explorer Du Chaillu first described a male gorilla "beating his chest in rage." Almost every hunter, traveler, and scientist who since that time has encountered gorillas in the wild mentions this striking display in which the animal rises on his hind legs and beats a rapid tattoo on its chest with its hands. But none of these observers noted that beating the chest is the climax of a complex series of actions, which more than anything else are typical of the gorilla and constitute the most exciting aspect of its behavior. The complete sequence, which is rarely given and then only by silverbacked males, consists of nine more or less distinct acts. At the beginning of the display, the male often sits, tips up his head, and through pursed lips emits a series of soft, clear hoots that start slowly but grow faster and faster until they fuse into a slurred growling sound at the climax of the display. The hoots seem to generate excitement in the male, helping him to build up to the desired climax, much as natives use a drum in their frenzied dances. The gorillas have a look of great concentration on their faces when they hoot, and if another member of the group interrupts the even rhythm of the vocalization in some way, the male may stop abruptly and look around as if annoyed before continuing his display. Sometimes the male stops vocalizing briefly and plucks a single leaf from a nearby plant and places it between the lips, an act of such daintiness and seeming irrelevance that it never ceases to amaze me. The females and youngsters in the group know that the hoots and the placing of a leaf between the lips are preliminary to rather vigorous, even violent, actions on the part of the male, and they generally retreat to a safe distance.

Just before the climax, the male rises on his short, bowed legs and with the same motion rips off some vegetation with his hand and throws it into the air. The climax consists of the chest beat, which is the part of the display most frequently seen and heard. The open, slightly cupped hands are slapped alternately some two to twenty times against the lower part of the chest at the rate of about ten beats a second. Gorillas do not pound their chests with the fists, as is often stated, except on very rare occasions. Chest beating is not at all stereotyped in its application, and the animal may slap its belly, the outside of its thigh, a branch, a tree trunk, or the back of another gorilla. One juvenile patted the top of its head about thirty times, and once a blackbacked male lay on his back with legs stretched skyward, beating the soles of his feet. Two females did not slap their chests directly, but rotated their arms, making their breasts flap in passing. While beating its chest, the gorilla often kicks a leg into the air.

Immediately after and sometimes during chest beating, the animal tends to run bipedally sideways for a few steps before dropping to quadrupedal position and dashing along. The male often slaps, breaks, and tears at anything in its path during the run, and this is dangerous, not only because of the violence of the act, but also because the male is not at all selective in what he swats. Any member of the group may be hit. One juvenile was picked up by a male and bowled down the slope. Even a man in the path of a running male may be swatted, as observed by Fred Merfield: "N'Denge was holding his gun loosely pointing downward, and was looking toward me, when a big male gorilla

suddenly crashed out of the bush and swept him aside with a terrible full blow in the face." The grand finale of the display consists of a vigorous thump of the ground with the palm of the hand. The performer then settles back quietly, the display completed. It is a magnificent act, unrivaled among mammals, which Dr. Emlen likened to a symphony when he wrote (in the Transactions of the Philadelphia Academy of Science): "The hooting comes first, an effective introduction, rich in restraint and suspense to the human connoisseur of sonata and symphony. This leads with dramatic crescendo into the powerful climax of the display as the animal leaps to its feet, hurls leaves and branches into the air, and then pounds out a resounding percussion on its massive chest. Then follows the crashing finale, a free-swinging run ending in a tremendous thump."

Infants display various acts at an early age. When only about four months old they rise shakily and very briefly on their hind legs and beat their chests, and at a year and a half they throw vegetation and place a leaf between the lips. Although all parts of the sequence, except for the hooting and possibly the kick, are given by the females as well as the males, the former display less frequently and less intensely. To what extent the display is inherited or learned, and how age and sex of the animal affects the behavior cannot be determined in the wild. Goma, the infant born at the Basel zoo, beat its chest and the ground without having had the opportunity to learn the act from other gorillas. This, and similar data, suggests that gorillas have an inborn tendency to beat something when excited.

A display like that of the gorilla poses some challenging problems of interpretation. The remarkable series of sounds, movements, and postures must be of survival value to the species or it would not have evolved or persisted. A clue to the function of the display and to its underlying cause can be obtained by noting the situations that elicit it. The most intense, prolonged, and diverse displays are given in response to the presence of man. Other situations include the proximity of another gorilla group or a lone male, an undetermined disturbance, displays by another member of the group, and play. The hooting, the bipedal stance, the thrown vegetation, the running—all are actions which draw attention to the animal and make it conspicuous. It seems to advertise its presence, to show off. Studies of many animals, especially birds, have shown that certain prominent gestures are of significance in signaling information to others of the same and even different species—they are a means of communication. Judging from the effect that the display of the gorilla has on other gorillas and on man, it appears to function in two ways: it is a communicatory signal, revealing, for example, that another group is in the vicinity, and it serves to intimidate other gorillas and human intruders.

But what is the motivation underlying this remarkable display? Intimidation and communication do not explain the cause. Why, for instance, does it occur in play and in situations where there is nothing to intimidate or communicate? The most general emotional term which encompasses all the diverse manifestations is excitement. During the display the gorillas find release for the tension which has accumulated in their system in an excitable situation. After the display, the level of excitement temporarily drops, and the animals behave calmly until a new accumulation of tension erupts in display.

The evolutionary derivation of the display is of particular interest, and my explanation of it is based on the concepts developed in recent years by Niko Tinbergen, Konrad Lorenz, and other behaviorists. When two conflicting impulses, such as attack and flight, operate at the same time, the result is often a displacement activity, an activity which seems irrelevant and out of context in the situation at hand. A conflict of this type may produce preening in birds; but in gorillas it results in feeding, scratching, yawning, and the tendency to beat something. Natural selection may act on such displacement activities by enhancing their effectiveness as communicatory signals; they may become stereotyped and be incorporated into a definite display—they become ritualized. The fact that the gorilla often places a leaf between its lips suggests that this curious gesture may be a ritualized act of displacement feeding, and beating the chest may be the fairly stereotyped outcome of the tendency to slap something.

Man behaves remarkably like a gorilla in conflicting situations. A marital squabble, for example, in which neither person cares to attack or retreat, may end with shouting, thrown objects, slamming doors, furniture pounded and kicked—all means of reducing tension. Sporting events, where man is excited and emotionally off guard, provide the ideal location for people-watching. A spectator at a sporting event perceives behavior that excites him. Yet he cannot participate directly in the action, nor does he want to cease observing it. The tension thus produced finds release in chanting, clapping hands, stamping feet, jumping up and down, and throwing objects into the air. This behavior may be guided into a pattern by the efforts of cheer leaders who, by repeating similar sounds over and over again with increasing frequency, channel the display into a violent and synchronized climax. Two of the functions of this display are communication with and intimidation of the opponent. Wherein lies the difference between gorilla and man?

Source:
From George B. Shaller, *The Year of the Gorilla*. New York: Ballantine, 1971, pp. 236–243.

Summary

1.

Anthropologists study the physical characteristics, the environment and the social relations among the ancestors of primates and *Homo sapiens* for a better understanding of the development of man and culture. When the early primates adapted to an arboreal environment, modifications in dental structure, sense organs, the brain, and the skeleton took place. Learned social behavior also aided in surviving in this environment. Chimpanzees are social animals and possess primitive social structure, communicate with audible signals, are good learners and can make tools. Gorillas, too, live in social groups and their social relationships have been studied.

2.

It is thought that the complex physical and social changes that took place in the early hominids evolved simultaneously through a process of mutual reinforcement. *Ramapithecus,* known from fossil remains, is considered to be the earliest man because of its teeth and jaws and is thought to have walked erect. *Australopithecus,* pygmy-like in size, was truly bipedal, walking erect, which freed his hands and raised his eye level for a better view, adaptations suited for hunting and gathering.

3.

Scientists are in agreement that *Homo erectus* is to be designated as a true man based on smaller teeth and a cranial capacity capable of language and culture. Charred bones of many different animals found with these fossil men indicate that *Homo erectus* was a mighty hunter who cooked his food. *Homo erectus* in Africa and Europe manufactured tools for use in hunting, processing hides, and cutting vegetables.

4.

Neanderthal man possessed the brain capacity to be considered a true *Homo sapiens.* He lived in a cold climate, used fire extensively and had evolved a larger nose as an aid in breathing cold air and a chunky body to expose less surface to the cold. He lived in small bands and communicated by speech. Cro-Magnon replaced the Neanderthal and possessed a body structure, brain and physical and facial appearance similar to our own. Cro-Magnon was an artist who decorated his tools and is credited with the remarkable cave paintings in southern France.

5.

Mesolithic man was the first to settle down. These people made permanent settlements on the banks of rivers and lakes, built boats and depended to a great extent on fish for food. In the Middle East there is evidence that Mesolithic man cultivated and stored grain.

6.

In the New Stone Age Neolithic man learned to grow crops and domesticate animals. Neolithic man invented pottery, weaving and was the first to build houses and make clothing. The irrigation practices of these people indicate the existence of social organization but it must have been an egalitarian society with little division of labor characterized by intimate social relationships.

Suggested readings

Bordes, Francois *A Tale of Two Caves*. New York: Harper & Row, 1972.
The archeological evidence found in two French caves of the Dordogne district forms the basis of this anthropological case study. The book discusses the interdisciplinary approach and methodology employed by French anthropologists and geologists. A complete history of the research done in these caves is traced, and the information gathered on the Acheulian and Mousterian cultures is reported. Various methods used to date the findings and to understand Paleolithic societies are considered.

Brace, C. Loring, Harry Nelson, and Noel Korn *Atlas of Fossil Man*. New York: Holt, Rinehart, and Winston, Inc. 1971.
The core of this atlas consists of a series of drawings which provide a pictorial survey of all the key fossils that form the basis of our knowledge of human evolution. Each drawing highlights the diagnostic character of the fossil find to facilitate comparison and is accompanied by notes on date, geological age, place of discovery, and interpretations. Maps showing the distribution of important sites and stone tool distributions are included for each stage.

Buettner-Janush, John *Origins of Man: Physical Anthropology*. New York: John Wiley & Sons, Inc., 1966.
This introduction to physical anthropology is divided into two parts. Part I contains a discussion of evolutionary theory and systematics and descriptions of fossil man and the major groups of living primates. Part II is devoted principally to *Homo sapiens'* culture, population, and genetics, and the effects of evolutionary processes on human populations.

Constable, George, and the Editors of Life *The Neanderthals*. New York: Time-Life, 1973.
Many misinterpretations of fossil remains of Neanderthal man have been made since their discovery in 1856. This part of the Time-Life Emergence of Man Series analyzes the old views in light of new evidence and discoveries. The tools, behavior, and ultimate evolution of the Neanderthal man into Cro-Magnon man is described.

Jolly, Alison *The Evolution of Primate Behavior*. New York: Macmillan, 1972.
In this book, Jolly attempts a survey of current knowledge about primate behavior and its relevance to human behavior. Part 1, entitled "Ecology," deals with habitat and locomotion, food, predation, interspecific relations, reasons for sociability and group range, size, and structure. "Society," Part 2, discusses learning and instinct, communication, status, affiliation and sex, mothers and infants, growing up in a troop, and violence and warfare. The volume concludes with "Intelligence," with sections on primate psychology, manipulation and tools, cognition, language, social learning, and the evolution of intelligence. The bibliography is also very useful.

Korn, Noel *Human Evolution*. New York: Holt, Rinehart and Winston, Inc., 1973.
The emphasis of this shortened edition is an ongoing survey of modern populations, with micro-evolutionary events studies in detail. An ecological and ethnological perspective on primate and human evolution is emphasized.

Lawick-Goodall, Jane Van *In the Shadow of Man*. New York: Dell Publishing Co., 1971.
Jane Van Lawick-Goodall's account of her ten years of study of wild chimpanzees in

Tanzania is written in a readable, informative style. The family life, sex, infant, and child-mother relations of chimps discussed thoroughly. The correspondence of primate behavior to human life is stressed.

Pilbeam, David *The Ascent of Man: An Introduction to Human Evolution.* New York: Macmillan, 1972.
This book summarizies much of the post-1940 research on primate fossil materials. Early hominids in South Africa and East Africa from the middle and later Pleistocene form the subject of this book. This book attempts to construct and present dynamic models of human evolution by relating it to primate studies.

Schaller, George B. *The Year of the Gorilla.* New York: Ballantine, 1971.
Schaller, who has written a scientific monograph on The Mountain Gorilla, describes here in popular form some of the results of his work in Africa. This is a personal book about gorillas and the way they behave. The author's simple line drawings and clear prose make this book a fine introduction to primate behavior.

White, Edmund, and the Editors of Life *The First Men.* New York: Time-Life, 1972.
The story of *Homo erectus* is the subject of this book. Prehistoric man's wanderings, development of speech, and discovery of fire are discussed. The book is well-illustrated and includes special chapters on Java man and Peking man.

2

Culture
and man

DICTIONARIUM BRITANNICUM:

Or a more Compleat

UNIVERSAL ETYMOLOGICAL

ENGLISH DICTIONARY

Than any EXTANT,

CONTAINING

Not only the Words and their Explication; but their Etymologies from the *Antient British*, *Teutonick*, *Dutch Low* and *High*, *Old Saxon*, *German*, *Danish*, *Swedish*, *Norman* and *Modern French*, *Italian*, *Spanish*, *Latin*, *Greek*, *Hebrew*, &c. each in its proper Character.

ALSO

Explaining hard and technical Words, or Terms of Art, in all the *ARTS, SCIENCES*, and *MYSTERIES* following. Together with *ACCENTS* directing to their proper Prouuntiation, shewing both the *Orthography*, and *Orthoepia* of the *English Tongue*,

VIZ. IN

AGRICULTURE, ALGEBRA, ANATOMY, ARCHITECTURE, ARITHMETICK, ASTROLOGY, ASTRONOMY, BOTANICKS, CATOPTRICKS, CHYMISTRY CHIROMANCY, CHIRURGERY, CONFECTIONARY, COOKERY, COSMOGRAPHY, DIALLING, DIOPTRICKS, ETHICKS, FISHING, FORTIFICATION, FOWLING, GARDENING, GAUGING, GEOGRAPHY, GEOMETRY, GRAMMAR, GUNNERY, HANDICRAFTS, HAWKING, HERALDRY, HORSEMANSHIP, HUNTING, HUSBANDRY, HYDRAULICKS, HYDROGRAPHY, HYDROSTATICKS, LAW, LOGICK, MARITIME *and* MILITARY AFFAIRS, MATHEMATICKS, MECHANICKS, MERCHANDIZE, METAPHYSICKS, METEOROLOGY, NAVIGATION, OPTICKS, OTACOUSTICKS, PAINTING, PERSPECTIVE, PHARMACY, PHILOSOPHY, PHYSICK, PHYSIOGNOMY, PYROTECHNY, RHETORICK, SCULPTURE, STATICKS, STATUARY, SURVEYING, THEOLOGY, *and* TRIGONOMETRY.

Illustrated with near Five Hundred CUTS, for Giving a clear Idea of those Figures, not so well apprehended by verbal Description.

LIKEWISE

A Collection and Explanation of *English* PROVERBS; also of WORDS and PHRASES us'd in our ancient Charters, Statutes, Writs, Old Records and Processes at Law.

ALSO

The Iconology, Mythology, Theogony, and Theology of the *Egyptians*, *Greeks*, *Romans*, &c. being an Account of their Deities, Solemnities, either Religious or Civil, their Divinations, Auguries, Oracles, Hieroglyphicks, and many other curious Matters, necessary to be understood, especially by the Readers of *English* POETRY.

Language
and communication

All normal humans learn to talk, and ordinarily they spend a considerable part of every day talking to each other. What are they saying? Listen to a speaker of Yoruba: *Kini se t'o ko da mi l'ohun?* A speaker of Papiamento: *Miedu ku e machete aki den mi man?* And a speaker of Korean: *Chogi kaso kugosul posio!* What do the languages of these people on three different continents have in common?

Language is a systematic code for the communication, in **symbols,** of any kind of information. Insofar as nonhuman animals also communicate certain kinds of information systematically, we may also speak of animal language. But symbol in our definition means any kind of sound or gesture to which we ourselves have given meaning as standing for something, and not one that has a natural or biological meaning, which we call a **sign.** A tear is a sign of crying, and crying is a sign of some kind of emotional or physical state; the word "crying," however, is a symbol, a group of sounds to which we have learned to assign the meaning of a particular action, and which we can use to communicate that meaning whether or not anyone around us is actually crying.

At the moment language experts are not certain whether to give credit to animals—bees, dolphins, or chimpanzees—for the ability to use symbols as well as signs, even though these animals and many others have been found to communicate in remarkable ways. At least one famous chimp, named Washoe, has apparently been able to learn and to use some human symbols. What are the implications of this fact for our understanding of the nature and evolution of language? No certain answer can be given until further investigation of animal communication gives more facts to work with. What we can be sure of is that human language is a remarkably universal form of human social behavior, intimately related to practically everything man is and does, and that a knowledge of the workings of language is essential to any kind of work in anthropology.

The nature of language

Any human language—English, Chinese, Swahili—is obviously a means of transmitting information and sharing with others both a cultural and an individual experience. Because we tend to take language for granted, it is perhaps not so obvious that language is also a systematic code that enables us to translate our concerns, beliefs, and perceptions into symbols that can be decoded and interpreted by others. The many such codes presently in existence all over the world—an estimated 3000 different languages—may well astound and mystify us by their great variety and complexity; but basically languages are all rational systems, invented, developed, and perpetuated by man, and we should be able to figure them out, if only we have the right methods and the time.

The modern scientific study of language began as early as the seventeenth century, in the age of exploration and discovery, with the accumulation of facts: the collecting of sounds, words, and sentences from as many different languages as possible, chiefly those encountered in exotic lands by European explorers, invaders, and missionaries. The great contribution of the nineteenth century was the discovery of system, regularity, and relationships in the data, and the tentative formulation of some laws and regular principles. In the twentieth century, while we are still collecting data, we have made considerable progress in the reasoning process, testing and working from new and improved theories. Insofar as theories and facts of language are verifiable by independent researchers looking at the same materials, there may be said now to be a science of linguistics, or the study of all aspects of language.

Linguistics

The field of linguistics in general has traditionally been approached by two different methods. The **historical** study of language investigates relationships between earlier and later forms of the same language, antecedents in older languages for developments in modern languages, and questions of relationships between older languages. It is a concern of historical linguistics, for example, to identify and explain the development of early medieval spoken Latin into later medieval French and Spanish, through both natural change in the original language and the influence of con-

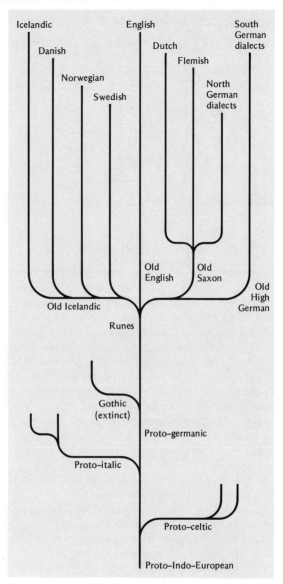

Figure 4-1. English is one of a group of languages in the modern Germanic family; this diagram shows its relationship to other languages in the same family. The root was an Indo-European language spoken by the early Aryans who spread westward over the European continent, bringing both their customs and their language with them.

tacts with the barbarian invaders from the North. The **descriptive** approach to language, on the other hand, is concerned with registering and explaining all the features of any one given language at any one time in history. A descriptive linguist concentrates, for example, on the way modern French or Spanish function now as closed systems, consistent within themselves, without any appeal to historical reasons for their development. Although Latin *ille* ("that") is identifiable as the origin of both French *le* ("the") and Spanish *el* ("the"), the descriptive linguist treats *le* and *el* only as they function in the modern language, where the meaning "that" is no longer relevant and very few people are aware that they are speaking a modern development of Latin. There is actually no ill will between historical and descriptive linguists, and presently the two approaches are recognized to be interdependent. Even a modern language is constantly changing, and it changes according to principles that can only be established historically.

Both the historical and the descriptive approaches to language are of interest to anthropology. Historical linguistics provides a means of dating (at least approximately) certain migrations, invasions, and contacts of peoples, and therefore of determining dates for the establishment of new or changed cultural groups. The concept of linguistic divergence, or the breaking up of an originally unified language with various local forms, for example, is used to identify the time at which one group of speakers of a language separated from another group. From a study of the use in rural French Canada of seventeenth-century French *icite* ("here") instead of modern French *ici,* one can date the separation of French colonists from the mother country at a specific time.

Glottochronology, also known as time-depth, introduced by linguists Swadesh and Lees, is a method of dating a more radical kind of divergence, when whole branches of language families separated from each other, such as Latin and Greek from a supposed earlier common language. Time-depth estimates rely on a complicated logarithmic formula for the number of words two languages should still have in common after they have been separated a given number of years.

Descriptive linguistics furnishes the anthropologist with both a framework for understanding, and the means to analyze, describe, and work with, the language of any people. A distinction should be made between **theoretical** and **field** linguistics, which are nevertheless interdependent and both considered to be under the general heading of descriptive linguistics. A theoretical linguist, such as the now celebrated Noam Chomsky of the Massachusetts Institute of Technology, makes a framework and a system for describing what happens in the whole encoding and sentence-making process. He hopes that his system will hold for all languages, though he may develop it in detail for only one.

The primary concern of the theoretical linguist is to answer the question of how language works rather than how to learn, use, or understand any particular language. The field linguist, on the other hand, collects raw data from speakers of a language, analyzes it, describes it in a coherent way, and typically also uses it in communicating with or about those speakers. He is a descriptive linguist by virtue of the fact that he begins by meticulously describing, to the best of his ability, and usually with special training, what is actually said in the language he is working on. He takes nothing for granted, and he learns to elicit natural responses that will illustrate every important aspect of a language. Descriptive in this sense is ordinarily opposed to prescriptive, or making a judgment about what ought to be done. For example, if the field linguist were working with a dialect group of English speakers who said consistently "he sa go tomorrow" and "I sa go next week," he would record the fact descriptively that the future for the dialect was regularly expressed by *sa;* he would not prescribe that it must or should be *shall* and that it was mispronounced or corrupted. It is the field linguist whose findings are most relevant to the concerns of anthropology, although the school of ethnosemantic anthropology, exemplified by the work of Lévi-Strauss, leans heavily on theoretical linguistics.

Theoretical linguistics

What happens when we talk? How do we make sentences? Current thinking highly favors the theory that most of our utterances are built up swiftly and unconsciously from basic two-part units, called in the terminology of Noam Chomsky the **deep structure**. The finished product, the complete utterance or sentence, is said to display **surface structure**, a complex web of transformed and integrated units from the deep structure. The principle is assumed to be the same for all languages, but the deep structures will differ, and the processes of getting from deep structure to surface structure should vary according to the habits, conventions, and social adaptations of different cultures. Understanding or explaining any language, according to this theory, should amount to identifying deep structure and establishing the rules whereby the deep structure is transformed into surface structure. A complete set of principles or rules should then be capable of generating or producing all possible sentences in the language. Using this terminology, Chomsky's theory is called **generative transformational grammar.**

Transformational grammar. Chomsky's theory has been widely acclaimed for bringing about a revolution in our thinking about language; indeed it provides the first consistent and logical model for a scientific description of the facts of language. The theory has been expanded, revised, and improved in detail over the past few years, and currently a considerable number of world languages are being put to a transformational analysis. Stages in the transformational process of using language have been compared to the operation of a super computer, with a series of yes-no decisions made in an elaborate program that no one has yet been able to put on paper, and with memory banks that are constantly updated and perhaps not always functioning properly. There is no doubt much truth in the analogy, considering what we do know about the functioning of the brain; but of course we have reason to believe

Figure 4-2,3. *Pictured below is a Sumerian cylinder seal. When rolled over tablets of wet clay, it produced an impression like the one shown above; the tablet was then baked or dried in the sun to make the record permanent. Opposite is a page from the Codex Mendoza, an early Spanish attempt to decipher Mexican writing, which like Sumerian was pictographic rather than syllabic.*

that emotions, biological changes, and an essential adaptability, among other things, make people somewhat different from computers.

To illustrate the theoretical process of transformational grammar in its application to a study of English, let us say for example that there is an unpleasant sensation in my head and that I want you to be aware of that fact for some reason. In encoding the message, I follow a basic pattern of English conventions in which a topic comes first (head), followed by a comment (hurt). The most important two-part unit in the deep structure will therefore be head-hurt. Because I want to identify the head in question as my own, another unit in the deep structure may be another topic and comment: head-mine. One transformational rule of English will make head-mine into my-head whenever that kind of statement is put into a larger sentence; another rule will put together the larger combination my-head-hurt; and a final rule will touch up the finished form of the utterance as my-head-hurts. The result is said to be a grammatical sentence, because it follows what we can identify as the rules or conventions of the language. Another speaker of the language can decode it effortlessly, and any native speaker could come up with the same utterance. An ungrammatical sentence would be hurts-head-my, which can be decoded with some little effort but would not ordinarily be produced by any native speaker of the language.

A practical disadvantage of transformational theory when applied to specific languages is that there turn out to be so many rules, and so many special conditions for the application of the rules, that a truly complete analysis of a moderately complex language such as English is probably humanly impossible. The computer program seems to have developed beyond the complete comprehension or control of the programmer. Furthermore, some of the simplest looking surface structures, or sentences, turn out on inspection to be enormously complicated and to require extensive and uneconomical analysis. Consequently the transformationalist has to be satisfied with a tentative and partial analysis, covering the

Figure 4-4,5. *In the photo above, the Yąnomamö speak into anthropologist Chagnon's tape recorder as he carries out studies in field linguistics. The other pictures relate to another aspect of the study of communication, the study of gestures and body movements. The sequence of four photos shows two men from different villages engaging in a ritual chest-pounding duel with closed fists. The intention is at once both friendly and also threatening—a reminder that they might hurt one another but are refraining from so doing. This field of communication study is called kinesics; anthropologists have found that many subtle shades of emotion can be communicated through body movements and facial expressions. Also important is the study of proxemics, or man's use of personal space.*

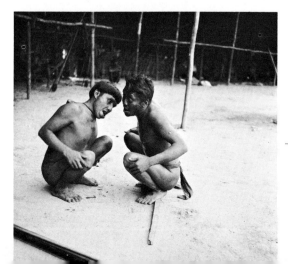

main ground but always subject to further refinement.

The origins of language. A knowledge of transformational grammar also leads to speculation about how language might have started in the first place: a computerlike brain, a versatile vocal mechanism, sounds, basic words, two-part structures, trial and error, conventions, surface structures—language. Who knows? The question of the origin of language has long been a very popular subject, and some reasonable and not so reasonable theories have been proposed: exclamations became words, sounds in nature were imitated, or people simply got together and assigned sounds to objects and actions. The main trouble with these theories, interesting and possible as some of them are, is that they account for word-making but not for sentence-making. Does transformational theory have the answer? The current attitude is generally that we have had enough speculation on the subject, that transformational theory offers some good new possibilities, and that we need to do some more work on the biological basis of language and communication before any conclusions about what might have happened can be drawn. The question of the origin of language has not been dismissed as hopeless or irrelevant: there is still the possibility of an intelligent reconstruction of the process.

The search for a truly primitive language that might show the processes of language just beginning or developing has been abandoned, no doubt permanently. Is there such a thing as a primitive language? So far, all the natural languages that have been described and studied, even among people with something approximating a Stone Age culture, appear to be highly developed, complex, and capable of expressing an immense range of experience, belief, and perceptions. At one time linguists thought they had found a truly primitive or archaic language, that of the central Australian tribe called the Arunta, described in 1930 when the tribe was on the point of extinction. The language was found to have

93

only three vowel sounds (a, i, and u), very few consonant sounds (p, t, k, m, n, l, r, ch), no names for objects but only for states or actions, and no connective words like our prepositions or conjunctions. On the other hand, the Arunta made use of at least four hundred different gestures to supplement the spoken language. What was "missing" verbally seems to have been supplied visually. In spite of the apparent simplicity of the language, it proved to be no less difficult to learn properly, or even to describe accurately, than any other language. The truth seems to be that people have been talking on this world for an extremely long time, and every language, wherever it is, now has a long history and has developed subtleties and complexities that strongly resist any label of primitivism. What a language may or may not express is no measure of its age, but of the kind of life of its speakers, reflecting what they want or need to share and communicate.

Generalizations about language.   Important contributions to theoretical linguistics have by no means come only from recent transformational theory. Other systems of analysis and description—traditional, structural, tagmemic, and stratificational grammars, for example—have given us nearly all of the basic vocabulary of language study and many necessary insights into functions and principles. Four important general principles have been established in modern descriptive linguistics, not by any one linguist, but cumulatively, through the work and observations of many. First, language is systematic, regular, and to a large extent predictable. Second, all living language is in a state of constant growth and change, with imperceptible but steady alteration of sounds, vocabulary and structure, and often with simultaneous development toward complexity in some areas and simplicity in others. Third, the changes that occur in language are not changes that can or should be prevented or judged; the actual changing usage of people is ultimately the only basis for correctness in a language, and a grammar that describes what was or what might have been is not an accurate description of a language.

Fourth, human language is above all an oral phenomenon, and the living spoken language is not to be identified in an absolute way with written representations, which tend to be conservative and formal, reflecting a different set of conventions. All of these generalizations have, at one time or another in the past, been the subject of doubt and debate. They are presently taken for granted by every working linguist, however; they may be thought of as the tenets of modern descriptive linguistics and as the starting point for practically all current theory and practice.

Field linguistics

How can an anthropologist, a missionary, a social or a medical worker approach and make sense of a language that has not already been analyzed and described, or for which there are no immediately available materials? There are hundreds of such languages in the world; fortunately some fairly efficient methods have been developed to help with the task. It is a painstaking process to unravel a language, but it is ultimately rewarding and often even fascinating for its own sake.

The process requires first a good ear and a thorough understanding of the way speech sounds are produced. Otherwise it will be extremely difficult to write out or make intelligent use of any data. To satisfy this preliminary requirement, most people ordinarily need special training in phonetics, the study of the production, transmission, and reception of speech sounds.

Phonemes.   In order to analyze and describe any new language, an inventory of all of its sounds and an accurate way of writing them down are needed. Some sounds of other languages may be very much like the sounds of English, others may be sounds that we have never consciously produced; but since we all have the same vocal equipment, there is no reason why we should not be able, with practice, to reproduce all the sounds that anyone else makes.

The first step in studying any particular language is distinguishing the sounds that make a difference in meaning, called **phonemes,** and the sounds that are merely variations of those sounds in different contexts, called **allophones.** This is done by a process called the minimal pair test: the linguist tries to find two short words that appear to be exactly alike except for one sound, such as *bat* and *pat* in English. If the substitution of *b* for *p* in this minimal pair makes a difference in meaning, which it does in English, then those two sounds have been identified as distinct phonemes of the language and will require two different symbols to record. If, however, the linguist finds two different pronunciations, recorded tentatively as *top* and *tawp,* and then finds that there is no difference in their meaning for a native speaker, he will consider the sounds represented by *o* and *aw* as allophones of the same phoneme, and for economy of representation will use only one of the two symbols to record that sound wherever he finds it. For greater accuracy and to avoid confusion with the various sounds of our own language, the symbols of the International Phonetic Alphabet, a set of about eighty symbols, can be used to distinguish between the sounds of most languages in a way comprehensible to anyone who knows the system.

Morphemes. The process of making an inventory of sounds may of course be a long task; concurrently, the linguist may begin to collect all groups or combinations of sounds that seem to have meaning. These are called the **morphemes** of the language. A field linguist can elicit morphemes and their meanings from speakers of a language by means of pointing or gesturing, but the ideal situation is to have an informant, a person who knows enough of a common second language, so that approximate translations can be made more efficiently and confidently. It is pointless to write down data without any suggestion of meaning for it. *Cat* and *dog* would of course turn out to be morphemes, or meaningful combinations of sounds, in English. By pointing to two of either of them, the linguist could elicit *cats* and *dogs.* This tells him that there is another mean-

ingful unit, an *-s,* that may be added to the original morpheme to mean "plural." When he finds that this *-s* cannot occur in the language unattached, he will identify it as a **bound morpheme;** because *dog* and *cat* can occur unattached to anything, they are called **free morphemes.** Because the sound represented as *s* is actually different in the two words (*s* in *cats* and *z* in *dogs*), the linguist will conclude that the sounds *s* and *z* are **allomorphs** of the plural morpheme: that is, they are two varieties of the same morpheme (even though they may be two different phonemes), occuring in different contexts but with no difference in meaning.

Grammar and syntax. The next step is putting morphemes together to form phrases or sentences. This process is known as identifying the syntagms of the language, or the meaningful combination of morphemes in larger chains or strings. Proceeding slowly at first, and relying on pointing or gestures, using a method called frame substitution, the field linguist can elicit such strings as *my cat, your cat,* or *her cat,* and *I see your cat, she sees my cat.* This begins to establish the rules or principles of phrase and sentence making, the **syntax** of the language.

Further success of this linguistic study depends greatly on individual ingenuity, tact, logic, and experience with language. A language may make extensive use of kinds of utterances that are not found at all in English, and which the linguist may not therefore even think of asking for. Furthermore, certain speakers may pretend not to be able to say (or may truly not be able to say) certain things which they consider to be impolite, taboo, or inappropriate for mention to outsiders. It may even be culturally unacceptable to point, in which case the linguist will have to devise roundabout ways of eliciting words for objects.

The **grammar** of the language will ultimately consist of all observations about the morphemes and the syntax. Further work will include establishing by means of substitution frames all the **form classes** of the language: that is, the parts of speech or categories of words that work the same way in any sentence. For example, we may establish a category we call "nouns" defined as anything that will fit the substitution frame "I see a —." We simply make the frame, try out a number of words in it, and have a native speaker indicate "yes" or "no" for whether the words work. In English the words *house* and *cat* will fit this frame and will be said to belong to the same form class, but the word *think* will not. Another possible substitution frame for nouns might be "The — died," in which the word *cat* will fit, but not the word *house*. Thus we can identify subclasses of our nouns: in this case what we can call "animate" or "inanimate" subclasses. The same procedure may be followed for all the words of the language, using as many different frames as necessary, until we have a lexicon, or dictionary, that accurately describes the possible uses of all the words in the language.

One of the strengths of modern descriptive linguistics is the scientific objectivity of its methods. A descriptive linguist will not approach a language with the idea that it must have nouns, verbs, prepositions, or any other of the form classes identifiable in English. The linguist instead sees what turns up in the language and makes an attempt to describe it in terms of its own inner workings. For convenience he may, and often will, label morphemes that behave approximately like English nouns and verbs as "nouns" and "verbs"; but if he thinks that the terms are misleading, he may instead call them "x-words" and "y-words" or "form class A" and "form class B."

The methods of field linguistics are important tools for the cultural anthropologist, even when he is working with a language that has already been described. No analysis of any language is ever complete, and improvements, fresh insights, and new interpretations are always possible.

Sociolinguistics

The whole question of the relationships between language and culture is the province of **sociolinguistics,** a field that has grown out of both

sociology and descriptive linguistics to become an area of almost separate enquiry. Sociolinguistics is concerned with every aspect of the structure and use of language that has anything to do with society and culture and human behavior. It is a term synonymous with both ethnolinguistics and anthropological linguistics. The field is fascinating and seemingly limitless.

Language and culture

An important sociolinguistic concern of the 1930s and 1940s was the question of whether language might indeed determine culture. Do we see and react differently to the colors blue and green, with different cultural symbolism for the two different colors, only because our language has different names for these two neighboring sections of the unbroken color spectrum? When anthropologists noticed that some cultures lump together blue and green with one name, they began to wonder about this question. The American linguist Edward Sapir first formulated the problem, and his student, Benjamin Lee Whorf, drawing on his experience with the language of the Hopi Indians, developed a full-fledged theory, sometimes called the Whorfian hypothesis. Whorf proposed that a language is not simply an encoding process for voicing our ideas and needs but rather a shaping force that guides our thinking and our behavior. The problem is a little like the old question of the chicken or the egg, and Whorf's theory about which came first has since been generally criticized as both logically unsound and not amenable to any experimentation or proof. Its primary value is that it did begin to focus attention on the relationships between language and culture.

An opposite point of view, that life fashions language, has been more recently and somewhat more rationally maintained by the British linguist Joshua Whatmough. Whatmough believes that there is nothing to show that concepts such as color, time, or space have been imposed by language, but rather that there is ample evidence that languages are creative, flexible, and adaptable to any new needs or changed perceptions of their users. If the people who make no distinction between the two colors of blue and green only had good reason to sort them out, he would argue, such as having to distinguish between a missionary's blue Ford and a doctor's green one, they could very well make their language do the job, and they might perhaps even begin to associate blue with religion and green with medicine.

Linguists are finding that although language is generally flexible and adaptable, once a terminology is established it tends to perpetuate itself and to reflect and reveal the social structure and the common perceptions and concerns of a group. For example, the English words for war and the tactics of war and the hierarchy of officers and men who fight, reflect what is obviously a reality for our culture. An observer from an entirely different and perhaps warless culture could understand a great deal about our institution of war and its conventions simply from what we have found necessary to name and talk about in our military terminology. Similarly, anthropologists have noted that in the Arabic dialects of Bedouin tribes in the Middle East there is an elaborate system of terminology for everything having to do with camels; with a certain amount of study we can determine from the naming system alone the importance of camels to the culture, attitudes toward camels (which are often treated with more care than people), and the whole etiquette of human and camel relationships. Cultural terminology is properly a concern of anthropology, and it is an example of one important area of sociolinguistics.

Kinship terms. In the same connection, considerable attention has been paid by anthropologists to the way people name their relatives in various societies: further observations on the question of kinship terms will be found in Chapter 18. In English we have terms to identify brother, sister, mother, father, grandmother, grandfather, granddaughter, grandson, niece, nephew, mother-in-law, father-in-law, sister-in-law, and brother-in-

law. Some people also distinguish first and second cousin, and great aunt and great uncle. Is this the only possible system for naming relatives and identifying relationships? Obviously not. We could have separate and individual words, as some cultures do, for younger brother and older brother, for mother's sister and father's sister, and so on. What we can describe in English with a phrase, if pressed to do so, other languages make explicit from the outset, and vice-versa: some West African languages use the same word to denote both a brother and a cousin, and a mother's sister may also be called one's mother.

What do kinship terms reveal? We can certainly learn from them how the family is structured, what relationships are considered close or distant, and sometimes what attitudes to relationships may be.

Figure 4-6. *This somewhat idealized portrait of the Cherokee chief Sequoia shows him pointing to the alphabet, the result of his single-handed efforts to find a way to write the Cherokee language.*

SE - QUO - YAH

Caution is required, however, in drawing conclusions from kinship terms. Just because we do not distinguish linguistically in English between our mother's parents and our father's parents (both are simply *grandmother* and *grandfather*), does that mean that in our culture we lump them all together as faceless old people or that we treat old people badly? Some people have argued that it is so. But in France, where there is reputedly considerably more respect and concern for older relatives, perhaps even exaggeratedly so by our standards, there is no more linguistic difference between a mother's mother and a father's mother than there is in English. Kinship terms can establish the limits of so-called extended families in certain cultures, and they can define the cultural relationships between families brought together by a marriage. Other implications are still uncertain, but the area has turned out to be a rich one for investigation.

Taboo words. Another interesting concern of sociolinguistics is the matter of taboo words, obscenities, and acceptable and unacceptable language in general. Just consider, for example, the question of whether this textbook should supply at this point a list of some vigorous obscenities in English to illustrate the point. The answer is obviously that it should not, though a more formal, technical article in a journal might very well do so. What makes words socially unacceptable or inappropriate in certain contexts in certain languages? There is no universal taboo about words related to sex and excrement, as in our culture, and some cultures find our obscenities to be only a little foolish or peculiar, as we do theirs. Consider, for example, the English obscenity "bloody" or the French one, *"Sacre bleu"* (blue rite); both sound odd to American ears. By determining what may or may not be said, and when and where, we can understand a great deal about beliefs and social relationships. An interesting study has been made recently by the British anthropologist Edmund Leach of the striking relationships between animal names, verbal abuse, and cultural taboos. Leach finds a relationship, for example, between a long-standing cultural belief in the dirtiness of a dog, the fact that it is insulting in English to call someone a dog, and the fact that we may not and do not eat the dog for meat (though some cultures do). What is meat and what is not, what is insult and what is not, what is dirty and what is not: all of these are important questions that may be answered in part in language, and they are likewise matters for investigation in sociolinguistics.

Social dialects

A somewhat broader concern of sociolinguistics is the matter of social dialects. A social dialect is the language of any group of people within a larger group of people, all of whom may speak more or less the same language. Technically all dialects are languages—there is nothing partial or sublinguistic about them—and the point at which two different dialects become distinctly different languages is roughly the point at which the speakers of one are almost totally unable to communicate with speakers of the other. Boundaries may be psychological, geographical, social, or economic, and they are not always very clear. There is usually a transitional territory, or perhaps a buffer zone, where features of both are found and understood, as between central and southern China. The fact is that if you learn the Chinese of Peking you cannot communicate with the waiter in your local Chinese restaurant who comes from Canton or Hong Kong, although both languages—or dialects—are conventionally called Chinese.

In addition to the larger problem of determining dialect boundaries, and trying to determine whether linguistic differences in any given case also reflect cultural differences, there is also the problem in dialect studies of why and how people in the same community, whether it be a large American city or a small African town, can and do speak the same language in different ways. Some people are able to speak one social dialect in one situation and one in another. As a rather extreme example, in New York City presently some second-generation immigrant children from Puerto Rico are able to speak the language of their parents at home, a dialect known as Puerto Rican "Spanglish" with their contemporaries, and New York English with their teachers. The process of changing from one level of language to another, whether it be from one language to another or from one dialect of a language to another, is known as code-switching, and it has been the subject of a number of studies in sociolinguistics. Almost all of us can switch from formality to informality in our speech, and the question of why and when such things are done in various cultures is only beginning to be investigated.

Of the many other concerns of sociolinguistics today we can only mention that we also find investigations of children's languages and word games, the structure of folk tales and folk songs, bilingualism and multilingualism, pidgin languages and creoles, linguistic borrowing and innovation, formulas of address and politeness, the language of gesture and intonation, secret languages, magic languages, and myth. The list increases and has begun to duplicate many of the concerns of other fields or disciplines. It can easily be seen that almost every aspect of anthropology and sociology has a linguistic side or a relevance to linguistics. This new field of sociolinguistics proves to be not one field but many, and it is providing an opportunity for some productive cooperation and sharing between disciplines.

ANIMALS, MAN, AND COMMUNICATION

Men have tried to distinguish themselves from the animals in many ways—as "featherless bipeds," as toolmakers, as the unique possessors of a soul—but perhaps it is our gift of language that most clearly sets us apart. Animals do communicate with one another. They cry, hoot, bleat, and coo, and to some degree these noises accomplish the same purposes as our language. They call infants, attract a mate, warn of danger, or cry in pain. Yet these animal noises are more like our human cries, screams, sighs, and grunts than they are like language. Language alone has an inherently meaningless set of sounds, which can be used to form a vast vocabulary; and language alone is productive of an infinite number of utterances and applicable to an infinite number of topics.

No animals speak in nature, and none can be taught to speak by man. Devoted researchers have tried to teach chimpanzees to say a few words, but after months of effort they will do little more than utter gruff noises, in a few situations where we might think a word would be appropriate. They never even come close to combining known forms into new combinations, a skill that is a crucial aspect of human speech and an ability that comes easily to every normal human child. The teeth, tongue, and larynx of a chimpanzee are adequate for speech, but his brain is not, and no amount of training can make up for this lack. All normal men on the other hand learn their first language with little direct instruction. Learn they must, but unlike the chimp they bring adequate equipment to the task.

In the several million years during which man has become differentiated from his fellow anthropoids, his brain has somehow developed a new and unique ability, an ability unknown elsewhere in the animal kingdom. Conceivably, it has been selection in favor of this ability that has brought much of man's unique development. It may even be that the expansion of the brain, a rather rapid development by usual evolutionary standards and a development that can be traced rather well through the record of fossil man, resulted from the progressive selection of ever more competent speakers. Once our barely human ancestors acquired the incipient beginnings of language, the individuals and the groups who were most skilled in speech must have had a considerable advantage when competing for limited resources. They could have cooperated more successfully, warned each other of dangers, and helped each other in time of need. Slowly but inexorably, the ever more skillful speakers would survive and pass on to their children their superior potential for speech. On the average, the better speakers probably had bigger brains, and perhaps this is why the human brain has doubled in size in the course of the last million or so years. It may even be fair to suggest that the unique character of the human brain and the trait that distinguishes it most clearly from other mammalian brains is its ability to produce language. It is hardly profitable to speculate on just how our brain accomplishes its task, but we cannot doubt that our ability to speak and the ways in which human vocal communication differs from that of our nearest nonhuman relatives rest squarely upon our biological organization.

Yet here lies a paradox, for our brains cannot produce speech without training: we must always learn our language. Any normal infant given a suitable opportunity can learn any language, and the languages we learn are certainly diverse. We can credit our biological capacity with our general linguistic abilities, but the varied details of a man's language depend upon his unique personal experiences. In the diversity of his behavior, man is again set apart from other animals, for man alone is capable of developing and perpetuating distinct traditions, or different "cultures," whether in language or in other aspects of his behavior. Other animals have but a limited capacity to learn varied forms of behavior, and virtually no ability to teach their juniors to follow them. Behavior varies from species to species, of course, and individual diversity in behavior among members of a single species is by no means negligible, but variation from band to band or from herd to herd appears to be a very minor matter.

It is here that man is strange. Surely the diversity in the behavior of various human groups, the diversity of tradition handed down to our children, is one of our most remarkable characteristics. In the past, these differences in tradition were sometimes attributed to the diverse biological or racial characteristics of the groups or believed to be dependent in some simplistic way upon the environment in which the group lived. Such explanations can no longer be taken seriously. Caught early enough, any child can learn any language and any culture. People with the same inherent capacities learn to eat different foods, to organize different sorts of families, to construct diverse political systems, and to speak Swahili, Mohawk, or English.

Figure 4-7a,b. *These photos of baboons show the range of communication possible through posture and facial expression. The photo on the right shows one juvenile establishing dominance through use of pseudosexual posture; the other photo shows two fear postures.*

Our human potential for learning such varied behavior and for teaching our children to follow us in similar behavior must itself rest upon our uniquely human nature. It is easy to imagine that the pressures of natural selection might have produced an animal with a complex form of language that was still uniquely determined by the biological organization of the species. All members of such a species would speak exactly the same sort of language, or at least any minor variability would depend only upon the random genetic variability among the individuals. One member of such a species would not even have to be in contact with others in order to learn to talk. His speech could be a spontaneous and automatic concomitant of his biological organization, like the cries of animals or of babies, which need not be learned, though they are nonetheless used for communication. But evolution did not take this path, for each human child must learn some particular form of speech, just as he must learn some particular cultural patterns. So complex are the things he must learn, that every child, even in the most primitive of societies, must spend long years before he knows enough to behave as a responsible adult. No other species is so burdened.

The central facts of human language, then, are also the central facts of human culture: our ability to speak, like all our other human abilities, rests firmly upon our unique human inheritance. Even our peculiar ability to learn and then to perpetuate different traditions of language and culture is attributable ultimately to the kind of animal we are. The particular traditions of language or of culture that any one of us acquires result from our own individual experiences. Since language is learned so early and since it is central to so much of our other learning, it is even tempting to wonder if our ability to learn a language does not somehow lie at the core of our other human abilities. Conceivably our very ability to perpetuate varying traditions in all aspects of our culture rests in part, at least, upon our ability to perpetuate varying traditions in that most human of all our abilities, our ability to speak.

If language is so central to man, it is hardly surprising to find so much of human life mirrored in language. Not only do we give names to things, but our languages come to symbolize our social divisions, our particular position in our social organization, our attitudes, our personalities. In the perpetuation of language, in its borrowing, and in the way it changes, we see reflected the general properties of human culture. Linguists have learned much about the internal organization of language, but grammar and phonology, as they have been studied by linguists, represent only the beginning of the real complexity and importance of language. Language is so involved with the rest of our lives that it penetrates everything we do, and everything we do penetrates language. We can never hope to fully understand either language or other aspects of human behavior, without attention to both.

Source:

From *Man's Many Voices: Language in its Cultural Context* by Robbins Burling. Copyright © 1970 by Holt, Rinehart and Winston, Inc. Reprinted by permission of Holt, Rinehart and Winston, Inc.

Culture and man ● part **2**

Summary

1.

Language is a code for symbolic communication. A symbol is any sound or gesture to which we give a meaning. It is an arbitrary representation of something else. Human culture as we know it cannot exist without language.

2.

Linguistics is the science that studies all aspects of language. There are two approaches to the study of linguistics. The historical approach investigates relationships between earlier and later forms of the same language. The descriptive approach registers and explains all the features of a language at any time in history. Historical linguistics provides a means of roughly dating certain migrations, invasions, and contacts of peoples. Descriptive linguistics gives the anthropologist a framework for understanding languages and the means to analyze, describe, and work with them.

3.

Noam Chomsky has provided the first consistent and logical model for scientifically describing the facts of language. His theory is called generative transformational grammar. Chomsky holds that we unconsciously build our utterances with basic two-part units, called deep structures. Complete utterances display surface structure, a complex web of deep structure units. The principle is assumed to be the same for all languages, but the deep structures differ. Understanding a language involves identifying deep structure and establishing how deep structure becomes surface structure.

4.

Four important general principles have been established in modern descriptive linguistics. First, language is systematic, regular, and to a large extent predictable. Second, all living language is constantly growing and changing. Third, the changes that occur in language cannot and should not be prevented. Fourth, human language is primarily an oral phenomenon. Descriptive linguistics also recognizes that human language consists of more than speech; it includes also such elements as gestures and voice inflection.

5.

To analyze and describe a new language, a linguist needs an inventory of all its sounds and an accurate way of writing them down. The first step in studying a language is distinguishing the sounds that make a difference in meaning, called phonemes, from variations of those sounds, called allophones. A linguist must list all the meaningful combinations of sounds of a language. These are called morphemes. He can then put morphemes together to form phrases or sentences. Meaningful combinations of morphemes are called strings. From a study of such strings, a linguist can identify the principles which make up a language's syntax. Grammar studies the ways a language operates and is constructed.

6.

Sociolinguistics, synonymous with ethnolinguistics and anthropological linguistics, deals with the relationship between language and culture. Some linguists, such as Benjamin Lee Whorf, have theorized that language shapes culture. Others, such as Joshua Whatmough, have theorized that culture shapes language. Culture-shapes-language theories are based on evidence that language is creative, flexible, and adaptable. Though linguists have found language flexible and adaptable, they have also found that once a terminology is established, it perpetuates itself.

7.
Anthropologists are interested in the way different societies name their relatives. Kinship terms help reveal how a family is structured, what relationships are considered close or distant, and what attitudes to relationships are held. Anthropologists are also interested in taboo words, social dialects, and code switching. A taboo word can reveal much about a society's beliefs and social relationships. A social dialect is the language of a group of people within a larger group of people, all of whom speak more or less the same language. Code-switching is the process of changing from one level of language to another.

Suggested readings

Bloomfield, Leonard *Language*. New York: Holt, Rinehart and Winston, 1933.
It is a somewhat dated standard text intended for general reader and beginning student in linguistics. An orderly survey covering a wide range of topics including meaning, syntax, phonetic and semantic change, cultural borrowing.

Burling, Robbins *Man's Many Voices: Language in its Cultural Context*. New York: Holt, Rinehart and Winston, 1970.
An investigation into the nonlinguistic factors that affect the use of language, such as kinship systems and the wider cultural context. It relies heavily on examples from South and Southeast Asia.

Carroll, John B., ed. *Language, Thought and Reality: Selected Writings of Benjamin Lee Whorf*. New York: John Wiley and Sons, 1956.
Whorf's emphasis is on the relationship between human language and human thought and the ways in which language can shape thinking. An important contribution to semantics.

Chomsky, Noam *Syntactic Structures*. The Hague: Mowton and Co., 1957. This readable introduction to Chomsky's work was the book that first established the outlines of his theory of deep structure.

Evans, Williams F. *Communication in the Animal World*. New York: Thomas Y. Crowell, 1968. This book surveys all major animal groups and reports in detail on the many systems of communication by which different creatures relate to one another and to their environment.

Gelb, Ignace J. *A Study of Writing*. London: Routledge and Kegan Paul, 1952.
The aim of this study is to lay a foundation for a new science of writing, grammatology. It attempts to establish general principles governing the use and evolution of writing on a comparative basis, and is the first systematic presentation of the history of writing based on these principles.

Gleason, H. A., Jr. *An Introduction to Descriptive Linguistics*. (rev. ed.) New York: Holt, Rinehart and Winston, 1966.
This book focuses on the descriptive approach, studying languages in terms of their internal structures. It is a lucid, well written introduction to the study of language.

Hall, Robert A., Jr. *Linguistics and Your Language*. (2nd rev. ed.) Garden City, New York: Anchor Books, Doubleday, 1960.
This is a brief popular discussion of some problems connected with language and linguistics. Emphasizes the implications of the science of language for modern society. Very interesting reading.

Hockett, Charles F. *A Course in Modern Linguistics*. New York: Macmillan, 1958.
A presentation of the generally accepted facts and principles of the field of linguistics. Hockett is influenced by Leonard Bloomfield and American linguistics in general. Contains studies on phonology, grammar, morphemic systems, phylogeny, and linguistic prehistory.

Labov, William *Language in the Inner City*. Philadelphia: University of Pennsylvania Press, 1972.
The author argues in favor of the existence of Black English Vernacular as a dialect of English. The book studies such art forms as the ritual insult and ritualized narrative.

Premack, Ann James and David Premack "Teaching Language to an Ape" in *Scientific American*: Vol. 227:4, Oct. 1972, pp. 92–99.
This interesting article tests the hypothesis that language is unique to the human species. It concludes that certain gestures of human speech belong to a more general system, and are capable of being understood by other primates. The program that was used to teach the chimpanzee Sarah to communicate has been successfully applied to people suffering certain types of brain damage.

Wardhaugh, Ronald *Introduction to Linguistics*. New York: McGraw-Hill, 1972.
The book attempts to provide beginning students with a basic knowledge of the kinds of questions asked by linguists about language. Includes chapters on communication, phonetics, phonology, morphology, language change, and variation. Each chapter concludes with notes indicating further reading on the topic; it includes a glossary of terms.

Personality and culture

A wide variety of attitudes and behavior patterns can be found in cultures throughout the world. Though every individual is a unique person, his personality is largely determined by the society in which he is raised. It is difficult to give a single, all-inclusive definition of personality, but for our purposes, personality may be defined as the distinctive way a person thinks, feels, and behaves. The individual personality is largely formed through an assimilation of ways of thinking and acting that are common to the group, a process called enculturation.

How is the individual enculturated or socialized by his society? Eric Wolf, who has examined peasant societies in his book, *Peasants,* has made a number of significant observations about the social "programming" process as it occurs in both extended and nuclear families, which are the foundations of societies.[1] According to Wolf, extended families, which consist of several husband-wife-children groups, usually occur in agricultural societies where they have access to a steady, reliable source of food. In such families, group cohesion and continuity are important if the group is to survive because a large number of individuals is required to work the land. The extended family's greatest problem is to assure that its members remain within it. To do this, the family has devised a number of reinforcements, particularly in the ways it socializes its young. Thus, the extended family favors enculturation techniques that render its members dependent on it. For example, the family indulges its children with oral gratification for relatively long periods of time. This practice, according to psychological theory, assures that the individual will continue to look to his family for the fulfillment of his needs, especially his future economic needs. The family also tends to curb expressions of aggression and sexuality, hoping to teach the child to control his impulses. Such control is an important requirement for group coordination, which the structure and survival of the extended family demand. Thus, enculturation prepares the child to become a permanent member of the existing family; it also prepares for the family's future when offspring who marry will not establish their own household but reside with the family to help it produce the food it needs.

On the other hand, the smaller nuclear family, consisting of a man, woman and their offspring,

[1] Eric Wolf, *Peasants* (Englewood Cliffs, N.J.: Prentice-Hall, Inc., 1966).

is usually found among societies whose food supply is unstable and impermanent, such as hunter-gatherers and industrial societies, where self-reliance is a most important trait for survival. Wolf observes that enculturation techniques of the nuclear family are just the opposite of those favored by the extended family. The nuclear family tends to place less emphasis on prolonged oral dependence and to encourage displays of aggression and sexuality in its offspring. Such early training allows the individual a great deal of freedom in his relations with others and readies him to be more independent; he will need such qualities later in his struggle to make a living from an environment which does not provide a dependable, steady food supply and where the prevailing rule is "every man for himself."

Thus, an intricate interrelation exists between a society, as represented above by the family, and each of its members. Anthropologists have sought to define more precisely the nature of this relationship. Can we describe a "group personality" or a "national character" without falling into stereotyping? Do cultures assume personality characteristics deriving from particular child-raising practices? What is the status of the person who cannot adapt to the cultural norm? That part of anthropology which focusses on such questions is called psychological anthropology or, more commonly, the study of culture and personality.

Group personality

Culture, said Ruth Benedict, is personality writ large. Every society unconsciously selects from the vast variety of human potentialities certain traits which are established as normative or ideal. Those who conform to these norms are rewarded; those who deviate are punished. The result is a certain homogeneity of world view and behavior, a sort of group "personality" that forms an overall cultural orientation within which there is considerable variation. The group personality is an abstraction, not to be found in pure form in any single individual, and so it is extremely difficult to define. Yet field ethnologists are frequently struck by the feeling of personality conveyed by the group they are studying.

Cultural configuration

The Kwakiutl Indians of the Northwest Coast, when they were studied by Franz Boas at the turn of the century, were a status-dominated people who saw life as a series of rivalry situations. Great feasts called "potlatches" were regularly held, in which enormous amounts of wealth were given away or destroyed—for example, by burning great quantities of valuable oil—to affirm the status of the feastgiver or to humiliate a rival who might not be able to give away or destroy a similar amount. The host would jeer his invited rivals with songs:

I am the great chief who makes people ashamed.
I am the great chief who makes people ashamed.
Our chief brings shame to the faces.
Our chief brings jealousy to the faces.
Our chief makes people cover their faces by what he is continually doing in this world,
Giving again and again oil feasts to all the tribes.

Among the Kwakiutl, the widespread practice of obtaining supernatural power in a dream or vision became a highly competitive situation. Men sought these visions by means of hideous self-tortures. They cut strips from the skin of their arms, they struck off fingers, they went without food and water for long periods. By inflicting great pain on themselves, they sought a mental state set apart from daily living in which to achieve their vision. Through excesses of suffering, each man tried to achieve the biggest and best vision.

The Zuni Indians of the American Southwest were in many ways the opposite of the Kwakiutl. Individuals were personally restrained, slow to anger, group oriented, and generally opposed to aggression and excessive behavior. They distrusted any kind of disruption, and did not understand self-torture. They had no rites in which

Figure 5-1. *This blanket is typical of the type of goods distributed by the host of a Kwakiutl potlatch. Woven of mountain goat wool and bark, it features the owner's totem.*

they sacrificed their own blood or used it for fertility. Drunkenness was repulsive to them. The old Zuni men voluntarily outlawed liquor after it was first introduced; the rule was congenial enough to be honored.

According to Ruth Benedict, in whose book *Patterns of Culture* these tribes are described, the Kwakiutl and the Zuni represented two opposite cultural configurations. Borrowing her terms from the German philosopher Friedrich Nietzsche, she called these two fundamental modes of ideology and behavior the "Dionysian" and the "Apollonian." The Dionysian, exemplified by the Kwakiutl, is characterized by ecstatic ritual, egocentrism, and extremely individualistic behavior. The Zuni represent the Apollonian response to life. The Zuni's rule is the Golden Mean; he wants no part of excess, no disruptive psychological states; he distrusts individualism. Benedict saw cultures as comparable to great works of art, possessing internal coherence and consistency. Cultures are far more than the sum of the individuals who adhere to them, because in them are developed and elaborated traits with greater intensity and richness than any individual would be capable of, even in a whole lifetime. Each person is heir to a rich cultural heritage. The variety of cultural and individual response is summarized by a myth of the Digger Indians:

> God gave to every people a cup, a cup of clay, and from this cup they drank their life. . . . They all dipped in the water, but their cups were different.[2]

Though *Patterns of Culture* had an enormous and valuable influence in popularizing the idea of cultural variation and the influence of culture upon individual personality, the book has been severely criticized. The Apollonian-Dionysian characterization, which Benedict saw as fundamental, applies only to a few, if any, cultures in the world. More significantly, the book characterizes cultures in terms of their most obvious aspects, ignoring subtleties that may be extremely important—a tendency which is very close to stereotyping. The Kwakiutl, for example, have a delightful sense of play and humor which is sometimes displayed in farces satirizing their own potlatches. Some of the supposedly mild-mannered, pain-avoiding Zuni practice sword swallowing and ritual walking over red-hot coals. The very richness of these cultures makes any simple summary necessarily incomplete.

Growing up

In Western society, adolescence is a period of tension and stress. The no-longer-child must come to terms with biological changes, with sexual desire, and the social demands for its iniation. He may begin questioning the "truths" he has been brought up with; he may rebel against pa-

---
[2]Ruth Benedict, *Patterns of Culture* (Boston: Houghton Mifflin, 1934) p. 21.

rental authority; he may come to see that injustices in the world do not correspond to the ideals he was raised to revere. Some writers believed that these conflicts arise out of the very nature of adolescence, and therefore are universal. But are they? In 1925 a young anthropologist named Margaret Mead went to Samoa to try to find the answer.

Samoan children learn that they can have their own way if they are quiet and obedient. Preference is given not to the arrogant, the flippant, the courageous, but to the quiet and demure boy or girl who "speaks softly and treads lightly." The standards of conduct are graded in this fashion: small children should keep quiet, wake up early, obey, work hard and cheerfully, play with children of their own sex; young people should work industriously and skillfully, not be presuming, marry discreetly, be loyal to their relatives, not carry tales nor be troublemakers; adults should be wise, peaceable, serene, generous, anxious for the prestige of their village, and conduct their lives with all good form and decorum.

Little girls move and play together, reacting to boys with antagonism or avoidance. As they grow up, however, these groups slowly begin to break up, and boys and girls begin to play and banter together good naturedly during parties and torch-fishing excursions. A few years after puberty, the girl may take the first of a series of lovers. Liaisons may last for some time, or adolescents may slip away together into the bush. As long as there is no breach of custom, such as incest or a boy's aspiring to love an older woman, society considers these premarital relations completely natural and pays little attention to them.

Consequently, Samoans grow up with minimal sexual or social stress, in a society characterized by peaceful conformity and a tolerant attitude toward sex. The transition from childhood to adulthood is relatively smooth. Generalizing, Mead concludes that "adolescence is not necessarily a time of stress and strain, but that cultural conditions make it so. . . ."

By providing strong evidence of the effect of childhood training on the formation of the adult

Figure 5-2. *Through their participation in society's culture, children learn its rules. This pair illustrates the Mauritanian custom of dressing in navy blue cloth by the age of 8.*

personality, Mead stimulated an interest in child-rearing not only as an anthropological problem, but also as a practical one. If a great deal of adolescent behavior is learned, rather than biologically induced, then in our own culture it might be possible to minimize the anxiety and antisocial behavior associated with adolescence by changing the culture. Also, the converse may be possible: by changing child-rearing practices, we may be able to change the structure of society. However, Mead cautions against thinking we can accomplish anything by simply copying the Samoans, because "unfortunately, the conditions which vex our adolescents are the flesh and bone of our society, no more subject to straightforward manipulation upon our part than is the language we speak."[3]

Development of personality

We have seen how the individual members of a society are carriers of the norms that are characteristic of the culture. But where do these norms come from in the first place? On the theory that personality is largely formed in infancy and childhood, some psychologists and psychologically oriented anthropologists have studied different societies to determine how child raising practices teach the norms to the individual child and reinforce them for the adults of the society.

Personality patterns

A person learns in childhood the patterns of behavior expected from him by the society in which he was born. Such predictable patterns of behavior are a result of cultural transmission. They provide a framework in which members of the society can make sense out of the motivations and the behavior of others.

[3]Margaret Mead, *Coming of Age in Samoa* (New York: William Morrow, 1961, 3rd ed.)

A certain minimum of cooperation is necessary for the group to survive. Whether the society chooses a culture which encourages competition and conflict or cooperation and harmony, or its own unique combination of values, the pattern of individual behavior will reflect that choice. There must be a consensus on norms and values for the group to go about its everyday round of activities. The goal of the ongoing society is to bring the individual into a general conformity with its prevailing view of the world.

Sigmund Freud. With *Totem and Taboo,* Freud expanded his theories of personality development from the psychoanalyst's couch to the vast domain of culture. In this work, he used the Oedipus complex, that is, the sexual desire of the son for his mother, which Freud saw as the most important factor in individual personality development, to explain the origins of culture and society. According to this scheme, early societies were strongly patriarchal, with the dominant man possessing exclusive sexual rights over his sisters and daughters. The sexually deprived sons rebelled, killed their father, and ate him. Overcome with guilt, the brothers then repressed their sexual desires toward their mothers, sisters and daughters. Thus came into being the incest taboo and exogamy. Through what Freud called the "racial unconscious," the sons inherited the primal guilt over the killing of the father.

Almost no anthropologist would accept this theory in its original form, because there is no evidence to substantiate it. However, one need not accept Freud's origin-of-society hypothesis in order to find in the Oedipus complex a possible basis for significant cultural norms and values. Some Freudian anthropologists, such as Geza Roheim, believe that tensions rising from the Oedipal family situation, in which the boy feels antagonistic toward his father and has to suppress his incestual desires toward his mother, are to be found in all societies, and are indeed the source of such cultural phenomena as the incest taboo and exogamy. According to Roheim, any anthro-

pologist who denies this is simply repressing his own Oedipus complex.

Bronislaw Malinowski. Bronislaw Malinowski was one of the first to challenge the universality of Freud's Oedipus complex theory with careful field research. The people of the Trobriand Islands, he pointed out, do not think of the child as belonging to his father's family. Because Trobriand society is matrilineal, the mother's elder brother functions as a child's disciplinarian and authority figure, while the father assumes the role of friend and companion to the child. Whereas the Oedipus complex is based on the triangular relationship between mother, father, and son, the true complex of relationships for the Trobriands is brother, sister and sister's son.

Whatever the final verdict on the Oedipus complex, Freud's beliefs have been accepted in other areas of psychological theory relevant to anthropology. As Edward Sapir said:

> Such relational ideas as the emotionally integrated complex, the tendency to suppression under the stress of conflict, the symptomatic expression of a suppressed impulse, the transfer of emotion and the canalizing or pooling of impulses, the tendency to regression, are so many powerful clues to understanding how the "soul" of man sets to work.[4]

Individual psychology and enculturation

Benedict and Mead emphasized the ways culture produces individual personality; Freud saw all culture as deriving from individual complexes. It remained for Abram Kardiner to seek a synthesis that would at once respect the theoretical contributions of both individual psychology and the influence of culture in the development of personality. Kardiner, a trained psychoanalyst, attempted to lift Freud's theories from their ethnocentric European matrix and enlarge the scope of

[4] Quoted in Marvin Harris, *Rise of Anthropological Theory* (New York: Thomas Y. Crowell, 1968) pp. 432.

these theories to account for cultural diversity. To do so, he rejected much of Freudian dogma, including the Oedipus complex, stages of infantile sexuality, and the emphasis on exclusively sexual aspects of human drives. What he retained was the importance of infantile experience for adult personality, and such Freudian psychological mechanisms as repression, or the suppression of unwanted feelings and emotions.

Rather than ascribing certain personality types to given cultures, Kardiner discussed the range of personalities to be found in a culture. According to this new scheme, the personality "types" described by Benedict and Mead are replaced by basic personality structures, or traits shared by nearly all group members and which are subject to wide variation even within a single society.

According to Kardiner, personalities differ because of the variation in cultural institutions. Following Malinowski's classification, Kardiner distinguishes between two kinds of institutions. Primary institutions, such as the quest for food and sexual gratification, are those which arise to fill fundamental human needs. Secondary institutions, such as government and religion, are those institutions which arise in response to needs stimulated by primary institutions. The interaction of these institutions with the personality shapes and is shaped by human culture. By explaining personality in terms of its interaction with cultural institutions, Kardiner accounts for variation of basic personality structures in different societies.

To test his thesis, Kardiner gathered from field workers the seemingly trivial details of social behavior which they might ordinarily notice but not report. The most complete source of ethnopsychological data he analyzed came from Cora Dubois' study of the Alorese culture of the South Pacific. Through their work, a correlation was discovered between the child-rearing techniques of the Alorese and the nature of their cultural institutions.

The Alorese. Alorese children were raised with a minimum of attention or affection. No effort was made during infancy to teach the child to talk. An adult might sing dance songs to soothe him, but there was no deliberate attempt to impart verbal training. The only word Dubois heard an adult direct toward a child was the repetition of its name.

Toilet training, too, was completely disregarded during the period before walking began. Adults exhibited no anger or disgust when a child soiled the carrying shawl or the body of a person caring for it. The caretaker cleaned up after the child with the most casual matter-of-factness, wiping off its buttocks with a bit of leaf, a corn husk, or a bamboo sliver.

Walking was not urged on the child. Crawling was confined to the relatively rare periods when the child was seated on a verandah, or in the living room, instead of being carried in a shawl. One child, whom Dubois watched develop, learned to stand by pulling himself up on his mother's leg in an effort to get her attention so that she would pick him up and nurse him.

Women were not merely indifferent to children, but were quite reluctant to have them. Consequently, babies received little attention even just after birth. As one informant put it, "We men are the ones who want children. Our wives don't. They just want to sleep with us."

Children were subjected to extremely severe forms of discipline. The Alorese ideal dictated that corporal punishment should only be administered by the parents, but in practice this ideal was ignored. All kinds of relatives, however distant, were almost as free as parents themselves in rapping children on the head, pulling ears, twisting mouths, tying children up, and administering other such forms of treatment.

Teasing, ridicule, and deception were also widely practiced, not only in disciplining children, but as a form of amusement, especially among young men. On one occasion, Dubois observed a man of about twenty-eight send a twelve-year-old boy to fetch a bunch of bananas he said he had left at the foot of the village. In return he promised the boy six of them. The boy raced gleefully to the indicated spot but returned saying he had not found them. He was sent off again, and when he returned the second time, he realized that he had been deceived. A group of six or seven grown men were sitting around watching the procedure and laughing heartily, to the boy's evident shame and anger.

As a result of their upbringing, the Alorese grow into aggressive and egocentric adults. This basic personality structure, induced by the lessons of early childhood, is reflected in every aspect of Alorese culture, from religion and warfare to personal relations.

One of the several formalized outlets for anger that helped to drain off the frustration and humiliations associated with the social system was a switch dance between young men. One partner stood as impassively as possible with one leg thrust forward while the other dancer, after many preliminary feints and flourishes with a rattan switch, hit him as hard as possible on the shin bone. From one to five blows were given, and then the partners changed roles.

From such data, Dubois later found it difficult to relate the personality of any individual Alorese to the supposed basic personality of the groups. The "basic" personality might be better represented as the "modal" personality. The personality which seems to characterize a culture is viewed as a statistical frequency, allowing for a wide range of individual variation. The modal personality represents the ideal, not necessarily the actual, within a given culture.

A cross-cultural approach

One way to deduce individual character and personality is to observe the way different people react to the same situation. Consider, for example, Americans who catch cold during a winter virus epidemic. One sufferer may tend to blame others for having so callously gone about in public while sick, hence giving him the disease. Another person might blame himself for having carelessly exposed himself by contact with others. Still another person might react emotionally, focusing on the different degrees of susceptibility to the dis-

Figure 5-3. *The Havasupi, Indians of the American Southwest, are gentle with children and treat them with great and obvious affection. Yet though the children are given much independence, they are also expected to learn the rules of their culture quickly and well. Adults do not intervene to save a child from the results of his errors.*

ease, saying essentially, "Why me?" Another person might blame himself for not keeping in better health. Why such various reactions to the same cold?

Anthropologist J. M. Whiting and psychologist I. L. Child suggest that the answer lies in child-rearing practices. A child's behavior is directed by means of positive and negative sanctions—that is, he is rewarded for those responses that correspond to culturally approved behavior, and he is punished for behavior that is culturally disapproved. The anxiety which the child experiences as a result of severe negative sanctions, such as spanking, may result in negative fixations, whereas excessive gratification may result in positive fixations. In other words, extreme practices during child-rearing may lend exaggerated psychological importance to certain ideas or events.

Since illness is an anxiety-causing phenomenon, a culture will tend to explain illness on the basis of the fixations established by child-rearing experiences. For this reason, Whiting and Child chose to study cultural attitudes toward illness as a key to understanding cultural fixations. Drawing data from a great number of societies, they assigned numerical values to the degree of oral, anal, sexual, dependent, and aggressive fixations. Thus they were able to correlate the effect of child-rearing techniques with each culture's approach to explaining illness.

They concluded that variations in reactions to illness among different individuals are likely to be in large part a product of general personality characteristics. But these reactions are also attributable to variations in the experience of different individuals in childhood. Such reactions are neither entirely cultural nor entirely individual.

National character

In popular thought, a national character is ascribed to the citizens of many different countries. Henry Miller epitomizes this when he says, "Madmen are logical—as are the French," suggesting that Frenchmen, in general, are overly rational. A Parisian, on the other hand, might view Americans as maudlin and unsophisticated. Similarly, we all have in mind some image, perhaps not too well defined, of the typical Russian or Japanese or Englishman. Essentially, these are simply stereotypes. But we might well ask if these stereotypes have any basis in fact. Is there, in reality, such a thing as "national character?"

Some anthropologists would answer, "yes." National character studies have focused, first, on discovering the modal characteristics of a people, and, second, on determining the child-rearing practices and education that shape such a modal personality. Margaret Mead, Ruth Benedict, and Geoffrey Gorer conducted national character studies using relatively small samples of informants. During World War II, techniques were developed for studying "culture at a distance" through intensive interviews with nationals living away from their native lands and through the analysis of newspapers, books, and photographs. By investigating memories of childhood and cultural attitudes, and by examining graphic material for the appearance of recurrent themes and values, researchers attempted to portray national character.

The Japanese

At the height of World War II, Geoffrey Gorer attempted to determine the underlying reasons for the "contrast between the all-pervasive gentleness of Japanese family life in Japan, which has charmed nearly every visitor, and the overwhelming brutality and sadism of the Japanese at war." Strongly under the influence of Freud, Gorer sought his causes in the toilet-training practices of the Japanese, which he believed were severe and threatening. He suggested that because Japanese infants were forced to control their sphincters before they had acquired the necessary muscular or intellectual development, they grew up filled with repressed rage. As adults, the Japanese were able to express this rage in their brutality in war. Another anthropologist, Weston La Barre, independently came to the same conclusions.

Neither Gorer nor La Barre was able to do fieldwork. When, after the war, the toilet-training hypothesis could be tested, it was found that the severity of Japanese toilet training was a myth. Children were not subject to severe threats or punishment. Nor were all Japanese soldiers brutal and sadistic in war; some were, but then so were

Figure 5-4. *These photos rather amusingly depict some of the stereotypes we hold of the national character of other countries. The Japanese tea ceremony and subway crowds, the French lovers and gendarmes, and the Englishman with his umbrella, bowler, and pipe are part of our mythology about these foreign countries. Yet we would surely protest foreign views of the typical American and protest the error of the stereotype.*

some Americans. Also, the fact that the postwar Japanese took the lead in the Far East peace movement hardly conformed to the wartime image of brutality.

This study was most important, not in revealing the importance of Japanese sphincters on the national character, but in pointing out the dangers of generalizing from minimal evidence and employing simplistic individual psychology to explain complex social phenomena.

The Russians

Despite severe criticism from some of their colleagues, a few anthropologists have continued their interest in the question of national character. They have both refined their techniques and expanded their sampling, with some interesting results.

One example of this sophisticated approach is the Harvard Project on the Soviet social system. Nearly 3000 Soviet citizens, who were displaced by World War II and who had decided not to return to the U.S.S.R., completed a long questionnaire. A few hundred of these were also extensively interviewed, and 51 were clinically studied in depth. What emerged from this study was one of the best portraits to date of the modal personality of a particular nation.

The strongest and most pervasive quality of the Russian personality is affiliation, or the need for interaction with other people in direct personal relationship. Unlike the average American, the Russian is liable to have a relatively small drive to achieve. Surprisingly, there are few pronounced differences between the basic attitudes of Russians and Americans in relation to authority, except that the Russians seem to have more fear of their authority figures and fewer positive expectations of them. Both Russians and Americans feel guilt and shame, but these emotions are aroused under different circumstances. An American feels guilty when he has failed to meet the formal rules of etiquette or procedural forms; the Russian does not care about formal rules, but feels guilt and shame for defects of character in interpersonal relations. In sum, the Russian personality is characterized by emotional aliveness, expressiveness, spontaneity, gregariousness, and a certain need for dependence on authority.

Objections to national character studies

Critics of national character theories have emphasized the tendency for such work to be based on unscientific and overgeneralized data. The modal personality has a certain statistical validity, they argue, but to generalize the qualities of a complex nation on the basis of such limited data is to lend insufficient recognition to the countless individuals who vary from the generalization. Further, such studies tend to be highly subjective; for example, the tendency during the late 1930s and 1940s for anthropologists to characterize the German people as aggressive paranoids was obviously a reflection of wartime hostilities and not of scientific objectivity.

It has also been pointed out that occupational and social statuses tend to cut across national boundaries. A French farmer may have less in common with a French factory worker than he does with a German farmer. The concept of national character may be a useful supplement to the concept of modal personality, but it demands a high degree of objectivity and factual investigation.

Abnormal personality

Each culture perpetuates a set of norms by encouraging some behavioral patterns and discouraging others. Such patterns vary so much from culture to culture that we may well ask whether there can be a universal standard of normalcy. The Dobuans of New Guinea and certain Plains Indian tribes furnish striking example of normal behavior radically different from ours.

Normal and abnormal behavior

The individual in Dobu whom the other villagers considered neurotic and thoroughly disoriented was a man who was naturally friendly and found activity an end in itself. He was a pleasant fellow who did not seek to overthrow his fellows or to punish them. He worked for anyone who asked him, and he was tireless in carrying out their commands. In any other Dobuan, this would have been scandalous behavior, but in him it was regarded as merely silly. The village treated him in a kindly fashion, not taking advantage of him, or making sport or ridiculing him, but he was definitely regarded as one who stood outside the normal conventions of behavior.

Among certain Plains Indians, a man, compelled by supernatural spirits, may assume woman's attire, perform woman's work, and even marry another man. Under the institution of the *berdache,* such an individual would find himself in conflict with his neighbors or the law; yet, although the *berdache* is rare among Indians, it is not looked upon as the behavior of an abnormal personality.

The standards that define normal behavior for any culture are determined by that culture itself. Obviously, no society could survive if murdering one's neighbor was looked upon as normal behavior; yet each culture determines for itself the circumstances under which murdering one's neighbor may be acceptable. What is judged to be murder in one society may be treated as justifiable homicide in another. Moral acts are those which conform to certain social standards of good and evil, and each society determines those standards for itself. Morality is thus based on culturally determined ideals.

Is this to suggest that "normalcy" is a meaningless concept as it is applied to personality? Within the context of a given culture, the concept of normal personality is quite meaningful. A. I. Hallowell somewhat ironically observed that it is normal to share the delusions traditionally accepted by one's society. Abnormality involves the development of a delusional system not sanctified by culture. The individual who is disturbed be-

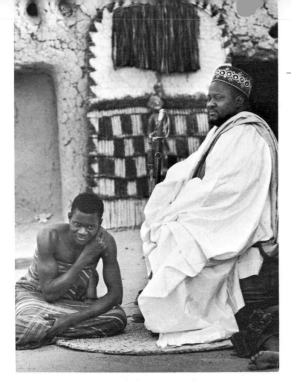

Figure 5-5. *The chief of the Mossi tribe lives in a palace and is served by slaves. The slaves must dress in women's clothing to symbolize their subordinate status; this custom gives us a clue to the way the society interprets the role of women.*

cause he cannot adequately measure up to the norms of society, and yet be happy, may be termed neurotic. When his delusional system is significantly different from that of his society and in no way reflects its norms, the individual may be termed psychotic.

Culturally induced conflicts can not only produce psychosis, but can determine the form of the psychosis as well. In a culture which encourages aggressiveness and suspicion, the madman is that individual who is passive and trusting. In a culture which encourages passivity and trust, the madman is that individual who is aggressive and suspicious. Just as each society establishes its own norms, each individual is unique in his perceptions. Many anthropologists see the only meaningful criterion for personality evaluation as the correlation between personality and social conformity.

However, the situation may not be so simple. Some radical psychologists, notably R. D. Laing, are questioning the sanity of society itself. We might well ask how a society which, for example, systematically pollutes its own air and water and poisons its own food with pesticides, can act as the arbiter of sanity. It has been suggested that some of the behavior which society calls "mad" may rather be a sane response to an insane society. In any case, the purely relativist viewpoint may be too easy an answer to an enormously complex question.

Current trends in personality studies

Culture and personality studies have come a long way since the descriptive studies of Ruth Benedict and Margaret Mead were considered important explanations of the ways culture and personality interacted. Benedict divided all cultures into Apollonian and Dionysian types, while Mead considered child-rearing practices of the highest importance in explaining cultural behavior and personality. Although the work of these anthropologists has come under heavy fire for being impressionistic rather than scientific and not susceptible of replication, their theories have contributed much to the realization that human behavior is relative. The theory of cultural relativity resulting from the study of many societies undermined the ethnocentrism common to all social groups. Anthropologists have established that cultures are indeed different and that their members possess personalities reflecting these differences.

Current studies in culture and personality go far beyond the traditional ethnographic descriptive approach of Benedict, Mead, and others. In his book, *Culture And Personality*, Anthony Wallace points out that current investigators are combining Freudian pyschoanalytically based theories with biological and social variables to discover, analyze, and explain the laws of cultural dynamics. Thus, current culture and personality studies are examining human genetic and ecological processes; these processes are entirely independent of culture, but they are the cause of change in the human biological system upon which culture depends. Further, Wallace points out, culture and personality studies are being broadened to include more than the study of motivation and affect and their causes; more attention is being given to the cognitive processes of the mind, which are the basic mechanisms responsible for such cultural expressions as language, myth and art.

HABITUATION AND EDUCATION

Into every culture and every civilization, year after year, hordes of uncultured "barbarians" descend in the form of newborn babies. In every society, a major —indeed, an overwhelming—amount of social energy must be spent in making cultured creatures out of this human plasm. Babies, whatever their potential may be, have few inborn abilities. They can grasp (a newly born baby can support its own weight by its grasp), but probably have to learn to utilize the capacity. They have to be taught to suck—for some, learning takes a minute or two, for others as much as a day or two. Some children are brighter than others, and the difference begins to show very early in life.

It is one of the characteristics of human beings that their children remain helpless for a very long period. Horses can walk and run a few hours after birth. Apes mature in about a third of the time that it takes human beings to mature. Even elephants, whose period of gestation is almost twice that of human beings, and whose life span is only a little shorter, are self-sufficient within about three years. Under minimal conditions, the human being requires ten or twelve years to become self-sufficient; under most conditions of culture, some fifteen years or so; and under our own system, with its complex material culture and vast need for training and education, somewhat longer than that.

Human beings, whether they are a few days old, a few years old, or a few decades old, have many needs because of the sheer fact that they are animals. Some of these needs, if left unfulfilled, will lead to the death of the animal. They must be fed, they must have a certain environmental temperature, and they need at least a certain minimal contact with others. If human babies are left without human contact, they die—even if their other needs are well attended.

Babies, being helpless, have their needs fulfilled for them. In the course of the fulfillment of these needs, the way in which the need is fulfilled comes to be almost as important as the fact of fulfillment. By the time a child is nearly adult enough to fulfill some of his own requirements for food and sleep, his habits are well established. These habits may be changed several times during the course of maturation, but even the need to change and the capacity to change are developed into habits. If it were not possible to change habits, any sort of "progress" or social change would be quite impossible.

The habits that are acquired by youngsters are part of the culture in accordance with which they are brought up. In one sense, the habits are the culture: if all the habits of all the people were changed, the culture would have changed.

There are, however, two ways in which culture can be "internalized." One is by habituation and the other by purposeful education. Western children are taught, rather systematically, to use a fork (a most clumsy instrument until you have mastered it); but they are not taught food preferences in the same purposeful way (although they may be taught, very purposefully indeed, what not to eat).

In habituation, human beings learn those aspects of culture that are not regarded in the culture as specifically learnable techniques. In education they are taught—specifically taught—the techniques. Education is usually defined as the directed learning process, either formally or informally carried out. The purpose here is not to make a pedantic distinction between these two aspects of education—many situations of human learning cannot be specifically set out as one or the other, but partake of both. It is merely to point out that human beings learn a great deal more than is specifically taught them: people pick up habits, without questioning them, because "that's the way it is done." Yet nobody picks up reading as a habit the way he picks up a taste for wheat bread and meat instead of millet porridge and fish.

Both of these processes—habituation and education—make it possible to live in the society in which we are born or in which we find ourselves. Neither stops, however, when the learner becomes a full-fledged member of adult society. Rather, he continues throughout his entire life to learn his culture—new culture or new fields of traditional culture. Education and habituation continue to the grave. There is no culture that it is possible completely to master, even though it is possible in some—but not in our own—to be "old and full of years," satiated with sufficient of one's culture that death is not an objectionable alternative to finishing the job.

Thus, as man's primary needs are cared for—those whose neglect would cause his death—he is habituated and educated. The habituation and education themselves set up a secondary set of needs for the primary needs to be cared for in certain ways. They may become as grave a need as the substantive needs.

Education may be carried on by any number of agencies. The family is probably the most important educating agency in every society. In some societies, a part of the job is taken over by professionals when the child is about six years old. Even in societies that lack any sort of formal schooling, the family may be assisted by other elements of the society when the child reaches about this age. Sometimes children are sent to their grandparents, because grandparents are thought in that culture, for one reason or another, to be the best formal instructors during certain periods of a child's life. In other societies, a child goes to his father's sister because it is thought that the parents themselves may be so fond of the child as to be too indulgent to insist on adequate training for coping with life and society. The father's sister, the evaluation in such a society runs, is a close kinswoman and hence will be kind and proffer some affection, but she is far enough removed that she will insist on the child's continuing education to the point of being strict if it is necessary. Some societies have formalized age associations that organize children to teach younger children.

Finally, the community as a whole may act as an habituating and educating agency simply by withholding its approval from people who do not behave "properly," or by rewarding behavior that is esteemed. The community may be to its members what Pavlov was to his dogs: in the end the individual learns to do what the community expects and even to like it, just as one of Pavlov's dogs told a peer who belonged to a different master: "I've got my guy trained to ring a bell every time he's about to feed me."

There are, of course, some failures. These are the people that the society brands neurotic, sick, criminal, or all three. Yet even these "failures" are habituated and to some degree educated: they rebel in terms of their own culture.

They speak the language, wear the clothes, eat the food of the society they are rebelling against. They sing songs written with the same scales and notes, and they recognize the same norms, even by valuing perversions of them.

Source:
From *Social Anthropology* by Paul Bohannan. Copyright © 1963 by Holt, Rinehart and Winston, Inc. Reprinted by permission of Holt, Rinehart and Winston, Inc.

Figure 5-6. *A child in a California commune learns a skill by watching and helping adults.*

Summary

1.

Society to a great extent determines an individual's personality. Personality is formed through enculturation, the assimilation of a group's ways of thinking and acting. Every society operates according to a series of norms and ideals. Those who conform to these norms are rewarded; those who deviate are punished. The result is a "group personality," within which there is considerable variation.

2.

Ruth Benedict, in *Patterns of Culture,* saw cultures as conforming to two general types: the "Dionysian" and the "Apollonian." The "Dionysian" is characterized by ecstatic ritual, egocentrism, and extremely individualistic behavior; the "Apollonian" is characterized by avoidance of excess and distrust of individualism.

3.

Margaret Mead, in her studies of foreign cultures, emphasized the effects of culture on personality. Her Samoan studies indicate that a great deal of adolescent behavior is learned. A child learns through cultural transmission how society expects him to behave. Cultural transmission produces predictable patterns of behavior. These patterns provide a member of a society with a framework for interpreting the motivations and behavior of other members. On the other hand, Sigmund Freud emphasized the shaping effects of individual psychology on personality and culture. He used the Oedipus complex to explain the origins of culture and society. Most anthropologists today would not accept his conclusions, but the Oedipus complex is still valuable in the study of personality development.

4.

Abram Kardiner attempted to use both psychology and culture to explain personality. He held that personality structures, or cultural norms, vary widely within a society. Personalities differ because cultural institutions vary. He distinguished between primary and secondary institutions. Primary institutions arise to fill fundamental human needs and in turn give rise to secondary institutions. The interaction of the institutions with the personality shapes human culture. The most complete source of ethnopsychological data he analyzed was Cora Dubois' study of the Alorese culture of the South Pacific.

5.

One way to deduce individual character and personality is to observe the way different people react to the same situation. Anthropologists Whiting and Child have suggested that a society's child-rearing practices can reveal a group's personality.

6.

National character studies have focused on the modal characteristics of a people. They have then attempted to determine the child-rearing practices and education which shape such a modal personality. During World War II, investigators interviewed foreign-born nationals and analyzed newspapers, books, and photographs in attempts to portray national character. Many anthropologists believe that national character theories are based on unscientific and overgeneralized data.

7.
A culture determines the standards that determine normal behavior. Within the context of a given culture the concept of normal personality is meaningful. Abnormality involves developing a delusional system not accepted by culture. Culturally induced conflicts can not only produce psychosis but determine its form as well.

8.
Current culture and personality studies are combining traditional psychoanalytically based theories with biological and social factors to explain culture and cultural dynamics. Attention is also being given to the cognitive processes of the mind which are the mechanisms responsible for such cultural expressions as language, myth, and art.

portfolio two

Seasons of the Eskimo

Of all the earth's regions, the Eskimos live in the
harshest and most forbidding. Summers are short, cool and
mosquito-plagued; winters long, dark, and cold. Yet despite
the murderous climate and ever-present threat of famine,
the Eskimo are gay, gregarious, good-natured, and amazingly
contented. Innuit, the people, Eskimos proudly call
themselves. Men, pre-eminent, the Original Men to whom earth
herself gave birth.

Eskimo society in the past was one of equals. They
acknowledged neither chiefs nor superiors; their language
lacks the terms. The closest they can come is to call a
man *ishumata*—he who thinks, a man whom others respect for
his wisdom. But power he had none. What power there was lay
within the community, in the rule of public opinion. The
approval and esteem of other members of his group were a man's
highest reward, ostracism his worst punishment.

The advent of the white man's culture destroyed the
fragile fabric of this ancient way of life. Its concepts
of master and servant, of material wealth as a measure of a
man's worth, subordinated one man's wishes to another
man's will and thus were alien and mystifying to the Eskimo mind.
And as the Eskimo settled in permanent communities and adopted
the white man's life, they lost touch with the cycle of the
seasons. Their children no longer learn the lore of hunting
and the ice and even sometimes do not learn their grandparents'
language. In some smaller communities, however, the
hunting-trapping life of the camps persists according to the

Winter camp in drifting snow.

Hunter wears slit-type bone goggles to protect his eyes from the intense glare of spring ice and snow.

Igloo for the night, built during a hunting trip.

Hunters with polar bear.

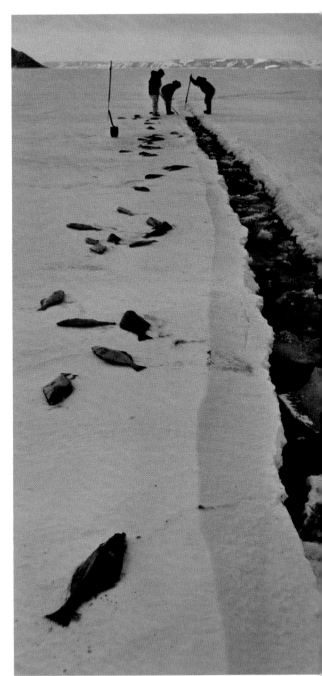

A hunter readies his harpoon; he has killed two seals already.

Eskimos gaff halibut that have floated up into a lead—
a break in the thawing spring ice.

Hunter in a kayak.

Grandmother.

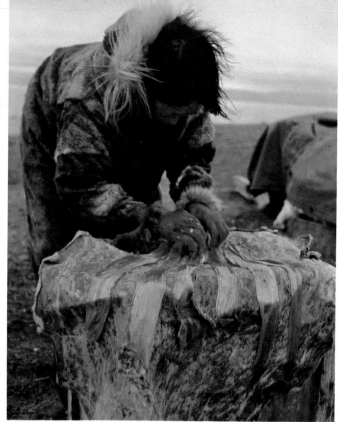

Drying caribou sinew; later it will be slit and used as thread to sew fur clothing.

Hanging split char (fish) to dry for preservation.

Women sew the sealskin cover onto a kayak frame.

Summer migration across the tundra with pack dogs.

immutable rules of old: to take from each season what each season brings; to share your food with all members of the group, as they will share theirs with you; to rise to superhuman efforts when the hunt requires it, and to live in quiet harmony with yourself and others when bad weather imprisons you in your tent; to do as you like and let others do as they like.

One of the last and largest camp areas in Canada, (pictured on the preceding pages) is Bathhurst Inlet in the Central Arctic, inhabited by fewer than ninety people living in eleven widely scattered camps. In winter they hunt seal at the breathing holes and fish through the ice. In spring, the caribou come from the taiga in the south across the vastness of the tundra to the Arctic shores. In summer, the men fish; in fall, the seals are fat and float when shot, the new clove-brown fur of the caribou is short and strong, ideal for winter clothes, and the animals are heavy after pasturing all summer on the Arctic meadows. Fat char ascend the rivers and ground squirrels, ready for their eight month winter sleep, look like plump, furred sausages with feet. It is the time to collect meat and fish for the dark, lean months of winter ahead.

Camp life is hard. It is an unpredictable life. One year spring comes, but the caribou do not. The people travel far, work hard, and find nothing. They may have to trap ground squirrels to subsist. The dogs become weak; traveling is curtailed. Another year, large numbers of caribou stay near the camps all year, seals are plentiful, life is relatively easy. To endure and succeed in such a life, a hunter must be resourceful and hardy, he must have faith in himself, a lot of optimism, a certain fatalism, and the ability to live each day and enjoy the good it brings and not spoil it with worry about the morrow. In the words of an Eskimo song:
And yet, there is only
One great thing,
The only thing:
To live;
To see in huts and on journeys
The great day that dawns,
And the light that fills the world.

Photographs by Fred Breummer
Text adapted from "Seasons of the Eskimo" by Fred Breummer

Suggested readings

Barnouw, Victor *Culture and Personality*. Homewood, Ill.: Dorsey Press, 1963.
Three approaches to personality determination form the background of this book: the childhood determinist, the situational, and the world view. The cultural and social determinants of personality are dealt with. Citing theories of such classic scholars as Benedict, Mead, and Malinowski, the author discusses some contemporary approaches as well as different methods of culture and personality research.

Hunt, Robert C., ed. *Personalities and Cultures: Readings in Psychological Anthropology*. Garden City, N.Y.: Natural History Press, 1967.
The eighteen articles included in this book focus on various aspects of culture and personality. Attention is given to psychological and sociocultural variables and the relationships between them.

Norbeck, Edward, Douglas Price Williams, and William McCord, eds. *The Study of Personality: An Interdisciplinary Appraisal*. New York: Holt, Rinehart and Winston, 1968.
The volume contains addresses given at Rice University in 1966. Its objective is to review and appraise knowledge and theories concerning personality in several scholarly fields (psychology, anthropology, sociology, philosophy of science, etc.). It also discusses factors that influence the formation of personality, and the personalities of social and psychiatric deviates.

Wallace, Anthony F. *Culture and Personality*. New York: Random House, 1970.
The logical and methodological foundations of culture and personality as a science form the basis of this book. The study is guided by the assumptions that anthropology should develop a scientific theory about culture, and that a theory pretending to explain or predict cultural phenomena must reckon with noncultural phenomena (such as personality) as well.

Whiting, John W. M., and I. Child *Child Training and Personality: A Crosscultural Study*. New Haven: Yale University Press, 1953.
How culture is integrated through the medium of personality processes is the main concern of this study. It covers both the influence of culture on personality and personality on culture. It is oriented toward testing general hypotheses about human behavior in any and all societies, rather than toward a detailed analysis of a particular society.

Patterns
of subsistence

Several times today you will interrupt your activities to eat or drink. You may take this very much for granted, but if you went totally without food for as long as a day, you would begin to feel the symptoms of starvation: weakness, fatigue, headache. After a month of starvation, your body would probably never repair the damage. A mere week to ten days without water would be enough to kill you.

All living beings, and man is obviously no exception, must satisfy certain basic needs in order to stay alive. Among these needs are food, water, and shelter. Man may not live by bread alone, but no man can live long without any bread at all; and no creature could long survive if its relations with its environment were random and chaotic. Living beings must have regular access to a supply of food and water and a reliable means of obtaining and using it. A lion might die if all its prey disappeared, if its teeth and claws grew soft, or if its digestive system failed. Although man faces these same problems, he has an overwhelming advantage over his fellow creatures; man has culture. If our meat supply dwindles, we can turn to some vegetable, like the soybean, and process it to taste like meat. When our tools fail, we replace them or invent better ones. Even when

our stomachs are incapable of digesting food, we can predigest food by boiling or pureeing. However, we are subject to the same needs and pressures as all living creatures, and it is important to understand human behavior from this point of view. The crucial concept that underlies such a perspective is **adaptation,** that is, how man manages to deal with the contingencies of daily life.

Adaptation

The process of adaptation establishes a moving balance between the needs of a population and the potential of its environment. One illustration of this process can be seen in the case of the Tsembaga, New Guinea highlanders who support themselves chiefly through slash-and-burn agriculture. Although they also raise pigs, they eat them only under conditions of illness, injury, warfare, or celebration. At such times the pigs are sacrificed to ancestor spirits, and their flesh is ritually consumed by those people involved in the crisis. (This guarantees a supply of high-quality protein when it is most needed.)

In precolonial times, the Tsembaga and their

Figure 6-1. *Throughout New Guinea, the killing of a wild pig is such an important event that it is surrounded by much ritual and symbolic action. The men of the Big Namba tribe turn out in their most elaborate costumes for the pig festival.*

neighbors were bound together in a unique cycle of pig sacrifices that served to mark the end of hostilities between groups. Frequent hostilities were set off by a number of ecological pressures in which pigs were a significant factor. Since very few pigs were normally slaughtered and their food requirements were great, they could very quickly literally eat a local group out of house and home. The need to expand food production in order to support the prestigious but hungry pigs put a strain on the land best suited for agriculture. Therefore, when one group had driven another off its land, hostilities ended and the new residents celebrated their victory with a pig festival. Many pigs were slaughtered, and the pork was widely shared between allied groups. Even without hostilities, festivals were held whenever the pig population became unmanageable, every five to ten years, depending on the groups' agricultural success. Thus the cycle of fighting and feasting kept the balance between men, land, and animals.

The term adaptation also refers to the process of interaction between changes made by an organism on its environment and changes made by the environment on the organism. The spread of the gene for sickle-cell trait is a case in point. Long ago, when central Africa was mostly covered by tropical forests, a genetic mutation appeared in the local human population, causing the manufacture of red blood cells that take on a sickle shape under conditions of low oxygen pressure. Since persons homozygous to this trait usually develop severe anemia and die in childhood, there was a selection pressure exerted against the spread of this gene in the local gene pool.

Then slash-and-burn agriculture was introduced into central Africa, creating a change in the natural environment that was conducive to the breeding of mosquitos that carry the parasite causing falciparum malaria. When transmitted to man, the parasites live in the red blood cells and cause a disease that is always debilitating and very often fatal. However, individuals who were heterozygous for sickle-cell trait turned out to have a specific natural defense against the parasite. Its presence in any red blood cell caused that cell to sickle; when that cell circulated through the spleen, which routinely screens out all damaged or worn red blood cells, the infected cell, and the parasite along with it, were destroyed. Since heterozygotes were therefore resistant to malaria, they were selected, and the sickling trait became more and more frequent in the population. Thus, while man changed his environment, his environment also changed him.

The unit of adaptation

The unit of adaptation includes both organism and environment: anthropologist Gregory Bateson calls it the "flexible organism-in-its-environment." By "flexible" is meant not just the flexibility of one individual, but the flexibility of a whole population to cope with variability and change within its environment. In biological terms, this means that different organisms within the population have somewhat differing genetic endowments. In cultural terms, it means that there is variation between individual skills, knowledge, and personalities. Organisms and environments form interacting systems. Men might as easily be farmers as fishermen; but we do not expect to find farmers in the Arctic Circle or fishermen in the Sahara Desert.

We might consider the example of a group of lakeside fishermen. The men live off the fish, which, in turn, live off smaller animals. Those animals, in turn, consume green plants; plants liberate minerals from water and mud, and, with energy from sunlight, transform them into proteins and carbohydrates. Dead plant and animal matter is decomposed by bacteria, and chemicals are returned to the soil and water. Some energy escapes from this system in the form of heat. Evaporation and rainfall constantly recirculate the water. Men add chemicals to the system in the form of their wastes, and, if they are judicious, help to regulate the balance of animals and plants.

Some anthropologists have borrowed the ecologists' term, **ecosystem.** An ecosystem is composed of both the physical environment and the organisms living within it. The system is bound by the activities of the organisms as well as by such physical processes as erosion and evaporation.

Human ecologists are generally concerned with detailed microstudies of particular human ecosystems; they emphasize that all aspects of human culture must be considered, not only the most obvious technological ones. The Tsembaga's attitude toward pigs and the cycle of sacrifices have important economic functions; we see them in this way, but the Tsembaga do not. They are motivated by their belief in the power and needs of their ancestral spirits. Although the pigs are consumed *by* men, they are sacrificed *for* ancestors. Human ecosystems must often be interpreted in cultural terms.

Evolutionary adaptation

Adaptation must also be understood from an historical point of view. In order for an organism to fit into an ecosystem, it must have the potential ability to adjust to or become a part of it. The Comanche, whose tribal history began in the harsh, arid plateau country of Montana, provide a good example. In their original home, they subsisted on wild plants, small animals, and occasionally large game. Their material culture was simple and limited to what could be transported by the women of the tribe. The size of their groups was restricted, and what little social power could develop was in the hands of the shaman, who was a combination of medicine man and spiritual guide.

At some point in their nomadic history, the Comanche reached the Great Plains, where buffalo were abundant and the Indians' potential as hunters could be fully developed. As larger groups could be supported by the new food supply, the need arose for a more complex political organization. Hunting ability thus became a means to acquire political power.

Figure 6-2. *Indian tribes of the American plains, such as the Sioux, Crow, Cree, Blackfoot, and Kiowa, share many culture traits because their means of subsistence are similar.*

Eventually the Comanche acquired the white man's horse and gun, which greatly extended their hunting prowess, and the great hunting chiefs became powerful indeed. The Comanche became raiders in order to get horses, for they were not horse breeders, and their hunting chiefs evolved into war chiefs. The once poor and peaceful hunter-gatherers of the plateau became wealthy pirates, dominating the Southwest from the borders of New Spain (Mexico) in the south, to those of New France (Louisiana) and the fledgling United States in the east and north. In passing from one environment to another, and in evolving from one way of life to a second, the Comanche made the best advantage of their developing potentials, or cultural **preadaptations.**

Many different societies develop independently, and some find similar solutions to similar

Culture and man ● part **2**

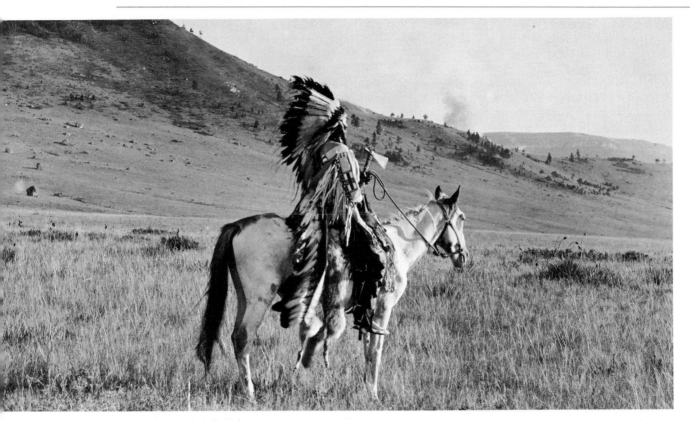

problems. The development of similar cultural adaptations to similar technoenvironmental conditions is called **parallel evolution.** To a large extent, the rise of great civilizations in China, northwest Mesopotamia, and Peru was made possible by the independent invention of irrigation agriculture in each of these areas. The problems of applying irrigation agriculture to making a living in similar environments—problems of labor and distribution—led to a number of parallels in the social and cultural development of those societies.

Culture areas

The Great Plains was an aboriginal **culture area,** a geographic region in which there existed a number of societies following a similar pattern of life. Thirty-one politically independent tribes faced a common environment, in which the buffalo was the most obvious and practical food source. Living close by each other, they were able to share new inventions and discoveries. They reached a common and shared adaptation to a particular ecological zone.

The Indian tribes of the Great Plains were, at the time of contact with the Europeans, invariably buffalo hunters, dependent upon this animal for food, clothing, shelter, and bone tools. The tribes were generally organized into a number of warrior societies, and prestige came from hunting and fighting skills. Their camps were typically arranged in a distinctive circular pattern. Many religious rituals, such as the Sun Dance, were practiced throughout the plains region.

Sometimes ecological zones are not uniform in climate and topography, and so new discoveries do not always diffuse from one group to another. Moreover, within a culture area, there are variations between local environments, and these variations favor variations in adaptation. The Great Basin of the southwestern United States is a case in point. The Great Basin Shoshone Indians were divided into a northern and a western group, both primarily migratory hunters and gatherers. In the north, a relative abundance of game animals favored the development of larger populations, requiring a great degree of cooperation between local groups. The western Shoshone, on the other hand, were almost entirely dependent upon the gathering of wild crops for a living, and as these varied considerably in their seasonal and local availability, the western Shoshone were forced to cover vast distances in search of food. Under such conditions, they could maintain groups of only a few families, only occasionally coming together with other groups, and not always with the same ones.

The Shoshone were not the only inhabitants of the Great Basin. To the south lived another closely related tribe, the Paiutes. They were also hunter-gatherers living under the same environmental conditions as the Shoshone, but the Paiute had discovered how to irrigate wild crops by diverting small streams. They did not plant and cultivate crops, but even without agriculture, the Paiute, unlike their northern neighbors, were able to secure a steady food supply. Hence, their populations were larger than those of the Shoshone and they led a settled existence.

In order to explain variations within culture areas, Julian Steward proposed the concept of **culture type,** a culture considered in terms of a particular technology and its relationship with the particular environmental features that technology is equipped to exploit. The example of the Great Plains shows how technology often decides just which environmental features will be useful. Those same prairies that once supported tribes of buffalo hunters now support grain farmers. The Indians were prevented from farming the plains not for environmental reasons, nor for lack of agricultural knowledge, since some of the plains tribes had been farmers before they came west. They did not farm because they lacked the steel-tipped plow that was needed to break up the compacted prairie sod. The farming potential of the Great Plains was simply not a relevant feature of the environment, given the available technology before the coming of the Europeans.

Culture core

Environment and technology are not the only factors that determine a society's way of subsistence; social and political organization also affect the application of technology to the problem of staying alive. In order to understand the rise of irrigation agriculture in the great centers of civilization, such as China and Mesopotamia, it is important to note, not only the technological and environmental factors that made possible the building of huge irrigation works, but also the social and political organization needed to mobilize large groups of workers to build and maintain the systems. It is necessary to examine the monarchies and priesthoods that organized the work and decided where the water would be used and how the agricultural products of this joint venture would be distributed.

Those features of a culture that play a part in the society's way of making its living are called its **culture core.** The culture core includes the society's productive techniques and its knowledge of the resources available to it. It encompasses the patterns of labor involved in applying those techniques to the local environment. For instance, do people work every day for a fixed number of hours, or is most work concentrated during certain times of the year? The culture core also includes other aspects of culture that bear on the production and distribution of food. An example of the way ideology can indirectly affect subsistence can be seen in a number of Moslem cultures. The religious beliefs of Moslems call for a four-week period of fasting during the spring;

no food can be eaten between sunrise and sunset. Because of the fasting, people can do very little heavy work. When the fast period coincides with the time crops should be planted, farmers plant less than they do normally and food is scarce for the next year.

A number of anthropologists, known as ethnoscientists, are actively attempting to understand the principles behind folk ideologies and the ways those principles help keep a people alive. The Tsembaga, for example, avoid certain lowlying, marshy areas because they believe these areas are inhabited by red spirits who punish trespassers. Modern Western science interprets those areas as the home of mosquitos, and the "punishment" as malaria. Whatever Westerners may think of the Tsembaga's belief in red spirits, it is a perfectly useful and reasonable one; it keeps them away from marshy areas just as surely as does a belief in malaria. If we want to understand why people in other cultures behave the way they do, we must understand their system of thought from their point of view as well as our own. Unfortunately, not all such beliefs are as easy to translate into our terms as is that of the Tsembaga red spirits.

The hunting-gathering life

At the present time, a scant quarter of a million people of a world population of three billion support themselves chiefly through hunting, fishing, and the gathering of wild fruits and vegetables. Although 250,000 is a sizable figure, it comprises only .003 percent of the total world population. Yet, before men discovered agriculture and the domestication of animals ten thousand years ago, all men must have supported themselves through some combination of plant gathering, hunting, and/or fishing. Of all the men who have *ever* lived, 90 percent have been hunter-gatherers.

Because man developed as a hunter-gatherer, we owe many of the important features of human society and culture to this way of life. Early man implemented the division of labor, food-sharing, toolmaking, and language. It seems obvious then that if we would know who we are and how we came to be, if we would understand the relationship between environment and culture, and if we would comprehend the institutions of more complex societies that have arisen since the development of agriculture and animal husbandry, we should turn to the oldest and most basic of fully human life-styles, the hunter-gatherer adaptation.

When hunter-gatherers were dominant some ten thousand years ago, they had their pick of the best environments. These have long since been appropriated by farming and, more recently, industrial societies. Today, most hunter-gatherers have been left to their traditional life only in the world's marginal areas—frozen arctic tundra, deserts, inaccessible jungles. These habitats, although they may not support large or dense agricultural societies, provide adequate support for hunting and gathering peoples.

Until recently, it was assumed that these areas did not provide the best way of living. But one anthropologist, Marshall Sahlins, has gone so far as to describe hunter-gatherers as the "original affluent society." In his view, their diets are ample, they have plenty of leisure time, and if their material comforts are limited, so are their desires. The !Kung Bushmen of South Africa's Kalahari Desert obtain a better than subsistence diet in an average work week of twelve to nineteen hours. Others have observed that this is clearly not true for all hunting and gathering societies. Some people, like the Birhor of India, work very hard indeed and still often go hungry. It is probably true that ancient hunter-gatherers lived in better environments with more secure and plentiful sources of food than do their modern counterparts.

All modern hunter-gatherers have had some degree of exposure to more technologically advanced neighbors. Modern hunter-gatherers often have metal and firearms, and some have learned to do a little farming. Even the Kalahari Bushmen have been known to plant corn when rainfall has

Figure 6-3a. *This photo shows a dry season camp of the !Kung Bushmen of south central Africa. The hut walls are thatched but the roof is open.*

Figure 6-3b. *Two Bushmen dig into the dried clay soil at the end of the rainy season to obtain roots and bulbs, foods eaten only when other plants are scarce.*

Figure 6-3d. *Two Bushmen carefully fasten down with wooden stakes the hide of a hartebeest; when it is dried, the hide will be scraped and tanned.*

Figure 6-3e. *This hut is built for the rainy season; unlike the dry season hut in 16-3a, it has a roof but remains open to the air since there the winds are not strong.*

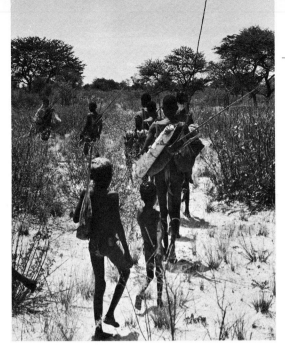

Figure 6-3c. *This photo shows a small band of Bushmen on the move to a new locale. They carry with them everything they own.*

Figure 6-3f. *These two Bushmen hunters carry with them the tools of their trade, virtually the only possessions they have— bow, arrows, digging stick, club, spear.*

been especially good. It also seems likely that some contemporary hunter-gatherers have only returned to this way of life after failing at agriculture. Such is thought to be the case of the Siriono of South America and the Veddas of Ceylon. Contact with other peoples has fundamentally changed, if not completely disrupted, the social organizations of many hunting and gathering societies. The Mbuti Pygmies of the Congolese Ituri rain forest live in a complex patron-client relationship with their agricultural neighbors, some Bantu and Sudani tribes. They exchange meat and military service for farm produce and manufactured goods. During part of the year, they live in their patron's village and are incorporated into his kin group, even to the point of allowing him to arrange their marriages.

Characteristics of the nomadic life

Hunter-gatherers are by definition people who do not practice animal husbandry or agriculture. Hence, they must accommodate their places of residence to naturally available food sources. This being the case, it is no wonder that they move about a great deal. Such movement is not aimless wandering but is done within a fixed territory or home range. Some, like the !Kung Bushmen who depend on the reliable and highly drought-resistant Mongongo nut, may keep to fairly fixed annual routes and cover only a restricted territory. Others, such as the Great Basin Shoshone, must cover a wider territory; their course is determined by the local availability of the erratically productive pine nut. A crucial factor in this mobility is the availability of water. The distance between the food supply and water must not be so great that more energy is required to fetch water than can be obtained from the food.

Another characteristic of the hunter-gatherer adaptation is the small size of local groups, twenty-five to fifty being the average number. Although no completely satisfactory explanation of group size has yet been offered, it seems certain that both ecological and social factors are involved. Among those suggested are the **carrying capacity** of the land, the number of people who can be supported by the available resources at a given level of food-getting techniques, and the **density of social relations,** roughly the number and intensity of interactions between camp members. More people means a higher social density, which, in turn, means more opportunities for conflict.

Both carrying capacity and social density are complex variables. Carrying capacity involves not only the immediate presence of food and water, but the tools and work necessary to secure them, as well as short- and long-term fluctuations in their availability. Social density involves not only the number of people and their interactions, but also the circumstances and quality of those interactions and the mechanisms for regulating them. A mob of a hundred angry strangers has a different social density than the same number of neighbors enjoying themselves at a block party.

Among hunter-gatherer populations, social density seems always to be in a state of flux, as people spend more or less time away from camp and as they move to other camps, either on visits or more permanently. This redistribution of people is an important mechanism for regulating social density as well as for assuring that the size and composition of local groups is suited to local variations in resources. Thus, cultural adaptations serve to help transcend the limitations of the physical environment.

In addition to seasonal or local adjustments, long-term adjustments to resources must be made. Most hunter-gatherer populations seem to stabilize in numbers well below the carrying capacity of their land. In fact, the territories of most hunter-gatherers can support from three to five times as many people as they typically do. In the long run, it may be more adaptive for a group to keep its numbers low, rather than to expand indefinitely and then suddenly be cut down by an unexpected disaster. It is not certain just how this stabilization is regulated, but among the population control methods used by hunting and gathering peoples are infanticide, abortion, prohibitions against sexual intercourse with nursing mothers, and various herbal drugs that interfere with fertility or conception. The population density of hunter-gatherer groups rarely exceeds one person per square mile, a very low density; yet, their resources could support greater numbers.

The impact of hunting on human society

Recently much has been written on the importance of hunting in shaping the supposedly competitive and aggressive nature of modern man. Although many anthropologists are unconvinced by these arguments, it does seem likely that three crucial elements of human social organization developed along with hunting. The first of these is the division of labor. Some form of division of labor by sex, however modified, has been observed in all human societies. There is some tendency in contemporary Western society to do away with such division. One may ask what the implications are for future cooperative relationships between men and women.

Hunting is universally a male occupation. This may be due to the fact that hunters must often travel long distances on foot, something which is not easily possible for nursing mothers and pregnant women. Women typically do the work of gathering; although it is often more arduous labor than hunting, it does not require long-distance travel.

Men, however, do not spend all or even the greatest part of their time in hunting. The amount of energy expended in hunting, especially in hot climates, is often greater than the energy return from the kill. Too much time spent at hunting might actually be counterproductive. A certain amount of meat in the diet guarantees high-quality protein that is not easily obtained from vegetable sources, but energy itself is derived primarily from plant carbohydrates; it is the female gatherer who brings in the bulk of the calories. Most modern hunting and gathering societies actually obtain 60 to 70 percent of their diets from vegetable foods, fish, and shellfish (a diet similar to that of prehuman primates); therefore, female food-getting activities are generally more important than male hunting.

Hunting, whether cooperative or not, seems to be correlated with food-sharing among adults, a very rare occurrence among nonhuman primates. Food-sharing is the second key feature of man's social organization. It is easy enough to see why sharing would be necessary if game is hunted cooperatively; but even individual hunters may find it in their interest to share what they cannot consume. Among the Hazda of northern Tanzania, a man will eat his fill at his killsite, then carry what he can back to camp. If the kill has been especially good, the camp may move to him. For the individual hunter, food-sharing is really a way of storing food for the future; his generosity gives him a claim on the future surpluses of other hunters. As a cultural trait, food-sharing has the obvious survival value of distributing resources needed for subsistence.

Although carnivores share food, the few examples of food-sharing among nonhuman primates all involve groups of male chimpanzees cooperating in a hunt and later sharing the spoils and even offering some to the females and infants. It is difficult to say how typical this behavior is for chimpanzees uninfluenced by human intruders, but it does suggest that the origins of food-sharing and the division of labor are related to a shift in food habits from rare meat-eating to a balance between hunting and gathering. This may have occurred among our earliest hominid ancestors.

Another distinctive feature of the hunting economy is the importance of the camp as the center of daily activity and the place where food-sharing actually occurs. Among nonhuman primates, activities tend to be divided between feeding areas and sleeping areas, and the latter tend to be shifted each evening. Hunting man, however, lives in camps of some permanence, ranging from the dry-season camps of the Bushmen that serve for the entire winter, to the dry-season camps of the Hazda, oriented around the hunt and serving for several days or a week or two. Moreover, human camps are more than sleeping areas; people are in and out all day, eating, working, and socializing in camps to a greater extent than any other primates. It is thought that the first camps were primarily places where the spoils of the hunt were butchered and then consumed over a period of several days. It would seem that it is to these earliest hunters that we owe the very concept of home.

Cultural adaptations and material technology. The mobility of hunter-gatherer groups may depend on the availability of water, as in the case of the !Kung; of pine nuts, as in the Shoshone example; or of game animals, as in the Hazda example. Hunting styles and equipment may also play a role in determining population size and movement. Some Mbuti Pygmies hunt with nets. This requires the cooperation of seven to thirty families; consequently, their camps are relatively large. The camps of those who hunt with bow and arrow number from three to six families. Too many archers in the same locale means that each must travel a great distance daily to keep out of the other's way. Only during midsummer do the archers collect into larger camps for religious ceremonies, matrimonial bargains, and social exchange. At this time the bowmen turn to communal beat-hunts. Without nets they are less effective than their neighbors, so it is only when the net-hunters are widely dispersed in the pursuit of honey that the archers can come together.

Egalitarian society. An important characteristic of the hunter-gatherer society is its egalitarianism. Hunter-gatherers are highly mobile and, lacking animal or mechanical means of transportation, they must be able to travel without many encumbrances, especially on food-getting expeditions. Their material goods must be limited to the barest essentials, which include weapons that serve for

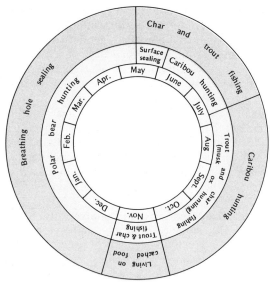

Figure 6-4. *The schematic diagram shows the cycle of subsistence activity among the Eskimo during the various seasons of the year.*

hunting, fighting, building, and toolmaking, and cooking utensils, traps, and nets. There is little chance for the accumulation of luxuries or surplus goods, and the fact that no one owns significantly more than another helps to limit status differences. Age and sex are usually the only sources of status differences in hunter-gatherer societies.

Hunter-gatherers make no attempt to accumulate surplus foodstuffs, often an important source of status in agricultural societies. To say that hunters do not accumulate food surpluses, however, is not to say that they live constantly on the verge of starvation. Their environment is their storehouse, and, except in the coldest climates, or in times of acute ecological disaster, there is always some food to be found in a hunter's territory. Because food resources are typically distributed equally throughout the group, no one achieves the wealth or status that hoarding might bring. In such a society, wealth is a sign of deviance rather than a desirable characteristic.

The hunter-gatherer's concept of territory contributes as much to social equality as it does to the equal distribution of resources. Most groups have territories or ranges which they exploit and within which access to resources is open to all members. If a Mbuti discovers a honey tree, he has first rights; but when he has taken his share, others have a turn. In the unlikely possibility that he does not take advantage of his discovery, others will. No one owns the tree; the system is first come, first served. Therefore knowledge of the existence of food resources circulates quickly throughout the entire group.

Families move easily from one group to another, settling in any group where they have a previous kinship tie. The composition of groups is always shifting. This loose attitude toward group membership promotes the widest access to resources and, at the same time, is a leveling device that promotes social equality.

The hunter-gatherer pattern of generalized exchange, or sharing without any expectation of a direct return, also serves the ends of resource distribution and social equality. A !Kung Bushman spends as much as two-thirds of his day visiting others or receiving guests; during this time, many exchanges of gifts take place. To refuse to share—to hoard—would be morally wrong. By sharing whatever is at hand, the !Kung achieve social leveling and assure their right to share in the windfalls of others.

The cold climate adaptation

The success of the hunter-gatherer adaptation depends on small, mobile groups, favoring the widest distribution of resources with considerable leeway for unexpected hard times. If the relationships we have been discussing were systematic, that is, were they interacting in consistent ways, we would expect that the replacement or addition of variables would have profound effects. This may have happened in some areas, when the discovery of animal husbandry and agriculture made available new sources of food and power.

Culture and man • part **2**

Figure 6-5a. *A family of the Copper Eskimo tribe moves camp at the beginning of winter. The sled on which their possessions are loaded is so heavy that both dogs and people must pull to move it.*

Figure 6-5b. *When the water is completely frozen over, the Eskimo wait by holes in the ice for seals to surface for a breath. This photo was taken just ten years ago; many Eskimos still observe their traditional ways.*

Figure 6-5c. *When the group moves camp during the winter, a new village must be built in their new location. Men and women of all ages work at cutting and placing the blocks of ice that form the houses.*

Figure 6-5d. *During the summer, a shelter is constructed of caribou hides, then in plentiful supply as a result of the hunt. The warmer temperatures of the season permit more casual construction of shelters.*

This raised the carrying capacity of the environment, permitting larger, denser populations with new systems for producing and distributing materials and energy, and this, in turn, affected social relations and culture. Some of these changes can be found even among contemporary hunter-gatherers, particularly those of the cold climate adaptation. Examples of this type of society can be seen among many Eskimo tribes; some of the food-getting adaptations of the Eskimo are depicted in Color Portfolio 2, between pages 127 and 130. The Lapps and some of the inhabitants of northern Russia also typify the cold climate adaptation.

People may have come to live in cold climates as a result of a slow but steady population increase during the Paleolithic era. Consequently, man developed a series of cold climate adaptations that increased his cultural variability. In the extreme latitudes, in climates similar to those first inhabited by man about seventy thousand years ago, vegetable foods are only rarely or seasonally available, and animal protein is the staff of life. Furthermore, the extra energy expended in hunting and the digestion of animal protein is a source of body heat. A greater dependence on animal foods requires a more complex tool kit, game fences, and fish traps; cold climate living requires greater complexity in clothing and shelter as well. These kinds of possessions limit a group's mobility; it can be regained only through further material advances, such as the canoe, kayak, and dog sled. Still, the cold climate hunter is less fully nomadic than his warm climate brothers; long, cold winters further restrict his mobility and keep him close to his home base.

The fear of starvation plays an ominous role in the folklore of cold climate peoples. In most cold climates, populations often shuttle between feast and famine. This was especially true of the salmon fishermen of the northwest Pacific Coast. Even in the best of years, and with good preservation technology, winter often outlasted the food supply. The norms that required sharing of food caught by any hunter helped to ensure that existing food supplies were distributed throughout the entire community.

Figure 6-6. *This husband and wife model the clothes once worn by Copper Eskimos. These summer outfits are made almost entirely from caribou hide; warmer winter clothing utilizes sealskin and fur. Clothes of this type are no longer worn by the Eskimos.*

Culture and man • part **2**

Cold climate peoples also had to solve the problems of intensive labor organization, redistribution of scarcer and less readily available resources, and redistribution of larger populations. There had to be some mechanism for motivating individuals to perform in a complex system. Among the solutions to these problems were the development of rich material cultures, complex systems of kinship and marriage, class systems, slavery, and chieftainships. One of the most dramatic solutions was the potlatch of the northwest Indians, a ceremony of conspicuous gift-giving, where giving was an honor and receiving a shame that could be resolved only by returning an even larger gift at a subsequent potlatch. (See the original study in Chapter 10 for a detailed description of a potlatch ceremony among the Kwakiutl Indians.) The potlatch is simply an extreme version of the obligation to share found in hunter-gatherer societies. Many of the "simple" hunters and fishermen of the cold latitudes, because of the pressures of their environment, were well on their way to the kinds of complex societies that developed in warmer areas only following the introduction of agriculture and the rise of urban civilizations.

Food-producing society

It was the invention of toolmaking that made man a successful hunter and gatherer. The next important event in his history, an event which also led to rapid cultural evolution, was the domestication of plants and animals. Man's transition from hunter and gatherer to food producer (the available evidence suggests this change began 9000 to 11,000 years ago) has been termed revolutionary. After this revolution, much of human society no longer depended on a capricious nature for food; by planting and harvesting crops and keeping domestic animals, man could choose the time and the place of his next meal.

One of the most significant results of this new way of life was the development of permanent settlements, in which families of farmers lived together. The task of food production lent itself to a different kind of social organization; the hard work of some members of the group could provide food for all, thus freeing certain people to devote their time to inventing and manufacturing the equipment needed for a new way of life. Harvesting and digging tools, pottery for storage and cooking, clothing made of woven textiles, and housing made of stone, wood, or sun-dried bricks were some of the results of this combination of new needs and free time.

The transition also brought important changes in social structure. At first, social relations were egalitarian and hardly different from those that prevailed among hunters and gatherers. However, as settlements grew and large numbers of men began to share the same important resources, such as land and water, society became more structured. Kinship groups such as clans, which do not commonly play a large part in the social order of hunter-gatherers, were probably the organizing unit for this kind of work; they provide a convenient way to handle the problems of land use and ownership that arise in a food-producing society.

Man adapted to his new settled life in a number of ways. For example, some societies became horticultural—small communities of gardeners working with simple hand tools and using neither irrigation nor the plow. Horticulturists typically cultivate different varieties of crops in small gardens they have cleared by hand. Technologically more complex than the horticulturists are the intensive agriculturists. They often employ irrigation, fertilizers, and the wooden or metal plow pulled by two harnessed draft animals, such as oxen or water buffalo, to produce food on larger plots of land. One of the more striking examples of man's adaptation to the environment is the pastoralist, who raises and herds domesticated animals such as cattle, sheep, horses, and camels. Pastoralism is usually an adaptation to heavy grasslands, mountains, deserts, or other regions not amenable to agriculture. In addition, pastoral societies are seasonally nomadic, moving with their herds over large territories in response to the annual weather cycle.

As a food producer, man has developed several major crop complexes: two adapted to seasonal uplands and two to tropical wetlands. In the dry uplands of Asia Minor, for example, he times his agricultural activities with the rhythm of the changing seasons, domesticating wheat, barley, flax, rye, and millet. In the tropical wetlands of the Old World, rice and tubers such as yams and taro are cultivated. In the New World, man has adapted to environments similar to those of the Old World, but has cultivated different plants. Maize, beans, squash, and the potato are typically grown in drier areas, whereas manioc is domesticated in the tropical wetlands.

Horticulture: the Gururumba

A typical example of a horticultural society that has exploited its environment successfully is the Gururumba, a tribe of 1121 people who live in six villages spread over 30 square miles in the Upper Asaro valley of New Guinea. Because of the elevation, the climate is cool and damp, and the area receives about 100 inches of rain a year.[1]

Each Gururumba village has a number of gardens separated by fences; several nuclear families may have plots inside each fenced area. Every adult is involved in food production, with a strict division of labor according to sex. Men plant and tend sugar cane, bananas, taro, and yams, while women cultivate sweet potatoes and a variety of green vegetables. A family's social prestige is partially based on the neatness and productivity of its garden. Crops are rotated, but fertilizers are not used. Each gardener maintains more than one plot and uses different soils and different ecological zones for different crops; thus, the gardens are ready for harvesting at different times of the year, assuring a constant food supply. (Another technologically simple cultivating technique used

[1] Most of the following information is taken from Philip L. Newman, *Knowing the Gururumba* (New York: Holt, Rinehart & Winston, Inc., 1965).

Figure 6-7. *Horticulturists like the Gururumba live in many different types of houses. This photo shows cliff dwellings of sun-dried brick constructed by prehistoric Indian horticulturists in Arizona. Closely-related kin groups shared single apartments.*

by many horticultural societies, but not the Gururumba, is the slash and burn method, in which trees are toppled, allowed to season several months, then set afire. The ashes provide nutrients for the soil, which is then seeded and cultivated.) Since rainfall is plentiful, the Gururumba do not irrigate their gardens, and although some plots are planted on slopes with angles of 45°, terracing is not practiced. Simple hand tools, such as digging sticks made of wood or ground stone, are used by the men to break the soil.

Like many such societies in this culture area, Gururumba society is knit together through a complex system of gift exchange, in which men lavish gifts on one another and so accumulate a host of debtors. The more a man gives away, the more is owed him, and hence the more prestige

Figure 6-8. *These illustrations indicate man's propensity to depict plant and animal domestication in his artifacts. In the sculpture above, a farmer grinds grain with a huge pestle; below, an early Greek coin shows a bee, domesticated for honey.*

he has. It is for this reason that every man keeps two gardens, one with crops to fulfill his everyday needs, and one with "prestige" crops for his exchange needs. Although the crops planted in the latter gardens are not special, particular care is given to this garden to assure crops of the finest quality. A man anticipates a major occasion when he will have to give a feast, such as a daughter's wedding or a son's initiation, by planting his prestige garden a year in advance.

The second major feature of the Gururumba subsistence pattern, also common throughout this culture area, is the keeping of pigs. Pigs are raised not primarily for food, but as gift-exchange items to raise social prestige. Every five to seven years, a huge pig feast, called an *idzi namo* ("pig flute") is held. Hundreds of pigs are killed, cooked, and distributed, simultaneously abolishing old obligations and creating new ones for the clan that gives the feast. As was the case among the Tsembaga whom we met earlier in this chapter, the pig feast helps the Gururumba get rid of a pig population that had grown too large to continue feeding; it also provides them with occasional animal protein in their diet.

Pastoralism: the Bakhtiari

In the south Zagros mountains of western Iran dwell a fiercely independent, hard-bitten tribe of some 50,000 to 150,000 pastoral nomads who tend herds of goats and fat-tailed sheep; they are the Bakhtiari. Although some of the tribesmen own horses and most own donkeys, these are used only for transport; the animals around which Bakhtiari life revolves are the sheep and goat. (For pictures of the Bakhtiari, see Color Portfolio three, page 160.)

The harsh, bleak environment dominates the lives of these people: it determines when and where they move their flocks, the clothes they wear, the food they eat, and even their dispositions—they have been called "mountain bears" by the Iranian townspeople. In the Zagros are ridges which reach altitudes of 12,000 to 14,000 feet. Their steep, rocky trails, and escarpments challenge the hardiest and ablest climbers; jagged peaks, deep chasms, and watercourses with thunderous torrents also make living and traveling hazardous.

The pastoral life of the Bakhtiari revolves around two seasonal migrations to find better grazing lands for the flocks. Twice yearly the tribe moves: in the fall, from their *sardsin,* or summer quarters in the mountains, and in the spring, from their *garmsin,* or winter quarters in the lowlands. In the fall, before the harsh winter comes to the mountains, the nomads load their tents, women, and children on donkeys, and drive their flocks down to the warm plains that border Iraq in the west; grazing land here is excellent and well-watered in the winter. In the spring, when the low-lying pastures dry up, the Bakhtiari return to the mountain valleys, where a new crop of grass is sprouting. For this trek, the tribe splits into five groups, each containing about 5000 individuals and 50,000 animals.

The return trip north is the more dangerous of the two because the mountain snows are melting and the gorges are full of turbulent, ice-cold water rushing down from the mountain peaks. This long trek is further impeded by the kids that are born in spring, just before migration. Where the water courses are not very deep, the nomads ford them. Deeper channels, including one river which is a half mile wide, are crossed with the help of inflatable goatskin rafts, on which are placed infants, the elderly and infirm, lambs and kids; the rafts are then pushed by the men swimming alongside in the icy water. If they work from dawn to dusk, the nomads can get the entire 5000 people and 50,000 animals across the river in five days. Not surprisingly, dozens of sheep are drowned each day at the river crossing.

In the mountain passes, where a biting wind numbs the skin and brings tears to the eyes, the Bakhtiari must make their way through slippery unmelted snow. Climbing the steep escarpments is dangerous, and the stronger men must often carry their own children and the newborn kids on their shoulders as they make their way over the ice and snow to the lush mountain valley that is their goal. During each migration, the tribe may cover as many as 200 miles, and the trek can take weeks because the flocks travel slowly and require constant attention. The nomads have fixed routes and a somewhat definite itinerary; generally, they know where they should be and when they should be there. On the drive, the men and boys herd the sheep and goats, while the women and children ride the donkeys along with the tents and other equipment.

When they reach their destination, the Bakhtiari live in black tents of goat's hair cloth woven by the women. The tents have sloping tops and vertical sides, held up by wooden poles. Inside, the furnishings are sparse: rugs woven by the women or heavy felt pads cover the floor. Against one side of the tent are blankets; containers made of goat skin, copper utensils, clay jugs, and bags of grain line the opposite side. Bakhtiari tents provide an excellent example of adaptation to a changing environment. The goat's hair cloth retains heat and repels water during the winter, and keeps out heat during the summer. These portable homes are very easy to erect, take down, and transport.

Sheep and goats are central to Bakhtiari subsistence. The animals provide milk, cheese, butter, meat, hides, and wool, which is woven into clothes, tents, storage bags, and other essentials by the women or sold in towns. The tribe also engages in very limited horticulture; it owns lands that contain orchards and the fruit is consumed by the nomads or sold to townspeople. The division of labor is according to sex. The men, who take great pride in their marksmanship and horsemanship, engage in a limited amount of hunting on horseback, but their chief task is the tending of the flocks. The women cook, sew, weave, care for the children, and carry fuel and water.

The Bakhtiari have their own system of justice, including laws and a penal code. They are governed by tribal leaders, or *khans,* who are elected or inherit their office. Most of the *khans* grew wealthy when oil was discovered on tribal lands around the turn of the last century, and many of them are well-educated, having attended Iranian or foreign universities. Despite this, and although some of them own houses in cities, the *khans* spend much of their lives among their people.

Urban life among nonindustrial peoples

As improved agricultural techniques lead to higher crop yields and increased population, an agricultural settlement may grow into a city. This leads to an entirely new way of life, involving intense specialization of labor. Individuals who had previously been engaged in agriculture were freed to specialize in other activities. Thus, such craftsmen as carpenters, blacksmiths, sculptors, basketmakers, and stonecutters contribute to the vibrant, diversified life of the city.

Unlike horticulturalists and pastoralists, city dwellers are only indirectly concerned with adapting to their natural environment. Far more important is the fact that they must adapt to living and competing with their fellow urbanites. Urbanization means more complex social organization: society becomes stratified and people are ranked according to the kind of work they do, or the family they are born into. As social institutions cease to operate in simple, face-to-face groups of acquaintances and friends, they grow more formal and bureaucratic, with specialized political institutions.

With urbanization came a sharp increase in the tempo of human cultural evolution. Writing was developed, trade intensified and expanded, and the wheel, the sail, metallurgy, and other crafts were invented. In many early cities, monumental buildings, such as royal palaces and temples, were built by thousands of men, often slaves taken in war; these feats of engineering still amaze modern architects and engineers. The inhabitants of these buildings—the ruling class composed of nobles and priests—formed a central government that dictated social and religious rules; in turn, the rules were carried out by the merchants, soldiers, artisans, farmers, and other citizens.

Figure 6-9. *Urbanization typically means advanced economic systems and permanant housing. Above, a market in a small town of the Yoruba tribe of West Nigeria; their tradition of urbanism makes the Yoruba unique among the world's small-scale societies. Below, the ruins of Machu Pichu, a city built by the Pre-Columbian Incas of Peru.*

Aztec city life

The Aztec empire, which flourished in Mexico in the sixteenth century, is a good example of a highly developed urban society among non-Western peoples. The capital city of the empire, Tenochtitlan (modern-day Mexico City), was located in a fertile valley 7000 feet above sea level. It is thought that the population of Tenochtitlan, and its satellite city, Tlatelolco, was about 300,000 in 1519, when Cortes first saw it. If this is true, then the Aztec cities were five times more populous than the city of London was at the time. The city sat in the middle of a salt lake which has since dried up, and two aqueducts brought in fresh water from nearby springs. A ten-mile dike rimmed the eastern end of the city to ward off the floodwaters originating in the neighboring lakes during the rainy season.

As in the early cities in Asia Minor, the foundation of Aztec society was agriculture, and corn was the principal crop. Each family, alloted a plot of land by its clan, cultivated any of a number of crops, including beans, squash, gourds, peppers, tomatoes, cotton, and tobacco. Unlike Old World societies, however, only a few animals were domesticated; these included dogs and turkeys (both for eating).

As Tenochtitlan grew and land became scarce, Aztec farmers developed an ingenious method to cope with this situation: they created *chinampas,* or reed-walled gardens, out of the marsh that surrounded the capital. Each *chinampa,* actually a small, man-made island whose soil was as fertile as that of the Nile Delta, was tended by farmers who paddled around the interconnecting canals in small dugout canoes. Even today, *chinampas* can be found at Zochimilco, a few miles outside Mexico City.

Aztec agricultural success led to an increasing population and the diversification of labor. Skilled artisans, such as sculptors, silversmiths, stone workers, potters, weavers, feather workers, and painters were able to make good livings by pursuing these crafts exclusively. Since religion was central to the operation of the Aztec social order, these craftsmen were continuously engaged in the manufacture of religious artifacts, clothing, decorations for buildings and temples. Other nonagricultural specialists included the warriors, the traveling merchants or *pochteca,* the priests, and the government bureaucracy of nobles.

As specialization, both among individuals and cities of the Aztec empire increased, the market became an extremely important economic and social institution. In addition to the daily markets in each city, there were larger markets in the various cities held at different times of year. Buyers and sellers traveled to these from the far reaches of the empire. The market at the city of Tlatelolco was so huge that Spanish soldiers compared it to those of Rome and Constantinople. At the Aztec markets, barter was the primary means of exchange. However, at times, cacao beans, gold dust, crescent-shaped knives, and copper were used. In addition to its obvious economic use, the market served social functions: people went there not only to buy or to sell, but to meet other people and to hear the latest news. A law actually required that each person go to market at least once within a specified number of days; this insured that the citizenry was kept informed of all important news. The other major economic institution, trade networks between the capital and other Aztec cities, brought goods such as chocolate, vanilla beans, and pineapples into Tenochtitlan.

Aztec social order was stratified into three main classes: nobles, commoners, and serfs. The nobles and commoners were also subdivided into clans. Within each clan, individual status depended on the degree of descent from the clan founder: those more closely related to the clan founder had higher status than those whose kinship was more distant. The third class in Aztec society consisted of serfs bound to the land, and porters employed as carriers by merchants. Lowest of this class were the slaves. Some had voluntarily sold themselves into bondage; others were captives taken in war.

The Aztecs were governed by a semidivine king, who was chosen by a council of nobles, priests, and leaders from among candidates of royal lineage. Although the king was an absolute monarch, the councillors advised him on affairs of state. A vast number of government officials oversaw various functions, such as the maintenance of the tax system, the courts of justice, management of government storehouses, and control of military training.

As in the modern city, housing in Tenochtitlan ranged from squalid to magnificent. On the outskirts of the city, on *chinampas*, were the farmers' hovels, huts of thatched straw and wattle smeared with mud. In the city proper were the houses of the middle class—graceful, multiroomed, single- and two-story stone and mortar buildings, each of which surrounded a flower-filled patio and rested on a stone platform for protection against floods. It is estimated that there were about 60,000 houses in Tenochtitlan. The focal points of the city were the *teocallis*, or pyramidal temples, at which religious ceremonies, including human sacrifice, were held. The 100-foot-high double temple dedicated to the war god and the rain god was made of stone and featured a steep staircase which led to a platform containing an altar, a chamber containing shrines, and an antechamber for the priests.

The typical Aztec city was rectangular and reflected the way the land was divided among the clans. In the center was a large plaza containing the temple and the house of the city's chief. At Tenochtitlan, with a total area of about 20 square miles, a huge temple and two lavish palaces stood in the central plaza, also called the Sacred Precinct. Surrounding this area were other ceremonial buildings belonging to each clan.

The palace of the emperor Moctezuma boasted numerous rooms for attendants and concubines, a menagerie, hanging gardens, and a swimming pool. Since Tenochtitlan sat in the middle of a lake, it was unfortified and connected to the mainland by three causeways. Communication among different parts of the city was easy, and one could travel either by land or by water. A series of canals, with footpaths running beside them, ran throughout the city. The Spaniards who came to this city reported that thousands of canoes plied the canals, carrying passengers and cargo around the city; these worldly Europeans were so impressed by the communication network that they called Tenochtitlan the Venice of the New World.

☐

Original study

YORUBA MARKETS AND TRADE

Nearly all Yoruba men engage in farming, but the production of many other goods is specialized. Weaving, dyeing, ironworking, brasscasting, woodcarving, calabash-carving, beadworking, leather-working and pottery, as well as hunting, fishing, drumming, divining, circumcising and cicatrizing, and the compounding of charms and medicines are crafts whose techniques are known only to a small group of professionals and are often protected as trade secrets by religious sanctions. Traders are also professionals, and in recent times sawyers, carpenters, brick makers, bricklayers, tailors, bicycle repairmen, automobile mechanics, shop keepers, letter writers and other professions have been added. Most of these specialists do some farming, but they supply all other members of the community with their goods and services.

Craft specialization makes each individual economically dependent upon the society as a whole. Craft specialization also meant the development of internal trade and town markets for the exchange of local produce. The size and importance of these markets, visited by many tens of thousands in the larger cities, impress the visitor today as they did the early explorers. Bowen, an early American missionary who traveled through parts of Yoruba country in the 1850s, wrote:

> The most attractive object next to the curious old town itself—and it is always old—is the market. This is not a building, but a large area, shaded with trees, and surrounded and sometimes sprinkled over with little open sheds, consisting of a very low thatched roof surmounted on rude posts. Here the women sit and chat all day, from early morning till 9 o'clock at night, to sell their various merchandise. . . . The principal marketing hour, and the proper time to see all the wonders, is the evening. At half an hour before sunset, all sorts of people, men women, girls, travelers lately arrived in the caravans, farmers from the fields, and artizans from their houses, are pouring in from all directions to buy and sell, and talk. At the distance of half a mile their united voices roar like the waves of the sea. . . . As the shades of evening deepen, if the weather allows the market to continue, and there is no moon, every woman lights her little lamp, and presently the market presents to the distant observer, the beautiful appearance of innumerable bright stars. . . . Every fifth day there is a "large market," when the few thousand people who attend daily are increased to a multitude (Bowen 1857:296–297).

The markets are composed of areas occupied by women selling the same commodities: poultry in basketry coops, tethered goats and sheep, yams, peppers, plantains, green vegetables, meat, salt, palm oil, palm wine, soap, cloth, pots, firewood, the varied ingredients of charms and medicines, and European cloths and other imported items. They are dominated by women traders, the principal exception being the men who butcher and sell cattle from the north. During the day, before the market reaches its peak, women hawk their wares through town or sell them in front of the house and at street corners. Many women prepare and sell cooked food in the streets or scattered through the market. Over a century ago Bowen (1857:301) observed, "No people are so much in the habit of eating in the streets, where women are always engaged in preparing all sorts of dishes for sale to passers by."

A farmer's wife may carry his produce to market and sell it for him, turning over the full sale price to her husband; but many women are professional traders. Some pay cash for their goods and others take their goods on credit; both trade for profit, bargaining with both the producer and the consumer in order to obtain as large a margin of profit as possible. Bargaining is a standard feature of Yoruba economic transactions. Other women traders are commissioned agents who deal regularly with a particular producer; a weaver, for example, may show his agent cloths that he wishes to be sold and tell her the price he expects to receive for them. If she believes that the price is right, she takes them on credit; when they have been sold she pays the weaver what he asked and in return she receives a commission, usually about five percent. If she cannot sell the cloths at the weaver's price, she can return them to him; but if she can sell them at higher prices, she earns a profit in addition to her commission.

A fourth system is followed by the women who sell palm wine, which cannot be sold when it is two days old, and brings only half price when it is a day old. Each palm wine tapper has a group of women who sell for him, each receiving the same amount each day to sell at the price set by the tapper. All

Figure 6-11. *Urbanization produces specialists able to develope sophisticated artistic techniques. Shown here is a Yoruba wood-carved cup, in the shape of a woman seated before a sacrificial cock, used for storing palm nuts.*

the money received on the first two days belongs to the tapper, and that received on the third day belongs to his agent. If she should drop her calabash on the way to market, she or the tapper takes the loss depending upon whose day it is. A tapper is not concerned about how well an agent does on her own day, but he demands that she be reasonably successful in selling on his days, and if she is not he refuses to deal with her again.

Although tradition speaks of a time when goods were bartered, for centuries, at least, money in the form of cowry shells was the basis of trade, and tradition also speaks of cowries being found in the lagoon. If the Yoruba did not have cowries before the Portuguese explored the coast, perhaps only in small numbers through trade from the Indian Ocean, one wonders what so quickly gave the Portuguese the idea that they were worth importing.

Credit was available from money lenders at high rates of interest, through the institution of indenture or "pawning" and, since the introduction of cocoa, through the "pawning" of cocoa trees. It also was and is available through the esusu, an institution which has elements similar to installment buying, a credit union, and a savings club. The esusu is a fund to which a group of individuals make fixed contributions of money at fixed intervals; and the total amount contributed each period is assigned to each of the members in rotation. The number of contributors, the size of the contributions, and the length of the contributions vary from one group to another; but if twenty members contribute one shilling each monthly, at the end of twenty months, which completes the cycle, each member will have contributed one pound and will have received one pound in return. There is neither gain nor loss; but the advantage to the members is that they have one pound in a lump sum (or larger amounts of money if there are more members or larger contributions) with which to purchase goods, pay for services, or repay debts. Except for the one who receives the fund at the end of a cycle, all members receive an advance on their contributions without having to pay interest. Moreover, an attempt is made to make the fund available to members at times when they have need for it, assigning it to a member who applies for it unless he has been tardy in making his payments or has already received the fund during the current cycle.

As noted initially, the foundations of the economy in precontact times were sedentary hoe farming, craft specialization, and farming. The rotation of crops and, particularly, the rotation of land through fallowing made possible a sedentary way of life and the development of large, dense, permanent communities and an urban way of life. Craft specialization led to trade, both within and between these communities, and made each individual economically dependent upon the society as a whole. Trade involved professional middlemen, formal markets, and money. The pecuniary nature of Yoruba culture and the importance of the profit motive are both apparent.

Source:
From *The Yoruba of Southwestern Nigeria* by William Bascom.
Copyright © 1969 by Holt, Rinehart and Winston, Inc.
Reprinted by permission of Holt, Rinehart and Winston, Inc.

Summary

1.

Needs and pressures force man to alter his behavior and adjust it to suit his environment. This adjustment is part of adaptation. Adaptation has two meanings. It means that there is a moving balance between the needs of organisms and the potential of their environment. It also means the process whereby the environment changes the organism and the organism changes the environment. The unit of adaptation includes both the organism and its environment. Adaptation takes place over long periods of time. To survive, organisms must be able to adjust to new environments and respond to changes in climate or biological environment.

2.

An ecological zone in which various societies follow similar patterns of life is known as a culture area. In culture areas, societies share inventions and discoveries. The climate and topography of an ecological zone often differ from area to area. Often each climate and topography require a different technology. As a result, in a diverse ecological zone, individual societies develop different technologies. A culture considered in terms of its technology and the ways it is applied to the environment is a culture type. Social and political organization also affect the application of technology to the problems of staying alive. Those features of a culture that play a part in the society's way of making its living are called its culture core. Anthropologists can trace direct relationships between types of culture cores and types of environment.

3.

Hunter-gatherers are people who do not practice animal husbandry or agriculture. They fish, hunt, and gather wild fruits and vegetables to sustain themselves. Although there are variations in hunter-gatherer activity, the consistency of the hunter-gatherer adaptation across cultures is a strong argument for subsistence activities as a determinant of social forms. There are two key features of the hunter-gatherer adaptation: (1) they move about a great deal to accommodate their living places to naturally available food sources, and (2) their groups are small. No completely satisfactory explanation for this has been given. One explanation contends small sizes fit land capacity to sustain the groups. Another contends the less people, the less chance of social conflict. Hunting styles and equipment may also play a role in determining population size and movement; efficiency of subsistence technology permits greater population size and stability.

4.

Ancient hunter-gatherers lacked animals or mechanical means of transportation. They traveled light, restricting themselves to the barest essentials. A territory belonged to all of its groups and group members were constantly shifting. Egalitarian societies developed. It is difficult to interpret modern hunter-gatherer activity. Today's hunter-gatherer has been exposed to at least some contact with more highly technological neighbors. He has been left to his traditional way of life only in the world's marginal areas—deserts, inaccessible forests, and frozen arctic tundra. Hunting and gathering in frozen regions has led to cold climate adaptation, whereby man's cultural variability increased. This adaptation features redistribution of scarcer and less readily available resources and redistribution of larger populations.

5.

Three elements of human social organization developed along with hunting. First, the division of labor. In hunter-gatherer societies, men hunted and women gathered. Second, food sharing. Hunters who hunted in teams shared what they killed. One reason an individual hunter shared what he killed was to stake a moral claim on other hunters' future kills. Third, the camp as a center of daily activity. Hunters shared their food at a camp where they also worked, slept, and socialized. These features had important consequences for the continued evolution of patterns of social organization.

6.

The agricultural revolution which took place some seven to nine thousand years ago encouraged the development of permanent settlements. Social organization changed to permit a greater division of labor. As the settlements grew larger the social structure became somewhat more stratified.

7.

Simple horticulture employed neither the plow nor irrigation. Intensive agriculture is more complex requiring irrigation, fertilizers and draft animals. Pastoralism is a means of subsistence which relies on raising herds of domesticated animals such as cattle, sheep and goats. Pastoralists are usually nomads, moving to higher ground in the summer.

8.

The Gururumba who live in the highlands of New Guinea are a successful horticulturist society. The men plant sugar cane, bananas, taro and yams and the women raise sweet potatoes and green vegetables. The demands of the culture necessitate an elaborate system of gift-giving and the men raise a second garden for "prestige" crops to enable them to participate in the giving of gifts. Pigs are raised too for gift exchange.

9.

In the mountains of Iran the Bakhtiari are pastoralists whose herds consist of sheep and goats. These fierce and proudly independent people spend the winter months in the lowlands where there is excellent grazing land. When this land dries up in the spring they make the arduous trip across the mountains to a high valley where they can graze their flocks. The animals provide milk, cheese, butter, hides and wool. The Bakhtiari practice a simple division of labor in which the men tend the flocks and the women cook, sew, weave, care for the children and carry fuel and water.

10.

Cities developed when improved agricultural techniques created a surplus, freeing individuals to specialize in other activities. The social structure becomes increasingly stratified with the development of cities and people are ranked according to the work they do and the family they are born into. Social relationships grow more formal and political institutions are formed.

11.

With the development of the first cities came a rapid cultural growth with the invention of writing, the wheel, the sail, metallurgy, monumental architecture and engineering. By the sixteenth century the Aztecs of Mexico had a highly developed urban society based on agriculture with corn as the principal crop. These people were subject to rule by an absolute monarch and their society was stratified into three groups: nobles, commoners and serfs. Their city was a source of wonder to the Spanish soldiers of Cortes' army who compared it with Venice, the most powerful city of Europe at that time.

portfolio three

The Persian nomads

Among the last remaining nomads on earth are the Bakhtiari of Iran, whom we met in Chapter six. These proud, independent people trace their lineage through 2500 years of Persian history to the most ancient Aryan peoples. Living on the fringes of the heartland of "civilization" near where the first cities of Sumer and Babylon flourished, they have resisted every attempt to change their way of life. In recent times, the father of the present Shah of Iran succeeded briefly in settling many Bakhtiari, but after his abdication in 1941, the tribesmen burned down their homes and went again to the mountains.

The Bakhtiari, or Lors as they are sometimes called, number nearly half a million in Iran today. They wander because they are herdsmen, and have always been. Spending the winter grazing their flocks of sheep and goats on the plains north of the Persian Gulf (where oil discoveries in 1908 made some of them very rich), the Bakhtiari drive their herds each spring some 250 miles into the high, lush pasturelands of the Zagros mountains, near Isfahan. Traditionally, the spring migration begins 14 days after Nowrouz, the Persian New Year, and at the time of the spring equinox. Leaving behind the increasingly sere plain, where temperatures reach 120 degrees in summer and grass withers to inedibility, the shepherds and their flocks climb almost 15,000 feet on a journey that may last over a month.

Such a journey is pictured on the following pages. Members of the Babadi, a subtribe of the Bakhtiari,

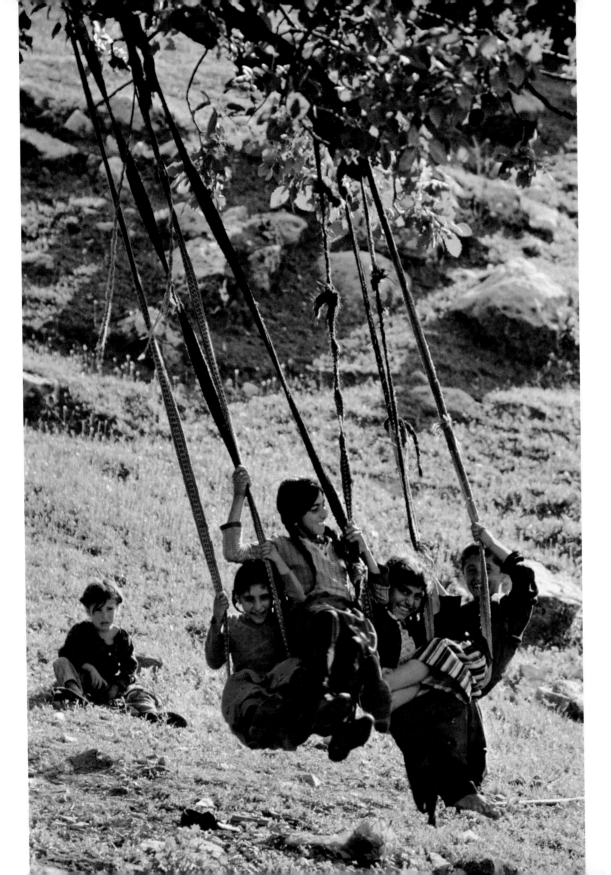

which consists of some 30,000 people subdivided into many clans,
are led by their Kalantar (Chief) Jafar Qoli from Lali,
their market town in the plains, to Kuh Rang,
their summer quarters near Zardeh Kuh, the
"Yellow Mountain."

By Bakhtiari standards, Jafar Qoli is a wealthy man.
He has about a thousand sheep and goats, maintains several
wives—one of whom, the shepherdess-wife, is seen in the
center pages of this portfolio—employs three shepherds
who earn about $1.25 per day, and owns some land. But it is
the sheep that represent a Bakhtiari's wealth. Goats give
milk and their hair is woven into tents, the black tents that
are the nomads' trademarks; mules are valued pack animals,
sure-footed and tough enough to survive the mountain
journeys. The land yields wheat, which is planted in
mountain valleys as the herdsmen travel upward, reaped some
40 days later and ground into flour in the autumn on the
return journey. Sheep are the most valuable because the ewes
bear lambs, which are sold for meat and wool. (Although Iran
desperately needs protein for the nation's diet, the
government has persisted in a policy of settlement for the
Bakhtiari, a policy which would both destroy a way of life
and waste a valuable resource. Some Bakhtiari, however,
believe that the Shah himself is sympathetic to them and
hope that they may maintain the old ways.)

On their migrations, the Bakhtiari travel in a maal,
the smallest tribal unit consisting of from two to eight
families. Each maal or Taefeh (clan) departs from its winter
or summer quarters at a different time so that the migration
route is not overgrazed. At various points along the journey,
in valleys large enough to support them, the groups meet and
the reunions are joyous. In the photograph on the opposite
page, clan children enjoy a swing on the ropes used to tie
down the pack burdens which the shepherds have thrown up into
a tree. The life is hard, the way is treacherous, but the
Bakhtiari prefer it to any other life they know.

Photographs by Anthony Howarth

Suggested readings

Bicchieri, M. G. ed. *Hunters and Gatherers Today: A Socioeconomic Study of Eleven Such Cultures in the Twentieth Century.* New York: Holt, Rinehart and Winston, 1972.
Both ecological-historical reconstruction and participant-observer ethnographies are contained in this volume. Each chapter is preceded by a short introduction pointing out the specific character and basic features of each of the studies.

Oswalt, Wendell H. *Habitat and Technology.* New York: Holt, Rinehart and Winston, 1972.
The author develops a taxonomy which permits precise cross-cultural comparisons of the complexity of manufactures. The research is based on a systematic analysis of the known manufactures of non-Western peoples. Shelters, tools, clothing, implements, and cultivated foodstuffs are considered.

Rappaport, Roy *Pigs for the Ancestors.* New Haven: Yale University Press, 1968.
This is a study of the functions of ritual among the Maring, a primitive farming people of New Guinea.

Steward, Julian *Theory of Culture Change: The Methodology of Multilinear Evolution.* Urbana: University of Illinois Press, 1972.
The author discusses concepts and methods needed to develop a general methodology for determining regularities in the interrelationships of cultural patterns and culture change among different societies. The basic theory is illustrated with examples from selected cultures (Shoshone Indians, Bushmen, etc.).

Vayda, Andrew, ed. *Environment and Cultural Behavior: Ecological Studies in Cultural Anthropology.* New York: Natural History Press, 1969.
The focus of the studies collected here is the interrelationship between cultural behavior and environmental phenomena. The writers attempt to make cultural behavior intelligible by relating it to the material world in which it develops. This volume includes articles concerning population, divination, ritual, warfare, food production, climate, and diseases.

part

3

The formation
of groups

Marriage and
the family

The family, regarded as an immutable social institution in American life, has surfaced as a matter for controversy and discussion. The women's movement, the new sexual freedom, and the soaring divorce and delinquency rates have raised questions about the functions of the American family and its ability to survive in a period of rapid social change. Evidence of the widespread interest in these questions can be seen in the popularity of books like *Open Marriage*, and television documentaries like *An American Family*.

Does the American family, as presently constituted, offer the best environment for bringing up children? Does it impose an inferior status on the woman, confined and isolated in the home, performing household and child-raising chores? Does the man, locked into an authoritarian role, suffer unduly in his personal development from bearing the sole responsibility of supporting the family? Are there adequate substitutes for people who have no family to care for them, such as old people and orphans? If the modern American family is found wanting, what are the alternatives?

Historical and cross-cultural studies of the family offer as many different family patterns as the fertile imagination of man can invent. These different family patterns are not just interesting products of human inventiveness; they are solutions to the different sorts of problems with which people must cope. Different family forms, at the same time, themselves present certain sets of problems which somehow must be dealt with. How men and women in other societies live together in families can be studied, not as bizarre and exotic forms of human behavior, but as evidence of the adaptive potential of culture.

Functions of the family

There is some disagreement among anthropologists as to the functions of the family unit, but all agree that the family in one form or another can be found in every known society. Our own notions of family are closely identified with marriage and romantic love. Thus we might conclude that the major function of the family is to control sexual behavior, limiting sexual access within the confines of the roles of husband and wife. Although this regulation is indeed one of the family's functions, it is safe to say that in human society the basic function of a family is the nurturance of children, which ensures the survival of society.

Nurturance of children

Primate babies are born helpless, and they remain dependent upon their parents for a longer time than any other animals. This dependence is not only for food and physical care but, as the studies of both Rhesus monkeys and human babies have revealed, for the physical nearness and response the mother provides.[1] Psychologist Harry Harlow separated baby Rhesus monkeys from their natural mothers and raised them with surrogate mothers— dummies made of wire or cloth. The baby monkeys preferred the soft dummies to the wire ones, whether or not the cloth ones were fitted out with baby bottles of milk—indicating the need for soft contact. More revealing, however, was the finding that monkeys who were nurtured only by surrogate mothers became emotionally disturbed; they were unable to interact with normally raised monkeys, cowered in a corner of the cage, and were unable to have sexual relations. After six months, this behavior became irreversible.

Another study, done in the early 1930s by Rene Spitz, compared four groups of human babies.[2] The study found that babies raised with parental affection were relatively healthy and hardy, even without any medical care. The babies raised in a clean, medically supervised orphan asylum were the most likely to sicken and die. These babies not only experienced the barest of human contact and interaction after they were weaned from the wet nurse, but there was nothing for them to look at but the ceiling, due to the arrangement of blankets hung on the sides of the cribs. Spitz concluded that human babies must have human contact and response, as well as some stimulation from the environment, for bare survival.

From such evidence it is apparent that children do not just "grow like Topsy" but that the care of at least a mother is essential to their growth. However, for the human infant, a mother alone

[1]Harry F. Harlow, "Social Deprivation in Monkeys," *Scientific American*, 206 (November, 1962), 1–10.
[2]Rene A. Spitz, "Hospitalism," in *The Psychoanalytic Study of the Child* (New York: International Universities Press), Vol. I (1945), pp. 53–72.

Figure 7-1. *These pictures implicitly contrast two different attitudes toward the raising of children. The photo on the left shows an American baby in a Skinner box, named after its designer, the famed behavioral psychologist B.F. Skinner. It is a mechanically controlled environment that keeps temperature and humidity constant in a sterile atmosphere. At right is a group of men on a New Guinea island; it is their responsibility to raise all male children.*

is not sufficient. This is because, in all known societies, adult male and adult female roles differ to some degree, due to sexual division of labor. In order to function properly as an adult, a child needs to be closely associated with an adult of the same sex to serve as a model for the proper adult role. Moreover, the social division of labor common to all societies means that the presence of both adult males and females is necessary for the economic maintenance of the child-rearing unit.

The family is an effective grouping for the purposes of child-rearing. It provides for a close mother-child relationship, as well as for the presence of an adult male. This is not to say, however, that the family is the only unit capable of providing these conditions. Theoretically, other arrangements might be possible. For example, groups of children might be raised by paired teams of trained male and female specialists: the Israeli kibbutz was a step in the direction of such an arrangement. So the child-rearing function alone cannot account for the universality of the human family, even though the function itself is universal. Obviously, other factors must be involved.

Control of sexual relations

Another problem faced by all human societies is the constant sexual receptivity of the human female. In this, the human female goes the other primates one better. Although frequent receptivity is characteristic of all female primates, only the human female is continually receptive. On the basis of clues from the behavior of other primates, anthropologists have speculated about the nature of the evolutionary advantage this trait might have. Among the species of primates most closely related to man, sexual activity seems to reinforce social bonds, which themselves seem based on individual likes and dislikes. If indeed sexual activity helps to tie together a group of individuals of different sexes and ages, it seems possible that as the social life of early hominids became more crucial to survival, a selective advantage was enjoyed by those groups with the strongest cohesion. To the extent that constant sexuality reinforced this, natural selection worked to favor this attribute in females.

At the same time that sexual activity can reinforce group ties, it can also be disruptive. This is due to the basic primate characteristic of male dominance. It is based on the fact that, on the average, males are bigger and more muscular than females, although this differentiation is less noticeable in modern *Homo sapiens* than it probably was in the earliest hominids. Because of the males' larger size, they tend to dominate females when the latter are at the height of their sexuality; this trait can be seen among baboons, gorillas, and, to a lesser extent, chimpanzees. With the continual sexual receptiveness of early hominid females, the dominant males may have attempted to monopolize the females; an added inducement could have been the prowess of the female at food gathering. Such a tendency would introduce a competitive, combative element into hominid groupings. The establishment of the family unit to regulate sexual access would counteract this potentially disruptive force and help to provide the harmonious social relationships on which human survival depends.

Rules of sexual access. We find that everywhere societies have behavioral norms controlling sexual relations. In our society, many people marry to insure a partner for sexual relations, since marriage in America is a form of contract whereby a person establishes a continuing claim to the right of sexual access to another person. But marriage is not a prerequisite to family life; there can be families which are not established through marriage, as, for example, among the Nayars of India.

Actually, the United States is among a very small minority—about 5 percent—of all known societies whose formal codes of behavior prohibit any sexual involvement outside of marriage.[3] Among the Kaingang, a very small society of 109 people living on a reservation in the high jungles of Brazil, studied by Jules Henry in 1932, there was a bare minimum of restriction placed on sexual activity or physical contact between members of the community. "Brothers and sisters, brothers- and sisters-in-law and cousins, sleep next to one another. . . . Marriages and love affairs (exist) among all classes of relatives. . . ."[4] In the traditional culture of the Eskimos, the sexual favors of the wife are offered to a visitor as a means of expressing hospitality and, in fact, a rejection of this offer is considered insulting. Despite these exceptions, the family plays an important role in providing a means of satisfying sexual drives that otherwise might be socially disruptive.

[3] F. Ivan Nye and Felix M. Berardo, *The Family: Its Structure and Interaction* (New York: The Macmillan Company, 1973) p. 173.

[4] Jules Henry, *Jungle People* (Locust Valley, N.Y.: J. J. Augustin, Inc., 1941).

Figure 7-2. *A wood engraving from a newspaper of the 1870s shows a community of Shakers dancing; some suggest it was a way to release sexual energies.*

The incest taboo. All societies at all times in history have formulated a rule, called the **incest taboo,** that prohibits sexual relations between members of the same family. The rule's universality has fascinated anthropologists and other students of human behavior. In all known societies, sexual relations are prohibited between parent and child and (with only a few very specific exceptions) between siblings as well. It has become a matter of serious import for social anthropologists to explain why incest should always be regarded with such horror and loathing.

Many explanations have been given. The simplest and least satisfactory is based on "human nature"—that is, some instinctive horror of incest.

It is also said that human beings raised together have less sexual attraction for one another, but this argument really substitutes the result for the cause. The incest taboo ensures that children and their parents, who are constantly in intimate contact, avoid regarding one another as sexual objects.

Early students of genetics thought that the incest taboo precluded the deleterious effects of inbreeding. This theory has been abandoned to a great extent because, as with domestic animals, inbreeding can increase desired characteristics as well as deleterious ones. Sigmund Freud accounted for the incest taboo in his psychoanalytic theory of the unconscious. The son desires the mother, creating a rivalry with the father. (Freud called this the Oedipus complex.) He must suppress these feelings or earn the wrath of the father, who is far more powerful than he. The attraction of the daughter to the father, or the Electra complex, places her in rivalry with her mother. Freud's theory can be viewed as an elaboration of the reasons for a deep-seated aversion to sexual relations within the family.

A truly convincing explanation of the incest taboo has yet to be advanced. Some biologists believe that it may be due to an instinctual preference for a genetically different mate. Such an instinct has been demonstrated among other animals—the fruit fly, for example—and would have an obvious adaptive value in maintaining a high level of phenotypic diversity within a population. Another recent theory focuses on the protection of the young. Some psychologists endorse the belief that young children can be emotionally scarred by sexual experiences, which they may have interpreted as violent and frightening acts of aggression. The incest taboo thus protects children against sexual advances by older members of the family. A closely related theory is that the incest taboo helps prevent girls who are socially and emotionally too young for motherhood from becoming pregnant.

Endogamy and exogamy. Another way to explain the value of the incest taboo is to examine its effects on social structure. Closely related to the prohibitions against incest are the rules against **endogamy,** or marriage within a group of related individuals. If the group is defined as just one immediate family, then all societies prohibit endogamy and practice **exogamy,** or marriage outside the group. However, if the family group is enlarged to include more members—second and third cousins, for example—then we find that endogamy may be a common practice. For example, Scottish Highlanders traditionally married within the network of alliances of the family clan, strengthening its political and economic position.

Sir Edward Tylor, in fact, advanced the proposition that alternatives to inbreeding were either

Figure 7-3. A woman of the Big Namba tribe is making a new wig by sewing together strips of leaves from the pandanus, or breadfruit tree; she wears an older model of the same type of wig. The sole function of this hairpiece relates to a taboo against incest. Whenever a woman meets one of her brothers-in-law, she must immediately adjust the wig to cover her face, thus preventing these relatives of her husband from taking any sexual interest in her.

The formation of groups ● part **3**

"marrying out or being killed."[5] Our ancestors, he suggested, discovered the advantage of inter-marriage to create bonds of friendship. Claude Lévi-Strauss elaborated on this premise. He made exogamy the basis of a distinction between early hominid life in isolated family groups and the life of *Homo sapiens* in a supportive society with an accumulating culture. The bonds with other groups, established and strengthened by marriage ties, make possible a sharing of culture.

In a roundabout way, exogamy also helps to explain the two exceptions to the incest taboo, that of brother and sister marriage within the royal family of ancient Egyptians, Incans, and Hawaiians. Members of such royal families were considered semidivine and their very sacredness usually kept them from marrying mere mortals. The brother and sister married to keep intact the godliness and purity of the royal line.[6]

Choice of mate

The institution of the family, and the rules that surround it, also regulate individual choice of a mate so as to promote and increase the social stability of the entire group. The American egal-itarian ideal that an individual should be free to marry whomever he or she chooses is an unusual arrangement, certainly not one that is universally embraced. Among the Arapesh, as described by Margaret Mead in *Sex and Temperament,* the father chooses his son's wife, who must be from another clan. Her brothers and her male cousins, who will be his son's brothers-in-law and his grandchildren's maternal uncles, must be "good hunters, successful gardeners, slow to anger, and wise in making decisions."[7] Rather than a neces-sary evil, the Arapesh regard marriage primarily as an opportunity to increase the warm family

circle within which one's descendants may then live.

In Gopalpur, a small village in southern India, marriage to any person related through the pa-ternal line is regarded as incest.[8] Marriage to relatives of a sister or a mother is looked for. Brides are usually brought in from another village and must be in the same caste.

The levirate and the sororate. If a husband dies, leaving a wife and children, it is often the custom that the wife marry one of the brothers of the dead man. This custom, called the **levirate,** not only provides social security for the widow and her children but also is a way for the hus-band's family to maintain their rights over her sexuality and her future children: it acts to pre-serve the bonds established. When a man marries the sister of his dead wife, it is called the **soro-rate.** In societies that have the levirate and soro-rate, the relationship between the two families is maintained even after the death of a spouse; in essence, the family supplies another spouse to take the place of the member who died.

Monogamy and polygyny. **Monogamy,** or the taking of a single spouse, is the form of marriage with which we are most familiar. It is also the most common, primarily for economic rather than moral reasons. A man must be fairly wealthy to be able to afford **polygyny,** or marriage to more than one wife. Among the Gusii of Western Kenya,[9] four wives was the ideal; such an ideal was actually realized only by some of the older men. Wives were desirable because they worked in the fields and increased a man's wealth, but young men could not afford to purchase more than one wife. In our country, the rich Mormons practiced polygyny; they were hounded from state to state until they finally gave up the cus-tom, so repugnant was it to our moral code.

Polyandry, the custom of a woman having sev-

---

[5]Quoted in Roger M. Keesing and Felix M. Keesing, *New Per-spectives in Cultural Anthropology* (New York: Holt, Rinehart and Winston, 1971) p. 183.

[6]*Ibid.,* p. 182.

[7]Margaret Mead, *Sex and Temperament in Three Primitive So-cieties,* 3rd ed. (New York: William Morrow, 1963) p. 67.

---

[8]Alan R. Beals, *Gopalpur: a South Indian Village* (New York: Holt, Rinehart and Winston, 1972) p. 25.
[9]Wendell H. Oswalt, *Other Peoples, Other Customs* (New York: Holt, Rinehart and Winston, 1972) p. 120.

eral husbands, is far less common, because man's life expectancy is shorter and male infant mortality is high. Group marriage, in which several men and women have sexual access to one another, also occurs in very rare cases. Even in communal groups today, among young people seeking alternatives to modern marriage forms, group marriage seems to be a transitory phenomenon, despite the publicity it has been receiving.

Economic and political function of the family

In many societies, economic considerations are often the strongest motivation to marry. A man of New Guinea does not marry because of sexual needs, which he can readily satisfy out of wedlock, but because he needs a woman to make pots and cook his meals, to fabricate nets and weed his plantings.[10] A man without a wife among the Australian aborigines is in an unsatisfactory position since he has no one to supply him regularly with food or fire-wood. In all societies, the smallest economic unit is the family.[11]

In societies where the family is the most powerful institution exercising social control over individuals, marriages are arranged for the economic and political advantage of the family unit, as for example in feudal Europe, traditional China and India, and until most recent times, in Japan. The marriage of two individuals who must spend their whole lives together and raise their children together is only incidental to the serious matter of making allies of two families by means of the marriage bond. Marriage involves a transfer of rights between families, including rights to property and rights over the children, as well as sexual rights.

In many societies, marriage and the establishment of a family are considered far too important

[10] Robert Lowie, cited by Leslie White, *The Science of Culture: a Study of Man and Civilization* (Garden City, N.Y.: Doubleday, 1969)
[11] Charles W. Hart and Arnold R. Pilling, *Tiwi of North Australia* (New York: Holt, Rinehart and Winston, Inc., 1960)

174

Figure 7-4a-d. *Polygyny is quite common in many parts of the world. The photo at the upper right shows a Bakhtiari tribesman with his three wives and many children; the Bakhtiari are unusual in this part of the world because the women go unveiled. The other photos are of various African tribes.*

to be left to the whims of children. The function of marriage in such cases is often economic in nature and, for wealthy and powerful families, political. In our own upper class, the children of powerful families are segregated in private schools and carefully steered toward a "proper" marriage. A careful reading of announced engagements in the society pages of *The New York Times* provides clear evidence of such family alliances.

The family strengthens the bonds of an individual to a society. The web of relationships and the social control that is exerted by families over the individual is an important force in integrating a society and making it cohesive. The problems of child-rearing, the regulation of sex, the need for cooperation between the sexes, the formation of political and economic alliances, need not all be performed by the same institution. But they are interrelated functions. Child-rearing follows from sexual activity, and it requires cooperation between man and woman, who cooperate in other ways as well. At the same time that economic cooperation takes place between adult men and women, it also takes place between adults and children, as well as between larger bands of adults who form an extended family group. A reasonable and logical approach to this network of social needs is to deal with them together in the context of the family, and that is the way that most societies function.

Form of the family

Perhaps it would be useful at this juncture to define a family. Raymond Firth says a family is regarded as being incomplete unless the three elements—father, mother, child—are present.[12] Ashley Montagu adds that the union among them must be more or less permanent.[13] But most anthropologists define the family as a group com-

[12] Raymond Firth, *Human Types: an Introduction to Social Anthropology* (New York: The New American Library, Inc., 1958) p. 88.
[13] Ashley Montagu, M. F. A. (Ed.), *Culture: Man's Adaptive Dimension* (New York: Oxford University Press, 1968).

175

Figure 7-5. *The political and economic significance of marriage bonds is demonstrated by this picture taken at the wedding of Princess (now Queen) Elizabeth of England and Prince Philip of Greece.*

posed of a woman and her children and at least one adult male annexed through marriage or blood relationship. The American family is a conjugal one, formed on the basis of marital ties between a husband and a wife. The basic unit of mother, father, and dependent children is referred to as the **nuclear family;** other forms of conjugal families are polygynous and polyandrous families, which may be thought of as aggregates of nuclear families with one spouse in common.

An alternative of the conjugal family is the consanguine family, which consists of women and their brothers, and the dependent offspring of the women. In such societies, men and women get married, but do not live together as husbands and mates. Rather, they spend their lives in the households in which they grew up, with the men "commuting" for sexual activity with their wives. Consanguine families are rare; the classic case is that of the Nayar peoples of India.

The nuclear family

In our society, the nuclear family has become the ideal. It is not considered desirable for young people to live with their parents beyond a certain age, nor is it considered a moral responsibility for a couple to take their aged parents into their home when the old people are no longer able to care for themselves. Additional family members are no longer an economic asset but an expense.

The nuclear family as the sole family form is also found in societies that live in harsh environments, such as the Eskimos. The Eskimo mother and father each have their work to do. In the winter, these little families roam the vast arctic wilderness in search of food. The father hunts and makes shelters. The mother cooks, is responsible for the children, and makes and keeps the clothing in good repair. One of her chores is to chew her husband's boots to soften the leather for the

next day, so that he can resume his search for game. The wife and her children could not survive without the husband, and life for a man is unimaginable without a wife. The Bushmen of the Kalahari Desert and the aborigines of the inhospitable Australian desert also have nuclear families.

Certain parallels can be drawn between the contemporary nuclear family in industrial societies and families living on the bare edge of survival. In both cases, the family is an independent unit that must fend for itself; this creates a strong dependence of individual members on one another. There is little help from outside in the event of emergencies or catastrophes. When their usefulness is at an end, the elderly are cared for only if it is feasible. In the event of death of the mother or father, life becomes precarious for the child. Yet this form of family is well adapted to a life that requires a high degree of mobility. For the Eskimo, this mobility permits the hunt for food; for Americans, it is probably the hunt for jobs and improved social status that requires a mobile form of family unit.

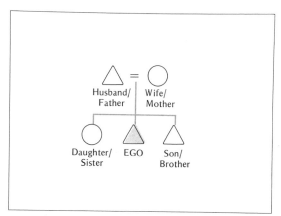

Figure 7-6. *Anthropologists use diagrams of this sort to illustrate the relationships formed through marriage. The diagram always begins with a hypothetical individual, called Ego, and then demonstrates the kinship and marital ties in his immediate family. This particular diagram shows the relationships in a nuclear family such as is found in our own society. Only two generations are represented, but all possible relationships between the various individuals can be determined from the diagram.*

The extended family

The small nuclear family of industrialized societies was evolved from the larger extended farm family, a combination of conjugal and consanguineous families, which might include grandparents, mother and father, unmarried brothers and sisters, perhaps a spinster aunt, and a stray cousin or two. All these people, related by various ties of blood or marriage, lived and worked together.

Horace Miner described such families in his study of French Catholics on the St. Lawrence River in Quebec, Canada, where a unified family effort is necessary and a large family is essential to work the farms.[14] Children and unattached adults were an asset on the farm. The older children left to work their own farms or to find employment in the city and were usually assisted by

[14]Horace Miner, *St. Denis: A French Canadian Parish* (Chicago: The University of Chicago Press, 1939).

the family until they were established. The land was capable of supporting a limited number of people, and even after the sons and daughters moved out of the immediate household, the relationship remained very strong.

The Tanala of Madagascar also formed extended families.[15] When the sons grew up and married, they brought their wives to live in houses close to the parental home. The head of the family was the father, who made the important decisions concerning the agricultural activities of the family. If the sons worked on the outside, they gave their earnings to the father for the purchase of new cattle or for other family needs. The family worked together as a group and dealt with outsiders as a single unit.

[15] E. Adamson Hoebel, *Anthropology: The Study of Man* (New York: McGraw-Hill, 1966) p. 434.

Figure 7-6a. *A variant on the simple nuclear family is the extended family. All the members of this Kentucky family are descended from the couple at the back of the photo.*

The formation of groups ● part **3**

Extended families living together in a single household were the most important social unit among the Zuni Pueblo Indians of New Mexico.[16] Usually, the head of the household was an old woman; her married daughters, their husbands, and their children lived with her. The women of the household owned the land, but it was tilled by the men (usually their husbands). When extra help was needed during the harvest, for example, other male relatives, or friends, or persons designated by local religious organizations, formed work groups and turned the hard work into a party. The women performed household tasks, such as the making of pottery, together.

A different form of the extended family was practiced by the Chukchi people of northeastern Siberia, who lived by herding reindeer.[17] The family consisted of perhaps ten couples of about the same age. The group was formed by the males, who were not related by blood, and lived in separate camps. The marriages of the group were ritualized in a ceremony in which a reindeer was killed, and the males were annointed with the blood. The relationship among the males in the group was stronger than that of true blood relatives. The men of such a family were called "companions in wives" and protected each other in time of need. The wives did not rotate, but were offered to a companion if he was visiting. Occasionally, men might exchange wives. Sharing of women created a strong bond.

It is interesting to note that a form of extended family arrangement is currently being experimented with by young people today who have found the nuclear family inadequate for their needs. Their families are groups of nuclear families who own property in common and live together; hence, it is a form of the extended family. It is further noteworthy that the life-style of these modern families often emphasizes the kind of cooperative family ties to be found in the rural American extended family of old, where this family pattern provided a manpower pool for the many tasks required for economic survival.

[16] Oswalt, op. cit., p. 294.
[17] Ibid., p. 167.

Residence patterns. Where some form of conjugal or extended family is the norm, incest taboos require that at least the husband or wife must move to a new household upon marriage. There are four common patterns of residence that a newly married couple may adopt:

(1) A woman may live with her husband and his father. This is called **patrilocal** residence.
(2) A man may live with his wife and her mother. This is called **matrilocal** residence.
(3) A married couple may have the choice of living with the relatives of the husband or those of the wife. This arrangement is called **ambilocal** or **bilocal** residence.
(4) A married couple may form a household in an independent location. This arrangement is referred to as **neolocal** residence.

Why do different societies practice different patterns of residence? The form of residence seems to be closely related to the nature of the economy.[18] Murdock proposed a direct correlation: matrilocal residence occurs where cooperation among women is crucial for subsistence; patrilocal residence occurs where men are the center of subsistence; and neolocal residence occurs where isolation of the nuclear family alone is emphasized. Ambilocality, on the other hand, allows for greater fluidity of social grouping, so that a population can move about in a way which optimizes the availability of resources and labor. The example of the !Kung Bushmen illustrates the way in which a hunting and gathering group can adjust itself to fluctuating resources.[19] The Bushmen typically live in one place for a few days until they have exhausted all available food resources. They then move as separate family units into camps where relatives with more abundant food resources are to be found. Ambilocality greatly enhances the Bushmen's opportunity to find food. For a people of low population density, ambilocality can be a crucial factor for survival.

[18] George P. Murdock, *Social Structure* (New York: The Macmillan Company, 1949).
[19] Lorna Marshall, "Sharing, Talking and Giving: Relief of Social Tensions among !Kung Bushman," *Africa*, Vol. 31 (1961).

By studying the differences between matrilocal and patrilocal societies, anthropologists have acquired further insight into the reasons that societies display the various patterns of residence. In patrilocal societies, both authority and lines of descent are centered on the male; consequently, males are responsible for and have authority in the communities within which they reside. In matrilocal societies, on the other hand, males retain the authority, but lines of descent are traced through the female. Thus, males live in the community of their mothers and sisters. Because they hold positions of responsibility in the community in which they are born, males cannot move too far away from their maternal communities. Furthermore, warfare is inconvenient in a matrilocal society. The question of residence involves not only economic factors but

Figure 7-7. *Some young Americans have attempted to recreate the extended family with an artificial family in a commune.*

The formation of groups ● part **3**

factors of social cohesion as well. The nuclear family's residence is determined largely by the best interests of society.

Serial marriage

Perhaps the most exotic and bizarre of marriage forms is our own serial marriage. In this form, the man or the woman either marries or lives with a series of partners. The term was used in the recent past by sociologists and anthropologists to describe the marital patterns of West Indians and lower class urban blacks. These black societies were matriarchal. A series of men fathered the children, who remained with the mother. An adult man's loyalties might be to his mother rather than his present wife, and he, too, might bring his children to his mother to care for. Usually, the grandmother was the head of the household (which amounted to a consanguine family); it was she who cared for all the children, while the daughters worked to support the whole group.

Middle class Americans have taken up a variant of this pattern. The children, born out of a series of marriages, remain with the mother. In a society such as ours, in which a major value is the well-being and happiness of the individual, divorce may not necessarily signal social disorganization, but, instead, a liberating of the individual. Serial marriage may be evolving as an alternative to the extreme form of the nuclear family as it exists in the United States.

Divorce

As with marriage, divorce in non-Western societies is a matter of great concern to the families of the couple. Since marriage is primarily not a religious but an economic matter, divorce arrangements can be made for a variety of reasons and with varying degrees of difficulty.

Among the Gusii of Kenya, sterility or impotence were grounds for a divorce. Among the Chenchu of Hyderabad and the Caribou Indians of Canada, divorce was discouraged after children were born, and a couple was usually urged by their families to adjust their differences. A Zuni woman might divorce her husband by placing his belongings outside the door to indicate he was no longer welcome in the household. Divorce was relatively common among the Yahgan, who lived at the southernmost tip of South America, and was considered justified if the husband was considered cruel or failed as a provider.

Divorce in these societies seems familiar and even sensible, considered in the light of our own entangled arrangements. In one way or another, the children are taken care of. An adult unmarried woman is almost unheard of in most non-Western societies; a divorced woman will soon remarry.

Sex roles

Margaret Mead was the first anthropologist to study sex roles in non-Western societies with the purpose of showing that the work, norms, and behavior of men and women is learned, not inherited, and varies from group to group. Other social scientists who have studied the personality and temperament of men and women tend to make the common characterization of women as nurturing, supportive, emotionally dependent, passive, and more verbal; whereas men are depicted as being dominant, competitive, positively sexed, innovative, and stronger. Mead wondered whether such stereotypes were universal.

Dr. Mead studied three tribes in New Guinea: the Arapesh, the Mundugumor, and the Tchambuli. She found the Arapesh men and women were trained to be "cooperative, unaggressive, responsive to the needs and demands of others."[20] Sex was not a powerful driving force for either men or women. The Mundugumor were totally unlike the Arapesh. Both men and women developed as "ruthless, aggressive, positively sexed . . . with the maternal cherishing aspects of the

[20]Margaret Mead, op. cit.

personality at a minimum." In the third tribe, the Tchambuli, she found a genuine reversal of the sex attitudes of our own culture. The woman was a "dominant, impersonal, managing partner," and the man the "less responsible and emotionally dependent" person.

Having carefully observed the different patterns of child-rearing in each of these societies, Dr. Mead concluded that "many, if not all, of the personality traits which we have called masculine or feminine are as lightly linked to sex as are the clothing, the manners, and the form of head-dress that a society at a given period assigns to either sex." This statement still strikes many ears as a radical assertion.

Dr. Mead was interested in the cross-cultural variation in personality and temperament as related to the assigned sex roles. Sex roles are also closely linked to the work that is performed in a society. Men and women perform complementary economic roles within the family unit. There are few tasks which virtually every society assigns to only men or women, as there is a great deal of overlap for most jobs. What is defined as a woman's job in one society may well be classified as a man's job in another. Jo Freeman points

Figure 7-8. *The concept of "women's work" varies from society to society. At left is an Englishwoman at work in a munitions factory; at right is an Ivory Coast woman pounding millet in a wooden mortar.*

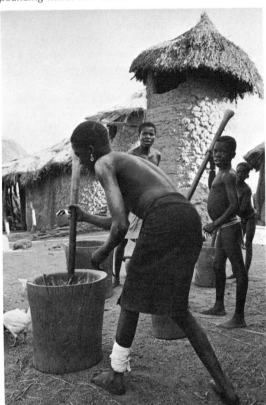

out that in societies in which great physical strength was necessary for survival—where hunting and warfare played an important role—the male, as physically stronger, tended to dominate.[21] But even after the necessity for male strength ceases, the superiority of the male becomes incorporated into the value structure of the society, and maleness continues to confer a higher personal status than does femaleness.

It has been suggested that in modern societies as well the tasks which are assigned to males are defined as more honorific. If so, this would suggest that a division of labor based on sex in a family or society comes close to racial or caste distinction. The low ranking class, or sex, is kept from doing certain types of prestigious work. The corollary to this is that jobs that women do automatically are ranked as less important. But the sexual division of labor, of course, is an ancient primate trait; it remains to be seen whether there is any adaptive value in cultural regulations that attempt to counteract this trait.

[21] Jo Freeman, "Growing up Girlish," *Transaction,* Vol. 8 (Nov./Dec. 1970).

Original study

NAMBIKWARA FAMILY LIFE

The Nambikwara have few children; childless couples are not uncommon, though one or two children constitute the norm, and it is quite exceptional for there to be more than three in one family. Sexual relations between parents are forbidden while their child remains unweaned: often, that is to say, until it is three years old. The mother carries her child astraddle on her thigh, and keeps it in place with a broad shoulder-strap of cotton or bark; as she also has to carry a large basket on her back, one child is clearly her maximum load. Living, as they do, a nomadic life in a very poor environment, the natives have to be very careful; and the women do not hesitate to resort to abortion of one kind or another—medicinal plants, or some mechanical device—in case of need.

They both feel and show, none the less, the liveliest affection for their children; and this affection is returned. Sometimes, however, this is masked by extreme nervousness; instability takes its toll. A little boy, for instance, is suffering from indigestion; between headache and vomiting he spends half his time groaning aloud and the other half in sleep. Nobody pays the slightest attention to him and he is left completely alone all day. But when evening comes his mother comes across to him, tenderly picks off all his lice as he falls asleep, signs to the others not to come near, and makes for him a kind of cradle with her arms.

Or, it may be, a young mother is playing with her baby. Playfully she gives him slap after little slap on the back; he loves it, and to make him laugh the louder she slaps harder and harder till he bursts into tears; then she stops and consoles him. . . .

When they are crossed, children often hit out at their mother, and their mother does nothing to stop it. The children are not punished, and I never saw one of them beaten—not even in pantomime—except by way of a tease. Sometimes a child cries because he's hurt himself, because he's hungry, because he's had a quarrel, or because he doesn't want to have his fleas picked off—but this last is rare: delousing seems to be as much fun for the patient as for the operator, and it is prized as a mark of interest and affection. A child—or husband—who feels in need of it will lay his head on the woman's knees, offering first one side and then the other. She will then part his hair, ridge by ridge, and peer through. A louse, once caught, is instantly eaten. Any child who cries during the proceedings is consoled by an older child or a member of his family.

And so there's a delightful gaiety in the spectacle of a mother with her child. Sometimes she dangles an object in front of him through the straw walls of their hut and whips it away just as he reaches out for it: "There—you missed it! Grab it at the front—or the back!" Or else she takes up the child and with great shouts of laughter threatens to throw him down to the ground. . . .

There's something correspondingly uneasy and exacting about the loving kindness with which the children surround their mother. They want to be quite sure that she gets her fair share of the spoils of the hunt. The child has lived very close to its mother. When they move camp she carries the child until it can walk; later, it hurries along at her side. It stays with her in their camp, or

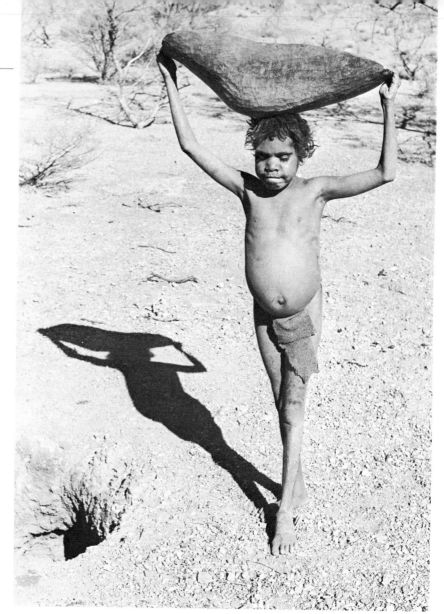

Figure 7-9. *In all cultures, children learn the tasks allotted to their sex through early practice.*

their village, while its father goes hunting. Eventually, however, certain distinctions of sex may be remarked. A father is more interested in his son than in his daughter, because his son has to be taught the techniques of manhood; and the same is true of mother and daughter. But the relations between father and children are marked by tenderness and solicitude; a father will take his child for a walk on his shoulder and carve for him weapons appropriate to his tiny arm.

It's also the father's duty to tell his children the traditional legends of the tribe—transposing them down, of course, in terms acceptable to the infant mind: "Everyone was dead! No one left! Not one man! Nothing!" Thus begins the South American children's version of the Flood in which all humanity was once engulfed.

In cases of polygamy a special relationship exists between the children of the first union and their youthful stepmothers: a free-and-easy comradeship which is extended to all the other girls in the group. . . .

Another special relationship exists between those children whose degree of cousinage is such that they are allowed to call one another "Husband" and "Wife." Sometimes they behave like a real married couple and, at nightfall, they leave the family circle, take a few warm logs into a corner of the camp, and light a fire. After which they "set up house" and demonstrate their affections, in so far as they can, just as their elders do; the grown-ups glance their way in amusement.

Source:
Claude Lévi-Strauss, *Tristes Tropiques*. Newly translated by John and Doreen Weightman. Translated from the French *Tristes Tropiques* © 1955 by Librairie Plon. English translation © 1973 by Jonathan Cape Limited. Reprinted by permission of Atheneum Publishers, New York.

Summary

1.
There is considerable disagreement among anthropologists as to the functions of the family. One of its functions is to control sexual behavior. But it is fairly safe to say that the most basic function of the family is the nurturance of children to ensure the survival of the society. Studies of primate and human babies have revealed that a baby's physical nearness to his mother and constant affection and interaction with her are essential for his normal emotional development. Lack of human contact and response and some stimulation from the environment may lead to a baby's death. Parental care is essential for a baby's development.

2.
Everywhere societies have behavioral norms controlling sexual relations. In our society, many people marry to ensure a partner for sexual relations. By definition, marriage is a form of contract whereby a person establishes a claim to the right of sexual access with another person. But marriage is not a prerequisite to family life; there can be families without marriage, as among the Nayars of India.

3.
In most non-Western societies, economic considerations strongly motivate an individual to marry. The family arranges marriages in societies in which it is the most powerful social institution. Marriage serves to bind two families as allies. The family serves to supply a society with new members, ensuring its survival.

4.
In all known societies, sexual relations are prohibited between parent and child and usually between brother and sister. No one has advanced a convincing explanation of the incest taboo. Endogamy is marriage within a group of related individuals; exogamy is marriage outside the group. If the group is limited to the immediate family, all societies can be said to practice exogamy. The arrangement whereby an individual chooses his marriage partner is rare. The levirate provides that a widow marry her husband's brother; the sororate provides that a widower marry his wife's sister. Monogamy is the taking of a single spouse. It is more common than polygyny, in which a man takes two or more wives, and polyandry, in which a woman takes two or more husbands. Polygyny and polyandry are uncommon, primarily for economic reasons.

5.
Most anthropologists define a family as a group composed of a woman and her children and the relatives annexed through marriage or consanguinity. The basic unit of mother and/or father and their children is called the nuclear family. The nuclear family follows four basic residence patterns: patrilocal, matrilocal, ambilocal, and neolocal. Residence patterns seem closely related to the nature of a society's economy.

6.
The industrial society evolved the small nuclear family from the larger extended family. An extended family is a combination of conjugal and consanguineous families. All of an extended family's members might not be related by blood or marriage, but all live and work together. The joint family is a kind of extended family.

Suggested readings

Fox, Robin *Kinship and Marriage in an Anthropological Perspective*. New York: Penguin, 1968.
> Professor Fox starts his argument with the universal biological bond between mother and child and imagines a process in which the husband intrudes into the basic group.

Goode, William J. *World Revolution and Family Pattern*. Glencoe, Illinois: Free Press, 1963.
> Important changes in family patterns that have occured during the twentieth century in Japan, China, India, the West, sub-Saharan Africa, and the Arab countries are described and interpreted in an effort to relate the changes to transformations in other social processes, such as industrialization, social change, class stratifications.

Goodenough, Ward Hunt *Description and Comparison in Cultural Anthropology*. Chicago: Aldine, 1970.
> The book illustrates the difficulties anthropologists confront in describing and comparing social organization cross-culturally. The author examines marriage and family, kindred and clan, sibling and cousin, in relationship to social structure.

Goody, John *Comparative Studies in Kinship*. Palo Alto, California: Stanford University Press, 1969.
> Kinship and marriage are discussed in a cross-cultural context. There is a classification of double-descent, inheritance, and social change. Professor Goody relies heavily on empirical and statistical data.

Mair, Lucy *Marriage*. New York: Penguin, 1972.
> Dr. Mair traces the evolution of marriage and such alternative relationships as surrogates and protectors. Commenting upon marriage as an institution and drawing her examples from primitive cultures, Dr. Mair deals with the function, rules, symbolic rituals, and economic factors of marriage. She also cites the inferior status of women and discusses the self-determining behavior of "serious free women" as an important factor in social change.

Needham, Rodney, ed. *Rethinking Kinship and Marriage*. London: Tavistock, 1972.
> This collection of essays is concerned with a definition of kinship and the marriage procedure. It deals cross-culturally with the practices and rituals, and the relationship of marriage to the entire social structure. Contributors include Edmund Leach, Francis Korn, David McKnight.

Stephens, William N. *The Family in Cross-Cultural Perspective*. New York: Holt, Rinehart and Winston, 1963.
> This book describes the institution of the family in different societies. It reports on a wide range of topics, including plural and arranged marriage, kin groups, adultery, roles of wife and husband, and child-rearing.

Kinship
and descent

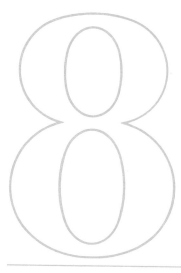

Human social groups have been classified in many different ways according to the function they perform in society; the family is one such social group. It is the chief organizational principle underlying every society—undoubtedly the primary human social group. The structural principle of the family may be further extended until it links every individual in a given society, placing all within a larger group of kinsmen called the kin group.

In small-scale or nonindustrial societies consisting typically of farmers, nomadic hunters, or pastoralists, a formal political system with administrative machinery and law courts does not usually exist. These societies lack the traditional chief to make and enforce laws, keep the peace, and perform other regulatory societal functions. Instead, the kinship system—the complex form of social organization which relates kinsmen and fulfills individual social and personal needs—is the organizing principle of society.

The importance of the kinship system in a non-Western society may be illustrated by the Ifugao of the Philippines. Among the Ifugao, the kin group consists of the descendants of an individual's four pairs of great-grandparents. It may include as many as 2,000 persons. In this case, prac-

tically the entire village is related in one way or another. In such a society, where the net of kinship, social, and political ties is very tight, it is extremely important that the individual know the exact nature of his relationship to each of his relatives—that he know, for example, who has the strongest claim on his loyalties, and to whom he may turn in time of need. This sorting out process is achieved through the society's kinship system, which lets an individual know exactly how he is related to others and what he can thus expect of them, and they of him. The kinship system structures the obligations and interests of its members: it dictates sharing economic and religious undertakings, provides psychological support in time of crisis, and legal help and defense when required. Among the Ila, a cattle-breeding people of Zambia studied by A. Tuden, for example, one's descent determines his rights in the use of farmland, his share in the distribution of grain and other goods, his place in the work force, and his treatment in disputes and quarrels.

An extreme example of the importance of the kinship system is found among the Jivaro Indians of South America. Among the Jivaro, a man's knowledge of his kin may be a matter of life and death. When an individual visits another tribe of

Jivaro, his host may casually question the visitor about his genealogy, attempting to ascertain whether the visitor belongs to a friendly or a hostile kin group. If the host determines the visitor is related to inimical kin, he may poison his beer or food, or ambush him when he leaves the village. Not surprisingly, Jivaro fathers drill their youngest sons in their genealogy for an hour before dawn each day.

Kinship studies also show that parts of a culture, such as political and economical spheres, are related to one another. For example, as societies grow larger, more mobile and dispersed, the importance of the kinship system as a social regulatory agency decreases, to be increasingly assumed by the state. Thus, in large-scale industrialized societies, such as our own, occupational specialization and complex systems of economic exchange are the rule, and business ceases to be confined to kinsfolk. Instead, relations with relative strangers—employer, doctor, merchant, teacher—become more important.

Rules of descent

The rules governing kinship and relationship among the members of a given society are known as rules of descent. Rules of descent arise because many societies must deal with problems which cannot be handled even by the largest of extended families. For example, it may be necessary for the members of one local group to be able to claim support and protection from individuals in another. Some way to share rights in means of production, such as farmland, is also essential. By application of a rule of descent, sets of kin are identified which can deal with such problems. Each individual can then trace a chain of parent-child links back to a common ancestor (who may be real or fictive) and, by so doing, establish his place in a descent group to which he has certain obligations and in which he has clearly defined rights and privileges.

To operate most efficiently, membership in a

Figure 8-1. *The society of the Jivaro, a South American tribe, illustrates an extreme dependence on kinship as a means of organization. The patrilineal family group, living under one roof, is the only existing social unit, except in times of war.*

descent group ought to be clearly defined. Otherwise, membership overlaps and it is not always clear where one's primary loyalty belongs. The most common determinant of kinship organization is sex. Instead of tracing membership back to the common ancestor, sometimes through men and sometimes through women, one does it exclusively through one sex. In this way, each individual is automatically assigned to his or her mother's or father's group, and that group only.

Unilineal descent

Unilineal descent (sometimes called unisexual or unilateral descent) establishes kinship exclusively through the male or the female line. In non-Western societies, unilineal descent groups are the most common form. The individual is assigned at birth to membership in a specific consanguineous—related by blood—kin group which may trace descent either **matrilineally,** through the female line, or **patrilineally,** through the male line. In patrilineal societies the males are far more important than the females, for it is they who are considered to be responsible for the perpetuation of the group. In matrilineal societies, the responsibility falls on the female members of the group.

There seems to be a close relationship between the descent system and the economy of a society. Generally, patrilineal descent predominates where the man is the breadwinner, as among pastoralists and full-time agriculturists. Matrilineal descent is important mainly among semi-agriculturists with societies in which female labor is a prime factor. Numerous matrilineal societies are found in South Asia, which may be a cradle of primitive agriculture in the Old World. Matrilineal systems exist in India, Ceylon, Indonesia, Sumatra, Tibet, South China, and many Indonesian islands.

It is now recognized that in all societies, the kin of both mother and father are important components of the social structure. In some societies, the relationship is quite clear; the membership in the descent group is traced through the mother, whereas succession to chieftainship is traced through the father's line. However, in most societies where unilineal descent prevails, there is a general overlapping of social responsibilities.

Patrilineal descent and organization. Patrilineal descent (sometimes called agnatic, or male, descent) is the more widespread of the two basic systems of unilineal descent. The male members of a patrilineage trace through the males their descent from a common ancestor. Ego and his sister belong to the descent group of their father's father, their father, their father's siblings, and their father's brother's children. Ego's son and daughter also trace their descent back through the male line to their common ancestor. In the typical patrilineal group, the power for training the children rests with the father or his elder brother. A female belongs to the same descent group as her father and his brothers, but her children cannot trace their descent through them. Ego's paternal aunt's children, for example, trace their descent through the patrilineal group of her husband.

The Tikopia: A typical patrilineal society. Among the Tikopia, a people of the western Pacific islands of Polynesia, studied extensively by anthropologist Raymond Firth, the patrilineal system prevails. The family, consisting of the father, mother, children, and usually the father's sister (if unmarried), lives near the house of the father's father. Residence, therefore, is patrilocal. As in most patrilineal societies, the father's brother and his sons exert a strong influence in the life of the father's male children. The children look upon their paternal uncle as a second father and behave toward him accordingly. The father's sister has a unique position towards her brother's children. She is looked upon as a secondary mother, acting as nurse, protector, and mentor; her authority and ritual powers are akin to those of her brother.

Every individual Tikopian family belongs to a larger group known as a *paito* (which means

Figure 8-2. *This diagram shows how patrilineal descent is traced. Only the individuals symbolized by a colored circle or triangle are in the same descent group as Ego. The abbreviation F stands for father, B for brother, H for husband, S for son, Si for sister, D for daughter and Wi for wife.*

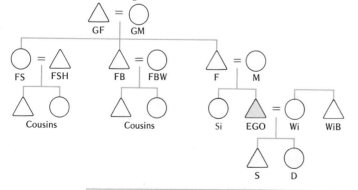

"house"). Each *paito* is composed of a number of families, the core members of which trace their descent through the male line to a common ancestor. The head of the *paito* is the senior living male descendant of this ancestor. A number of *paitos* combine to form the *kainana*, or clan, the largest social group on the island.

The position of an individual within the *paito* determines his social status. The kind of instruction he will receive as a child and his rights to the produce of the land depend on this. As an adult he will be entitled to a share in the land and other property, a house-site, and a given name when he marries. Membership in his family *paito* also entitles him to economic and ritual assistance when required, as well as use of religious formulae and certain prerogatives when he appeals to his principal ancestral deities. Moreover, the *paito* determines the individual's rank in the *kainana*.

The patrilineal system reaches throughout Tikopian social relations and determines legal matters of succession and inheritance. Succession to the position of *paito* head is solely in the male line; under no circumstances can a person belong to the *paito* of the mother rather than that of his father. On the death of an elder or chief, the kin group goes to the farthest limits of male descent and explores the collateral lines to the utmost to find an heir. The immediate sister's son is never even considered; he is excluded because his mother married into another patrilineage.

Each *paito* has its own economic organization. Its members are responsible for the production and consumption of food, the exchange of property, or ownership. Political activities of the *paito* involve the transmission of cultural goods, tradition, rank, and property as well as judicial matters such as the settling of disputes, both internal and external. The *paito* meets also on social and religious occasions, such as marriages, births, deaths, and initiation ceremonies. The patrilineal kinship group is indeed the backbone of Tikopian society.

Matrilineal descent and organization. In all respects but one, matrilineal descent is the exact

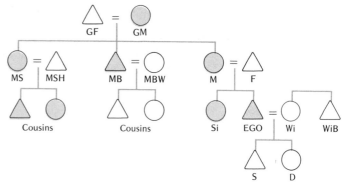

Figure 8-3. *This diagram, which traces descent through the matrilineal line, can be compared with Figure 8-2, showing patrilineal descent. The two patterns are virtually mirror images. Note that Ego cannot transmit his own descent.*

opposite of patrilineal descent: descent is reckoned through the female line and residence is matrilocal. The group resulting from the union of several matrilineages is the matriclan.

The matrilineal pattern differs from the patrilineal in that descent does not confer authority. Although descent passes through the female line, females do not exercise authority in the kin group; the males do. Apparently, the adaptive purpose of the matrilineal system is to provide continuous female solidarity within the female work group. Matrilineal systems are usually found in farming societies in which women perform much of the productive work. Because the food provided by the women is important to the subsistence of the society, matrilineal residence and descent prevail.

In the matrilineal system, Ego and his sister belong to the descent group of the mother's mother, the mother, the mother's siblings, and the mother's sister's children. Males belong to the same descent group as their mother and sister, but their children cannot trace their descent through them. For example, the children of Ego's maternal uncle are considered members of his wife's matrilineage. Similarly Ego's own children belong to his wife's, but not his, descent group.

The matrilineal system has one serious disadvantage: it is the source of a great deal of family tension and creates weak ties between husband and wife. The wife's brother, and not the husband-father, distributes goods, organizes work, settles disputes, administers inheritance and succession rules, and supervises rituals. The husband has legal authority not in his own household but in that of his sister. He is strongly tied to his natal household even though he and his wife may live elsewhere. Thus, brother-sister bonds are strengthened at the expense of husband-wife bonds. Moreover, family tension further arises from the fact that the father's property and status are not inherited by his own son but by his sister's son. It is not surprising that divorce, even though frowned upon, is often common in matrilineal societies.

Matrilineal organization among the Ashanti.
An example of a matrilineal system is found among the Ashanti, a horticultural people of Ghana. Among the Ashanti, a boy lives with his parents until he reaches adult status; then he moves to the house of his mother's brother, where his legal claims to a livelihood rest. After marriage, his wife lives with her mother and he lives with his father. In later years, the couple may establish their own household, usually on land that belongs to the wife's matrilineage.

In Ashanti society, the male head, chosen by consensus of both sexes in the lineage, governs the matrilineage. He may be assisted by a senior woman, called the Queen Mother, who oversees the conduct of the women in the lineage, administers the ritual matters of the females, and helps arbitrate family quarrels.

The male leader, with the further assistance of a kind of council of senior males, supervises the social, religious, and economic undertakings of the lineage. He also allocates the right to use property owned by the matrilineage, arbitrates quarrels, and approves all marriages, divorces, and remarriages. The male head also supervises funerals, enforces inheritance rules, and represents the matrilineage in its relations with other groups in the society.

Each segment of an Ashanti matrilineage is composed of the matrilineal descendants of an ancestress, and inheritance and mutual aid are generally restricted to this group, which owns its own land and other property. There is no legally recognized head within the segment, but the mother's brother is generally accepted as its voice or leader. The mother's brother, called the "house father," performs rituals for the family ancestors, arbitrates household disputes, and administers family property. One of the senior males who supervises the lineage's property is regarded as the leader of the entire lineage. Each lineage, in turn, belongs to one of the eight Ashanti clans.

In most matrilineal societies, the mother's brother has extensive legal authority over his nephews and nieces. He may bargain away or sell his nephews and nieces, he can deny them permission to marry, and, once they are married, he can deny them divorce should they seek it. Moreover, the children's father has no authority over them, nor can he transmit to them status or property. Among the Ashanti, however, the father's role in the family limits the influence of the mother's brother. The father-son relationship is very affectionate, and Ashanti fathers generally love their own sons more than the sons of their sisters. Thus, the role of the sister's brother, usually strong in a matrilineal society, is weak among the Ashanti.

Double descent

Double descent, or double unilineal descent, whereby descent is reckoned both patrilineally and matrilineally, is very rare. In this system, descent is matrilineal for some purposes and patrilineal for others. Generally, where double descent is reckoned, each lineage takes corporate action in different spheres of society.

For example, among the Yakö of eastern Nigeria, property is divided between patrilineal line possessions and matrilineal line possessions. The patrilineage owns perpetual productive resources, such as land, whereas the matrilineage owns consumable property, such as livestock. The legally weaker matrilineal line is somewhat more important in religious matters than the patrilineal line. Because of the existence of the double descent rule, a Yakö individual might inherit grazing lands from the father's patrilineal group and certain ritual privileges from the mother's matrilineal line.

Bilateral descent and the kindred

Bilateral descent, a characteristic of Western society, relates a person to other close relatives through both sexes; in other words, the individual traces descent through both parents simultaneously. Theoretically, all relatives on both the mother's and father's sides of the family are his relatives. Thus, this principle relates an individual lineally to all eight great-grandparents and laterally to all third and fourth cousins. Since such a huge group is too big to be socially practical, the group is usually reduced to a small circle of paternal and maternal relatives, called the kindred. The kindred may be defined as a group of people closely related to one individual through both parents. Unlike unilineal descent groups, the kindred is laterally rather than lineally organized. That is, Ego, or the focal person from whom the degree of each relationship is reckoned, is the center of the group. We are all familiar with the kindred; we simply call them "relatives." It includes the relatives on both sides of the family whom we see on social occasions, at family reunions, and at funerals. Most of us can identify the members of our kindred up to second cousins and grandparents. In our society, the limits of the kindred are variable and indefinite; no one is ever really certain which relatives to invite to a social function and which to exclude. The kindred is thus amorphous and vague, lacking the distinctiveness of the unilineal descent group. (It is also temporary, lasting only as long as the function it has been assembled to attend.)

The kindred possesses one feature which sets it apart from all other descent groups: because of its bilateral structure, a kindred is never the same for any two persons except siblings (brothers and sisters). Thus, no two people (except siblings) belong to the same descent group. Ego's father's kindred, for example, range lineally to the father's grandparents and laterally to cousins too distant for ego to know; the same is true of his mother, and his maternal and paternal aunts and uncles. Thus, the kindred is not composed of people with an ancestor in common, but of people with a relative in common—Ego.

The Ego: Center of the kindred. Kindreds are referred to as "ego-centered" or "ego-focussed" groups because Ego, or the person viewing the group, is at its center. Even in relation to Ego, the membership of the group is constantly changing as Ego moves through life. When he is young, it consists of his parents, siblings, and other close consanguineous relatives, most of whom are usually older than he is. As Ego grows older and has children, the composition of his kindred changes; it consists of his descendants and the remaining relatives of his own generation. Thus, because of its vagueness, temporary nature, and changeable-

Figure 8-4. *Here the kinship pattern of the kindred is illustrated. These people are related not to a common ancestor but to a common relative, Ego. The squares represent persons of either sex; degree of relationship is not sexually determined.*

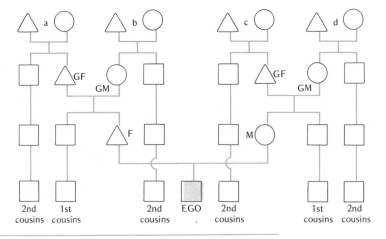

The formation of groups ● part **3**

ness, the kindred is a weaker social unit than other descent groups. For example, it cannot function as a group except in relation to Ego. Unlike other descent groups, it is not a self-perpetuating group—it ceases with Ego's death. It has no constant leader, nor can it hold, administer, or pass on property. In most cases, it cannot organize work, nor can it administer justice or assign status. In non-Western societies, for example, headhunting and trading parties are composed of kindred groups. The group is assembled, goes on the hunt, shares the spoils, then disbands. Thus, kindreds assemble only for a specific purpose.

Because of its shortcomings, the non-Western bilateral group usually exists side by side with more useful unilineal descent groups. Kindreds are found mostly in complex societies, such as our own, where mobility weakens contact with relatives. Individuality is emphasized in complex societies, and a strong kinship system is not as important as it is among non-Western peoples.

Cognatic descent

Unilineal descent provides an easy way of restricting descent group membership, so as to avoid problems of divided loyalty and the like. A number of societies, many of them in the Pacific and Southeast Asia, accomplish the same thing in other ways, though perhaps not quite so neatly. The resultant descent groups are known as non-unilineal, or cognatic, descent groups. Cognatic descent provides a measure of flexibility not normally found under unilineal descent; each individual has the option of affiliating with either the mother's or the father's descent group.

Cognatic descent among the Iban.
An example of a cognatic society is found among the Iban of the Balek region of Sarawak, studied by J. D. Freeman. The Iban descent group is called the *bilek*. The husband and wife, when newly married, may affiliate with the *bilek* of either set of parents, depending on their choice of residence.

Thus, the land rights, ritual obligations, and other activities controlled by the *bilek* are decided at marriage. A couple that affiliates with one *bilek* relinquishes its claim on the other; there can be no overlapping membership. Their children can belong only to the *bilek* of their parents, and like the parents, when the children marry, they must decide with which *bilek* they will live. The distinctive trait of the cognatic descent group is the possibility of changing one's permanent affiliation by changing one's residence. A person can decide to his own advantage whether or not he will honor his original group obligation.

Among the Iban, an individual may belong at any one time to only one *bilek;* thus, Iban society is divided into discrete and separate groups of kin. However, other cognatic societies, such as the Samoans of the South Pacific and the Bella Coola and the southern branch of the Kwakiutl of the Pacific Northwest Coast, allow overlapping membership in a number of descent groups. As George Murdock notes, too great a range of individual choice interferes with the orderly functioning of any kin-oriented society:

> An individual's plural membership almost inevitably becomes segregated into one primary membership, which is strongly activated by residence, and one or more secondary memberships in which participation is only partial or occasional.[1]

Generally, cognatic groups appear to be closer in structure to unilineal descent groups than they are to bilateral kindred groups.

Types of descent groups

In many parts of the world, a descent group is more than just a group of relatives providing warmth and a sense of belonging; it may be a

[1]George P. Murdock, "Cognatic Forms of Social Organization," in G. P. Murdock (ed.), *Social Stratification in Southeast Asia,* (Chicago: Quadrangle Books, 1960) p. 11.

tightly organized working unit providing security and services in the course of what is often a difficult, uncertain life. The tasks performed by descent groups are manifold. One of their most important social functions is generally the regulation of marriage by establishing which person a member of the group may marry. Since unilineal descent groups are usually exogamous, members of the group must look beyond its membership for eligible mates. In Truk society, in the western Pacific, for example, the largest group is the matriclan; therefore, a person cannot marry a member of his matrilineage or matriclan. Instead, he must go outside his descent group to seek a partner.

The descent group also acts as an economic unit providing mutual aid to its members; it may support the aged and infirm or help in case of marriage or death. But the unity of the descent group is perhaps most apparent on a political level, especially in time of war. The descent group also acts as a repository of religious traditions. Ancestor worship, for example, is a powerful force acting to reinforce group solidarity.

Lineage

A **lineage** is a corporate descent group composed of consanguineous kin who claim descent from a common ancestor and who are able to trace descent genealogically through known links. The term is usually employed where some form of unilineal descent is the rule, but there are similar cognatic groups.

The lineage is ancestor-centered; membership in the group is recognized only if relationship to a common ancestor can be traced and proven. In many societies, an individual has no legal or political status except as a member of the lineage. Since "citizenship" is derived from lineage membership and legal status depends on it, political and religious power are thus derived from it as well. Important religious and magical powers, such as those associated with the cults of gods and ancestors, may also be bound to the lineage.

Figure 8-5. *These photos show modern versions of the kindred. The top photo is a French family attending a wedding of one of its members; the bottom photo shows members of the family of Magnus McDonald in Marion, Illinois, enjoying their annual family reunion.*

The formation of groups ● part **3**

The lineage, like General Motors or Polaroid, is a corporate group, because it continues after the death of members as new members are continually being born into it. This perpetual existence enables a lineage to take corporate actions such as owning property, organizing productive activities, distributing goods and manpower, assigning status, and regulating relations with other groups. Thus, the lineage is a strong, effective base of social organization.

Clan

A second type of descent group is the **clan.** The term clan, and its close relative, the term **sib,** have been used differently by different anthropologists, and a certain amount of confusion exists about their meaning. The clan (or sib) will here be defined as a noncorporate descent group in which each member assumes descent from a common ancestor (who may be real or fictive) but is unable to trace definite genealogical links back to the ancestor. A clan differs from a lineage in two respects: a clan cannot trace its descent links with certainty and it lacks the residential unity that tends to be characteristic of the lineage. As in the lineage, descent may be traced through either the male or female line exclusively.

The clan, unlike the lineage, does not usually hold property corporately. Rather, it acts more as a unit for ceremonial matters, assembles on certain occasions, and has a recognized head or leader. Moreover, clans often develop from splitting of lineages that have grown too large. Clans, like lineages, are usually exogamous.

Clans, lacking the residential unity of lineages, depend on symbols—of animals, plants, natural forces, and objects—to provide members with solidarity and a ready means of identification. These symbols, called **totems,** are often associated with the clan's mythical origin and provide clan members with a means of reinforcing the awareness of their common descent. The word "totem" comes from the Ojibwa American Indian word *ototeman,* meaning "he is a relative of mine."

Totemism has been defined by A. R. Radcliffe-Brown as a set of "customs and beliefs by which there is set up a special system of relations between the society and the plants, animals, and other natural objects that are important in the social life."[2] Creek Indian matriclans bear such totemic names as Alligator, Arrow, Bird, Corn, Deer, Red Paint, Spanish Moss, and Wind.

Totemism is a changing concept that varies from clan to clan. Evidence of totemism may even be found in our own society where baseball and football teams are given the names of such powerful wild animals as Bears, Tigers, and Wildcats. Totemism extends to the Democratic Party's donkey and the Republican Party's elephant, to the Elks, the Lions, and other fraternal and social organizations. Our animal emblems, however, do not involve the same notions of descent, nor are they associated with the various ritual observances associated with clan totems.

Phratries and moieties

A third type of descent group is the phratry or the moiety. A **phratry** is a unilineal descent group composed of two or more clans who are supposedly related, though they may not be. Like individuals of the clan, members of the phratry are unable to trace accurately their descent links to a common ancestor, though they believe such an ancestor exists.

If the entire society is divided into two and only two major descent groups, be they equivalent to clans or phratries, each group is called a **moiety** (after the French word for "half"). Members of the moiety believe themselves to share a common ancestor but are unable to prove it through definite biological links. As a rule, the feeling of kinship among members of lineages and clans is stronger than that felt among members of phratries and moieties. This may be due to the larger size of the latter groups.

[2]A. R. Radcliffe-Brown, "Social Organization of Australian Tribes." *Oceania Monographs,* No. 1. (Melbourne: Macmillan, 1931) p. 29.

Rise of the cognatic descent group

It appears that ambilocality, ecology, and the rise of cognatic descent groups are interrelated. Cognatic descent groups are often associated with ambilocality, in which the newlywed couple may live with either the wife's kinsmen or the husband's kinsmen. In the case of ambilocal families, two different relationships between cognatic descent groups and ecology have been pointed out in an effort to account for the rise of the cognatic group. Cognatic groups may have arisen as a result of pressure from overcrowding. An excellent example of this relationship is found on the Gilbert Islands of Micronesia. The cognatic extended family on the islands is the corporate landholding unit related to other social units through a series of cognatic kin ties and supported by ambilocal residence. This unit held title to certain garden plots which it cultivated; when the family cultivating a particular plot grew too large to share in the profits derived from the plot, the entire family, or some members, would leave the corporate unit to join similar units with which it had kin ties.

Another theory regarding the emergence of cognatic descent groups is that they act as a means of increasing populations where certain important resources are found in abundance. For example, anthropologist M. J. Harner found that among the Indians of the Northwest Pacific Coast, important resources such as salmon and sea mammals occurred in vast numbers, but only sporadically. The ambilocal residence pattern of the Indians' cognatic descent group allowed populations to adjust to the uncertainties of this situation by changing residences, so that these food sources could be exploited wherever and whenever they appeared.

Evolution of the descent group

Just as different types of families occur in different societies, so do different kinds of descent systems. Descent groups, for example, do not ap-

Figure 8-6. These posts stand by the house of a Kwakiutl man; he believes his ancestors speak through the totem to advise him.

pear at all in simple hunting and gathering societies, where marriage acts as the social mechanism for integrating individuals within the society. In horticultural, pastoral, or many intensive agricultural societies, however, the descent group provides the structural framework upon which the fabric of the society rests.

Lewis Morgan and other nineteenth century anthropologists believed that the descent group progressed in an evolutionary manner from promiscuity to matrilineal to patrilineal organization. In so-called promiscuous societies, paternity was never certain and descent could be traced only through the mother; hence the emergence of the matrilineal group. The accumulation of wealth, in the form of land and other valuable material possessions, was responsible for the rise of the patrilineal system, for wealth resided in the males. A means of passing wealth from male to male down the generations was required. Finally, civilization, with its complex patterns of individuality, specialization of labor, and greater mobility, brought with it the consideration of both paternal and maternal descent rules. This combination resulted in the bilineal or bilateral kinship system of modern Western civilization.

Morgan's evolutionary sequence was declared invalid by George Murdock, who found that the simplest of arctic hunter-gatherers practiced bilateral descent. Descent rules, according to Murdock, bore no relation to the level of technological or social development. Most scholars agree that Morgan's evolutionary thesis is incorrect. However, some relation between a society's subsistence pattern and its descent system does exist.

Kinship terminology

The ways in which kinship relationships are defined in any society are subject to elaborate cultural rules. Each society has a particular way of assigning the individual to his place in the descent group; a set of terms designates the individual's position within the groups to which he belongs. These labels are called kinship terms, and the whole classificatory system is called the system of kinship terminology.

There are a number of factors at work in each system of kinship terminology that help differentiate one kin from another. These factors may be sex, generational differences, or genealogical differences. In the various kinship terminology systems, any one of these factors may be emphasized at the expense of others. But regardless of the factors emphasized, all kinship terminologies accomplish two important tasks. First, they group particular kinds of persons into single specific categories; secondly, they separate different kinds of persons into distinct categories. Generally, two or more kin are merged under the same term when similarity of status exists between the individuals. These similarities are then emphasized by the application of one term to both individuals.

Six different systems of kinship terminology result from the application of the above principles: the Hawaiian, Eskimo, Iroquois, Omaha, Crow, and Sudanese systems. Each of these six systems can be identified according to the way cousins are classified.

Hawaiian system

The Hawaiian system of kinship terminology, practiced mainly in Hawaii and other Malayo-Polynesian speaking areas, is the least complex system, in that it uses the least number of terms. The Hawaiian system is also called the generational system, since all relatives of the same generation and sex are referred to by the same term. For example, in one's father's generation, one's father, his brother, and one's mother's brother are all referred to by the single term "father." Similarly, one's mother, her sister, and one's father's sister are all called "mother." In Ego's generation, male and female cousins are distinguished by sex and are equated with his brother and sister.

The Hawaiian system reflects the absence of a strong unilineal descent group and is usually associated with cognatic descent. Because cognatic descent rules trace descent through both sides of the family, and members on both father's and mother's side of the family are looked upon as being more or less equal, a certain degree of similarity is created among the father's and the mother's siblings. Thus, they are all simultaneously recognized as being similar relations and are merged together under a single term. In like manner, the children of the mother's and father's siblings are considered related to oneself in the same way as one's brother and sister are.

Eskimo system

The Eskimo system of kinship terminology, comparatively rare among all the systems of the world, is the system used by Anglo-American cultures. It is also used by a number of hunting and gathering peoples. The Eskimo system, or lineal system, of terminology emphasizes the nuclear family by specifically identifying mother, father, brother, and sister, while merging together all other relatives such as maternal and paternal aunts, uncles, and cousins, without differentiating among them. For example, one's father is distinguished from his father's brother (uncle); but one's father's brother is not distinguished from his mother's brother (who is also called uncle). In addition, one calls all the sons and daughters of his aunts and uncles "cousin," without distinguishing their sex or the side of the family to which they belong.

Unlike other descent terminologies, the Eskimo system provides separate and distinct terms for each member of the nuclear family. Perhaps this is because the Eskimo system is generally found in societies where the dominant kin group is the bilateral kindred, in which only the closest members of the family are important. This is especially true of our society, in which the family is independent, living apart from, and not directly involved with, other kin except on ceremonial occasions. Thus, we distinguish between our closest kin (our parents and our siblings) but use the same terms (aunt, uncle, cousin) for other members on both sides of the family.

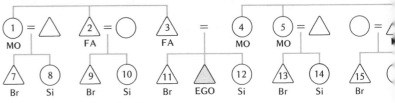

Figure 8-7. *The Hawaiian Kinship system is shown in the diagram above. The men numbered 2, 3, and 6 are all called "father" by Ego; the women numbered 1, 4, and 5 are all called "mother." All cousins of the same generation (7–16) are considered brothers and sisters.*

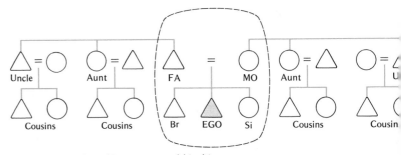

Figure 8-8. *The Eskimo system of kinship terminology emphasizes the nuclear family (here separated by the dotted circle). Ego's father and mother are distinguished from his aunts and uncles, and his siblings are distinguished from his cousins.*

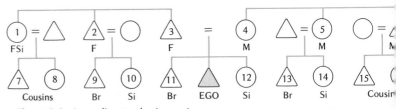

Figure 8-9. *According to the Iroquois system of kinship terminology, the people numbered 2 and 3 are called father; 4 and 5 are called mother; but 1 and 6 are aunt and uncle. 9–14 are all considered siblings, but 7, 8, 15, and 16 are called cousins.*

The formation of groups ● part **3**

Iroquois system

In the Iroquois system of kinship terminology, one's father and his father's brother are referred to by a single term (father), as are one's mother and one's mother's sister (mother); however, one's father's sister and one's mother's brother are given separate terms. In one's generation, brothers, sisters, and parallel cousins[3] of the same sex are referred to by a single term, whereas cross cousins are distinguished by separate terms.

Such a method of differentiating is called a bifurcate-merging system, a strange term which simply means some of the family members are separated (or bifurcated) and given different names, while other kin are combined (or merged) under a common term. The Omaha and the Crow systems are also examples of bifurcate-merging forms.

Iroquois terminology is very widespread and is usually found with unilineal descent groups, particularly in weak matrilineal systems of social organization. However, the Iroquois system has also been found among other types of descent groups as well.

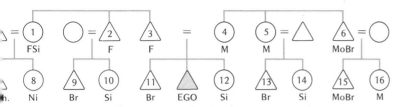

Figure 8-10. *In the Omaha system, 2 and 3 are father, 4 and 5 are mother, but 1 and 6 are aunt and uncle. In Ego's generation, the children 9–14 are all considered siblings, but 7, 8, 15, and 16 receive separate terms. 15 and 16 are equated with the older generation of the parents.*

Omaha system

In the preceding terminology systems, some relatives were grouped under common terms, while others of the same generation were separated and given different labels or terms. In the Omaha and Crow systems, another variable enters the picture: both systems ignore the distinction that occurs between generations among certain kinsmen.

The Omaha system, found in many parts of the world, is associated with a pattern of strong patrilineal descent and thus groups differently relations on the father's side and relations on the mother's side of the family. Cross cousins on the maternal side are merged with the parental gen-

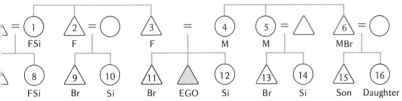

Figure 8-11. *The Crow Indians use a system that is the obverse of the Omaha system in Figure 8-10. 4 and 5 are merged under a single term, as are 2, 3, and 7. Ego's parallel cousins (9,10,13,14) are referred to in the same way as his brothers and sisters (11 and 12).*

[3] Parallel cousins are the offspring of parental siblings of the same sex. One's mother's sister's children and one's father's brother's children are one's parallel cousins. Cross cousins are the offspring of siblings of the opposite sex. One's mother's brother's children and one's father's sister's children are one's cross cousins.

eration (mother's sister or mother's brother), while those on the paternal side are merged with the generation of Ego's children. Otherwise, the system is much like the Iroquois system.

From our point of view, such a system is terribly complex and illogical. Why does it exist? The Omaha system is found where strong patrilineal descent is the rule. Thus, maternal cross cousins are terminologically merged with the lineage of Ego's mother, the lineage which, figuratively speaking, sired Ego. Ego's lineage, in turn, stands in the same relationship to the children of his father's sister and Ego's own sister; they are "sired" by Ego's lineage.

Crow system

The Crow system, named after the North American Indian tribe, is the matrilineal mirror image of the patrilineal system. Thus one's mother and one's mother's sister are called by the same term, whereas one's father and one's father's brother and father's sister's son are merged together under a common label, as are one's father's sister and one's father's sister's daughter. Similarly, one's male parallel cousins receive the same term as one's brother; one's female parallel cousins receive the same term as one's sister.

Sudanese system

In this relatively rare system, one's mother's brother is distinguished from one's father's brother, as is one's mother's sister from one's father's sister. Each cousin is distinguished from each other, as well as from siblings. It is therefore more precise than any of the other systems. This may be one reason why it is so rare. In few societies are all one's aunts, uncles, cousins, and siblings treated differently from one another.

☐

Kinship behavior among the Western Pueblos may be comprehended most easily by a discussion of the extended matrilineal household where an individual receives his first and lasting cultural orientation. The household normally consists of a woman and her husband, married daughters and their husbands, unmarried sons, and children of the daughters. The women are the important members of the unit; they own the house, are responsible for the preparation and distribution of food, make all the important decisions, and care for the ritual possessions of the family. The oldest woman of the household enjoys the most respect, and the members of the unit look to her for instructions and seek her advice in times of trouble. Next in importance is her oldest daughter, who assumes the duties and responsibilities of the household when her mother is away. Men born into the household and lineage leave the house when they marry, although they return frequently, exercise considerable authority in religious matters, and may discipline their sister's children when asked. The husbands contribute to the economic support of the household, teach their children the techniques of making a livelihood, and provide warmth and affection toward their children; but in disciplinary matters and economic decisions, they defer to their wives and their wives' brothers and uncles.

Interaction with the father's relatives goes on almost simultaneously with those of the matrilineal household. These relatives, particularly father's mother and father's sisters, are frequent visitors and the child, in turn, frequently visits the home of his paternal grandparents and sisters. These relatives exert little authority and do not discipline, but they provide love, comfort, and aid during crucial and anxious periods of his life.

The Western Pueblo matrilineal extended household in the past occupied a series of adjacent rooms. With the increasing importance of wage work and livestock activities in recent years, this situation has changed. Families living on farms and ranches during the summer are now essentially of the elementary type: husband, wife, and children, and in some cases a widowed grandmother, a divorced daughter, or other relative. Off-reservation employment restricts the size of the household even more drastically. Although it is not uncommon to have one or even both parents of the wife living with a nuclear family on a farm or ranch, older people refuse to make their home with children who live in government quarters or rented houses in towns and cities. The large extended household of the Pueblos generally has thus tended to become a smaller and less integrated unit in recent years; nevertheless, there is keen awareness of all the relatives that comprise the household group. Modern forms of transportation afford resumptions of extended-household living. Frequent ceremonies draw members back to the village enabling close relatives to interact with one another and thus renew and strengthen the bonds of friendship.

The lineage is the living and functional representation of a particular clan; its members are in intimate contact with one another and bound together by deep loyalties. Marriages remove the men to the various households of their wives, but they renew lineage ties frequently to visit with maternal relatives and to attend ritual duties. Women of the lineage never permanently leave the village and constantly interact fulfilling household and clan responsibilities. An older woman of one of the lineages is the head of the clan and her brother or maternal uncle usually performs the necessary rituals for the clan. Upon the death of the female head, the position goes to the next senior woman of the same household and lineage, but prominent members of the clan in the village may decide to designate as her successor a mature woman from another household and lineage. This is unlikely, however, for Pueblo custom tends to favor procedures deeply rooted in time and tradition. Among the Western Pueblos succession of important offices ordinarily remains within one household and lineage except where lineages have become extinct. The custom of having one household and/or lineage acting as the custodian of ritual paraphernalia and of providing the clan heads, both male and female, has tended to give a status ranking to lineages and clans. The village or town chief, an important official in all of these pueblos, although without the authority of his counterpart among the Eastern Pueblos, comes from a specific clan in most of the Western Pueblos: Bear clan, Hopi and Hano; Dogwood clan, Zuni; Antelope clan, Acoma, and perhaps Laguna.

Formerly, households of the lineage occupied a block of contiguous rooms, a pattern that has broken down in recent years, but the intimate bond of kinship remains even though the member households may be dispersed. Since each pueblo recognizes affiliation with other pueblo clans having the same name, lineages of equivalent clans in other pueblo villages are also considered legal kinfolk and the ordinary clan relations are extended to members of such lineages. Clans are land-holding units, each one having lands set aside for the use of its members. The control of ceremonies and their ritual paraphernalia are in the keeping of certain lineages. Adopted children retain the clan of their mothers; in most cases, however, children are adopted by members of their own clan. Marriage between members of the same clan is forbidden, as is marriage with a member of an equivalent Pueblo clan. In addition, marriage is disapproved with a member of father's clan. Violations of these latter restrictions occur, however, especially in recent years; but the rule that forbids marriage with a member of one's own clan is rarely violated.[1]

A Hano lineage is the living and functional representation of a particular clan; its members are in intimate contact with one another and bound together by deep loyalties. While marriages remove the men to the various households of their wives, they renew lineage ties frequently to exercise ceremonial responsibilities. Women of the lineage are, of course, constantly together. The lineages of the Hano are small and some are simply the matrilineal members of an extended household. A senior woman of one of the lineages is the head of the clan and her brother ordinarily performs the necessary rituals for the clan. Upon the death of the clan head, the position is usually assumed by the next senior woman of the same household and lineage, but prominent members of the clan in the village may decide to designate as her successor a mature woman from another household and lineage. Formerly households of the lineage occupied a block of houses adjacent to one another, a pattern that has broken down in recent years, but the intimate kinship bond remains even though the household members may be dispersed. Since the Tewa recognize affiliation with Hopi clans having the same name, lineages of equivalent clans in the Hopi villages are also considered lineal kinfolk and the ordinary clan relations are extended to members of these lineages.

Characteristics of Hano clan organization are revealed in the following statement by a Bear clansman:

I am of the Bear clan. Our mothers' mothers' mothers and our mothers' mothers' mothers' brothers were Bear clan people. They came a long, long, time ago from *Tsawadeh,* our home in the east. Our sisters' daughters' daughters' children, as long as women of my clan have children, will be of the Bear clan. These are our clan relatives, whom we trust, work with, and confide in. My mother's older sister guards the sacred fetish which is the power and guardian of our clan and which was brought in the migration from *Tsawadeh.* My mother's older sister feeds our fetish and sees that the feathers are always properly dressed. At important ceremonies, my mother's brother erects his altar and sets our fetish in a prominent place within the altar. My mother's older sister and my mother's brother make all the important decisions for our clan, and such decisions are accepted with respect and obedience by all Bear clan members. My mother's older sister and her brother are called upon to advise, to reprimand, and to make decisions on land and ritual affairs for all of us who are of the Bear clan. My mother's older sister's house is where our fetish is kept, and therefore it is a sacred house to us and there we go for all important matters that concern our clan.[2]

Sources:
[1] From *The Pueblo Indians of North America* by Edward P. Dozier. Copyright © 1970 by Holt, Rinehart and Winston, Inc. Adapted and reprinted by permission of Holt, Rinehart and Winston, Inc.
[2] From *Hano: A Tewa Indian Community in Arizona* by Edward P. Dozier. Copyright © 1966 by Holt, Rinehart and Winston, Inc. Reprinted by permission of Holt, Rinehart and Winston, Inc.

Summary

1.
The family is the chief organizational principle underlying every society, and is the primary human social group. Kinship is a powerful organizing principle in small or nonindustrial societies. As societies grow larger, more mobile and dispersed, the state increasingly assumes the function of kinship system.

2.
The rules governing kinship are called rules of descent. Unilineal descent establishes kinship exclusively through the male or female line. Patrilineal descent is traced through the male line; matrilineal, through the female. Generally, patrilineal descent predominates in societies in which the male is the breadwinner.

3.
The male members of a patrilineage trace through the males their descent from a common ancestor. A female belongs to the same descent group as her father and his brother; but her children cannot trace their descent through them. The Tikopia have a patrilineal system. The family is patrilocal, living near the house of the father's father. Individual Tikopian families belong to a *paito*. Each *paito* is made up of families whose members trace their descent through the male line to a common ancestor. The head of the *paito* is the senior living male descendant of this ancestor. A number of *paitos* form the *kainana,* or patriclan, the largest social group on the island.

4.
In all respects but one, matrilineal descent is the exact opposite of patrilineal. Matrilineal families are matrilocal and form matriclans. However, in a matrilineal society, though descent passes through the female line, males exercise authority in the kin group. The Ashanti have a matrilineal system. Segments of an Ashanti matrilineage are composed of the matrilineal descendants of an ancestress. The mother's brother is generally accepted as the leader of a segment.

5.
Double descent is reckoned patrilineally and matrilineally. Double descent is matrilineal for some purposes, and patrilineal for others. The Yako have a double descent system. Among the Yako, the patrilineage owns the land whereas the matrilineage owns the livestock.

6.
Bilateral descent is traced through both parents simultaneously. It is characteristic of Western society. An individual is lineally related to all eight grandparents and laterally to all third and fourth cousins. Such a large group is socially impractical. It is usually reduced to a small circle of paternal and maternal relatives, called the kindred, which is laterally organized. A kindred is never the same for any two persons except siblings.

7.
Cognatic descent is traced either matrilineally or patrilineally, according to the individual. The Iban have a cognatic descent system. The Iban descent group is the *bilek*. Upon marriage, a husband and wife select the *bilek* of one set of parents, relinquishing claims on the other. Children belong to the *bilek* of their parents until marriage.

The formation of groups ● part **3**

8.

In many parts of the world, a descent group may be a tightly organized working unit providing security and services. A lineage is a corporate descent group made up of consanguineous kin who claim descent from a common ancestor and can prove it. A clan or sib is a noncorporate descent group, each member of which assumes descent from a common ancestor, but cannot prove it. The phratry or moiety is a unilineal descent group of two or more clans which are supposedly related.

9.

The rise of cognatic descent groups appears to be related to ambilocality and ecology. In the case of ambilocal families, cognatic groups may have arisen in response to over-crowding, or as a means of increasing populations where an abundance of natural resources called for it.

10.

Different types of descent systems occur in different societies. In hunter-gatherer societies, descent groups do not appear at all, whereas in intensive agricultural societies they provide a structural framework for society.

11.

Defining kinship relationships in a society is subject to elaborate cultural rules. Factors such as sex, generational differences, and genealogical differences help differentiate one kin from another. The Hawaiian system is the least complex of kinship systems. All relatives of the same generation and sex are referred to by the same name. The Sudanese system is the most complex. One's mother's brother is distinguished from one's father's brother, as is one's mother's sister from one's father's sister. Each cousin is distinguished from each other.

Suggested readings

Fox, Robin *Kinship and Marriage*. Baltimore: Penguin, 1968.
An excellent introduction to the concepts of kinship and marriage, outlining some of the methods of analysis used in the anthropological treatment of kinship and marriage. Updates Radcliffe-Brown's *African Systems of Kinship and Marriage* and features a perspective focused on kinship groups and social organization.

Homans, George C. and David M. Schneider *Marriage, Authority and Final Causes: A Study of Unilateral Cross-Cousin Marriage*. Glencoe: Free Press, 1955.
This is a study of "preferential marriage"—a system of unilateral cross-cousin marriage in which a male is expected to marry one specific female cousin. A discussion of the theories of Lévi-Strauss is included with examples from the Karienda.

Needham, Rodney, ed. *Rethinking Kinship and Marriage*. New York: Barnes and Noble, 1972.
This is a collection of papers dealing with various aspects of the concept of kinship and marriage. Although fairly technical, it provides an introduction by the editor on present issues in theory and practice in the field of social anthropology.

Nimkoff, M. F. *Comparative Family Systems*. Boston: Houghton Mifflin, 1965.
Major variations in the organization of the human family, such as what differences they make, what they are, what causes them are discussed. Verbal and quantitative, descriptive and analytical approaches are combined. The book examines comparative studies on family, analyzes family life in a particular society, and traces recent trends in family structure in industrializing and fully industrialized societies.

Radcliffe-Brown, A. R., ed. *African Systems of Kinship and Marriage*. London: Oxford University Press, 1950.
The purpose of the volume is to present a general view of the nature and implications of kinship in Africa. It consists of a general introduction to kinship and marriage, and several chapters of detailed study of particular social systems (Swazi, Zulu, Lozi, Tswana, Bantu, Ashanti, etc.)

Schusky, Ernest L. *Manual for Kinship Analysis*. New York: Holt, Rinehart and Winston, 1965.
A widely used book that discusses the elements of kinship, diagramming, systems, classification, descent and lineage with specific examples from American, Crow, and Omaha Indian societies.

Other forms
of social organization

As traditional ways are forced to vie with new ones, the importance of kinship diminishes to a great degree. One or more members of a family may be forced to leave their village for work in the cities or the mines, or are drawn away from home by a desire for adventure and excitement. The United States is not, after all, the only country faced with the problem of how to keep the young people down on the farm after they have read about the East Village, or Nairobi, or Johannesburg. Old ways may be abruptly dropped in such a move, or they may be snatched away, as under colonial rule or the coming of the missionaries.

Occasionally such changes, especially when they are involuntary, are catastrophic. Laurens van der Post, in a study of the lives and mythology of the Kalahari Bushmen, writes of the tragedy that results from the imprisonment of a Bushman for an act whose illegality he could not comprehend—hunting "out of season." Today the very survival of the Bushmen is threatened, in part because their social structure contains no mechanisms for cultural adaptation to their changing social environment.

Tribal or village organizations, initiation cults and other traditional groups help maintain stability at a time when the simplest as well as the most sophisticated institutions are challenged by rapid social change. The source of this strength may have been detected by A. R. Radcliffe-Brown in his work on *The Andaman Islanders:*

> A society depends for its existence on the presence in the minds of its members of a certain system of sentiments by which the conduct of the individual is regulated in conformity with the needs of the society. Every feature of the social system itself and every event or object that in any ways affects the wellbeing or the cohesion of the society becomes an object of this system of sentiments. In human society the sentiments in question are not innate but are developed in the individual by the action of the society upon him. The ceremonial customs of a society are a means by which the sentiments in question are given collective expression on appropriate occasions. The ceremonial (i.e. collective) expression of any sentiment serves both to maintain it at the requisite degree of intensity in the mind of the individual and to transmit it from one generation to another. Without such expression the sentiments involved could not exist.

Whether or not this explanation is sufficiently

comprehensive, observations do consistently show that where such functions are not served by kinship, other forms of association arise to take its place. Among these forms of nonkinship social organization we will examine age grouping, voluntary associations, and stratification.

Age grouping

Age grouping is so familiar and so important that one anthropologist calls it and sex the only two universal factors in social status. Our first friends generally are children our own age. Together we are sent off to school where together we remain until our late teens. At a certain age we become "legally adult," meaning that we can vote, should support ourselves and must, if required, go off to war if male or lend moral support if female. Until that time we cannot drink liquor, drive a car, or do any number of things reserved for our elders. We are "teenagers," "middle-aged," "senior citizens," whether we like it or not, and for no other reason than our age.

Age classification also plays a significant role in non-Western societies. There the term "coming of age" is possibly even more meaningful than in our own society, especially if it is associated with becoming a warrior. Old age too has profound significance, often bringing with it the period of greatest respect (for women it may mean the first social equality with men), although it may also in some cases mean abandonment—psychological, as in the United States, or literal, as in certain Eskimo tribes.

The institutionalization of age, as P. Gulliver points out, makes it clear that cultural rather than biological factors are of prime importance in determining social status. All human societies recognize a number of life stages; precisely how they are defined will vary from one culture to another. Out of this recognition they establish patterns of activity, attitudes, prohibitions, and obligations. In some instances, they are designed to help the transition from one age to another, to teach

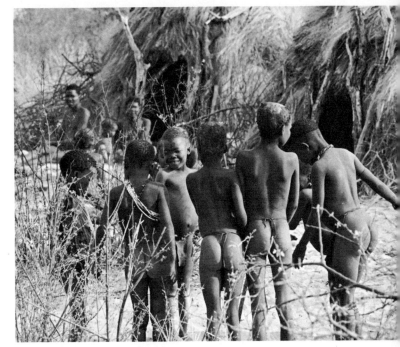

Figure 9-1. *In many societies, it is common for children of the same age to play, eat, and learn together, like this group of African boys. Such a group forms the basis of age-set organization.*

needed skills, or to lend economic assistance. Often they are designed to help structure a society and to meet its particular needs.

Institutions of age grouping

An **age category** is a generalized role disposition into which specific roles may be built. Anthropologists recognize three such distinctions: age class, age grade, and age set. An **age grade** is generally defined as a category of persons who fall within a particular, culturally distinguished age range. The collection of people currently occupying an age grade form an **age class**. The term **age set** is used to describe a group of persons initiated into an age grade who move through some or all of life's stages together. Age-ascribed roles may be specific, defining and limiting the nature of relationships between persons in different age grades. The total range of age-defined roles may constitute a graded system that emphasizes the progressive movement from role to role.

A specific time is often ritually established for moving from a younger to an older grade. Although members of senior groups commonly expect deference from and acknowledge certain responsibilities to their juniors, all such age-grade levels imply ascribed rather than achieved status, since one grade is no "better" or "worse" or even more important than another, and no ranking is achieved through individual effort. There can be standardized competition (opposition) between

Figure 9-2. *Some forms of age-set organization can be found in American society, as illustrated here by the annual tug of war between the freshman and sophomore classes at Dartmouth.*

age grades, such as between sophomores and freshmen on American college campuses. One can, comparably, accept the realities of being a "teenager" without feeling the need to "prove anything."

Whether by age set, class, or group, all peoples in some way distinguish the main stages of individual development. Such divisions may be as simple as youngsters, mature adults, and elderly peoples, such as among the Kalahari Bushmen; or as complex as the system of the Kikuyu of Central Kenya, who have six age-categories for men and eight for women. Within the three grades for men of the Masai—uncircumcised boys, circumcised bachelors, and married men—there are an indefinite number of classes; for example, all boys circumcised during the same four-year period form a set whose solidarity continues for life. This latter instance is also an example of the way an elaborate classification can spring up spontaneously, requiring only a name or procedure, such as circumcision, to fix it into a definite bond.

In the face of such obvious distinctions, a certain amount of controversy has arisen over the relative strength, cohesiveness, and stability that go into an age grouping. To Gulliver in particular, the age-group notion implies strong feelings of loyalty and mutual support that emphasize a corporate nature. Because such groups may possess property, songs, shield designs, and rituals, and are internally organized for corporate decision-making and leadership, he calls for a distinction between them and simple age-grade groupings. Gulliver also distinguishes between transitory age groups, which initially concern younger men (sometimes women too) but become less important and disintegrate as the members grow older, and the comprehensive systems that affect people through the whole of their lives. Among his other distinctions are that entry into and transfer out of age grades may be accomplished individually, either by a biological distinction, such as puberty, or by a socially recognized status, such as marriage or childbirth. Whereas age-grade members may have much in common, engage in similar activities, cooperate with one another, and share the same orientation and aspirations, their membership may not be entirely parallel with physiological age. Other anthropologists do not generally make such a distinction, which is considered one of degree rather than kind.

Age groupings in African societies

An example of a simple, traditionally defined age class of a relatively unsophisticated kind is the Nuer of Kenya, as described by Edward Evans-Pritchard. Among the Nuer, the position of every male in relation to every other male Nuer is defined only in terms of seniority, equality, or juniority. Initiation has no educational or moral purpose. At initiation a boy receives a spear from his father or uncle and becomes a warrior; he is given an ox and becomes a herdsman. Once initiated, he remains in this grade for the rest of his life. His new status implies no administrative, judicial, or other political or military functions; other than a taboo against milking, his domestic duties remain largely unstructured until marriage. His membership does have certain definite ritual observations and avoidances; for example, a man may not marry or have sexual relations with the daughter of an age mate, for she is regarded as his "daughter" and he as her "father." In matters of etiquette and division of food, his behavior is carefully structured according to seniority. These distinctions have no connotation of privilege, but only of stratification, and are superseded only by kinship.

Embodying many of Gulliver's notions of age groupings are the Swazi of Swaziland and the Afikpo Ibo of Eastern Nigeria. In Swazi, men's age groups (libutfo) were formed roughly every five to seven years according to the need for a group of immature youths to be available for state rituals. Each group had its own name, insignia, songs, barracks, and officials; every Swazi male was automatically enrolled and remained a member of the same libutfo from its inception until his death. Libutfos were originally sufficiently powerful to cut across the boundaries of local chiefs and the bonds of kinship, and incorporated individuals into a wider state unity. Although their primary activity was warfare, they took part in a number of civic functions and public works. Since their rituals and morality ran contrary to the teachings of the Christian missionaries, their influence ultimately waned, though they survive in attenuated forms.

The social organization of the Afikpo Ibo is well developed among both sexes. A village men's society, the Ogo, is found in every Afikpo village.

Figure 9-3. *Among the Pitjandara, a tribe of hunter-gatherers, the men in an age set undergo rituals together; these young men are participating in rather painful initiation rites. Such shared experiences create strong and lasting social bonds.*

The formation of groups ● part **3**

All initiated males perform religious, moral, and recreational functions involving the overall society, including the establishment of rules of conduct for all villagers. Also influential to a certain degree are age sets, which consist of persons living in one village born within approximately three years of one another. Men's and women's sets are paired and support one another in feasting and ceremonial activities. Age grades, composed of several contiguous age sets, form a larger body with important social and economic functions, strong feelings of loyalty, and mutual support. Age sets are formed on a village basis; age grades are organized on the basis of both the village and village group. Women's age sets and age grades exist at less highly organized levels and are subject to rulings of the men's age grades. Since the 1940s, village improvement associations and village group unions have also arisen.

Among the Afikpo, age grouping applies primarily to males. Girls' age groups sometimes occur, but the rights and obligations individually acquired in marriage and motherhood effectively curtail further relationships by age. Affairs purely for women are often organized by married women's groups, but age is an infrequent criterion, and the groups are weakly developed. Men's age grades determine the relationships for both men and women. In Swazi, even before the devitalization of traditional groups, a girl's marriage age had always been determined by her own parents rather than the rules of age grouping. Informal age groups do exist, but have flexible membership functions, and serve largely for temporary tasks. In contrast to this situation is the marked participation of women in voluntary associations.

The role of age groups varies considerably as these examples show; yet they are always of great importance in maintaining social continuity, in providing "performers" for various social roles from generation to generation, and in transmitting the social and cultural heritage of a society. This importance tends to increase in societies in which kinship fails to provide a workable solution to a society's need for functional divisions among its members. This may be, hypothesizes S. N. Eisen-

Figure 9-4. *Graduation from one age grade to another is often marked by elaborate rites. The top photo shows a group of young girls from the Ivory Coast who are returning home from ceremonies initiating them into full adult status; judging from the things they are carrying, the rites must have lasted quite a while. The other photo shows a young Burmese boy on his way to a temple initiation.*

Figure 9-5. *This photo shows a "captain" of the warrior age class in the Aboure tribe of the Ivory Coast dancing with other members of the grade. Other villagers look on and cheer the dancers.*

based on age. So strong is the force of age grouping that it is capable of cutting across and conflicting with both political and kinship ties, and with the possibilities of specialization and the achievement or privilege by effort and good fortune in a stratified society. In such instances, kinship dominates only where conflict might arise through antipathetic age roles.

Age, therefore, must be accepted as a force creating social units. Yet it may play only an indirect role in grouping; its influence is limited by sex division, and systems for social organization exist outside both age and kinship grouping.

Voluntary associations

The rise of voluntary associations, whether out of individual predilection or community need, is a theme intimately associated with world urbanization and its attendant social upheavals; our own society's fondness for joining is incontestably related to its complexity. This phenomenon poses a major threat to the inviolability of age and kinship grouping. An individual is often separated from his brother or age mate; he obviously cannot obtain their help in learning to cope with life in a new and bewildering environment, in learning a new language or mannerisms necessary for the change from village to city if they are not present. But such functions must somehow be met. Because voluntary associations are by nature quite flexible, they are increasingly, both in the cities and in the tribal villages, filling this gap in the social structure.

Kinds of voluntary associations

The diversity of voluntary associations is astonishing. Their goals may include the pursuit of friendship, recreation, and the expression and distinction of rank (usually among relatively small and technologically simple groups) as well as governing function and the pursuit or defense of

stadt from his comparative study of African age sets, because age is a criterion that can be applied to all members of society in the allocation of roles. Moreover, since age relationships have no contractual bond to begin with, there is no obstruction to setting up standards of behavior economic interests. Traditionally, associations have served for the preservation of tribal songs, history, language, and moral beliefs; the Tribal Unions of West Africa, for example, continue to serve this purpose. Similar organizations, often operating clandestinely, have kept traditions alive among American Indian tribes undergoing a resurgence of ethnic pride despite generations of reservation schooling. Also a significant force in the formation of associations is the supernatural experience common to all members; the Crow Tobacco Society, the secret associations of the Kwakiutl Indians of British Columbia with their cycles of secret rituals, and the Katchina Cults of the Pueblo Indians are well-known examples. Among other traditional forms of association are military, occupational, political, and entertainment groups that parallel such familiar groups as the American Legion, labor unions, block associations, and "co-ops" of every kind.

Such organizations are frequently exclusive, but a prevailing characteristic is their concern for the general well-being of an entire village or village group. Membership may connote prestige but never economic advantage. The rain that falls as a result of the work of Pueblo rainmakers nourishes the crops of members and nonmembers alike.

Men's and women's associations. Traditionally, women's contributions to voluntary associations have been regarded as less significant than men's. Although research, such as Phoebe Ottenberg's study of age grouping among the Afikpo Ibo, tends to support such an assumption, the thinking behind it is undergoing marked revision. Schurtz's theory that underlying the differentiation between kinship and associational groups is a profound difference in the psychology of the sexes was widely accepted for years. To Schurtz, women were eminently unsocial beings who preferred to remain in kinship groups based on sexual relations and the reproductive function, rather than form units on the basis of commonly held interests. Men, on the other hand, were said to view sexual relations as isolated episodes, an

attitude that fostered the purely social factor that makes "birds of a feather flock together."

Today, needless to say, this kind of thinking is being heatedly challenged by scholars of both sexes. It is suggested that women have not formed associations because of the demands of

Figure 9-6. *In American society, voluntary associations are a common form of social organization. These ladies are members of a church group, holding its annual Christmas bazaar to raise funds.*

raising a family and their daily activities. But given the plethora of women's clubs of all kinds in the United States for several generations, one wonders how this belief of women as unsocial survived as long as it did. Earlier, of course, when women had to stay at home in rural situations, with no near neighbors, they had no chance to participate in voluntary associations. Moreover, some functions of men's associations—like military duties—may be culturally defined as purely for men or simply repugnant to women.

But, as Robert Lowie and others clearly point out, women do play important roles in associations of their own and even in those in which men predominate. Among the Crow, women participate even in the secret Tobacco Society as well as in their own exclusive groups. Throughout Africa, women's social clubs complement the men's, and are concerned with educating women and with crafts and charitable activities. In Sierra Leone, where once-simple dancing societies have developed under urban conditions into complex organizations with a set of modern objectives, the dancing *compin* is made up of young women as well as men, who together perform plays based on traditional music and dancing and raise money for various mutual benefit causes. The Kpelle of Liberia maintain initiation of "bush" schools for both young men and women; women also alternate with men in ritual supremacy of a chiefdom. The cycle of instruction and rule (four years for males, three for females) that marks these periods derives from the Kpelle's association of the number four with maleness and three with femaleness rather than from a notion of sexual superiority.

Women's liberation organizations, consciousness-raising groups, and professional organizations for women are examples of some of the voluntary associations arising directly or indirectly out of today's social climate. These groups cover the entire range of association forming, from simple friendship and support groups to political, guildlike, and economic (the publication of magazines, groups designed to influence advertising) associations on a national scale. If an unresolved point does exist in the matter of women's partici-

pation, it is in determining why women are excluded from associations in some societies, whereas in others their participation is essentially equal with men.

Associations in the urban world

The importance of voluntary associations in areas of rapid social change is considerable. Increasingly such organizations assume the roles and functions formerly held by kinship or age groups; in many areas they hold the key both to individual adaptation to new circumstances and to group survival. Where once groups were organized to preserve tribal ways and structure against the intrusion of the modern world, urban associations accept the reality of such an intrusion and help their members to cope both socially and economically. Members may turn to such associations for support and sympathy while unemployed or sick; the groups may also provide education or socialization. An important need met by many of these associations is economic survival; to achieve such ends they may help raise capital, regulate prices, discourage competition, and organize cooperative activities.

Always the keynote of these groups is adaptation. As Kenneth Little observes, adaptation implies not only the modification of institutions but also the development of new ones to meet the demands of an industrial economy and urban way of life. Modern urbanism involves the rapid diffusion of entirely new ideas, habits, and technical procedures, as well as a considerable reconstruction of social relationships as a consequence of new technical roles and groups created. Age-old conventions yield to necessity, as women and young people in general gain new status in the urban economy. Women's participation, especially in associations with mixed membership, involves them in new kinds of social relationships with men, including companionship and the chance to choose a mate by oneself. Young persons on the whole become leaders for their less westernized and sophisticated counterparts. Even in rural areas, such voluntary associations thrive, reflecting the increasing consciousness of the outer world. With an irony implicit in many former colonial situations, the European contact that so frequently shattered permanent age and kinship groups has, partly through the influence of education, helped remove restrictions in association membership both in age and sex.

In our own culture, voluntary associations such as women's clubs, Boy and Girl Scouts, Kiwanis, Rotary, and PTA abound. Elements of secret initiatory cults survive, to some extent, among the Masonic lodges, and fraternity and sorority initiations. Women's associations recently seem to have proliferated. Although we may think of our own groups as more complex and highly organized than those of primitive societies, many of the new urban voluntary associations in Africa, for example, are elaborately structured and rival many of our secular and religious organizations. Such traditional groups, with their antecedents reaching far back in history, may have served as models for associations familiar to us; now, in becoming westernized, they promise to outstrip our own in complexity, an interesting phenomenon to watch as the non-Western countries become "modernized."

Figure 9-7. *This pair of pictures furnishes implicit evidence of the value of voluntary associations in bringing benefit to the group members. Above is a turn-of-the-century factory scene; below is the meeting of a powerful modern labor union.*

Social stratification

The study of social stratification involves the examination of distinctions that may seem perplexing. But social stratification is a common and powerful phenomenon among many of the world's peoples and must, at least in part, be viewed dispassionately.

Basically a **stratified society** is one in which members of the same sex and equivalent status do not have equal access to the basic resources that sustain life (as opposed to unstratified societies that rank individuals merely on the basis of age, sex, and kinship). The possibility for nonstratification does exist within both the **egalitarian** society, characteristic of hunters-gatherers, in which as many positions for prestige exist in any given age/sex grade as there are persons capable of filling them, and the **rank society,** which sharply limits its positions of prestige without affecting the access of its entire community to the basic resources of life. Such societies, though, are rare. The Kalahari Bushmen is the best known example of an egalitarian society; the noncontemporary Nootka Indians of the American Northwest Coast are an example of a rank society.

One widely accepted definition of a stratified society contains the following elements: hierarchically ranked groups that maintain relatively permanent positions, have differential control of the sources of power relative to their ranking, are separated by cultural and individual distinctions, and have an overreaching ideology that provides the rationale for the entire system. Such societies can be distinguished by a relative degree of inequality of rewards and privileges.

Class and caste

Most persons, hearing the word "caste," automatically think of India. Many anthropologists, however, question whether caste—widely used to describe random groups within rigid systems of social stratification—and the caste system should be defined in terms of the Hindu system alone, or whether the structure should be broadened to include features also found in societies of Arabia, Polynesia, North and South Africa, Guatemala, Japan, aboriginal North America, and the contemporary Unites States. Gerald D. Berreman, for example, defines a caste as a network of status-equal interactions in a society characterized by a network of hierarchical interaction between birth-ascribed groups. His approach makes possible the inclusion of a broader range of systems under the term "caste" than is possible with concepts derived only from stratification theory. The essential attributes of his caste naming include birth-ascribed, hierarchically ranked, ordered and culturally distinct groups, differential evaluation, differential rewards, and differential associations.

The basic difference between class and caste is that in the latter (a special kind of class) mobility is severely restricted, and endogamy is particularly marked.

In a large society, the groups constituting a caste system are often economically interdependent and occupationally specialized. Their members view themselves and are viewed by others as relatively homogeneous elements in a system of different ranked component parts, rather than independent and mutually unranked self-contained systems. Members of each caste share such common characteristics as group name, skin color, language, occupation, dress, or place of residence. Individual attributes in a caste system are irrelevant; caste membership is birth-determined, universal, and lifelong. Individual mobility is impossible. Thus, although caste shares certain characteristics with age grouping, membership may be more subjective, containing such exalted notions as purity (as in India) or honor (as in Swat). Almost all social interaction—who may become one's friend, mate, neighbor, master, servant, client, or competitor—is largely a matter of caste. Taboos against interaction are strong.

The **plural society** is in essence a simplified variation of the caste system. Such a society is composed of cultural sections, each of which is really a little society in itself, with its own kinship, family, and socialization systems, recreational activities, religious beliefs and practices, values, and language variants. The whole system, while in many ways sounding like a collection of voluntary groups, is generally thought to be held together by the political domination of one section. However, in the view of the social scientist Talcott Parsons, consensual interests and values, rather than political domination, are the cohesive force.

Examples of pluralistic societies can be found in postcolonial Africa, where black Africans exercise control over Indians and Chinese, and in the class-color hierarchies of West Indian societies. In the latter cases, classes are separated not merely by color and status, wealth and power, but also by diverse cultural patterns and social frameworks

Figure 9-8. *Although India's once-rigid caste system has changed considerably, members of the lowest caste are still barred from many kinds of social opportunity. Rapid change in the system may benefit such individuals but it also creates much social confusion.*

involving legal, religious, educational, and family institutions. Dominating are upper class Creoles —of North European, African, and mixed descent—who rule over such groups as aboriginal American Indians, Portuguese, Chinese, East Indian, Javanese, and Syrian immigrants.

Determinants of stratification

Social stratification can be based on many criteria —wealth, cultural level, legal status, birth, personal qualities, ideology. The Natchez Indians used to maintain an elaborate system of social class based on three ranked groups of nobility and a single commoner class. Obligatory inter-class marriage kept the nobility small and replenished the commoners. The Aztec society at the time of the Spanish Conquest was divided into nobles and commoners, who in turn were divided into elaborate classes according to urban or rural settlement and occupation, from warriors through merchants and craftsmen. Three slave classes also existed. The entire scheme was administered by an elaborate bureaucracy of nobles and warriors.

Although economic determinists, such as Karl Marx, stress ownership of land and capital as the

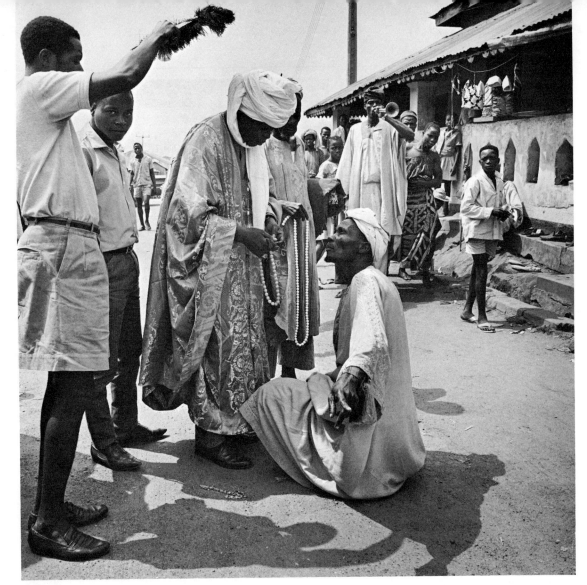

Figure 9-9. *Evidence of social stratification in Nigeria can be seen in the homage paid by the kneeling village chief, an important man in his own right, to the turbaned king.*

determinant of social stratification, others, such as Max Weber, include the nature of the external standard of living. Hyman Rodman incorporates both objective and subjective working criteria. The expression of attitudes associated with difference in status and role show marked differences from one culture to another. Harold Driver notes that on the whole American Indian societies were far more democratic than those of Africa, but indicates that there were nevertheless marked differences in rank and status in some areas and true social classes in other areas. In all societies, as we have seen, each individual possesses a multiple number of statuses simulta-

The formation of groups ● part **3**

neously, possibly ranked according to wealth, social heredity, proficiency, supernatural sanction, or any number of these factors in combination. Ideally, all statuses should be considered in giving an individual a place in a particular social class, but obviously this is rare. A point perhaps not as obvious is that for a society to be a "class" society at least two classes must exist; a one-class system is essentially classless.

The evils in social stratification of any kind may tend to overshadow the good; they at least appear to make life oppressive for large segments of a population. Often, the lower classes are placated by means of religion, which offers them a tolerable existence in the hereafter. If they have this to look forward to, they are more likely to accept the "here and now." In considering social stratification, we must, however, reckon with such deep-seated human drives as the desire to excel one's fellows. Although the impulse is suppressed by a few peoples, such as the Pueblo Indians, it is intense in most societies. Even in relatively democratic societies, certain goals stressed eventually become culturally fixed. Among the Winebago and Hopi Indians, the Sherente and Ugan-dan peoples, clan superiority and kinship lineages are recognized in electing chiefs, performing sacred rituals, and other special tasks, whether or not membership entails any economic advantages. Even functions not related to class may contain within themselves the germ of class differentiation. Ethnic differences often lead to diverse classes and even castes, as members of our own society have experienced through the racial stereotyping that leads to social and economic disadvantages.

Classes perform an integrative function in society. They may cut across some or all lines of kinship, residence, occupation, and age group, depending on the particular society, thus counteracting potential tendencies for society to fragment into discreet entities. Stratification may also provide a means for an alien group to dominate large members of people. Those who dominate are aided by their acknowledged "upper class" status. They are respected by the lower classes, who "know their place" and let themselves be dominated.

☐

TIRIKI
AGE GROUP

The Tiriki age group organization is directly borrowed from the Nilo-Hamitic Terik who border the Tiriki to the south. There are seven named aged groups (Kabalach, Golongolo, Jiminigayi, Nyonje, Mayina, Juma, and Sawe), each embracing approximately a fifteen-year age span. In addition, each age group passes successively through four distinctive age grades. The system is cyclical, each age group being reinstated with new initiates approximately every 105 years.

Perhaps the easiest way to grasp the difference in age groups and age grades is to review the nature of our college class system. Freshmen entering college in the autumn of 1958, for example, immediately become known as the Class of 1962—the year when they were due to graduate. Thenceforth, for as long as they live, they are known as the Class of 1962. While in college, however, members of the Class of 1962 must pass in successive years through four ranked grades: freshman, sophomore, junior, and senior.

In Tiriki each age group contains those men who were initiated over a fifteen-year age span, not simply during one year. The initiation rites, it will be recalled, traditionally extend over a six months' period, and are held every four years; thus each age group receives recruits from three or four successive initiations. The four traditional Tiriki age grades are *bandu bi lihe, balulu* (the warriors) *balulu basaxulu* (the elder warriors) *basaxulu bi biina, basaxulu bu luhya* (the judicial elders), and *basaxulu basaalisi* (the ritual elders). Before they were prohibited by the British about 1900, handing-over ceremonies were held at about fifteen-year intervals in conjunction with the closing of an age group to more initiates. At this time the age group just closed to initiates became formally instated in the warriors age grade, the age group that had just been the warriors' moved on to the elder warrior grade, the former elder warriors moved on to the judicial elder grade, and the former judicial elders moved on to the ritual eldership.

The cyclical aspect of Tiriki age groups can also be readily compared with the system of college classes, if one substitutes the Tiriki age group name for "Class of __," and remembers that each Tiriki age group embraces fifteen years. The Class of '62 at Harvard, for example, has been reinstated every 100 years for several centuries with a new group of college men, and thus can be viewed as part of a cyclical process. In Tiriki each cycle lasts 105 years instead of a century, because the seven age groups, each embracing fifteen years, cover a total span of 105 years. The Sawe age group, for example, open for initiates from 1948 to 1963, was previously instated and open to initiates from roughly 1843 to 1858.

The *warriors* were formally given the responsibility of guarding the country. They were said "to hold the land". An age group's lasting reputation was principally earned while it was occupying the warrior age grade. Similarly the reputation accompanying a man throughout the remainder of his life and then remembered by his posterity was primarily based on the leadership, courage, and good fortune he exhibited while a warrior.

The duties and perogatives of the *elder warriors* were neither as glorious nor as well defined as those of the warriors. They had relatively few specialized social tasks, but they gradually assumed an increasing share of administrative type activities in areas that were basically the responsibility of the elder age groups. For example, at public post-funeral gatherings held to settle property claims, usually a man of the elder warrior group was called upon to serve as chairman. His duty was to maintain order, to see that all the claims and counterclaims were heard, to initiate compromises, but always to seek and defer to the judgment of the elders in matters that were equivocal or a departure from tradition. Members of this age grade also served as couriers and envoys when important news needed to be transmitted between elders of different subtribes.

The age group occupying the *judicial elder* age grade fulfilled most of the tasks connected with the arbitration and settlement of local disputes. This included everything from delinquent or contested bridewealth payments to cases of assault or accidental injury. Any major disturbance or legitimate complaint by the head of a household served as sufficient reason for the community judicial elders to gather at the local meeting ground to hear the plaintiff and defendant, question witnesses, and give a judgment.

The *ritual elders* presided over the priestly functions of the homestead ancestral shrine observances, at subclan meetings concerning inheritance and the like, at semiannual community supplications, and at the initiation rites. Also, the ritual elders were accredited with having access to magical powers. They were the group who expelled or killed witches, or at least who were counted on to neutralize their evil powers, and they also were the group who underwrote the death through sorcery of anyone cursed by the community for violating the initiation secrets or for committing some other heinous crime. The advice of the ritual elders was sought in all situations that seemed to hold danger for or entail the general well-being of the community or the tribe. For example, the warriors solicited the auguries of the ritual elders before embarking on a major raid, and postponed the raid if the omens were bad.

Today, over sixty years after the last formal handing-over ceremony, the age group cycle still continues, kept alive by the regular performance of the initiation rites. The four graded statuses are still manifest in informal social behavior and in current social ideology and action, albeit in relatively informal and altered form. Young men whose age group according to traditional reckoning would now be warriors, are still occasionally called, or referred to as "warriors," but only in a spirit of friendliness and flattery. Today, instead of fighting, young men of this age grade find a modicum of excitement and adventure through extended employment away from the tribe. A fortunate few are pursuing secondary or advanced studies, teaching school, or holding clerical jobs; but in most cases they, too, are employed or are studying off-tribe. Members of the warrior age grade are no longer held in such esteem as formerly, and no one ever speaks of them as "holding the land." Their active participation, however, in the new and rapidly changing world beyond tribal boundaries still lends the warrior age grade a bit of glamour.

In contrast to that of the warriors, the relative status of those occupying the elder warrior age grade has increased dramatically during the last fifty years.

Men of this age grade have assumed nearly all the new administrative and executive roles created by the advent and growth of a centralized tribal administrative bureaucracy. With few exceptions they hold all the salaried offices in the tribal administration. It is quite in keeping with traditional age grade expectations that members of this age grade should occupy the executive and administrative positions, but pre-European conditions provided only a minimal number of such roles.

The judicial elders still serve as the local judiciary body, although their authority was somewhat altered and curtailed by the British colonial administration.

The ritual elders have suffered a severe diminution of their functions and powers. During the last twenty years, ancestor worship has declined until today the formal aspects of the cult are virtually extinct. They, like the warriors, have been deprived of a major part of their traditional age grade activity; but unlike the warriors, they have not found any substitute activity. The positions of leadership in the Christian church have been assumed by a small number of men, mostly of the elder warrior age grade. The ritual elders continue, however, to hold the most important positions in the initiation ceremonies, and their power as sorcerers and witchcraft expungers remains almost universally feared and respected.

Source:
From "The Bantu Tiriki of Western Kenya," by Walter H. Sangree, in *Peoples of Africa,* edited by James Gibbs, Jr. Copyright © 1965 by Holt, Rinehart and Winston, Inc. Reprinted by permission of Holt, Rinehart and Winston, Inc.

Summary

1.

Age groupings are important forms of nonkinship organizations. There are three age categories: age class, age grade, and age set. An age grade is a category of persons within a particular, culturally distinguished age range. The people currently occupying an age grade form an age class. An age set is a group of persons initiated into an age grade, who move together through some or all of life's stages. A specific time is often ritually established for moving from a younger to an older age grade. Anthropologists agree that all peoples distinguish the main stages of individual development. There is controversy, however, over the relative strength, cohesiveness, and stability of age groups; in many societies, they are relatively unimportant.

2.

An example of a simple, traditionally defined age class is found in the Nuer of Kenya. Among the Nuer, the position of each male is defined only in terms of seniority. More sophisticated age groupings are found in the Swazi of Swaziland and the Afikpo Ibo of Eastern Nigeria. Among the Swazi, men's age groups are formed roughly every five to seven years, depending on the need for immature youths to be available for state rituals. Each man remains a member of the same age group from its inception until his death. Among the Afikpo Ibo, age sets are made up of persons living in one village who are born within approximately three years of one another. Age grades, made up of several contiguous age sets, form a larger body with important social and economic functions in the context of the society at large.

3.

Voluntary associations are a form of nonkinship organization which has risen mostly as a result of world urbanization. Voluntary associations have traditionally served to preserve a society's cultural heritage. There is a current controversy over whether women have contributed as much to the development of voluntary associations as men. Women do play important roles in associations of their own and even in those in which men predominate. Among the Crow, women participate in the men's secret Tobacco Society, as well as in their own exclusive group.

4.

Voluntary associations are particularly important in areas of rapid social change. They are increasingly assuming the roles and functions formerly held by kinship or age groups. Urban associations help their members cope, both socially and economically, with the intrusions of the modern world. The keynote of these groups is always adaptation, implying not only the modification of institutions but also the development of new ones. Such groups are common in modern industrial societies.

5.

A socially stratified society is one in which members of the same sex and equivalent status do not have equal access to life-sustaining resources. The egalitarian society has as many positions in an age/sex grade as there are persons to fill them. The rank society sharply limits its positions to a selected few, but gives its entire community access to life-sustaining resources. Stratified societies contain hierarchically ranked groups. These groups maintain relatively permanent positions. Power is related to rank; it is conferred by the holding of certain social statuses.

6.

Caste is a kind of class in which mobility is severely restricted and endogamy is particularly marked. In a large society, the groups making up a caste system are often economically interdependent and occupationally specialized. Members of a caste system view only other members as equals. The plural society is essentially a simplified variation of the caste system. It is made up of cultural sections, each a society in itself. The whole system is generally thought by its members to be held together by a dominant group, but this need not be true in all cases.

7.

Social stratification can be based on many criteria, such as wealth, cultural level, legal status, birth, personal qualities, and ideology. A rigidly stratified society in which mobility is limited can make life oppressive for large segments of a popultion.

Suggested readings

Eisenstadt, S. N. *From Generation to Generation: Age Groups and Social Structure*. Glencoe, Illinois: Free Press, 1956.
Various social phenomena known as age-group and youth movements are analyzed to ascertain whether it is possible to specify the social conditions in which they occur. The analysis is based on a study of various societies—primitive, historical, and modern. The basic hypothesis of the book is that age groups exist in universalistic societies in which the family is not the basic unit of the social division of labor.

Friedenberg, Edgar *Coming of Age in America: Growth and Acquiescence*. New York: Random House, 1965.
A study of the effects of life in a mass society on the values of the people who share it. It is specifically an analysis of student values as these affect and are expressed in the choices made about school situations and attitudes toward secondary schools.

Lenski, Gerhard E. *Power and Privilege*. New York: McGraw-Hill, 1966.
Who gets what and why is explained by the distributive process and systems of social stratification in industrial nations: U.S., U.S.S.R., Sweden and Britain. Using a broadly comparative approach, the author makes heavy use of anthropological and historical material as well as the usual sociological materials on modern industrial societies. The basic approach is theoretical and analytical; the book builds on certain postulates about the nature of man and society, seeking to develop in a systematic manner an explanation of a variety of patterns of stratification. The theory presented is a synthesis of the two dominant theoretical traditions of the past and present, currently represented in both Marxian and functionalist theory.

Lowie, Robert H. *Social Organization*. New York: Holt, Rinehart and Winston, 1948.
This is a classic, though somewhat dated, study of social organization. The author discusses social organization on a cross-cultural basis, including age grading and voluntary associations.

4

Social integration

Economic systems

It is perhaps in the study of the economy of non-literate peoples that we are most apt to fall prey to interpreting anthropological data in terms of our own technologies, our own values of work and property, and our own determination of what is rational. For example, many of us would say that certain West African people act like children in their seeming inability to plan ahead. These people conventionally and traditionally use up so much of their food feasting during the dry season that, when the wet season comes and they must break up the land for new planting, they do not have enough food. We might term the Kogi Indians superstitious because of the way they use their land. The Kogi, who inhabit the Sierra Nevada range of Colombia, are faced with a scarcity of land. In these mountain ranges, however, there are many terraces built by earlier inhabitants; using them as farm land would save the Kogi much moving from one place to another. Yet the Kogi will not use these terraces. "There are many spirits of the dead there," they say.[1]

In order to understand how the schedule of wants or demands of a given society is balanced against the supply of goods and services available,

[1]Melville Herskovits, *Economic Anthropology: A Study in Comparative Economics* (New York: Knopf, 1952) 2nd edition.

it is necessary to introduce a third variable—the anthropological variable of culture. In any given economic system, economic processes cannot be interpreted without culturally defining the demands and understanding the conventions that dictate how and when they are satisfied.

In the last thirty years, anthropologists have borrowed theory and concepts from the discipline of economics in an attempt to understand certain relationships of nonliterate people. Since economics is the study of the allocation of scarce goods and services in industrial society, it is a matter of controversy as to what modifications must be made in order for economic theory to be applicable to nonindustrial societies. Do nonindustrial societies have economic systems? Can we speak of the profit motive, savings, capital goods, and all the other concepts that economists use, in relation to nonindustrial societies?

There are anthropologists who adhere to the point of view that there is little to be learned from the study of market economies, where the principal motivation is profit, in studying people who do not exchange goods for gain. This position is called **substantivism.**

Other scholars, called **formalists,** take a different view. Formalists claim that economic theory really has to do with the ways people get the greatest personal satisfaction in saving things and in distributing scarce resources. If this is true, then economic theory is certainly general enough to apply to all societies.

An economic system may be defined as a set of institutions and regulations through which goods are produced and distributed within a given technology and social system. Almost every society produces a surplus, be it ever so minimal by our standards. Among nonindustrial peoples, the forms of production, distribution, and surplus may be so closely linked with institutions, such as religion and kinship obligations, that we scarcely discern them. Nevertheless, all societies produce a living and consume goods and at some times have leftovers.

Resources

In every society there are customs and rules governing the kinds of work that are done, which people do the work, who owns the land and tools, and how the work is accomplished. Land, labor, capital, and technology are the productive resources that a social group may use to produce desired goods and services. The rules surrounding the use of these resources are embedded in the culture and determine the way the economy operates.

Patterns of labor

Every society has rules to govern the allotment of work. There is always a division of labor along sex and age categories; such division is simply a further development of the patterns found in all higher primates. Whether men or women do a particular job varies from group to group, but much work is set apart as the work of either one sex or the other. The sexual division of labor in nonliterate societies has been studied extensively in anthropology, and some researchers have at-

Figure 10-1. *This Yanomamo woman is carrying a pack with all the possessions of her entire family. Here this task, which does require considerable physical strength, is considered women's work.*

tempted to make generalizations along physiological lines; for example, the women do the lighter work, the men hunt because they are stronger, the women stay nearer home because they feed and care for the children. Melville Herskovits, one of the first anthropologists to apply economics to anthropology, says, however, that a study of the work done by men and women in particular groups soon shows that "the specific forms taken by sex division of labor must be referred to the historical development of the particular body of traditions by which a particular people order their lives."[2] It is not possible to make such sweeping generalizations about the division of labor according to sex; rather each society must be studied to observe the assignment of work.

In Northern Australia, among the Tiwi, where the wealthier men usually had several wives, the women, with their baskets and perhaps a baby on their backs, spent the day gathering food—chiefly vegetables, grubs, and worms. Even the smallest household would contain at least one elder wife who knew the bush like the palm of her hand. These old women supervised and trained the younger women in the gathering and preparation of food for the household. The husband never interfered in matters concerning the work of the women. "If I had only one or two wives, I would starve," the head of a large household told a missionary who was preaching against plural marriage, "but with my present ten or twelve wives I can send them out in all directions in the morning and at least two or three of them are likely to bring back something at the end of the day; then we all can eat."[3] The vegetable foods obtained by the women gatherers were the everyday staples. The meat the men brought in was considered a dividend or extra. In such a culture, polygyny confers an adaptive advantage since it enables all members of the family unit to remain relatively well fed.

The men of the Copper Eskimos, who lived in the Northwest Territories in Canada, provided the food for the household.[4] In these northerly regions, there was scarcely any vegetable food. From May until November the men hunted caribou and fished. The rest of the year was devoted to hunting the ringed seal, except for a few weeks in early December, which were spent sewing clothes for the winter.

[2] *Ibid.*, p. 132.
[3] C. W. M. Hart and Arnold R. Pilling, *The Tiwi of North Australia* (New York: Holt, Rinehart and Winston, 1960) p. 34.
[4] M. G. Bicchieri (ed.), *Hunters and Gatherers Today: A Socioeconomic Study of Eleven Such Cultures in the Twentieth Century* (New York: Holt, Rinehart and Winston, 1972) pp. 12-19, 41-44.

The entire community participated in caribou drives. Shouting women and children drove the caribou toward the bowmen, who lay in wait in pits behind stones and poles set up like scarecrows to resemble men. The men hunted the seal in groups, waiting for them at a blowhole. When a seal was speared through the hole, help from another man was needed to pull the heavy animal out of the water onto the ice.

The women devoted much of their time to taking care of the children. They also cooked, prepared skins for clothing, fished, and were expected to do such heavy work as pitching and breaking camp, pulling sledges with the dogs, and backpacking considerable loads in the summer. However, during the long winter days, when the men were hunting seal, they spent much of the day visiting and gossiping with the other women.

There may also be a division of labor according to age. Among the Tiwi, for example, the men who were too old to hunt manufactured the tools and artifacts of the tribe. The older men, those with large households and therefore a large labor force, had leisure time to develop skills in the manufacture of canoes, baskets, digging sticks, and beautifully made artistic creations, such as grave posts and ceremonial spears. These men also composed songs and dances.

Among the Copper Eskimos, old age was a difficult time because the harsh climate and migratory life were special hardships for the old. The cold and the damp accelerated aging, apparently, and the old suffered the most during famines. There was little work easy enough for the old of either sex to accomplish, so old people and children constituted more of a burden for the Eskimos than for people in a more salubrious climate. Eskimo boys began to make an economic contribution in their late teens, and a ceremonial event was made of the killing of their first seal.

In many nonliterate societies, both children and older people make a greater contribution to the economy in terms of work and responsibility than is common in our own. In South Vietnam, for example, young children not only look after their younger brothers and sisters but help with housework as well. "An American would be horrified to see a child, four or five years old, handling a chopping knife or lighting an oil lamp, but in Vietnam it is common."[5] Unlike the elderly Eskimos, old people in South Vietnam retain economic responsibilities. The grandmother, for example, holds the purse strings, markets, cooks, and cleans the house. A similar allocation of responsibility used to be common in rural American households, where the work load was heavy and the labor pool small.

Cooperation. Cooperative work groups can be found everywhere in nonliterate, nonindustrial, and nonpecuniary societies. Often, if the effort involves the whole community, there is a festive spirit to the work. Jomo Kenyatta described the time of enjoyment after a day's labor in Kenya. "If a stranger happens to pass by, he will have no idea that these people who are singing and dancing have completed their day's work. This is why most Europeans have erred by not realizing that the African in his own environment does not count hours or work by the movement of the clock, but works with good spirit and enthusiasm to complete the tasks before him."[6]

In Dahomey, the iron workers cooperate in the operation of their forges. Each man owns his own iron, and the members of the forge work on the iron of one man at a time. The product belongs to the man who provided the iron, and he is free to sell it in the market for personal gain, reinvesting his return in more iron. Meanwhile, he works at the forge for each other man until his turn comes again.[7]

Cooperative work is not necessarily voluntary. It may be part of fulfilling duties to in-laws; it may be performed for chiefs or priests, by command. The institutions of family, kinship, religion, and the state all may act as organizing elements that define the nature and condition of each worker's cooperative obligations.

[5] Randy Gellerman in *The New York Times*, July 24, 1973, p. 40.
[6] Herskovits, *op. cit.*, p. 103.
[7] *Ibid.*, p. 108.

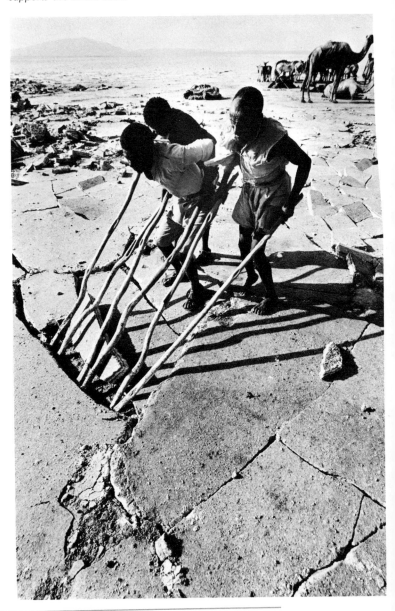

Figure 10-2a. *The Danakil tribe in Ethiopia have a very narrow economic specialization; they obtain salt from the ground and sell it to neighboring tribesmen; this work, which calls for cooperative effort of all the men, supports the entire tribe.*

Social integration ● part **4**

Figure 10-2b,c. *Once the salt crust is broken up and removed (hard work in the hot sun and high temperatures), it is cut into smaller slabs that serve as the basic unit for trade. These slabs are then loaded on camels, and a caravan takes the salt across the desert to the coast and highlands to be sold.*

Craft specialization.

In nonindustrial societies, where division of labor occurs along lines of age and sex, each person in the society has knowledge and competence in all aspects of work appropriate to his age and sex. Yet in every society there is some specialization of craft. Among the Trobriand Islanders, for example, the artisans of one village specialize in stone blades for adzes, whereas their neighbors may specialize in decorating pots or carving wooden handles for the stone blades.

An example of specialization can be seen among the Puluwats, who live in the Carolines: the most respected member of the society is the master mariner, a naval architect. He designs the frail *proas* that make long ocean voyages. He carves out logs into shapes as sophisticated as the limited technology will allow. He also makes the sails, blocks, and spars. During voyages, he is skipper of the craft and the navigator, finding his destination, perhaps three or four hundred miles away, across open water, to another tiny island like the one he came from. When asked by a European sea captain, "How did you find the island?" one master navigator is said to have replied, "I didn't find the island, sir. It has always been there."[8]

In Puluwat there are different schools of thought as to the best shape for a *proa,* and a young man desirous of becoming a navigator will apprentice himself for many years to a master navigator whose work he admires, in order to learn this specialty. An American anthropologist studied navigation for eighteen months with a master navigator in Puluwat and found that even after that length of time he scarcely began to understand the rudiments of *proa* building and of navigation. Specialties even in simple technologies are lifetime occupations and demand a high order of intelligence, knowledge, and skill.

Land ownership

All societies have regulations that determine the

[8] Thomas Gladwin, *East is a Big Bird: Navigation and Logic on Puluwat Atoll* (Cambridge, Mass.: Harvard University Press, 1970).

way that valuable land resources will be allocated. Small-scale hunter-gatherer societies must determine who can hunt game and gather plants, and where these activities take place. Horticulturists or food growers must decide how their farmland is to be acquired, worked, and passed on. Pastoralists require a system that determines rights to watering places and grazing land, as well as the right of access to land over which they move their herds. Full-time or extensive agriculturists must have some means of determining title to land and access to water supplies for irrigation purposes. In our own industrialized Western society, the system of private ownership of land and the rights to natural resources prevails. Elaborate laws have been established to regulate the buying, owning, and selling of land and water resources.

In nonindustrialized societies, individual ownership of land is rare; generally it is owned by one lineage or tribe. For example, among the Tiwi, all land is owned by one of nine bands. Each band of about two to three hundred people lived on roughly 200 square miles of land which they considered to be their territory—their own country. The territorial boundaries between bands were well-known, although they might strike Westerners as vague and imprecise. Anthropologists Hart and Pilling comment:

> All pieces of country—clumps of jungle, stretches of grassland, sections of thick woods —had names. A thickly wooded area belonged to one band, while the more open country that began where the woods thinned out belonged to another; thus the boundary was not a sharp line but a transitional zone—perhaps several miles—where the change from trees to savannah became noticeable. The Tiwi thought of the landscape as a sort of spectrum where a man moved gradually out of one district into another as he passed from one type of landscape into another.[9]

The adaptive value of this attitude toward land ownership is clear; the size of the band territories,

[9] Hart and Pilling, op. cit., p. 12.

as well as the size of the bands themselves, can change in size to adjust to change in amount of resources in any given place. Such adjustment would be more difficult under a system of individual ownership of land.

Among some West African horticultural tribes, a feudal system of land ownership prevails, by which all land belongs to the head chief. He allocates it to various subchiefs, who in turn distribute it to lineages; lineage leaders then assign individual plots to each farmer. Just as in medieval Europe, the African people owe allegiance to the subchiefs (or nobles) and the principal chief (or king). The people who work the land must pay taxes and fight for the king when necessary. The people, in a sense, "own" the land and transmit their ownership to their heirs. However, an individual cannot give away, sell, or otherwise dispose of his plot of land without approval from the elder of his lineage. When an individual no longer needs the land allocated to him, the lineage head rescinds title to it and re-allocates it to someone else in the lineage. The important operative principle among such farmers is that such a system extends the right to the individual to use land for a certain period of time, and the land is not "owned" outright.

Capital

Economists use the term **capital** to describe any resource that is not used up in the process of producing goods. In our society, capital means steel furnaces, drill presses, and jigsaws, as well as the money that will buy such tools. But even nonindustrial societies have means of creating and allocating the tools and other artifacts used in the production of goods and passed on to succeeding generations. The number and kinds of tools that a society uses are limited by the life-styles of its members. Hunter-gatherers and nomads, who are frequently on the move, have fewer and simpler tools than the more sedentary agriculturist, because a great number of complex tools would decrease their mobility.

Figure 10-3. *A grandmother of the !Kung tribe supervises the cooking efforts of a young girl; both young and old contribute.*

Hunters and gatherers make and use a variety of weapons, many of which are ingenious in their effectiveness. (For a look at some of the tools of such a society, see the color portfolio on the Eskimo, p. 128). They usually make for themselves the tools they need and so have first rights to their use. They may give or lend tools to others in exchange for the products of their use. For example, a bushman who gives his arrow to another hunter has a right to a share in any animals that the hunter may kill. Game is thought to "belong" to the man whose arrow killed it.

Among horticulturists, the slashing knife and the digging stick or hoe are the primary tools. Since these tools are relatively easy to produce, every man can make them himself and thus has first rights to their use. When he is not using them, any member of his family may ask to use them and usually is granted permission to do so. To refuse would mean the tool-owner would be treated with scorn for his singular lack of concern for others. If another kinsman helps raise the crop that is traded for a particular tool, he becomes part owner of the implement, and it may not be traded or given away without his permission.

As tools and other productive goods become more complex, more difficult and costlier to make, individual ownership in them usually becomes more absolute, as do the conditions under which owners may borrow and use such equipment. It is easy to replace a knife lost by a kinsman during palm cultivation, but much more difficult to replace an iron plow or a power-driven threshing machine. Rights to the ownership of complex tools are more rigidly applied; generally the man who has supplied the capital for the purchase of a complex piece of machinery is considered the sole owner and may decide how and by whom it will be used.

Technology

The economy of any society is dependent on the level of technological knowledge. In literate societies, this knowledge is preserved in books; in nonliterate societies it is retained in the minds of the living members of the group.

The division of labor is a method by which much of the technology can be apportioned among the members so that it will not be lost and can even be improved. Knowledge of various plants, when they can be harvested, where they are found, which parts are edible, and how they should be prepared and cooked, is learned by the children as they watch the adults. Lévi-Strauss reports that small children may have a knowledge of the names and uses of hundreds of plants.[10] The behavior and habits of animals, how to track them, how to use their bones and skin, how to make arrows or spears for the hunt, all are bits and pieces of the technology of nonindustrial people. It is on this technology that their livelihood rests, and all of it must be learned and passed on to the next generation in order for the group to survive.

Production—the yearly economic cycle

In an agricultural society, the patterns of work involved in the production of farm goods follow the seasons. The yearly economic cycle in a small village in modern Greece is a good illustration of production in an economic system.

The crops of the village are grown both for home consumption and for the market. The first event of the agricultural year is the pruning of the grape vines, which is commenced at the end of the winter rains. Pruning, followed by deep handhoeing, is considered a man's occupation and must be completed quickly so that the men can turn to plowing the cotton fields. Cotton is a commercial crop, whereas the grapes are grown for the wine made and consumed by the household. Cotton is usually plowed by rented tractors; the planting is done by hand.

Once the cotton starts to grow, the hoeing be-

gins. This arduous labor is performed by the girls and women of the household. Other women from the village or even from neighboring villages may be hired if the crop is a large one. This work does not excuse the women from their regular housework.

In June the wheat which was planted in the late fall is harvested by machines that are owned and operated by people outside of the village. Payment is in kind, 8 percent of the amount of wheat threshed. The wheat, made into bread and consumed at home, is still, literally, the staff of life, the basic food for the people of the village. The chaff and straw are used for the animals.

In late June and early July the tobacco, which was planted at about the same time as the wheat, is ready to be picked and strung for drying—a task welcomed by the women after the hot, backbreaking work of hoeing the cotton. They can sit in the shade near their houses.

Irrigation work in the cotton fields starts for the men in July. Each field is irrigated about three times. In October and November the cotton is picked, which requires prolonged work by many hands as the cotton does not ripen uniformly. Women do this job and again may be hired if necessary. The farmer's problem is to get the cotton picked before the winter rains set in.

Meanwhile, the vines have ripened, and winemaking takes place in October. This is an occasion much enjoyed because the men, women, and children all pick the grapes together, talk and joke, and eat a little of the produce.

The round of productive activities starts again for the next year. The Greek farmer, like any peasant, is really running a household rather than a genuinely commercial enterprise. He is motivated by a desire to protect the welfare of his own family; and the family, as the economic unit, works as a group to maintain or improve its common position. The villagers measure prestige and honor by the degree to which a family succeeds in fulfilling its obligations. The natural environment, the technology, and the work roles of the family members each exert an influence on the success from year to year of the family efforts.

[10] Claude Lévi-Strauss, *The Savage Mind* (Chicago: The University of Chicago Press, 1966).

Social integration ● part **4**

Distribution and exchange

In our own money economy, there is a two-step process between labor and consumption. The money received for labor must be translated into something else before it is directly consumable. In societies with no medium of exchange, the rewards for labor are usually direct. The workers in a family group consume what they harvest; they eat what the hunter brings home; they use the tools that they make. But even where there is no formal medium of exchange, some distribution of goods takes place. Karl Polanyi, an economist, classified the cultural systems of distributing material goods into three modes: reciprocity, redistribution, and market exchange.

Reciprocity

Reciprocity refers to a transaction between groups within a community in the form of gifts and countergifts presented in a manner prescribed by ritual and ceremony. In non-Western societies, pure altruism in gift-giving is as rare as it is in our own society. The overriding motive is to fulfill social obligations and perhaps to gain a bit of social prestige in the process. It might best be compared in our society to a hostess who gives a dinner party. She may compete within her social circle in the gourmet food she prepares, the originality of her decorations, and the quality of wit and conversation of her guests. Her expectation is that she will be invited to similar parties by some, although perhaps not all, of the guests.

Social customs dictate the nature and occasion of gift-giving. When an animal is killed by a group of hunters in Australia, the meat is divided among the families of the hunters and other kinsmen. Each person in the camp gets a share, the size of which depends on his relationship to the hunters. The least desirable parts may be kept by the hunters themselves. When a kangaroo was killed, the left hind leg went to the brother of the hunter, the tail to his father's brother's son, the

Figure 10-4. An Australian hunter of the Walmadgeri tribe prepares to build a fire and cook a kangaroo. He will later supervise the customary distribution of the meat to members of his family group.

loins and the fat to his father-in-law, the ribs to his mother-in-law, the fore-legs to his father's younger sister, the head to his wife, and the entrails and the blood to the hunter. If there were arguments over the apportionment, it was because the principles of distribution were not being followed properly. The hunter and his family would seem to fare badly according to this arrangement, but they would have their turn when another man made the kill. The giving and receiving was obligatory, as was the particularity of the distribution. Such sharing of food reinforces community bonds and ensures that everyone eats. It might also be viewed as a way of saving perishable goods. By giving away part of his kill, the hunter gets a social IOU for a similar amount of food in the future. It is really quite similar to putting money in a time-deposit savings account.

Reciprocity in which neither the value of the gift is calculated nor the time of repayment specified is **generalized reciprocity. Balanced reciprocity** is not part of a long-term process. The giving and receiving, as well as the time involved, are more specific. Examples of balanced reciprocity among the Crow Indians are related by Robert Lowie.[11] A woman, skilled in the tanning of buffalo hides, might offer her services to a neighbor who needed a new cover for her tepee. It took an expert to design a tepee cover, which required from fourteen to twenty skins. The designer might need as many as twenty collaborators, whom she instructed in the sewing together of the skins and whom the tepee owner might remunerate with a feast. The designer herself would be given some kind of property by the tepee owner. In another example from the Crow, Lowie relates that if a married woman brought her brother a present of food, he might reciprocate with a present of ten arrows for her husband, which rated as the equivalent of a horse.

Negative reciprocity is a third form of gift-giving, in which the giver tries to get the better of the exchange. In Malekula, according to Her-

skovits, "a gift is at most a venture, a hopeful speculation."[12] At the very least, the gift-giver has placed the recipient under an obligation.

Giving, receiving, and sharing constitute a form of social security or insurance. A family contributes to others when they have the means and can count on receiving from others in time of need. A leveling mechanism is at work in the process of reciprocity. Social obligations compel a family to distribute their goods, and no one is permitted to accumulate too much more than the others. Greater wealth simply brings a greater obligation to give.

Barter and trade

Reciprocity in the form of obligatory gift-giving takes place within the group. When exchange takes place between two groups, there is apt to be greater hostility and competition. Such an exchange takes the form of trade, by which scarce items from one group are bartered for desirable goods from the other group. Relative value is calculated, and, despite an outward show of indifference, sharp trading is more the rule when compared to the reciprocal nature of the exchanges within the group.

An arrangement that partook partly of reciprocity and partly of trade existed between the Kota, in India, and three neighboring tribes who traded their surplus goods and certain services with the Kota. The Kota were the musicians and artisans for the area. They exchanged iron tools with the other three groups and provided the music essential for ceremonial occasions. The Toda furnished to the Kota ghee (a kind of butter) for certain ceremonies and buffalo for funerals; relations between the Kota and the Toda were friendly. The Badaga were agricultural and traded their grain for music and tools. Between the Kota and Badaga there was a feeling of great competition, which sometimes led to some unfair trading practices; it was usually the Kota who procured the advantage. The forest-dwelling Kurumba, who

---

[11]Robert Lowie, *Crow Indians* (New York: Holt, Rinehart and Winston, 1956, original edition 1935) p. 75.

[12]Herskovits, *op. cit.,* p. 157.

were dreaded sorcerers, had honey, canes, and occasionally fruits to offer, but their main contribution was protection against the supernatural. The Kota feared the Kurumba, and the Kurumba took advantage of this fact in their trade dealings, so that they always got more than they gave. Thus there was great latent hostility between these two tribes.

Silent trade is a specialized form of barter in which no verbal communication takes place. The earliest and best-known description was given by Herodotus, who told of silent trade between the Carthaginians and the people who lived on the western coast of Africa, beyond the Pillars of Hercules. In California, an instance of silent trade occurred between the Tubatulabel and the other tribes with whom they had peaceful relations. They would trade piñon nuts and tobacco for lengths of white clamshell disks which passed for currency among all the tribes of that region. The reasons for silent trade can only be hypothesized, but perhaps trade was silent for lack of a common language, to avoid hostility, or because of problems of status which made verbal communication unthinkable. In any event, it provides for the exchange of goods between groups in spite of potential barriers.

The Kula ring

The classic example of trade among nonliterate people is the Kula of the Trobriand Islanders, first described by Malinowski.[13] The Kula is a trading system that involves the exchange of scarce goods, competition for prestige, and the all-important ceremonial exchange of highly-valued necklaces and armshells. Some of the first-class necklaces and armshells have names and histories, like Stradivarius violins, and, as Malinowski said, "always create a sensation when they appear in a district." The trade takes place throughout the islands, with the necklaces traveling in a clockwise fashion from island to island and the arm-

[13]Bronislaw Malinowski, *Argonauts of the Western Pacific* (New York: E. P. Dutton & Co., 1932).

Figure 10-5. *The ceremonial trading of necklaces and armbands in the Kula ring encourages trade throughout Melanesia.*

shells traveling counterclockwise. No one man holds these valuables very long, and each employs strategies to improve his position. It is the Trobriand Island version of how to win without actually cheating. But a man cannot be too crafty or no one will trade with him.

A few men on each island participate in the Kula and have trading partners on the other islands. An important man may have as many as one hundred trading partners. These partnerships are lifetime relationships. Much ceremony and magic are attached to the Kula.

The Kula involves ocean voyages of fifty miles or more, and, as might be expected, more than necklaces and armshells are exchanged. A man may simply exchange necklaces and armshells with his Kula partner, but he is free to haggle and barter over other goods he has brought along on the trip for trading. In this way these island people have access to a whole range of material goods not found on their own islands.

The Kula is a most elaborate complex of ceremony, social relationships, economic exchange, travel, magic, and social integration. To see it only in its economic aspects is to misunderstand it completely. The Kula demonstrates once more the close interrelationship of cultural factors that is especially characteristic of non-Western societies.

Redistribution

In nonliterate groups, where there is a sufficient surplus to support a government, income will flow into the public coffers in the form of gifts, taxes, and the spoils of war; then it will be distributed again. The chief or king has two motives in disposing of this income: the first is to maintain his position of superiority by a display of wealth; the second is to assure those who support him an adequate standard of living.

The administration of the Inca empire in Peru was highly efficient both in the collection of taxes and methods of control. A census was kept of the population and resources. Tributes in goods and, more importantly, in services were levied. Each craftsman had to produce a specific quota of goods from materials supplied by overseers.

Figure 10-6. *This frieze from the staircase of Persepolis illustrates the wealthy Persians bringing goods and livestock in tribute to the king; he redistributes the wealth to others.*

Forced labor might be used for agricultural work or work in the mines. Forced labor was also employed in a program of public works which included a remarkable system of roads and bridges throughout the mountainous terrain, aqueducts that guaranteed a supply of water, and storehouses that held surplus food for use in times of famine. Careful accounts were kept of the income and expenditures. A governmental bureaucracy had the responsibility of seeing that production was maintained and that commodities were distributed according to the regulations set forth by the ruling powers.

Through the activities of the government, **redistribution** took place. The ruling class lived in great luxury, but goods were redistributed to the common people when necessary. Redistribution then is a pattern of distribution by which the exchange is not between individuals or between groups, but, rather, by which a proportion of the products of labor is funneled into one source and is parceled out again as directed by a central administration. The progressive income tax in the United States is our method of redistribution;

Figure 10-7. *These great piles of yams are a sign of a good harvest in a New Guinea village. Many will not be eaten but rather displayed as a form of accumulated wealth.*

wealthy people theoretically pay relatively higher taxes and this money is redistributed through programs such as Social Security and aid to dependent children. For a process of redistribution to be possible, a society must have a fairly complex system of political organization and a substantial economic surplus.

Distribution of wealth

In nonliterate societies living barely above the subsistence level, gradations of wealth are small and systems of reciprocity serve to distribute in a fairly equitable fashion what little wealth exists.

Display for social prestige, what economist Thorstein Veblen called **conspicuous consumption,** is a strong motivating force for the distribution of wealth in societies where some substantial surplus is produced. These displays often take the form of feasts. The individual hosting the feast acquires status and prestige; his accumulated goods are dispersed throughout the group.

On Guadalcanal, one of the Solomon Islands, an ambitious young man plans a long-term strategic course to become an important person. His material goals are to have a fine, large house and to accumulate enough food to celebrate with a lavish feast. The building of the house may require as many as a hundred young men, all of whom have to be fed, along with his relatives who also assist in the work. His first move is to increase his gardens and accumulate livestock. The animals will require more labor, but they can be fed from the produce he has previously cultivated. After a few years, he lets it be known that he intends to erect his house. He is helped by all because of the excellent food they will get during the work and because they enjoy working together. Upon the completion of the house, a festival takes place which requires two weeks for preparation. An observer of one of these festivals counted 257 separate presentations of food.

In this instance, a surplus was created for the express purpose of gaining prestige by the display and the giving of food. Yet it also served as a levelling mechanism providing a distribution of wealth and preventing hoarding of goods that would make them unavailable for consumption. Conspicuous consumption in its most exaggerated form was exhibited in the nineteenth-century rivalry potlatch ceremonies of the Indians of the northwest United States and Canada. After a grandiose display of wealth by a person of high status, there was not only a great feast and generous gifts given to representatives of other groups, but a destruction of valuables such as canoes, blankets, and particularly European goods (including money), which had only recently been introduced into the society. There was competition for social prestige among chiefs and other persons of high status in the quantity of goods given away and destroyed.

Market exchange

The flow of goods passing from owner to owner in the marketplace, as a form of exchange, is familiar to Americans and is readily observable in foreign places. In fact, in the United States, there has been a revival and proliferation of "flea markets" where anyone, for a small fee, may display and sell handicrafts, second-hand items, farm produce, and paintings. There is excitement in the search for bargains, and an opportunity for

Figure 10-8a. *In nearly every society, the market is an important focus of social as well as economic activity. In our own society, going shopping is a popular weekend social occasion for groups of family and friends. The fact that many shoppers dress up in their best clothes emphasizes the social aspect of the excursion. This photo shows a Spanish market.*

Social integration ● part **4**

Figure 10-8b. *She sells sea snails by the sea shore of the Ivory Coast.*

Figure 10-8d. *This street in the bazaar of Marrakesh is devoted only to metalworkers.*

Figure 10-8c. *A bazaar in Delhi sells nuts and bolts and bicycle parts.*

Figure 10-8e. *This muddy food market is located in a Hong Kong slum.*

10 chapter ● **Economic systems**

haggling. A carnival atmosphere prevails with eating, laughing, and conversation, and items may even be bartered without any cash passing hands. These flea markets, or farmers' markets, are similar to the markets of non-Western societies.

The first and most basic characteristic of the market in non-Western societies is that it always means a marketplace, a specific site where the actual goods are exchanged. In non-Western societies, the marketplace is totally different from what is known in modern economy as the principle of market exchange. The market principle involves the system of establishing prices by the powers of supply and demand, no matter where the transactions are made. Although some of our market transactions do take place in a specific identifiable location—much of the trade in cotton, for example, takes place in New Orleans' Cotton Exchange—it is also quite possible for an American to buy and sell goods without ever being on the same side of the continent.

This difference between "principle" and "place" clearly separates the market economy of modern industrial societies from the kind of marketing which prevails in traditional non-Western societies. When people talk about a market in today's world, the particular place where something is sold is often not important at all. For example, think of the way people speak of a "market" for certain types of automobiles, or for mouthwash.

The chief goods exchanged in non-Western markets are material items produced by the people. The people bring to the market the produce and animals they have grown and raised and the handicrafts they have made. These they sell or exchange for items they want and cannot produce themselves. Land, labor, and occupations are not bought and sold as they are through the Western market economy. In other words, what happens in the marketplace has nothing to do with the price of land, the amount paid for labor, or the cost of services. The market is local, specific, and contained. Some noneconomic aspects of marketplaces in nonindustrial societies overshadow the strictly economic aspects. Social relationships are as important in the marketplace as they are in other aspects of the economy. For example, dancers and other entertainers perform in the marketplace. It is customary for people to gather there to hear news. In ancient Mexico, under the Aztecs, people were required by law to go to market at specific intervals, in order to be informed as to what was going on. Chiefs held court and settled judicial disputes at the market. Above all, the market is a gathering place where people renew friendships, see relatives, gossip, and keep up with the world.

Original study

THE POTLATCH

Among the Kwakiutl Indians of British Columbia, the potlatch is the most important public ceremony for the announcement of significant events and the claiming of hierarchical names, hereditary rights, and privileges. Such announcements or claims are always accompanied by the giving of gifts from a host to all guests. The guests are invited to witness, and later to validate, a host's claims, and each receives gifts of varying worth according to his rank.

Potlatches are held to celebrate births, marriages, deaths, adoptions, or the coming of age of young people. They may also be given as a penalty for breaking a taboo, such as behaving frivolously or performing ineptly during a sacred winter dance. A potlatch to save face can be prompted by an accident even as trivial as the capsizing of a canoe or the birth of a deformed child. Among the most extravagant potlatches are those given for rivalry or vengeance.

All potlatches are public. The host, with the support of his family, numima (the next largest tribal subdivision), or tribe invites other families, numimas, or tribes. The size of the gathering reveals the affluence and prestige of the host. At the ceremony, he traces his line of descent and his rights to the claims he is making. Every name, dance or song used by the host must be acknowledged and legitimized by the guests. No announcement or claim is made without feasting and the distribution of gifts. Gifts are given to guests in the order of their tribal importance and of a value relative to this prestige. Clearly, high-ranking chiefs receive more gifts than lesser men. But the value and quantity of gifts distributed at a potlatch reflect less on the recipients than on the donor. The gifts he gives away—or in some cases the property he publicly destroys—are marks of his wealth, rank, generosity, and self-esteem. Over a period of time, they also measure the power and prestige that he will be able to maintain over others of high status. For, at a later potlatch, each high-ranking guest will try to return as much, or preferably more, than he received. To keep track of the gifts distributed and the precise hierarchy of guests, each donor has the assistance of a "potlatch secretary" whose records are needed to maintain correct social form and avoid offense.

Potlatch gifts vary widely, from money to property. They include boats, blankets, flour, kettles, fish oil, and, in former times, slaves. More recently, gifts have included sewing machines, furniture, even pool tables. Probably the most valuable potlatch material has little intrinsic worth but enormous symbolic value. These are coppers—large pieces of beaten sheet copper shaped like shields with a ridge running down the center of the lower half. They are painted with black lead and a design is incised through the paint. Each copper has a name and its potlatch history determines its value. One copper, called "All other coppers are ashamed to look at it," had been paid for with 7500 blankets; another known as "Making the house empty of wealth," was worth 5000 blankets.

During a potlatch, which can last several days and long into each night, speeches, songs, and dances are mixed with the giving of gifts, snacks and more lavish feasting. The host is not the only speaker; usually high-ranking guests also speak or supervise the singing, dancing, and drumming. Elaborate ceremonial costumes are worn by the speaker—who holds a "speaker's staff"—

by dancers and musicians; the hall where the potlatch is held is decorated with painted hangings and tribal insignia.

All potlatch ceremonies are marked by exacting standards of etiquette and behavior. Impropriety, whether intentional or accidental, requires an immediate response. Mistakes in procedure, public quarreling, or an accident witnessed by others brings a sense of shame and indignity on its perpetrator, who must immediately "cover (or wipe off) the shame," making a payment to reestablish his self-esteem. Often, blankets are torn into strips and each witness is given a piece.

The Kwakiutl respond similarly to insults. Potlatchers sometimes deliberately insult a guest by calling his name out of order, by spilling oil on him, by throwing him his gift, or by presenting him with an inappropriate portion of food. The offended guest retaliates immediately by giving gifts himself, or by destroying something valuable of his own while denouncing the potlatcher. Violence sometimes erupts. On some occasions the host ignores a face-saving

Figure 10-9. *The blankets given away at a potlatch often feature this type of totemistic design.*

Social integration ● part **4**

gesture of a guest and this may precipitate a rivalry potlatch. If a host mistakenly offends, a guest restores his pride by giving the host a reprimand gift. Embarrassed by his carelessness, the correct host will make restitution in double the amount of the reprimand gift.

Rivalries also develop when two men compete for the same name, song, or other privilege. Each contestant recites his closest genealogical connection with the claim and tries to outdo his rival in the amount of property he can give away. In the heat of such rivalries, contestants sometimes break off a piece of copper, thereby destroying its value, and give the piece to their rival. The rival might then bring out his own copper of at least equal value, break it, and give both pieces back to the opponent. Great merit came to the man who threw his copper into the sea, "drowning it," thus showing his utter contempt for property and implying that his importance was such that what he destroyed was of little concern to him. At times this ostentatious destruction of property included canoes, house planks, blankets, and even slaves, in former days.

The witnesses to these dramatic acts of the potlatch act as judges to the claims; ultimately, they decide the victor. A powerful and prestigious man can sway public opinion by recognizing the claim of one contestant over another at a subsequent potlatch. Indeed, this is a basic principle of the potlatch; a successful potlatch in itself cannot legitimize a claim. It is the behavior of other hosts at later potlatches that validates a claim for once and for all.

Source:
From *The Kwakiutl: Indians of British Columbia* by Ronald P. Rohner and Evelyn C. Rohner. Copyright © 1970 by Holt, Rinehart and Winston, Inc. Adapted and reprinted by permission of Holt, Rinehart and Winston, Inc.

portfolio four

The Indian's story

Paintings on the following pages by European
and American artists depict in brief the history of the
American Indian—from tribal ways and existence on
the land, to increasing encroachment by white settlers,
armed conflict, and tragedy. The following speech, abridged
only slightly, was made by the Seneca Chief Red Jacket in response to
an address by a white missionary at Buffalo, New York, in 1805:

Brother, listen to what we say. There was a time when our
forefathers owned this great island. Their seats extended
from the rising to the setting sun. The Great Spirit had
made it for the use of the Indians. He had created the
buffalo, the deer and other animals for food. He made the
bear and the beaver, and their skins served us for clothing.
. . . He had caused the earth to produce corn for bread. All
this he had done for his red children because he loved them.
If we had any disputes about hunting grounds, they were
generally settled without the shedding of much blood: but
an evil day came upon us; your forefathers crossed the great
waters and landed on this island. Their numbers were small;
they found friends, not enemies; they told us they had fled
from their own country for fear of wicked men, and come here
to enjoy their religion. They asked for a small seat; we
took pity on them, granted their request, and they sat down
among us; yet we did not fear them, we took them to be
friends; they called us brothers, we believed them and
gave them a larger seat. At length their number had greatly
increased; they wanted more land; they wanted our country.

Rosa Bonheur, *Buffalo Hunt*

George Catlin, *Indian Meeting*

Charles M. Russell, *The Wagons*   Jules Tavernier, *The White Man's Weapon*

Erneste Etienne Narjot, *Colonel J. C. Cremony Leading a Fight Against the Apaches*

Charles M. Russell, *"Her heart is on the ground"*

Our eyes were opened, and our minds became uneasy. Wars took place; Indians were hired to fight against Indians, and many of our people were destroyed.

Brother, our seats were once large, and yours were very small; you have now become a great people, and we have scarcely a place left to spread our blankets; you have got our country, but you are not satisfied; you want to force your religion upon us.

Brother, continue to listen. You say that you are sent to instruct us how to worship the Great Spirit . . . you say that you are right and we are lost; how do we know this to be true? We understand that your religion is written in a book; if it was intended for us as well as you, why has not the Great Spirit given it to us, and not only to us but why did he not give to our forefathers the knowledge of that book with the means of understanding it rightly? . . . We also have a religion which was given to our forefathers and has been handed down to us their children. . . . It teaches us to be thankful for all the favors we receive; to love each other and to be united. We never quarrel about religion.

Brother, the Great Spirit has made us all; but he has . . . given us a different complexion and different customs. . . . Since he has made so great a difference between us in other things, why may we not conclude that he has given us a different religion according to our understanding. . . . Brother, we do not wish to destroy your religion, or take it from you; we only want to enjoy our own.

Brother, we are told that you have been preaching to white people in this place; these people are our neighbors, we are acquainted with them; we will wait a little while and see what effect your preaching has upon them. If we find it does them good, makes them honest and less disposed to cheat Indians, we will then consider again what you have said. . . . As we are going to part, we will come and take you by the hand and hope the Great Spirit will protect you. . . .

The minister refused to join hands, insisting "that there was no fellowship between the religion of God and the works of the devil." And the Indians left politely.

From Samuel G. Drake, Biography and History of the Indians of North America, 1851: as found in "The Winged Serpent," an anthology edited by Margot Astrov.
Paintings courtesy Kennedy Galleries, New York

Summary

1.

The study of the economics of non-Western societies can be undertaken only in the context of the total culture of each society. Each society solves the problem of getting its living within the limitations of its resources of land, capital, and technology, and distributes its goods according to its own priorities.

2.

The work people do is a major productive resource and the allotment of work is always governed by rules according to sex and age. Few generalizations can be made covering the kinds of work performed by men and women. The cooperation of many people working together is a typical feature of non-Western peoples. Specialties requiring a great skill and knowledge are important even in societies with a very simple technology.

3.

Capital in non-Western economies is primarily in the form of land which is usually owned by the group—the family, the lineage, or the tribe—rather than by individuals. The technology of a people in the form of the tools they use, their knowledge of plants and animals, and their ability to control the environment determines the way they gain their livelihood.

4.

Production is dependent upon the natural environment. Hunters and gatherers will follow the migrations of animals and the seasonal occurrences of fruits and vegetables. The yearly cycle of planting and harvesting circumscribes the productive activities of horticulturists and agriculturists.

5.

Non-Western people consume most of what they themselves produce. But there is an exchange of goods. The processes of distribution which may be distinguished are reciprocity, redistribution, and market exchange. Reciprocity is the giving and receiving of gifts, not necessarily of equal value, according to rules fixing obligations.

6.

Barter and trade take place between groups. There are elements of reciprocity in trading exchanges but there is a greater calculation of the relative values of goods exchanged. A classic example of exchange between groups which partook of both reciprocity and sharp trading was the Kula ring of the Trobriand Islanders.

7.

A complex economic and political organization is necessary for redistribution to take place. The government assesses each citizen a tax or tribute, uses the proceeds to support the governmental and religious elite, and redistributes the rest in the form of public services.

8.

Exchange in the market place serves to distribute goods in a district. The market place also functions as a social gathering place and a news medium.

Suggested readings

Bohannan, Paul, and George Dalton, eds. *Markets in Africa.* Evanston, Ill.: Northwestern University Press, 1962.

Essays on the market system of African economic life. Studies economic activities ranging in complexity from aboriginal to present day marketing systems. Discusses the noneconomic function of African markets. One article deals with current changes in Africa as they affect markets.

Clark, J. G. D. *Prehistoric Europe: The Economic Basis.* Palo Alto, Calif.: Stanford University Press, 1962.

The book is concerned with the ways in which early man, in competition with other forms of life, maintained himself since the end of the Pleistocene Ice Age. It discusses how man managed to raise his standards from those of hunters to those of peasants ready to support the full weight of urban civilization. Combines natural science and historical approaches.

Clough, S. B., and C. W. Cole *Economic History of Europe,* 3rd ed. Boston: Heath, 1952.

The authors have undertaken a study of economic developments to gain an understanding of the past. They use economic history as a thread which leads the student through important historical events and provides an understanding of human activity. They begin with the Middle Ages, convinced that most of the important elements of modern economic life had their roots then, and proceed with an analysis of European history to modern times, covering feudalism, guilds, commerce, capitalism, mercantilism, etc.

Heilbroner, Robert L. *The Making of Economic Society,* 4th ed. Englewood Cliffs, N.J.: Prentice-Hall, 1972.

This book attempts to present some of the basic content of economics in the light of theory and history. Emphasis is on the rise and development of the market system, the central theme of Western economic heritage. It begins with the premarket economy of antiquity and carries the study through the market society, industrial revolution and technology, to capitalism and modern economic society.

Nash, Manning *Primitive and Peasant Economic Systems.* San Francisco: Chandler Publishers, 1966.

This book studies the problems of economic anthropology, especially the dynamics of social and economic change, in terms of primitive and peasant economic systems. The book is heavily theoretical, but draws on field work done by the author in Guatemala, Mexico, and Burma.

Tuma, Elias H. *European Economic History: Theory and History of Economic Change.* New York: Harper & Row, 1971.

In the light of several competing theories of economic development and decline, this book examines the scale and methods of production and trade in Europe from the tenth century to the present. The medieval firm, living standards, territorial expansion, population growth, and technology are among the subjects that come in for extended discussion.

Vogt, Evon *The Zinacantecos of Mexico*. New York: Holt, Rinehart and Winston, 1970.
A case study in anthropology concerning the Zinacantecos, a Maya tribe in Mexico who have a highly ceremonialized life-style. An interesting study of their society, culture, religion, economic system, and social structure.

Wolf, Eric R. *Peasants*. Englewood Cliffs, N.J.: Prentice-Hall, 1966.
This book is concerned with the peasant stage in the evolution of human society—midway between primitive tribal and industrial society. The author discusses the economic and social aspects of peasantry, levels in religious traditions, and some peasant movements.

Political
organization

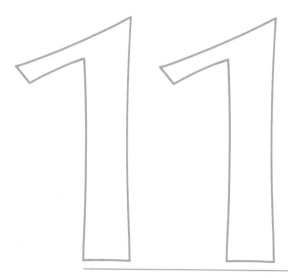

"I am the State," proclaimed Louis XIV. With this sweeping statement, the king declared absolute rule over France; he believed himself to be the law, the lawmaker, the courts, the judge, jailer and executioner—in short, the seat of all political organization in France.

Louis took a great deal of responsibility on his royal shoulders; had he actually performed each of these functions, he would have done the work of thousands of men, the number required to keep the machinery of a large political organization such as a state running at full steam. As a form of political organization, the state of seventeenth-century France was not much different from many that exist in modern times, including our own. All large states require rigid, elaborate, centralized structures involving hierarchies of executives, legislators, and judges who initiate, pass, and enforce laws for large numbers of people.

But such complex structures have not always been in existence, and even today, there are societies that depend on much less formal means of organization. In such small-scale societies, flexible and informal kinship systems with no designated leaders prevail. Social problems such as homicide and theft are perceived as serious "family quarrels" rather than affairs that affect the entire community. Between these two polarities of political organization lies a world of variety, including societies with chiefs, Big Men, or charismatic leaders, and segmented tribal societies with multicentric authority systems. Such disparity prompts the question, "What is political organization?"

The term "political organization" refers to those aspects of social organization specifically concerned with the management of the affairs of public policy of a society, whether it be organizing a giraffe hunt or raising an army. In other words, political organization is the system of social relationships that provides for the coordination and regulation of behavior insofar as that behavior is related to the maintenance of public order. Government, on the other hand, consists of an administrative system having specialized personnel which may or may not form a part of the political organization, depending on the complexity of the society. Some form of political organization exists in all societies, but it is not always a government.

The political organization of a society cannot be properly understood in isolation from its ecological and technoeconomic components; nor can it be meaningfully analyzed apart from its social and ideological context. Modern political anthropology, therefore, seeks to understand political systems not apart from, but rather in connection with, the other components of culture.

Kinds of political systems

Political organization is the means through which a society maintains social order and reduces social disorder. Such organization assumes a variety of forms among the peoples of the world, but scholars have simplified this complex subject by identifying four basic kinds of political systems. These are (in order of complexity) bands, tribes, chiefdoms, and states. The first two forms are uncentralized sociopolitical systems; the latter two are centralized systems.

Uncentralized political systems

Most non-Western peoples have neither chiefs with established rights and duties, nor any fixed form of government. The strong web of kinship forms the chief means of social organization among these peoples. The economies of these societies are of the subsistence type, so populations are typically very small. Leaders do not have real authority to enforce the society's customs or laws, and individual members conform out of fear that they will be ostracized or made the target of scorn and gossip. Important decisions are usually made in a democratic manner by a consensus among adult males; dissenting members may decide to act with the majority, or they may choose to adopt some other course of action if they are willing to risk the social consequences. This form of political organization provides great flexibility, which in many situations confers an adaptive advantage.

Band organization. The band is a small autonomous group; it is the least complicated form of political organization. Bands are usually found among hunter-gatherers and other nomadic societies in which there are factors that limit the size of the group. Bands are kin groups, composed of related men or women and their spouses and unmarried children; the closeness of the group is indicated by the fact that there are usually rules that prohibit marriage among band members. Bands may be characterized as associations of related nuclear families who occupy a common territory and who live together on it so long as environmental and subsistence circumstances are favorable. Some anthropologists believe that the band is the oldest form of political organization since all men were once nomadic hunters and gatherers, and remained so until the development of agriculture and pastoralism about 10,000 years ago.

Figure 11-1. *In the Ivory Coast, older tribal traditions of singing and dancing are mixed with the new custom of electioneering.*

Social integration ● part **4**

Since band members are typically hunter-gatherers who often must range far and wide to search for food sources, they are generally on the move most of the year, following herds and harvests. This migratory mode of existence is correlated with a second important feature of the band: its small size. Population density of the band is quite low, varying from a handful to a few hundred individuals; its size depends on the methods employed in gathering food. The more food the group is able to find, the more individuals it can support, and the larger the band. During seasons when food is scarce, the band may disperse over a broad area, perhaps dividing into several smaller groups.

Bands are generally quite democratic: no band member may tell another individual what to do, how to hunt, or whom to marry. There is no private ownership (except in the case of a few weapons or tools), and game and other foods are shared by all members of the group. Rank (other than age and sex status differentiation), the specialization of labor, and formal political organization are not found in this form of society. Generally, the band lacks the social techniques that would be necessary to integrate its members into larger political groups. Decisions in the band are usually made by a consensus of all adult members of the group, and so they require little formal implementation. The decision to undertake a hunting expedition or to begin a ritual celebration is reached after a meeting of the band's senior adult males.

Band leaders are usually older men whose courage, success in hunting, or ability to placate supernatural forces is recognized and admired by other members. The leader is followed not because he has coercive power, but because members know that in the past he has demonstrated good sense, skill and success; when he fails to lead well and make the right decisions, members will choose to follow another leader. The band leader is simply the first among equals, a leader with personal authority that stems from his abilities.

An example of the informal nature of leadership in the band is found among the !Kung Bushmen of the Kalahari Desert. Each !Kung band is comprised of a group of families who live together, linked to one another and to the headman through kinship. Although each band owns its territory and the resources within it, two or more !Kung bands may range over the same territory. The headman, called the *kxau* or owner, is the focal point for the band's ownership of the territory. The headman does not himself own the land or resources, but he symbolically personifies the rights of band members to them. If the headman leaves a territory to live elsewhere, he ceases to be headman, and some other member of the band takes his place.

The headman coordinates the band's movements when resources are no longer adequate for subsistence in a particular territory. His chief duty is to plan when and where the group will move; when the band moves, the headman's position is at the head of the line. He chooses the site for the new settlement, and he has the first choice of a spot for his own fire. He has no other rewards or duties. For example, the headman does not organize hunting parties, trading expeditions, the making of artifacts, or gift giving; nor does he make marriage arrangements. Individual band members instigate their own activities. The headman is not a judge, nor is he obligated to punish other band members. Wrongdoers are judged and regulated by public opinion, usually expressed by gossip among band members. If a headman is too young or too old or loses the desired qualities of leadership, band members will turn to another man to lead them.

Tribal organization. The second type of uncentralized or multicentric authority system is the tribe. Midway between the simple band and the more complex chiefdom or state, the tribe typically produces its goods through some form of agriculture or herding. Since these methods of production are more efficient and thus yield more food than those of the hunter-gatherer band, the tribe is able to support a greater number of individuals. The tribe has greater population density than the band; this brings a new set of problems to be solved at the same time that it permits new kinds of solutions.

Each tribe consists of one or more small autonomous units; these may then form alliances with one another for various purposes. As in the band, political organization in the tribe is informal and of temporary nature. Whenever a situation requiring political integration of all or several tribal groups arises, they join to deal with the situation in a cooperative manner. When the problem is satisfactorily solved, each group then returns to its autonomous state.

Leadership among tribes is also informal. Among the Navajo Indians, for example, the individual did not think of his government as something fixed and all-powerful, and leadership was not vested in a central authority. A local leader was a man respected for his age, integrity, and wisdom. His advice was therefore sought frequently, but he had no formal means of control and could not enforce any decision on those who asked for his help. Group decisions were made on the basis of public consensus, with the most influential man usually somewhat more responsible than others for the final decision. Among the social mechanisms that induced members to abide by group decisions were withdrawal of cooperation, gossip, criticism, and the belief that disease was caused by antisocial actions.[1]

The separate units of the tribe may be integrated by a number of pantribal factors. For example, organization can be based on membership in a kinship or descent group, an association or secret society, an age-set system, or territorial groups such as wards or towns.

Kinship organization. In many tribal societies, the organizing unit and seat of political authority is the clan, an association of kinsmen who trace descent from a common ancestor. Within the clan, elders or headmen are responsible for regulating the affairs of members and represent their kinship group in relations with other kinship

[1] Elman Service, *Profiles in Ethnology.* (New York: Harper & Row, 1958).

Figure 11-2a. *Sultan's palace in Cameroun.*

Figure 11-2b. *King's home in Cameroun.*

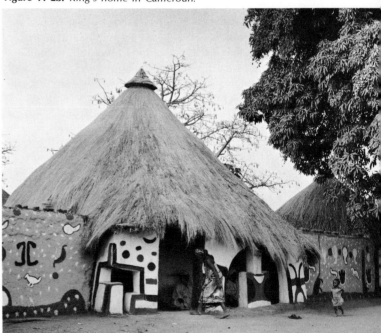

Social integration • part **4**

Figure 11-2c. *A tribal king in Dahomey wears traditional crown and French sunglasses.*
Figure 11-2d. *Another tribal king and crown.*

Figure 11-2e. *The royal family of an Ivory Coast tribal society.*
Figure 11-2f. *Dahomey king with noseguard to protect him against evil spirits.*

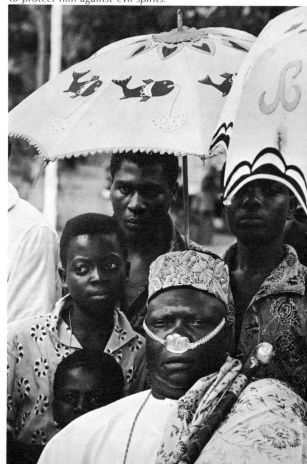

groups. As a group, the elders may form a council that acts within the tribe or for the tribe in dealings with outsiders. In some societies, the strategic and tactical planning for warfare rests in the hands of the clan.

Another form of tribal kinship bond that provides political organization is the segmentary lineage system. This system is similar in operation to the clan, but it is less extensive and is a relatively rare form of political organization. The economy of the segmentary tribe is generally just above subsistence level. Production is small-scale, and the tribe probably has a labor pool just large enough to provide necessities. Since each lineage group in the tribe produces the same goods, none depends on another for goods or services. Political organization among segmentary lineage societies is usually informal: there are neither political offices nor chiefs, although older tribal members may exercise some personal authority. In his study of the Tiv and the Nuer, Marshall Sahlins describes the way that the segmentary lineage form of political organization works.[2] According to Sahlins, segmentation is the normal process of tribal growth. It is also the social means of temporary unification of a fragmented tribal society to join in an action. The segmentary lineage may be viewed as a substitute for the fixed political structure which a tribe cannot maintain.

Among the Nuer, a tribe numbering some 200,000 people living in the swampland and savanna of the Sudan, there are at least twenty clans. Each clan is patrilineal and is segmented into lineages which are further segmented. A clan is separated into maximal lineages; maximal lineages are segmented into major lineages which are segmented into minor lineages, which in turn are segmented into minimal lineages. The minimal lineage is a group descending from one great grandfather or a greatgreat grandfather.

The lineage segments among the Nuer are all equal, and no real leadership or political organization at all exists above the level of the autonomous minimal or primary segments. The entire superstructure of the lineage is nothing more than an alliance, active only during conflicts between any of the minimal segments. In any serious dispute between members of different minimal lineage segments, members of all other segments take the side of the contestant to whom they are most closely related, and the issue is then joined between the higher order lineages involved. Such a system of political organization is known as complementary or balanced opposition.

Disputes among the Nuer are frequent, and under the segmentary lineage system, they can lead to widespread feuds. This possible source of social disruption is minimized by the actions of the "leopard skin chief," or holder of a ritual office of conciliation. The leopard skin chief has no political power and is looked on as standing outside the lineage network. All he can do is try to persuade feuding lineages to accept payment in "blood cattle" rather than taking another life. His mediation gives each side the chance to back down gracefully before too many people are killed; but if the participants are for some reason unwilling to compromise, the leopard skin chief has no authority to enforce a settlement.

Age-set organization. Age-set systems provide a tribal society with the means of political organization beyond the kin group. Under this system, youths, usually at puberty, are initiated into the first age set. They then pass as a set from one age grade to another when they reach the proper age. Age sets cut across territorial and kin groupings and are the chief means of political organization.

Political matters of the tribe are in the hands of the age sets and their officers. An example of the age-set system as a form of political organization is found in A. Prins' study of the Kipsigis in his book *East-African Age-Set Systems*. Among the Kipsigis, there are two principal age sets: that of *murenik* or warrior, and that of *poysiek* or senior elder. Secondary age-set groups are the junior warriors (males below the age of puberty), junior elders, and retired elders. Young men are initiated into the warrior age class at puberty, at

[2]Marshall Sahlins, "The Segmentary Lineage: An Organization of Predatory Expansion" in *American Anthropologist* 63:322-343.

which time they are taught tribal customs and religious codes. The tasks of the warriors are military and economic: they must defend the country and enrich and strengthen the tribe by begetting many children and capturing many cattle. The principal tasks of the elders are military, administrative, judicial, and religious. They may fight in defensive battles, and certain of them serve as chiefs of staff, organizing and advising the army.

Most political authority among the Kipsigis is vested in the age set of the elders who serve in the hamlet, village, and territorial group. In the hamlet, an elder versed in law mediates disputes. If the case cannot be resolved at the hamlet level, it is sent up to the village level, where a council of elders judges the case. Certain elders also preside at initiation ceremonies, and at those ceremonies where one age set is retiring and another rising to take its place.

Association organization. Sodalities, secret societies, and other associations that function as politically integrative systems within tribes are found in many areas of the world, including Africa, Melanesia, and India. Perhaps the best example of association organization may be found during the nineteenth century among the Indians of the Western plains of the United States, such as the Cheyenne. For these Indians, the basic territorial and political unit of the tribe was the band, but seven military societies, or warriors' clubs, were common to the entire tribe; the clubs functioned in several areas. A boy could join one of these societies when he achieved warrior status, whereupon he became familiar with the society's particular insignia, songs, and rituals. In addition to their military functions, the warriors' societies also had ceremonial and social functions. Among some plains Indians, notably the Arapaho, the warriors' societies were age-graded so that a man automatically passed from one society to another until he finally passed into the society of elders, which had great political and ceremonial importance.

The Cheyenne warriors' routine, daily tasks consisted of overseeing movements in the camp, protecting a moving column, and enforcing rules against individual hunting when the whole tribe was on a buffalo hunt. In addition, each of the warrior societies had a repertoire of dances that the members performed on special ceremonial occasions. Since identical military societies bearing identical names existed in each Cheyenne band, the societies thus served to integrate the entire tribe for military and political purposes.[3]

The Melanesian Big Man. Throughout much of Melanesia there appears a type of leader called the "Big Man." The Big Man combines a small amount of interest in his tribe's welfare with a great deal of self-interested cunning and calculation for his own personal gain. His authority is personal; he does not come to office nor is he elected. His status is the result of acts which raise him above most other tribe members and attract to him a band of loyal followers.

An example of this form of political organization can be seen among the Kapauku of West New Guinea. There the Big Man is called the *tonowi,* or "rich one." To achieve this status, one must be male, wealthy, generous, and eloquent; physical bravery and skills in dealing with the supernatural are also frequent characteristics of a *tonowi,* but they are not essential. The *tonowi* functions as the headman of the village unit.

The Kapauku culture places a high value on wealth, so it is not surprising that a wealthy individual is considered to be a successful and admirable man. Yet the possession of wealth must be coupled with the trait of generosity, which in this society means not gift-giving but the willingness to make loans. Wealthy men who refuse to lend money to other villagers may be ostracized, ridiculed, and, in extreme cases, actually executed by a group of warriors. Due to this social pressure, economic wealth is rarely hoarded, but is distributed throughout the group.

It is through the loans he makes that the *tonowi*

---

[3] E. A. Hoebel, *The Cheyennes: Indians of the Great Plains. Case Studies in Cultural Anthropology.* (New York: Holt, Rinehart and Winston, 1960).

Figure 11-3a. *The king of Akure holds court. His household consists of 156 wives and literally countless children; he rules over a large province of Nigeria and has about 230,000 subjects.*

Figure 11-3b. *The king of Akure is also a lawyer who was educated in England; here he wears the traditional wig and gown of the British barrister.*

Figure 11-3c,d. *The king drives up in his Chevrolet to his palace door; note the cement sculptures that decorate the palace, including the statue of a Nigerian in a British army uniform. The top photo shows the king stepping out of the palace with his retinue. The man on the far right, wearing Western dress, is the king's secretary; the man on the left is his page.*

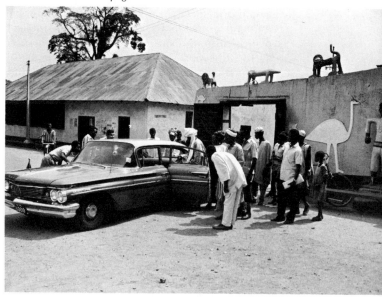

acquires his political power. The other villagers comply with his requests because they are in his debt (often without paying interest), and they do not want to have to repay their loans. Those who have not yet borrowed money from the *tonowi* are probably hoping to do so in the future, and so they too want to keep his goodwill.

The debtors of the *tonowi* are always his loyal supporters. This is in part due to their gratitude for his generosity; it is also due to the fact that debts can be inherited, and if anything happens to the *tonowi,* his heirs will probably ask for immediate repayment of all loans. Other sources of support for the *tonowi* are the apprentices whom he has taken into his household for training. They are fed, housed, given a chance to learn the *tonowi's* business wisdom, and given a loan to buy a wife when they leave; in return, they act as messengers and bodyguards. Even after they leave his household, these men are tied to the *tonowi* by bonds of affection and gratitude. Political support also comes from the *tonowi's* kinsmen, whose relationship brings with it varying obligations.

The *tonowi* functions as a leader in a wide variety of situations. He represents the group in dealing with outsiders and other villages; he acts as negotiator and/or judge when disputes break out among his followers. Leopold Pospisil, who studied the Kapauku extensively, notes:

> The multiple functions of a *tonowi* are not limited to the political and legal fields only. His word also carries weight in economic and social matters. He is especially influential in determining proper dates for pig feasts and pig markets, in inducing specific individuals to become co-sponsors at feasts, in sponsoring communal dance expeditions to other villages, and in initiating large projects, such as extensive drainage ditches and main fences or bridges, the completion of which requires a joint effort of the whole community.[4]

The *tonowi's* wealth comes from his success at

[4] Leopold Pospisil, *The Kapauku Papuans of West New Guinea* (New York: Holt, Rinehart and Winston, 1963). pp. 51–2.

pig breeding, for pigs are the focus of the entire Kapauku economy. Like all kinds of cultivation and domestication, raising pigs requires a certain amount of strength and skill, as well as some luck. It is not uncommon for a *tonowi* to lose his fortune rapidly, due to bad management or bad luck with his pigs. Thus the political structure of the Kapauku shifts frequently; as one man loses wealth and consequently power, another gains it and becomes a *tonowi*. These changes confer a degree of flexibility on the political organization, but prevent long-range planning and thus limit the scope of the *tonowi's* political power over the rest of the villagers.

Centralized political systems

Among bands and tribes, authority is uncentralized and each group is economically and politically autonomous. Political organization is vested in kinship groups and in other organizations. Populations are small, because the technological means of production permit no more. But as a society's social life becomes more complex, as population rises and technology becomes more complex, as the specialization of labor and trade networks produces surpluses of goods, the need for definite, stable permanent leadership becomes greater. In such societies, political authority and power are concentrated in a single individual—the chief—or in numerous groups of individuals—the state. The state form of organization is best suited to a complex heterogeneous society.

Chiefdoms. A chiefdom is a ranked society in which every member has a position in the hierarchy. An individual's status in such a community is determined by membership in a descent group: those in the uppermost levels, closest to the chief, are officially superior and receive deferential treatment from those in lower ranks.

The office of the chief may or may not be hereditary. Unlike the headmen of the band and lineage, the chief is generally a true authority figure, and his authority serves to unite his community in all affairs and at all times. For example, a chief can distribute land among his community and recruit members into his military service. In chiefdoms, there is a recognized hierarchy consisting of major and minor authorities who control major and minor subdivisions of the chiefdom. Such an arrangement is, in effect, a chain of command linking leaders at every level. It serves to bind tribal groups in the heartland to the chief's headquarters, be it a mud and dung hut or a marble palace.

On the economic level, a chief controls the productive activities of his people. Chiefdoms are typically redistributive economic systems; the chief has control over surplus goods and perhaps even the labor force of his community. Thus, the chief may demand a quota of rice from farmers which he will redistribute to the entire community. Similarly, he may recruit laborers to build an irrigation works, a palace, or a temple.

The chief may also amass a great amount of personal wealth and pass it on to his heirs. Land, cattle, and luxury goods produced by specialists can be collected by the chief and become part of his power base. Moreover, high ranking families of the chiefdom may engage in the same practice and use their possessions as evidence of status.

An example of this form of political organization was found in Hawaiian society. There was a class of nobles, rigidly differentiated in rank and specialized in occupation; they led the army and served as religious and political officials. Status was hereditary, and the gradations of status were so distinct that even children of the same parents were ranked in the order of their birth. The nobles near the top of the hierarchy were so important and powerful that ordinary people were required to throw themselves face down on the ground whenever one passed.

At the top of the hierarchy of nobles was the chief. It was believed that he was given the right to rule by the gods, to whom he was related. Around each chief was gathered a group of loyal nobles, who administered the affairs of politics, warfare, and religion. The nobles all paid some kind of tribute—goods and money—to the chief; they in turn collected tribute from inferior nobles, who collected tribute from the commoners. The chief's wealth gave him additional power and permitted him to undertake large-scale projects, such as wars of conquest. The chief had the right of life and death over all his subjects; he could also take away their property at will.

Although such a system would seem very stable, political power in Hawaiian society changed frequently. War was the way to gain territory and maintain power; great chiefs set out to conquer one another in an effort to become the paramount chief of all the islands. When one chief conquered another, the loser and all his nobles were dispossessed of all property and were lucky if they escaped alive. The new chief then appointed his own supporters to positions of political power. Thus there was very little continuity of governmental or religious administration.

State systems. The state, the most formal of political organizations, is one of the hallmarks of civilization. Inherent in the concept of the state is the idea of true, permanent government, public and sovereign, by which the state can use legitimized force to regulate the affairs of its citizens as well as its relations with other states. Found only in large, complex societies, the state has a central power and a formal rigid system of law and order administered by the central power.

An important aspect of the state is its delegation of authority to maintain order within and without its borders. Police, foreign ministries, war ministries, and other branches of the government function to control and punish such disruptive acts as crime, terror, and rebellion. By such agencies, authority is asserted impersonally and objectively in the state.

The state is found only in societies with numerous diverse groups, social classes, and associations; it brings together under a common rule many kinds of people. Typically, the state society is divided into social classes and strata, and economic functions and wealth are distributed unequally. A market economy involving money as

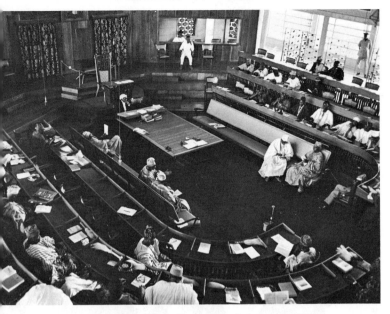

Figure 11-4. One of the duties of the king of Akure is attending sessions of the House of Chiefs, a legislative body modelled on the House of Lords in Great Britain. The Nigerian government also consists of a trained bureaucracy, such as these officials of the Department of Health.

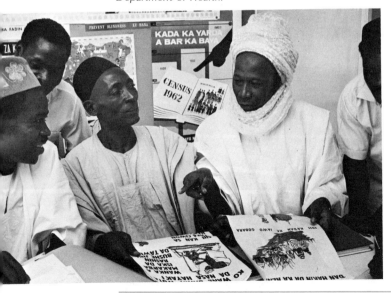

a medium of exchange is an integral part of the state, as are vast surpluses of goods and services and the intense specialization of labor.[5]

Our form of government, of course, is a state government and its organization and workings are undoubtedly familiar to everyone. An example of a not so familiar state is found in Hilda Kuper's study, *The Swazi Of Swaziland*. The Swazi are a Bantu-speaking people who live in Southeast Africa. They are primarily agriculturists, but the activity of cattle raising is more highly valued than agriculture: the ritual, wealth, and power of their authority system are all intricately linked with cattle.

The Swazi authority system is characterized by a highly developed dual monarchy, a hereditary aristocracy, and elaborate rituals of kinship as well as by state-wide age sets. The king and his mother are the central figures of all national activity, linking all the people of the Swazi state: they preside over higher courts, summon national gatherings, control age classes, allocate land, disburse national wealth, take precedence in ritual, and help organize important social events.

Advising the king are the senior princes, who are usually his uncles and half brothers. Between the king and the princes are two specially-created *tinsila*, or blood brothers, who are chosen from certain common clans. These men are his shields, protecting him from evildoers and serving him in intimate personal situations. In addition, the king is guided by two *tindvuna*, or counselors, one civil and one military. The people of the state make their opinions known through two councils: the *liqoqo*, or privy council composed of senior princes; and the *libanda*, or council of state, composed of chiefs and headmen and open to all adult males of the state. The *liqoqo* may advise the king, make decisions, and execute them. For example, they may rule on such questions as land, education, traditional ritual, court procedure, and transport.

Government extends from the smallest local unit—the homestead—upwards to the central ad-

[5]L. Krader, *Formation of The State* (Englewood Cliffs, N.J.: Prentice-Hall, 1968).

ministration. The head of a homestead has legal and administrative powers: he is responsible for the crimes of those under him, controls their property, and speaks for them before his superiors. On the district level, political organization is similar to that of the central government. However, the relationship between a district chief and his subjects is personal and familiar; he knows all the families in his district. The main check on any autocratic tendencies he may exhibit rests in his subjects' ability to transfer their allegiance to a more responsive chief. Swazi officials hold their positions for life and are dismissed only for treason or witchcraft. Incompetence, drunkenness, and stupidity are frowned upon, but they are not considered to be good enough reasons for dismissal.

The functioning of the political unit

Whatever form the political organization of a society may take, it must solve certain problems in order to permit the smooth functioning of the group. Chief among these problems is the need to obtain the people's allegiance. In small, loosely organized groups, in which every member participates in the making of all decisions, loyalty and cooperation are freely given, since each person considers himself a part of the political system. But as the group grows larger, and the organization becomes more formal, the problems of obtaining and keeping public support become greater.

Elements of political organization

Many political theorists suggest that the political process is based on the use of some form of coercion to insure that decisions are carried out. This coercion may be a threat of force; it could just as easily be scorn, ridicule, or social neglect; in real life, names can often be as hurtful as sticks

Figure 11-5. *The legitimacy of any government rests on the consent of the people. This tribal ruler of Ghana is an Englishman who was once a colonial official; villagers asked him to assume the position of chief.*

Figure 11-6. *Legitimacy of political authority may be demonstrated by symbolic attire, such as this aged helmet.*

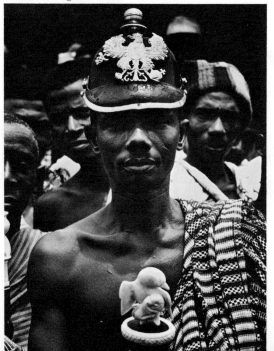

274

and stones. However, the reliance upon force as the most important instrument of political implementation tends to lessen the effectiveness of a political system. For example, the staff needed to apply force must often be large and may itself grow to be a political force. The emphasis on force often creates resentment on the parts of those to whom it is applied and so lessens cooperation. Thus police states are rare; most societies choose less extreme forms of social coercion.

Also basic to the political process is the concept of legitimacy, or the right of the political leaders to rule. Like force, legitimacy is a form of support for a political system; unlike force, legitimacy is based on the values which a particular society believes most important. Thus among the Kapauku, the legitimacy of the *tonowi's* power comes from his wealth; the kings of Hawaii, and England and France before their revolutions, were thought to have a divine right to rule; the chief of the Dahomey tribe of West Africa acquires legitimacy through his age, as he is always the oldest living male of the tribe.

Legitimacy grants the right to hold, use, and allocate power. Power based on legitimacy may be distinguished from power based on force: obedience to the former results from the belief that obedience is "right"; compliance to power based on force is the result of fear of the deprivation of liberty, physical well-being, life, material property. Thus, power based on legitimacy is symbolic and depends not upon any intrinsic value, but upon the positive expectations of those who recognize and accede to it. If the expectations are not met regularly (if the shaman fails too many times or the leader is continuously unsuccessful in preventing horse or camel theft), the legitimacy of the recognized power figure is minimized and may collapse altogether.

Religion and politics. Religion is intricately connected with politics Religious beliefs are often the basis for the society's social and political goals. Religious beliefs may also influence laws: acts which people believe to be sinful, such as sodomy and incest, are often illegal. Fre-

quently, it is religion that legitimizes government.

In both small-scale and industrial societies, belief in the supernatural is important and is reflected in the governments of these peoples. The effect of religion on politics is perhaps best exemplified by medieval Europe. Holy wars were fought over the smallest matter; immense cathedrals were built in honor of the Virgin and other saints; kings and queens pledged allegiance to the Pope and asked his blessing in all important ventures, be they marital or martial. In the pre-Columbian Americas, the Aztec society was a religious state, or theocracy, that thrived as a result of the theological need for human sacrifices to assuage or please the gods. In Peru, the Inca emperor proclaimed absolute authority based on the proposition that he was descended from the sun god. In our own country, the Declaration of Independence, which is an expression of the social and political beliefs of the American people, stresses a belief in a Supreme Being. This document states that "all men are created (by God) equal," a tenet that gave rise to our own form of democracy because it implied that all men should participate in governing themselves. The fact that the American head of state takes his oath of office by swearing on a Bible is another instance of the use of religion to legitimize political power.

In many small-scale societies, religion is even more closely related to the political system. Among the Afikbo Ibo of Nigeria, for example, religion is a political force even though priests and diviners are not politically active and officials do not require supernatural approval to hold office. The political power of religion is vested in the Afikbo guardian *erosi,* the impersonal spirits connected with nature. These awesome spirits are instrumental in such important affairs as prosperity, fertility, and general welfare. Politically, the *erosi* reinforce the men's village society which is charged with maintaining order within the village. For example, if a person accused of a crime denies his guilt, he must swear his innocence on an *erosi* shrine. If he refuses, he is considered guilty; if he swears and is lying, the Afikbos believe the *erosi* will kill him or make him seriously ill within a short span of time.

War

One of the responsibilities of the state is the organization and execution of the activities of war. Throughout history, men have engaged in a seemingly endless chain of wars and intergroup hostilities. Why do wars occur? Is the need to wage war an instinctive feature of the human personality? What are the alternatives to violence as a means of settling disputes between societies?

Everyone shares certain fundamental needs. In order to survive, each of us requires sufficient food, water, and living space. Because these resources are available only in limited quantities, every society is faced with the problem of securing them for its members. Therefore, it is believed that a significant factor in human aggression is the stress related to population pressures. In societies with relatively efficient means of food production, it often happens that population increases faster than living standards improve. Obviously, a large population will need more food, water, and space than a small one. As population density rises, stress rises not only within a society, but between societies as well. War is one method of regulating and redistributing population.

There is reason to suppose that war has become a serious problem only in the last 10,000 years, since the improvement of food production techniques, the rise of the city, and the invention of centralized states. Among hunters and gatherers, warfare is not a common method of relieving population pressures; some sort of voluntary redistribution is much more likely. Because territorial boundaries and membership among hunting and gathering bands are usually fluid and ill-defined, a man who hunts with one band today may hunt with a neighboring band tomorrow. Warfare is further rendered impractical by the systematic interchange of women among hunting and gathering groups—it is likely that someone in each band will have a sister or a cousin in a

Figure 11-7. *The Pope's status in the political hierarcy of the church is supported by Catholics' religious faith. The Shah of Iran is considered both a political and a religious leader, so he is treated with great deference.*

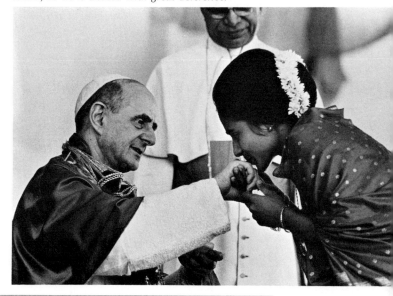

Social integration ● part **4**

neighboring band. Where property ownership is minimal and no state organization exists, the likelihood of warfare is greatly diminished.

Despite the traditional view of the agriculturist as a gentle tiller of the soil, it is among farming and pastoral populations that warfare is most prominent. As a result of the commitment to the land inherent in farming, agricultural societies tend to be far more centralized and stable in their membership than hunting and gathering societies. Moreover, these societies are often rigidly matrilocal or patrilocal, and each new generation is thus bound to the same territory.

The availibility of virgin land may not serve as a sufficient detriment to the outbreak of war. Among slash-and-burn agriculturalists, for example, competition for land cleared of virgin forest frequently leads to hostility and armed conflict. The centralization of political control and the possession of valuable property among agriculturalists provide much more stimuli for warfare.

On a broader scale, the difference between hunting and farming populations may be viewed as a difference in world view. As a general rule, hunters and gatherers tend to conceive of themselves as a part of nature and in balance with it. When a Bushman kills a giraffe, it is a serious and somber occasion, for the Bushman recognizes that the death of any creature upsets the balance of nature. This attitude may be referred to as a naturalistic world view.

The Bushman's respect for nature contrasts sharply with the world view prevalent among agriculturalists, who do not find their food in nature but take steps to produce it. The attitude that nature exists only to be used by man may be referred to as an exploitative world view. By extension, a society which adopts such a world-view may find nothing wrong with manipulating other societies in order to assure its own survival. The exploitative world view, prevalent among food-producing peoples, is an important prerequisite to intersocietal warfare.

A naturalistic world view is virtually nonexistent among modern industrial societies. Although technology and contraception have the potential to greatly reduce population pressures, the large populations of Western societies have created a great deal of stress both internal and external. Through the systematic exploitation of underdeveloped lands, European and American societies have largely overcome the need to fight for food and water and compete instead for power and influence. Despite the ability to control population, the elimination of war has yet to be achieved; value systems would therefore seem to be a crucial element in the existence of warfare.

War is not a universal phenomenon. Throughout the world, from the Bushmen of Africa to the Arapesh of New Guinea to the Hopi of North America, societies exist in which warfare as we know it is not practiced. Almost invariably, peaceful societies are those which have some form of naturalistic world view.

☐

Original study

TRIBAL ORGANIZATION OF THE BLACKFEET

A child born to Blackfeet parents began to learn the patterns of social interaction. He was first of all a member of a household—the occupants of a single tepee—which included the parents, unmarried brothers and sisters, and perhaps one or two other relatives as well, such as a grandparent, a maiden aunt, or other wives of the household head.

As the child grew older it learned that its family was the minimal economic unit of the Blackfeet society. The father was the decision maker, the one responsible for the protection and good behavior of its members; the first wife was the owner of the tepee, responsible for the other wives if any, for the care of the children, maintenance of the tepee and other duties within the women's realm. The child learned too about other kinsmen, that he had important relatives on both sides of the family—in other words, kin were recognized bilaterally.

As acquaintances were made beyond the household, he or she learned that there were other families that regularly lived near and traveled with one's own. These were members of the band, the day in and day out hunting and gathering group that was the basic economic and political unit of the Blackfeet. It was the band that moved according to the requirements of the yearly round, camped alone through the winter, joined with other bands in the summer for the tribal hunt. The child learned the band name and identified with it: he was a child of his parents and one of the Small Robes, Skunks, Lone Eaters or whatever his band might be. Over the years he learned too that the people who gathered during the summer hunt were fellow Piegan, and that among other people encountered on occasion were some who spoke his language, did things his way, were Blackfeet of the other divisions—the Siksika and the Kainah—who often came to the aid of the Piegan in times of conflict.

While kin ties were basic to band formation, friendship and self-interest played a part as well, and people changed bands when they felt it advantageous to do so. [Anthropologist John C.] Ewers believes that this shifting band allegiance had developed with the inequal distribution of wealth that followed the acquisition of the horse. Poor people became more dependent upon the generosity of the wealthy few and attached themselves to the bands of those men who could best provide for them.

Band membership then was based first of all upon kin ties, but with no absolute rule of descent. Wives usually joined the band of their husbands and children belonged to that of their father, but it was not unusual for a man to join his wife's group. A widow could choose to remain in her husband's band or to return to that of her parents. A man could change band affiliation "even in middle life . . ." (Wissler 1911). Other persons attached themselves to the band for various reasons, and long residence with a band, and acceptance by its members, was tantamount to band membership.

The tribe was a larger association of individual bands whose members recognized common ties of language, kinship and culture. It was an organized unit only during the few weeks of the summer hunt, and tribal discipline operated only at this time. Even here the bands retained their spatial and functional autonomy; each band had its habitual place in the camp circle and continued to operate as an economic and political unit with only a part of its powers surrendered to the tribal organization.

Like other Plains Indians, the Piegan had a series of men's organizations, or societies, of which there were three basic types: age-graded warrior societies, religious societies and cults, and the less formal dance association.

The named warrior societies (Mosquitoes, Pigeons, Braves, All-Crazy Dogs, etc.) were corporate groups, that is, they continued over time, surviving the individual members. Groups of young men of a similar age sometimes started a new society, or, more usually, got together and bought memberships in an ongoing society. Similarly the old members would in turn buy into the next age-rank. The transfer was between individuals and such purchases could occur at any time. It was customary, however, for several men to transfer at the same time. Periodic transfers of this kind made possible a progressive movement of membership from a lower to a higher ranking society as men grew older. The oldest society might continue as its ranks were renewed from below, or eventually die out as its members passed away.

These were the groups granted policing powers at the summer encampment. In addition they served to promote the military spirit of the members through war games and intersociety competition in races, dancing and games.

The medicine men's societies and related cults were less formally organized gatherings of men who owned important medicine bundles and powers. These men conferred together to aid in the organization and presentation of the Sun Dance and to promote the spiritual and material welfare of the tribe. The dance organizations were social clubs made up of young men who organized for the purpose of staging social dances during the time of the summer encampment.

Membership in one or more of these organizations created loyalties that cut across the ties of kinship and band affiliation, and helped to contribute to tribal solidarity. In other words, a person identified first with his kinsmen and with his band, but later established additional and potentially conflicting ties of loyalty by marrying someone from another band and by membership in a society that drew its members from many bands.

Band and tribal leadership was not inherited but open to all who could command a following. A band headman gained a position of influence by displaying the qualities valued in his society and by his continued exercise of these attributes. His influence depended upon his power to persuade others, and the support of many followers increased this ability. He conferred with family heads and all decisions were reached by mutual agreement.

Band leaders formed a council during the tribal encampment and one of them, by election or selection, came to be considered the chief of the tribe. The chief had no institutionalized authority and little disciplining power. His chiefly functions were to guide the council to agreement and to mediate in cases of conflict and uncertainty.

There were no formalized institutions for social control except for the policing duties of the associations under special regulations put into effect at the summer encampment. Conflict was first of all a matter between individuals, then a concern of the families and finally of the bands. The delinquent person was cautioned, ridiculed, gossiped about, and shamed into conformity. Ostracism and violence were the ultimate penalties within the band, but usually gossip and shame served to restore order. Boys and girls growing up in Piegan society were urged to achieve the ideals of that society. Boys were told to be brave, to be good fighters, able to defend themselves against their peers and to protect younger children. They were praised for skills and daring, even for sexual exploits. Girls were urged to be quiet, dutiful, sober, hard-working, and to protect their virginity. Both were rewarded with praise when they achieved, and punished with sarcasm and gossiped about when they misbehaved or failed. These sanctions contributed to a developing concern with their own identity and to a strong sense of shame, and such concerns in turn gave added force to these mechanisms of social control. Gossip and shame were also used to curb intratribal conflicts among adults. A cluster of tepees made an ideal setting for effective ridicule. Wissler describes a process of "formal ridicule" that was used to curb "mild persistent misconduct." When the people were quietly settled in of an evening, a headman would call out to a neighbor asking him if he had heard about that silly fellow two tepees down who had been mistreating his wife? Men in other tepees would join in telling what they thought of the man and his behavior, all to the discomfort of the victim and the enjoyment of everyone else. Sarcasm, ridicule, and the accompanying laughter, added up to an evening of entertainment for all but the victim, who was soon highly motivated to mend his ways.

In the more serious cases of adult disputes, force and physical punishment were employed if gossip failed. In cases of murder, a revenge killing might take place if a high payment was not offered in retribution and accepted. A person who disrupted the summer hunt might be beaten and have his clothing and weapons destroyed. An adulterous woman might have her nose cut off, or be put to death by the members of her husband's warrior society.

These forces contributed to the development of some general personality characteristics of the Blackfeet. [George Bird] Grinnell found them, like other Plains Indians, to be "talkative, merry, and lighthearted," and fond of joking, even though they appeared reserved and quiet when with strangers. Wissler commented on their fondness for jest and practical jokes. In addition, I get a picture of a brave, resourceful people, industrious and aggressive, yet much concerned with self, jealous, and easily shamed. These characteristics and their expression were further reinforced by the Blackfeet beliefs.

Source:
From *Modern Blackfeet: Montanans on a Reservation* by Malcolm McFee. Copyright © 1972 by Holt, Rinehart and Winston, Inc. Reprinted by permission of Holt, Rinehart and Winston, Inc.

Summary

1.

In all societies, social control and power is vested in a system of social relations or in a selected group for the purpose of maintaining social order. No group can live together without persuading or coercing its members to conform to the agreed upon rules of conduct. Political organization exists in every society to manage public affairs.

2.

In order of complexity, political organization ranges from the uncentralized bands and tribes to the centralized chiefdoms and states. The band is a small, autonomous group of hunters and gatherers made up of associated families or kin groups occupying a given territory. Political organization in bands is democratic and an informal social control is exerted by public opinion in the form of gossip. Leadership is transitory.

3.

The tribe, as a form of political organization, has an agricultural or livestock-raising economy with a larger population than the band, and the family units within the tribe are autonomous and egalitarian. Social control is informal but the authority of leadership is somewhat greater than in the band. Leadership within the clan may be based on kinship and is exercised by a group of elders. Another system of leadership which cuts across kinship and lineages is the authority vested in men in the group who shared the experience of initiation into the tribe at the same time. As these groups of men get older they become the effective leadership.

4.

Some tribes vest political authority in voluntary associations or men's clubs. A boy joins one or another men's club upon his initiation as a warrior. The men's organizations administer the affairs of the tribe. Another variant of authority in tribes is the Big Man, who privately builds up his wealth and political power until he must be reckoned with as a leader.

5.

Chiefdoms are centralized political systems in a hierarchical society in which rank is based on kinship membership.

6.

The state is a political unit which has a monopoly on the legitimate use of political force. States are permanent, with a large bureaucracy to administer the government, the authority to assess and collect taxes, to administer justice, and to make and enforce laws.

7.

Until quite recently political organization with a separation of church and state was rare. Religion is so intricately woven into the life of the people that its presence is inevitably felt in the political sphere. Fear of the supernatural is a form of social control and in the more complex chiefdoms and states, the head of state was often the head of the church or a demigod.

Suggested readings

Cohen, Ronald and John Middleton, eds. *Comparative Political Systems*. Garden City, New York: Natural History Press, 1967.
The editors have selected some twenty studies in the politics of nonindustrial societies by such well-known scholars as Lévi-Strauss, S. F. Nadel, Marshal Sahlins, and S. N. Eisenstadt.

Fortes, M. and E. E. Evans-Pritchard, eds. *African Political Systems*. New York: Oxford University Press, 1961.
This classic on comparative research on native African political systems focuses on areas formerly administered by the British. Among the peoples discussed are the Zulus of South Africa, the Bemba of Rhodesia, and the Nuer of southern Sudan. The editors' introduction outlines many of the fundamental issues of political anthropology.

Fried, Morton *The Evolution of Political Society*. New York: Random House, 1967.
The author attempts to trace the evolution of political society through a study of simple, egalitarian societies. The character of the state and the means whereby this form of organization takes shape is considered in terms of pristine and secondary states, formed because pre-existing states supplied the stimuli or models for organization.

Swartz, Marc J., Turner, Victor W. and Arthur Tuden *Political Anthropology*. Chicago: Aldine Press, 1966.
This reader in political anthropology attempts to trace the changes in the field since the publication in 1961 of Fortes and Evans-Pritchard's *African Political Systems*. The papers included illustrate the trend away from a classification of political structures and functions and toward an understanding of political processes.

Social
control

Few of us would admit to blindly following the dictates of our society; indeed, we may purposely attempt to assert our nonconformity in the way we speak, look, act, and think. Yet as much as we may flaunt our individuality, most of our behavior is restricted to some degree by certain fundamental cultural guidelines. As members of a society, each of us is obliged to conform to certain rules and regulations.

Society determines not only the limits of acceptable behavior, but the penalties for exceeding those limits as well. Thus a society that forbids adultery will also have some means of punishing the adulterers. A Blackfoot who discovers that his wife has been unfaithful may either cut off the woman's nose or demand damages from the man who has offended him. An Eskimo in the same situation may kill his wife's lover, or he may prefer to challenge him to a song contest in which the two men will settle their dispute by competing in the composition of mutually abusive songs. Both the Blackfoot and the Eskimo are responding to a personal offense in a manner condoned by their societies.

In every society, institutions are developed to encourage members to behave in certain ways and not in others. Through social controls, a group of people encourages conformity to its norms and values, thereby perpetuating its culture and maintaining its system of social relations. Thus the group establishes a certain predictability of behavior, which is essential for social living. In this chapter, we shall examine some of the questions which arise in connection with the problem of social control.

The study of social control

The process of social control is probably older than culture itself. In other higher primate groups, dominant males seem to police the other individuals in certain ways. When fights break out, they rush to the scene of the quarrel; in most cases, their presence is enough to restore order.

Before the twentieth century, anthropologists based their concept of social control on the theories of the Victorian jurist, Sir Henry Maine. In *Ancient Law,* originally printed in 1861, Maine expressed the belief that, in "primitive" societies, interpersonal relationships are determined by ascribed social status, and not by contract, as they are in more "advanced" societies. That is, "primitive" people conform to the rules of society out of a blind obedience to custom and tradition. "Advanced" people, on the other hand, base their interpersonal relationships not on traditional beliefs but on mutually advantageous agreements; the model for this was Thomas Hobbe's social contract.

Émile Durkheim also focused on the supposedly different bases for social sanctions in Western and non-Western societies. In *The Division of Labor,* Durkheim argued that, in simple societies, everyone performs much the same kind of work and produces much the same kind of goods. In such circumstances, order is maintained by submission to certain universally acknowledged rules of behavior. As a society becomes more complex, and its work force more specialized, members become increasingly dependent upon one another for goods and services. The individual, no longer able to provide for all of his own needs, must contract with other producers and sellers. In such a society, relationships are determined by the exchange of goods and services, not by submission to an all-inclusive code of law. Contractual relationships, according to Durkheim, form the basis of civil law in complex societies.

This clear-cut distinction between social control in "primitive" and "advanced" societies was refuted in the early twentieth century largely through the work of Bronislaw Malinowski. In *Crime and Custom in Savage Society,* Malinowski described the maintenance of social order among the people of the Trobriand Islands. Malinowski argued that the factors which motivate conformity in more simple societies are the same factors which motivate conformity in more complex societies. According to Malinowski, the universal basis of social order is the principle of reciprocity. Each individual understands that if he behaves properly towards his neighbor, his neighbor will find it advantageous to behave properly towards him. On the other hand, if a man fails to cooperate with his neighbors, he realizes that they may withdraw their cooperation as well. Although Malinowski may have attributed undue importance to the reciprocal principle, his emphasis on

the universality of this principle represented a major advance in our understanding of the mechanisms of social control. Much has since been written on social control—most notably by Hoebel in his study of the Cheyenne—but much research remains to be done on non-Western societies.

Internalized controls

People seem to behave as they are expected to mainly because of the implicit threat of the consequences of doing otherwise. Indeed, in all societies, the breaking of rules and laws is met with some kind of predictable counteraction. In some cases, the counteraction is visible and authoritative—a jail sentence, dismissal from an organization or club, the mark of the Scarlet Letter A, or a symbolic mutilation. Such punishment is imposed by the community, and the offender is properly shamed before his peers.

There are, however, forms of social control imposed on the guilty individual without the direct intervention of society. In such instances, controls have been so thoroughly built in to the individual that he provides his own punishment, and experiences a private shame. For example, in our society, people refrain from committing incest not so much from fear of legal punishment as from a deep abhorrence of the act and the shame they would feel in performing it. Built in or internalized controls rely on such deterrents as the fear of divine punishment, and magical retaliation. The individual expects that he will be punished by these forces even though no one in his community knows of his wrongdoing.

A society that strongly relied on internalized controls was that of the Penobscot Indians, a tribe that inhabited the northeastern part of North America. The Penobscots held a very strong belief in the effectiveness of magic. Every person was thought to have the potential for working magic—though some were more practiced than others. If a person secretly committed a crime, it was thought that sooner or later, the aggrieved party

Figure 12-1. *The top photo shows a group of Bakhtiari tribesmen holding a trial for one of their members who employed a professional thief to steal for him. The bottom photo is a trial of a !Kung Bushman accused of stealing a cow. The trial, held by the rival Tswana, is probably not a fair one, but it indicates an attempt to work within a legal system.*

would find out about it; he would then take some form of magical retribution. In fact the crime may have been of such a petty nature that it could never be discerned. Nevertheless, the wrong-doer's belief put him in a frame of mind wherein he expected to be discovered and punished. The first thing that happened out of the ordinary was therefore interpreted as retribution, and to escape worse punishment, the offender quickly took measures to rectify the wrong. Here equilibrium is achieved and social control effected not so much by direct legal processes of society but by the guilty party, acting alone.

Internalized controls as strong as these of the Penobscots tend to be reflected in, and supported by, other institutions in society. For example, the Penobscot religion posits a world inhabited by all sorts of spirits and superhumans. The tribe's mythology is rich with tales in which these super-humans punish people and other creatures for transgressions of the moral code. Myth-telling was a major recreational pastime, so the Penob-scot learned from earliest childhood exactly what happened to people who "didn't do right." Not only did the myths state a body of precedent for action, but they also presented the threat that, whatever else happened, an individual could at least expect divine retribution for any misdoing. A belief in magical and divine retribution achieved an internal control for crimes such as petty thievery and trespassing; only in more serious instances were direct actions undertaken by society as a whole.

Externalized controls

Because internalized controls are not wholly sufficient even in a society like that of the Penobscot, every society develops institutions designed to encourage conformity to social norms. These institutions are referred to as **sanctions;** they are externalized social controls. According to Radcliffe-Brown, "a sanction is a reaction on the part of a society or of a considerable number of its members to a mode of behavior which is thereby approved (positive sanctions) or disapproved (negative sanctions)." Furthermore, sanctions may be either formal or informal and may vary significantly within a given society.

Each group and subgroup within a society tends to develop its own distinctive pattern or usages and the means of maintaining them without necessary recourse to the municipal law. Sanctions there come to operate within every conceivable set of group relationships: they include not only the organized sanctions of the law but also the gossip of neighbors or the customs regulating norms of production that are spontaneously generated among workers on the factory floor. In small scale communities . . . informal sanctions may become more drastic than the penalties provided for in the legal code . . .[1]

Sanctions then operate within social groups of all sizes. As we shall see, they need not be enacted into law in order to play a significant role in social control. If a sanction is to be effective, it cannot be arbitrary. Quite the opposite: sanctions must be consistently applied, and their existence must be generally known by the members of the society.

Negative and positive sanctions. Social sanctions may be categorized as either positive or negative. Positive sanctions, by which we mean such incentives to conformity as awards, titles, and recognition by one's neighbors, seem generally to be of less significance in determining social behavior than negative sanctions. In most societies, the threats of imprisonment, corporal punishment, or ostracism from the community for violation of social norms are stressed far more heavily than are the advantages of social conformity. People are more willing to conform to society's rules than to accept the consequences of not doing so.

Formal and informal sanctions. Sanctions may also be categorized as either formal or informal,

Figure 12-2. *These Portuguese army officers seem satisfied with the positive sanctions— medals, honor, wealth—they have won.*

depending on whether or not a legal statute is involved. The man who wears tennis shorts to a church service may be subject to a variety of informal sanctions, ranging from the glances of the clergyman to the chuckling of nearby women. But if he were to show up without any trousers at all, he would be subject to the formal sanction of arrest for indecent exposure. Only in the second instance would he have been guilty of breaking the law.

Informal sanctions of the negative sort are very effective in enforcing a large number of seemingly unimportant customs. Because most people want to be totally accepted, they are willing to acquiesce to the rules that govern dress, eating, conversation, even in the absence of actual laws.

Organized and diffuse sanctions. According to Radcliffe-Brown, sanctions may further be classified either as organized or diffuse. Organized sanctions are those which reward or punish be-

[1] A. L. Epstein, "Sanctions" in *International Encyclopedia of Social Sciences*, 1968, Volume 14, p. 3.

havior through precisely regulated social procedure. Organized positive sanctions, such as military decorations or monetary awards, generally play a much smaller role in encouraging desirable behavior than do organized negative sanctions. This latter category of sanctions may include loss of status or rank, exclusion from social life and its privileges, seizure of property, imprisonment, and even bodily mutilation or death. When these sanctions are imposed by an authorized political body, they are referred to as **legal sanctions.** We shall have more to say about this special category of sanctions shortly.

Diffuse sanctions, defined by Radcliffe-Brown as "spontaneous expressions of approval or disapproval by members of the community acting as individuals," may assume a great many different forms. Often, diffuse sanctions involve patterns of behavior which, although they are enacted by no official authority, are, in fact, more or less institutionalized. In the *vito,* an old Spanish custom paralleled among various Mediterranean peoples, an individual who has offended community standards may be visited by a noisy delegation of his neighbors in the middle of the night. This unwelcome group of visitors may proceed to make such abusive noises or subject the offender to such inconveniences that he cannot possibly mistake or ignore his neighbors' disapproval of his behavior. The mockery of one's neighbors and the loss of honor act as powerful inducements to proper behavior. The *vito* exemplifies the **satirical sanction,** or the sanction of ridicule.

Witchcraft beliefs may also act as a powerful agent of social control in some societies. An individual would naturally hesitate to offend his neighbor when that neighbor might retaliate by resorting to black magic. Among the Azande of the Sudan, a man who thinks he has been bewitched may consult an oracle who, after performing the appropriate mystical rites, may then establish or confirm the identity of the offending witch. Confronted with this evidence, the "witch" will usually agree to cooperate in order to avoid any additional trouble. Should the victim die, his relatives may choose to make magic against the witch, ultimately accepting the death of some villager both as evidence of guilt and the efficacy of their magic. For the Azande, witchcraft provides not only a sanction against antisocial behavior but also a means of dealing with natural hostilities and death. No one wishes to be thought of as a witch, and surely no one wishes to be victimized by one. By institutionalizing their emotional responses, the Azande are able to successfully maintain social order.

Another important social control, and one that is likely to be internalized, is the religious sanction. Just as a devout Christian avoids sinning for fear of Hell, so do other worshippers tend to behave in a manner intended not to offend their powerful supernatural beings. The threat of punishment—either in this life or in the next—by gods, ancestral spirits, or ghosts is a strong incentive for proper behavior. In some societies, it is believed that ancestral spirits are very much concerned with the maintenance of good relations among the living members of their lineage. Death or illness in the lineage may be explained by reference to some violation of tradition or custom. Religious sanctions may thus serve not only to regulate behavior but to explain unexplainable phenomena as well.

Primary and secondary sanctions. According to Radcliffe-Brown, sanctions may be further classified either as primary or secondary. Primary sanctions involve direct community action against an individual; secondary sanctions are those which are directed at a person (or a group of people) by another person (or group of people) backed by the support of the community. The institution of the duel exemplifies the secondary sanction. In this case, the two involved parties settle their differences directly without the overt mediation of an official representative of the community. Secondary sanctions do not necessarily involve the use of physical force. Among the Trobriand Islanders, for example, a man may shout out his accusations against a neighbor in the middle of the night, informing the entire village of his complaint. So powerful is this sanction that people so accused have been known to commit suicide rather than face shame and dishonor.

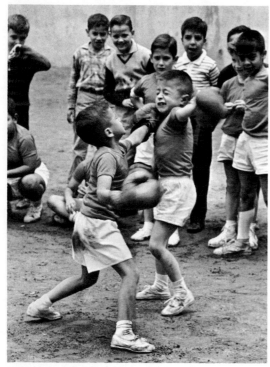

Figure 12-3. *Secondary sanctions leave the individuals involved in a dispute to work out their own solution; this may lead to some form of regulated combat, as seen here in a picture of Mexican schoolboys settling a quarrel with boxing gloves.*

Function of sanctions

Sanctions are introduced in order to formalize the adherence to norms, including adherence to formal law. A society may be composed of many different groupings of individuals, each with its own needs and interests; yet despite these differences, all are bound by certain common norms and values. It is the function of sanctions to integrate the various social factions and to insure maximum harmony in the community. John Beat-

tie wrote about the sanctions found in Bunyoro, a kingdom in Africa:

> Thus in Bunyoro disputes between fellow-villagers are often settled by an informal group of neighbors who have the traditional right to impose a penalty on the party judged to be in the wrong, but lack any formal means of enforcing their judgements. The judgement is always a payment of meat and beer, which must be brought to the successful litigant's house on an appointed day. There it is consumed by both parties to the dispute, as well as by those neighbors who were concerned in the settlement.[2]

The object of such a procedure is not to administer punishment but rather to restore unity to a disrupted village. In most cases, sanctions are primarily intended not to restrict behavior but rather to prevent damage to the social fabric and to mend such damage when it occurs.

Law in non-Western societies

The Ifugaos are a tribe of head-hunters living in the mountains of Luzon. Among the Ifugaos, an individual who is unable to settle a dispute with another man through personal negotiations may enlist the aid of a professional go-between known as a *monkalun*. If a settlement cannot be agreed upon with the assistance of the *monkalun*, the plaintiff and his kinsmen may attempt to kill the defendant or his kinsmen. Among the Ifugaos, the alternative to peaceful negotiation is feud. Ultimately, there is no binding legal authority.

In Western society, on the other hand, a man who commits an offense against another man is subject to a series of complex legal proceedings. He will be arrested by the police; tried before a judge and, perhaps, a jury; and, if his crime is serious enough, he may be fined, imprisoned, or even executed. Throughout this chain of events,

[2]John Beattie, *Other Cultures: Aims, Methods and Achievements.* (New York: The Free Press, 1964).

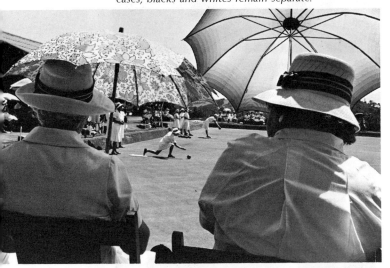

Figure 12-4. *In South Africa, law and custom intertwine to regulate racial behavior. The sign in the park (bottom photo) indicates the complexity of discriminatory rules. In most cases, blacks and whites remain separate.*

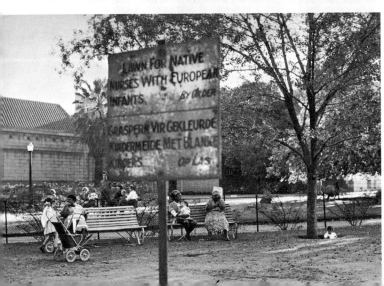

the accused party is dealt with by presumably disinterested policemen, judges, jurors, and jailers who may have no personal acquaintance whatsoever with the plaintiff or the defendant. How strange this would seem to the Ifugao! Clearly, the Westerner and the non-Westerner are operating under distinctly different assumptions.

Each society establishes institutions to encourage conformity to its norms and to define proper action in the event of breach of those norms. Through its sanctions, a society exercises a degree of control over the behavior of its members. An important part of a society's total system of social controls is that aspect referred to as law.

Definition of law

When two Eskimos settle a dispute by engaging in a song contest, the result of the contest is binding; that is, the affair is closed. No further action need be expected. Would we choose to describe the outcome of such a contest as a legal decision? If every law is a sanction, but not every sanction is a law, how are we to distinguish between social sanctions in general and those to which we will apply the label "law?"

The definition of law has been a lively point of contention among anthropologists in the twentieth century. In 1926, Malinowski argued that the rules of law are distinguished from the rules of custom in that "they are regarded as the obligation of one person and the rightful claim of another, sanctioned not by mere psychological motive, but by a definite social machinery of binding force based . . . upon mutual dependence." An example of one rule of custom might be seen in the dictate that guests at a dinner party should repay the host with entertainment in the future. A host who does not receive a return invitation may feel cheated of something he thought was owed to him, but he has no legal claim against his ungrateful guest for the $12.67 he spent on food. However, if he was cheated of the same sum by his grocer when he was shopping, he could invoke the law. Although Malinowski's definition introduced several important elements of law, his failure to adequately distinguish between legal and nonlegal sanctions left the problem of formulating a workable definition of law in the hands of later anthropologists.

An important pioneer in the study of primitive law was E. Adamson Hoebel. According to Hoebel, "a social norm is legal if its neglect or infraction is regularly met, in threat or in fact, by the application of physical force by an individual or group possessing the socially recognized privilege of so acting." In stressing the legitimate use of physical coercion, Hoebel de-emphasized the traditional association of law with a centralized court system. Although judge and jury are fundamental features of Western jurisprudence, they are not the universal backbone of human law.

In his study of the Kapauku Papuans, Leopold Pospisil defined law in terms of four basic attributes:[3]

1) A legal decision is backed by authority. Some individual or group of individuals must possess sufficient influence to insure the conformity of disputing parties to its decisions.

2) A legal decision is intended to have universal applicability; that is, it is expected that a legal decision made today will apply to comparable situations in the future.

3) A legal decision determines the rights of one party and the duties of the other. Law recognizes the two-sided nature of every dispute.

4) A legal decision determines the nature and degree of sanctions. Legal sanction may be physical—such as imprisonment or confiscation of property—or psychological—such as public ridicule or avoidance.

Some anthropologists have proposed that the precise definition of law is an impossible—and perhaps even undesirable—undertaking. When we speak of "the law," are we not inclined to fall back on our familiar Western conception of rules enacted by an authorized legislative body and enforced by the judicial mechanisms of the state? Can any concept of law be applied to such so-

[3] Leopold Pospisil, *The Kapauku Papuans* (New York: Holt, Rinehart and Winston, 1963).

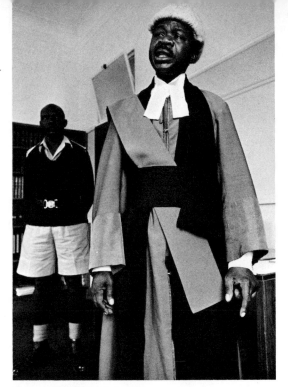

Figure 12-5. *In a tribal society, such as that of the Akure in Nigeria, it is the king who acts as judge (bottom photo) in all questions of law. More complex societies, such as that of the nation of Zambia, require the creation of legal specialists, such as this Zambian lawyer who has just been elected to a seat on the nation's Supreme Court.*

cieties as the Nuer or the Ifugao for whom the notion of a centralized judiciary is virtually meaningless? How shall we categorize duels, song contests, and other socially condoned forms of self-help which seem to meet some but not all of the criteria of law?

Ultimately, it seems of greatest value to consider each case within its cultural context. That each society exercises a degree of control over its members by means of rules and sanctions, and that some of these sanctions are more formalized than others, is indisputable; yet, in distinguishing between legal and nonlegal sanctions, we should be careful not to allow questions of terminology to overshadow our efforts to understand individual situations as they arise.

Functions of law

In *The Law of Primitive Man* (1954), Hoebel writes of a time when the notion that private property should be generously shared was a fundamental precept of Cheyenne life. Subsequently, however, some men assumed the privilege of borrowing other men's horses without bothering to obtain permission. When Wolf Lies Down complained of such unauthorized borrowing to the members of the Elk Soldier Society, the Elk Soldiers not only had his horse returned to him but also secured an award for damages from the offender. The Elk Soldiers then announced that, to avoid such difficulties in the future, horses were no longer to be borrowed without permission. Furthermore, they declared their intention of retrieving any such property and administering a whipping to anyone who resisted their efforts to return improperly borrowed goods.

The case of Wolf Lies Down and the Elk Soldier Society clearly illustrates three basic functions of law. First, law defines relationships among the members of society, determining proper behavior under various circumstances. Knowledge of the law permits each member of society to know his rights and duties in respect to every other member of society. Second, law allocates the authority to employ coercion in the enforcement of sanctions. In most complex societies, such authority is generally vested in the government and its court system. In simpler societies, the authority to employ force may be allocated directly to the injured party. Third, law functions to redefine social relations and to insure social flexibility. As new situations arise, law must determine whether old rules and assumptions retain their validity and to what extent they must be altered. Law, if it is to operate efficiently, must allow room for change.

In actual practice, law is rarely the smooth and well-integrated system described above. In any given society, various legal sanctions may apply at various levels of society. Because each individual in a society is usually a member of numerous subgroups, he is subject to the various dictates of these diverse groups. The Kapauku individual is, simultaneously, a member of a family, a household, a sublineage, and a confederacy, and is subject to all the laws of each subgroup. In some cases, it may be impossible for an individual to submit to contradictory legal indications:

> In one of the confederacy's lineages, incestuous relations between members of the same sib were punished by execution of the culprits, and in another by severe beating, in the third constituent lineage such a relationship was not punishable and . . . was not regarded as incest at all. In one of the sublineages, it became even a preferred type of marriage![4]

Furthermore, the power to employ sanctions may vary from level to level within a given society. The head of a Kapauku household may punish a member of his household by means of slapping or beating, but the authority to confiscate property is vested exclusively in the headman of the lineage. An example of a similar dilemma in our own society occurred in Oklahoma, a state in which the sale of liquor by the drink is illegal. State officials arrested several passengers and workers on an Amtrak train passing through the state; these people knew their actions were legal

[4] Ibid., p. 36.

under federal law but were unaware that they could be prosecuted under state law. The complexity of legal jurisdiction within each society casts a shadow of doubt over any easy generalization about law.

Crime

As we have observed, an important function of sanctions, legal or otherwise, is to discourage the breach of social norms. A man contemplating theft is aware of the possibility that he will be captured and punished; yet, despite the severity of sanctions, individuals in every society sometimes violate the norms and subject themselves to the consequences of their behavior. What is the nature of crime in non-Western societies?

In Western society, a clear distinction can be made between offenses against the state and offenses against an individual. Henry Campbell Black said:

> The distinction between a crime and a tort or civil injury is that the former is a breach and violation of the public right and of duties due to the whole community considered as such, and in its social and aggregate capacity; whereas the latter is an infringement or privation of the civil rights of individual merely.[5]

Thus a reckless driver who crashes with another car may be guilty of a crime in endangering public safety; he may also be guilty of a tort, in causing damages to the other car, and he can be sued for their cost by the other driver.

In many non-Western societies, however, there is no conception of a central state. Consequently, all offenses are conceived of as offenses against individuals, rendering the distinction between crime and tort of little value. Indeed, a dispute between individuals may seriously disrupt the social order, especially in small groups where the number of disputants may be a relatively large proportion of the total population. Although the

Mbuti Pygmies have no effective domestic or economic unit beyond the family, a dispute between two tribesmen will disrupt the effectiveness of the hunt and is consequently a matter of community concern. The goal of judicial proceedings in most cases is to restore social harmony and not punish an offender. In distinguishing between offenses of concern to the community as a whole and those of concern only to a few individuals, we may refer to offenses as public or private rather than distinguishing between criminal and civil law. In this way, we may avoid values and assumptions which are irrelevant to a discussion of non-Western systems of law.

Perhaps the most fruitful path to understanding the nature of law lies in the thorough analysis of individual dispute cases, each within its own unique social context. Basically, a dispute may be settled in either of two ways. On the one hand, disputing parties may, by means of argument and compromise, voluntarily arrive at a mutually satisfactory agreement. This form of settlement, which may or may not involve the mediation of a third party, is referred to as **negotiation** or **mediation.** The Penobscot Indians sometimes used this technique. The mediator was a person who commanded personal respect and therefore wielded real authority. Generally the mediator was the tribal chief. Although he had no coercive power, he usually effected a settlement through his judgments.

On the other hand, an authorized third party may issue a binding decision which the disputing parties will be obligated to respect. This process is referred to as **adjudication.** The difference between negotiation and adjudication is basically a difference in authorization. In a dispute settled by negotiation, the disputing parties present their positions as convincingly as they can, but they do not participate in the ultimate decision making.

Although the adjudication process is not characteristic of all societies, every society employs some form of negotiation in the settlement of disputes. Often, negotiation acts as a prerequisite or an alternative to adjudication. For example, in the resolution of American labor disputes, striking

---

[5] Henry Campbell Black, *Black's Law Dictionary* (St. Paul, Minn.: West Publishing Company, 1968).

workers may first negotiate with management, often with the mediation of a third party. If the state decides that the strike constitutes a threat to the public welfare, the disputing parties may be forced to submit to adjudication. In this case, the responsibility for resolving the dispute is transferred to a presumably impartial judge.

The work of the judge is difficult and complex. Not only must he sift through the evidence which is presented before him, but he must consider a wide range of norms, values, and earlier rulings in order to arrive at a decision which he hopes will be considered just not only by the disputing parties but by the public and other judges as well. In most tribal societies, a greater value is placed on reconciling disputing parties and resuming tribal harmony than on administering awards and punishments. Thus, "tribal courts may . . . work in ways more akin to Western marriage conciliators, lawyers, arbitrators, and industrial conciliators than to Western judges in court."[6]

In many societies, judgment is thought to be made by incorruptible supernatural powers, through a trial by ordeal. An example of such a trial was described by James L. Gibbs, Jr., who studied the Kpelle in Liberia:

> When there is some reason to doubt the testimony of a witness, or where the testimony of witnesses is in conflict, . . . a messenger is ordered to administer a spoonful of *katu* to the witness(es): *Katu* is a colorless liquid kept in a stoppered whiskey or wine bottle and is believed to have supernatural potency. In taking it, the witness swears over it, "If I bear false witness, then the *sale* [spirits] should kill me." It is believed that a person who breaks such an oath will be "caught" by the *katu*. His stomach will swell and he will die, or some other sickness will eventually strike. In the tropics, such a misfortune often occurs fairly soon, thereby supporting the belief in the efficacy of the liquid.[7]

[6]Max Gluckman, *The Judicial Process among the Barotse of Northern Rhodesia* (Glencoe, Ill.: The Free Press, 1955).
[7]James L. Gibbs, Jr., "The Kpelle of Liberia" in *Peoples of Africa* (Holt, Rinehart and Winston, 1965) p. 224-5.

Systems of social control

As we have seen, the mechanisms of social control are many and varied, and our societies utilize some combinations of internalized controls, which are part of the individual's enculturation, and externalized controls, which are administered by social institutions, such as the lineage or the state. It might be of interest here to compare two very different systems of social control. The Mbuti Pygmies and the Aztecs furnish a good comparison.

The Mbuti Pygmies

The Mbuti Pygmies are a tribe of hunters and gatherers situated in the Ituri forest of Central Africa. Although the Mbuti recognize no formal economic or political unit beyond the family and the band of which the family forms a part, the need for social cooperation binds the Mbuti into a closely knit community. Whether hunting with bows and arrows or with nets, the Mbuti are highly dependent upon each other for their day-to-day survival.

Despite the absence of any formal political structure, an informal hierarchy of social authority exists among the Pygmies. Leadership in various activities is determined largely by factors of age, sex, and marital status. Younger married men tend to lead the hunt, for example, while the younger married women generally assume responsibility for the gathering of mushrooms and nuts. Young unmarried men and women, on the other hand, tend to have little voice in group discussions. Nevertheless, every adult in the camp is free to express his point of view in reference to any situation.

Because the acquisition of food is a cooperative and communal activity, every individual understands that he is hunting for the band and not for himself. To be selfish or to withhold food from the band is a major offense among the Mbuti. Members of the band may noisily argue about their proper share of the day's food, but each claims only what is properly due him. Cooperation for the common good is the foundation of Mbuti society. Every man, woman, and child is made to understand that "a noisy camp is a hungry camp."

The Mbtui recognize no formal judicial process for the settling of disputes, and no such process seems to be necessary. Disputes between individuals are invariably harmful to the success of the band as a whole, and the Pygmy who jeopardizes the welfare of the group may find himself subject to public insult and ridicule. To be laughed at and humiliated may serve as a far more effective reprimand than a fine or a thrashing. After an offender has been appropriately chastised for his misbehavior, he is reunited with the band and quietly resumes his social role. There is no room in Mbuti

society for lingering punishments or for the bearing of grudges. The threat of social ostracism, however brief that ostracism may be, functions as a powerful instrument of social control among the Mbuti.

Resort to permanent exile is virtually unknown among the Pygmies. In most cases, disputes can be quickly resolved by an appeal to the common welfare. Although the mechanisms of punishment exist, the internal controls which are deeply instilled within each individual are usually sufficient to discourage any prolonged dispute. Conflicts are frequently resolved by the intervention of an impartial elder and the reminder that noise and hostility are harmful to the hunt and, consequently, to the welfare of the band. The maintenance of social control among the Pygmies is not achieved through any formal code of law; rather,

Figure 12-6a. *This photo shows the relative stature of Mbuti Pygmies and Europeans; the fellow primate on the right is a gorilla.*

Figure 12-6b. *These Mbuti men and boys are seated near the entrance of a leaf hut on the edge of the Ituri forest.*

it is understood that cooperation is a fundamental part of being Mbuti.

The Aztecs

The Aztec empire was a complex civilization which flourished in Mexico until the early sixteenth century. In contrast to the Mbuti, the Aztecs represented a highly structured and stratified society based on formally ritualized laws and customs. The Aztecs developed rigid and externalized mechanisms of social control, administered by the state.

Politically, the society of the Aztecs was a complex hierarchy including nobles, merchants, farmers, and slaves. Each individual had a clearly defined role to play within the civil and spiritual social structure. Church and state were tightly interwoven, and no distinction was made between the laws of the state and the laws of the gods. An offense against one was an offense against the other.

The Aztec court system was an elaborate and powerful instrument of law. Each town elected judges whose principal function was to settle minor disputes and to keep those disputes out of the two higher courts of appeal. Above the highest court was the emperor himself who, as Supreme Justice, was the final authority in all disputes. In addition to the regular courts, special courts for merchants and military leaders were established to serve the special needs of certain individuals.

Proper procedure in courts of law was carefully prescribed by law and custom. Judges were chosen from the ranks of respected nobles and warriors and served as intermediaries between the defendant and the gods. Lying under oath was punishable by death, as was the rendering of an unjust sentence due to partiality on the part of a judge. Aztec law was generally characterized by the swift and brutal administration of harsh penalties for violation of the law. Adulterers might be burned, thieves stoned, and homosexuals hanged. Strict laws governed every phase of Aztec

Figure 12-7. *This pair of pictures is from the Codex Florentino, a missionary book that attempted to explain the practices of the Aztecs.*

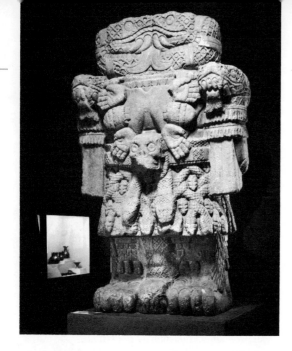

Figure 12-8. *This stone statue represents Coatlicue, mother of the Aztec gods. Her necklace is made of human hearts and hands; her skirt features writhing snakes.*

life. The efficiency of Aztec justice rendered private vengeance unnecessary, nor could such vengeance be tolerated in a complex state with many interdependent parts.

Despite their detailed body of laws and elaborate system of enforcement, the Aztecs naturally valued the prevention of conflict over its resolution. In order to insure conformity to social norms, Aztec culture was designed to continually re-enforce the values and standards of society.

> Crime was prevented by the system of domestic and public education, by constant vigilance of clan elders, by special inspectors and police, and by long speeches on all ceremonial occasions from the priests, the military leaders, and the ruler, which constantly reiterated the morals and ethics of the tribe.[8]

Characterized by self-discipline and obedience to authority, the social order of the Aztecs was maintained through a combination of continual reiteration of social standards and by the severe punishment of those who violated those standards. Unlike the Mbuti, the Aztecs were motivated to behave properly primarily by external controls.

[8] Frederick A. Peterson, *Ancient Mexico* (New York: Putnam, 1959) p. 73.

INFORMAL SOCIAL CONTROL IN AN IRISH VILLAGE

The informal social control system of Inis Beag comprises the parish priest and curate, the headmaster of the school—chosen and strictly regulated by the parish priest, and a "king." The position of king is not hereditary and not supported by a majority of the population as in some other Irish islands, but is self-assumed and based on a number of factors to be considered shortly. Not only is king strictly a term of reference, but it is employed by the folk only when they are most critical of his actions; it also is used by certain outsiders who are frequent visitors to Inis Beag and are aware of the power structure there, but always out of earshot of the islanders.

The folk are devoutly Catholic, despite the fact that they are extremely critical of their priests and retain and reinterpret pagan religious forms. They are proud of their strength of belief, with its attendant morality, and of the sanctity of "Inis Beag of the Saints," and they look to the curate for spiritual comfort, as well as political guidance in several spheres, and are uncomfortable in his absence. His presence, it is believed, provides supernatural protection for the island, while his absence invites possible anti-social behavior, and harm to the soul of one who dies suddenly and is deprived of Extreme Unction at his deathbed. The compensatory rite performed later for the deceased who has been interred while the curate was away is thought to be less efficacious in shortening the stay of the soul in Purgatory.

The techniques of social control utilized by curates are many and mostly negative; they include weekly sermons, lectures to students in the school, talks with individuals who need guidance or reprimand, the use of informers and confessions, the allocation of indulgences, and, in extreme cases, the refusal of sacraments, and the placing of curses. It is difficult to overestimate the degree of fear of the clergy and anti-clericalism which have been inculcated among the folk by the more immoderate measures employed by priests during the last century. Sermons deal both with spiritual messages based on the scriptures and church pronouncements, and with instruction and censure directed toward past or anticipated actions of the islanders in concert or of particular persons. Talks with individuals may take place in their or the curate's home, and often result from information received by the priest from informers or the confessional. The informers, it is said, are usually the housekeeper of the curate and her family, and children who are intimidated by the priest to reveal talk and behavior of their parents and others; however, certain folk are known to bear tales to the clergy and are shunned for this reason. Well aware of the power that the confessional gives the priest over their lives, islanders are outspoken in its condemnation, and many will not confess particular sins, especially those of a sexual nature, to a curate known to assign severe penances and to carry matters beyond the confessional.

The awarding of indulgences represents a positive social control method and has been used frequently, I was told, to obtain needed monetary contributions and services from the folk. Although the priest cannot excommunicate a recalcitrant parishioner, he can achieve the same objective by forbidding confession and absolution and the other sacraments to him, and the islanders report its threat and use as a sanction several occasions in the past. Even more feared is the "priest's curse," which in Co. Clare ". . . can bring ruin upon a prosperous house; can turn an unbeliever's head upon his shoulders; strike blindness . . ." (Arensberg 1937:28). In Inis Beag, it is called "reading the Gospel (or Bible) at," and can bring illness or death and ultimate damnation within a prescribed time; the folk reason that if a cleric can cure with prayer, he also can cause illness and death by its use.

It is difficult to ascertain today whether the headmaster or the king should be accorded the dominant position, after the curate, in the informal social control system of Inis Beag; for in recent years, the power and prestige of the former have been waxing and those of the latter waning. Headmasters were formerly older men with families whose tenure was long, who were much involved in local affairs and worked closely with the curate, who was politically active and backed candidates and tried to influence island voters, and who maintained social distance although considered "one of the people." For their teaching and other services, they were provided with food, given *curach* transportation without charge, and afforded other amenities by the folk. The house that they and their families occupied until recently is located in Castle Village, near both the old and new schools, and was owned by the diocese. Headmasters now are younger and often single, and are more independent of the curate (One in recent years quit his post, it is held, because he chafed at restrictions imposed on him by the priest.); also, they are apolitical and participate less in the gamut of local affairs. The prestige of the headmaster derives from his having been selected by the parish priest who supports his actions, his status as a "scholar," and the discipline that he exerts in the school with its vestigial effects on those who have graduated. Few islanders will openly contest his decisions in school and civic matters.

The important nonacademic tasks performed by the headmaster are signing official forms—a duty that he shares with the bailiff, drawing up and witnessing the signing of wills, writing letters for the islanders, especially those directed to the county council and departments of the central government, and giving advice on such matters as the advisability of emigrating and of matrimonial matches. Like the curates, the headmasters seldom have tried to direct community projects and social affairs, other than dances and inter-island competitions. The present headmaster considers himself atypical in many respects, in that he is youthful, has exceptional skill in playing the accordian, likes companionship and the festivities of party and pub, and has rapport with older boys and young men with whom he associates more than did his predecessors; as a result, he is the prime mover in social events—organizing dances and donating his musical talent. Older islanders often find him aloof and will apologize for "taking his time" when seeking favors of him.

Parents have little contact with the headmaster as regards the education of their children, and, although permitted and sometimes urged to do so, they seldom visit the school. They will consult with him about such matters as health problems of their children, but not about educational policies; nor do they complain to him of his role as pedagogue—"What the teacher does is right." Because of the severity of his discipline, and that of the other two teachers, and the fear that it arouses in his pupils, parents use him as a threat in disciplining their children at home.

Whereas the headmaster attracts the least amount of anti-authority sentiment of any other figure who regulates to a marked degree the lives of the folk, the king attracts the most. The latter is the senior of the two publicans, in age and role, whose home in Low Village accommodates guests as well as the shop and pub.

A personable man of great charm, the king has a measure of charisma which commands deference and respect, and it is said that had he chosen to become a priest or businessman on the mainland, he would now be a bishop or captain of industry. His business acumen is acclaimed, and many have become his customers because they believe him to be more "clever" than city merchants and well able to deal with them to the advantage of the islanders. The sources of his power are many. He began his career as a shopkeeper in the 1920s, with money provided him by a brother living in the United States (or, as claimed by some, with the insurance money that he received as a beneficiary when his brother was killed while serving in the armed forces of this country). Two brothers older than himself—the eldest the landholder—live in Inis Beag with large families, and he has their support and that of his many other kin. He gained a large following during the depression years of the 1930s by extending credit to customers for months without charging interest; many folk still show gratitude for this gesture by buying only from him and by acquiescing to many of his wishes, although covertly they may resent being in his debt and under his influence.

In Ireland, the term "gombeen" is used to demean the usurious shopkeeper, but this word is directed against the king only by those who most dislike him, and then to connote what they consider a combination of piety and avarice in his behavior rather than his economic practices. His role as moral guardian, with frequent instruction and reprimand as to manners and misdemeanors to men in the pub and children visiting the shop, is deeply resented by many. He does not care to have women make purchases in the shop, where they can observe men drinking and be observed in turn, ostensibly on moral grounds; he urges that children do the marketing instead, not for the convenience of their mothers, it is said, but because he can overcharge and shortchange them more easily. To dissuade women from shopping, he reads out their lists and talks with them about family affairs in a loud whisper, so that they have no privacy. The men complain not only of his alleged practice of overcharging and shortchanging them late at night when the pub is overcrowded with "light headed" drinkers, but also of his criticizing their actions in public, his frequent closing of the pub before midnight, and his refusal to serve those whom he feels have "taken too much" or those about to attend a party where more drinks will be proffered them.

Among the traits attributed to Inis Beag folk by nativists and primitivists are self-reliance, independence, and individualism. But the self-reliance of the islanders has become undermined increasingly since 1891 by a benevolent government; their independence is severely curtailed by restrictions imposed on them by curate, headmaster, king, and their fellows; and their individualism is a figment of literary imagination disguising a strict conformism. Inis Beag as much as any community is characterized by gossip, ridicule, and opprobrium, which gain their effectiveness as social control mechanisms from the deep concern of the folk with "saving face," and which serve to limit freedom of action and behavioral idiosyncracy. When asked to rank the major deficiencies of island life, the people almost without exception place the prevalence of malicious gossiping, along with poverty and the intrusion of the clergy into secular affairs, at the head of their list.

No matter how much the islanders detest gossiping when they are its victims, they nevertheless welcome every opportunity to engage in it. News of an event passes quickly by word of mouth from Low to Terrace Villages, and variations in the description of the event are usually numerous due to the distortions of rumor. In order to circumvent gossip, parties are organized at the last moment and invitations issued by small boys moving quietly from door to door in the night; persons will leave the island—sometimes to emigrate, visit the hospital with a serious illness, or enter an order—without previous announcement, running from their homes to the strand to board the last canoes for the steamer; and mail is posted just prior to the arrival of the steamer and picked up immediately after it is carried to the post office, for fear that the postmaster will open letters and talk publicly of their contents (or take money from them). It is customary for boys and young men to hide themselves in the darkness or behind fences in order to overhear conversations of passersby, or witness their misbehavior, which can be reported; this compels folk who move about after dark to conceal their faces and talk in whispers or low tones. When a person hidden in the darkness is accosted suddenly, he will vault a fence, run away, or crouch down and hide his face or draw a raincoat over his head and shoulders to avoid being recognized. Most social events and visiting take place after sundown, so that movements from one house to another will be unobserved.

Summary

1.

Social controls enable a group of people to encourage conformity to group norms and values. Conformity to these norms and values perpetuates the group's culture and maintains its system of social relations. Social control is older than culture itself. Nonetheless, the anthropological study of social control in non-Western societies is a relatively recent development. The misconception that there is a basic difference between social control in "primitive" and "advanced" societies was refuted by Malinowski in the early twentieth century. Malinowski said that the universal basis for social order is the principle of reciprocity: if a man treats his neighbor well, his neighbor will treat him well.

2.

There are two kinds of social controls, internalized and externalized. Internalized controls are imposed by a guilty individual on himself. These built-in controls rely on such deterrents as the fear of God and the threat of magical retaliation. Internalized controls are insufficient. Every society develops externalized controls, called sanctions. Positive sanctions are societal reactions to a member's behavior which show approval; negative sanctions are societal reactions to a member's behavior which show disapproval. Societies stress negative sanctions more heavily than positive sanctions.

3.

Formal sanctions are codified in legal statutes: informal sanctions are not. Organized sanctions reward or punish behavior through a precisely regulated social procedure; diffuse sanctions are the immediate approving or disapproving reactions of individual community members to a fellow member's behavior. Primary sanctions are direct community actions against an individual; secondary sanctions are community-backed sanctions directed by one person or group of persons at another person or group of persons.

4.

Law is an important part of a society's social controls. Some anthropologists have proposed that to define law is impossible. E. Adamson Hoebel said that social norms are legal when they are regularly enforced by "socially recognized" enforcers. Leopold Pospisil said that the law has four basic attributes: the backing of authority; universal applicability; the recognition of rights and duties; determination of the nature and degree of sanctions.

5.

Law serves three basic functions: it defines relationships among the members of a society; it allocates the authority to employ coercion in the enforcement of sanctions; it redefines social relations and insures social flexibility.

6.

Western societies clearly distinguish offenses against the state, called crimes, from offenses against an individual, called torts. Crimes are public offenses; torts are private offenses. Many non-Western societies have no conception of a central state and conceive of all offenses as offenses against individuals. All societies use negotiation to settle individual disputes. Negotiation involves the parties to a dispute themselves reaching an agreement, with or without help. Adjudication, not found in some societies, involves an authorized third party issuing a binding decision.

Suggested readings

Bohannan, Paul, ed. *Law and Warfare: Studies in the Anthropology of Conflict.* New York: Natural History Press, 1967.
Examples of various ways in which conflict is evaluated and handled in different cultures are brought together in this book. It examines institutions and means of conflict resolution including courts, middlemen, self-help, wager of battle, contest, and ordeal. It also has a selection discussing war—raids, organization for aggression, tactics, and feuds.

Hoebel, E. Adamson *The Law of Primitive Man: A Study in Comparative Legal Dynamics.* Cambridge: Harvard University Press, 1954. Atheneum, 1968.
This book combines the study of law and anthropology to develop a setting of ideas and methods for the study of law in primitive society. It then analyzes seven primitive cultures (including Eskimo, Commanche, Trobriand Islanders, and Ashanti) with reference to the underlying legal forms which govern each. It ends with a discussion of the interrelationship between law and society.

Nader, Laura, ed. "The Ethnography of Law" in *American Anthropologist,* 1965, Vol. 67, Part II, No. 6.
This special publication is the result of a conference held in Stanford, California in 1964 on anthropology and law. The discussion centered on problems and approaches to law in an anthropological context. It includes discussion on aspects of law, including "double institutionalization," law mechanisms, common law, and problems in cross-cultural comparisons of methodology.

Nader, Laura, ed. *Law in Culture and Society.* Chicago: Aldine Press, 1969.
This is a well-balanced and thorough collection of articles on law in different cultures and societies.

Religion
and magic

According to their origin myth, the Tewa Indians of New Mexico emerged from a lake far to the north of where they now live. Once on dry land, they divided into two groups, the Summer People and the Winter People, and migrated south down both sides of the Rio Grande. During their travels, they made twelve stops, before finally being reunited into a single community.

For the Tewa, all existence is divided into six categories, three human and three supernatural. Each of the human categories, which are arranged in a hierarchy, is matched by a spiritual category, so that when a man dies, he immediately passes into his proper spiritual role. Not only are the supernatural categories identified with human categories; they also correspond to divisions the Tewa make in the natural world.

From a Judeo-Christian vantage point, such a religion may seem, at best, irrational and arbitrary. It is neither—as has been shown by Alfonso Ortiz, a native-born Tewa anthropologist. Ortiz argues that his native religion is not only logical and socially functional, it is the very model of Tewa society.[1] The Tewa have one of the few extant "dual organization" societies in the world; it is

[1] Alfonso Ortiz, *The Tewa World* (Chicago: University of Chicago Press, 1969), p. 43.

divided into two independent moieties, each having its own economy, rituals, and authority. The individual is introduced into one of these moieties, which are not based on kinship, and his membership is regularly reinforced through a series of life-cycle rituals that correspond to the stops on the mythical tribal journey down the Rio Grande. The rites of birth and death are shared in by the whole community; other rites differ in the two moieties. The highest status of the human hierarchy belongs to the priests, who also help integrate this divided society; they not only mediate between the human and spiritual world, but also between the two moieties.

Tewa religion enters into virtually every aspect of Tewa life and society. It is the basis of the simultaneously dualistic/unified world view of the individual Tewa. It provides numerous points of mediation through which the two moieties can continue to exist as a single community. It sanctifies the community by providing a supernatural origin, and it offers divine sanction to those "rites of passage" that soften life's major transitions. In providing an afterworld that is the mirror image of human society, it answers the question of death in a manner that reinforces social structure. In short, Tewa religion, far from being arbitrary or illogical, gives a solid foundation to the stability and continuity of Tewa society.

All religions fulfill numerous social and psychological needs. Some of these needs—the need to confront and explain death, for example—appear to be universal; indeed, Malinowski has gone so far as to say that "there are no peoples, however primitive, without religion and magic."[2] Unbound by time, religion gives meaning to individual and group life, drawing power from the time of the gods in the Beginning, and offering continuity of existence beyond death. It can provide the path by which man transcends his arduous earthly existence and attains, if only momentarily, a spiritual selfhood. The social functions of religion are no less important than the psychological functions. A traditional religion reinforces group norms, provides moral sanctions for individual conduct, and furnishes the substratum of common purpose and values upon which the equilibrium of the community depends.

Because religion fulfills important psychological and social functions, it has survived the various onslaughts of anticlericalism, rationalism, science, and technology. Nineteenth century evolutionists believed that science would ultimately destroy religion by showing people the irrationality of their myths and rituals. But an opposite tendency has occurred, and traditional religious institutions continue to attract new members. And there are many new options: the fundamentalist, anti-rationalist cults, such as the so-called "Jesus freaks," who are trying to revive the mystical communion of earliest Christianity; the Eastern religions; astrology and occultism. Science, far from destroying religion, seems to have contributed to the creation of a veritable religious boom. It has done this by removing many traditional psychological props, while at the same time creating, in its technological applications, a host of new problems—pollution, atomic weapons, rapid travel and communications—which people must now deal with. In

[2] Bronislaw Malinowski, *Magic, Science and Religion* (Garden City, N.Y.: Anchor Books, 1954).

Figure 13-1. *This young Orthodox Jew is preparing to take part in an ancient rite.*

Figure 13-2a. *The Hare Krishna sect has attracted some young American believers.*

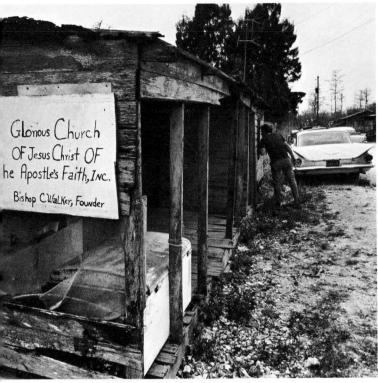

Glorious Church OF Jesus Christ OF he Apostle's Faith, Inc.
Bishop C. Walker, Founder

Figure 13-2b. *This shack is the church of a new fundamentalist sect in Georgia.*

Figure 13-2c. *An Indian guru speaks to his disciples, many from foreign countries.*

the face of these new anxieties, religion offers social and psychological support.

The persistence of religion in the face of Western rationalism clearly reveals that it is a powerful and dynamic force in society. Although the anthropologist is not qualified to pass judgment on the metaphysical truth of any particular religion, he can attempt to show how each religion embodies a number of "truths" about man and society.

The anthropological approach to religion

Melford E. Spiro defined religion as "an institution consisting of culturally patterned interaction with culturally postulated superhuman beings."[3] In other words, religion is that part of a group's cultural heritage that mediates between the profane world of everyday life and the sacred world of supernatural beings and powers. The interaction between these two worlds lies in a system of values, by which humans try to imitate the supposed values of the supernatural beings, and in a system of ritual consisting of symbolic activities which are designed to break down the barriers between the earthly and supernatural.

Talcott Parsons, a leading contemporary sociologist, has listed five factors which he believes all religions will be found to include. First, every religion encompasses a set of sacred entities which are set apart from ordinary objects and events of everyday life. Second, it has a system of expressive symbols, which are supposed to elicit sacred emotional states, and are typical of religions everywhere. Third, a religion always includes certain definite ritual activities, such as confession in Catholic Christianity, which are obligatory, or at least extremely important. Fourth, there is a feeling of collectivity or social solidarity among the religion's believers. Finally, there is a

[3]Melford E. Spiro, "Religion: Problems of Definition and Explanation" in Michael Bauton, ed., *Anthropological Approaches to the Study of Religion* (London: Tamstoch Publications, 1966), p. 96.

sense of some relationship between the supernatural world and the believer's moral values, goals, and rules of conduct.

These definitions of religion obviously differ from those one would expect from a theologian or a philosopher. The social scientist approaches religion from a particular point of view. The emphasis in anthropological definitions is on culture; religion is viewed not as an isolated institution existing within society, but as an integral part of society which affects and is affected by every other social institution, whether moral, economic, or political. According to Paul Radin:

Religion is thus not a phenomenon apart and distinct from mundane life nor is it a philosophical inquiry into the nature of being and becoming. It only emphasizes and preserves those values accepted by the majority of a group at a given time. It is this close connection with the whole life of man that we find so characteristically developed among all primitive cultures. . . . Only when other means of emphasizing and maintaining the life-values are in the ascendant, does religion become divorced from the whole corporate life of the community.[4]

The early evolutionists

Nineteenth century anthropologists, struck by the seemingly universal practices of magic that existed without the benefit of intercultural contact, explained their observations through the theoretical perspective of cultural evolutionism. Unfortunately, this perspective was especially inappropriate to the study of religions. For one thing, most theorists approached religion from a distinctly Christian viewpoint, seeing all other religions as "lower" on the evolutionary scale. Neither anthropological research nor popular opinion today supports this assumption. Moreover, evolutionism automatically implied the search for the origins of religion—a search futile from the start—and for stages of development

[4]Paul Radin, *Primitive Religion* (New York: Dover Publications, 1937), pp. 5–6.

310

Figure 13-3. *The worship of holy animals is a feature of many religions. The Ainu keep bears captive in log cages and ritually kill the cubs with many apologies to the Bear Spirit. The Indian temple shown below is sacred to the worship of holy rats.*

leading, of course, to Christian monotheism. Despite these lapses, such "armchair anthropologists" as Sir Edward Tylor, R. R. Marett, and Sir James G. Frazer made some significant contributions to the study of religions.

Animism

In his search for the origin of all religious beliefs, Sir Edward Tylor came upon the concept of **animism.** Essentially, animism (from "anima" or "soul") is a belief in personal spirits which are thought to animate nature. Tylor, writing in 1873, noted many examples of animism. For example, the Dayaks of Borneo believed rice had a soul, and they held feasts to contain the soul securely in order to prevent crop failure. Fijian women, until the turn of the century, were expected to willingly submit to death when their husbands passed away, so they could remain at their husbands' sides in the other world. The Koriaks of Asia, after killing a bear, would flay the animal, dress one of their people in the skin, and dance around chanting that they were not really responsible for killing the bear, and that the Russians killed it.

Primitive men, Tylor suggested, were profoundly impressed by two groups of biological problems:

> In the first place, what is it that makes the difference between a living body and a dead one; what causes waking, sleep, trance, disease, death? In the second place, what are those human shapes which appear in dreams and visions? Looking at these two groups of phenomena, the ancient savage philosophers probably made their first step by the obvious inference that every man has two things belonging to him, namely, a life and a phantom.[5]

Thus is born the idea of soul, or anima. By extension, animals and plants are seen to embody

[5]Sir Edward B. Tylor, "Animism" in V. F. Calverton, ed., *The Making of Man: An Outline of Anthropology* (New York: The Modern Library, 1931), p. 635.

souls, for they also live and die. Through further analogy, stones, weapons, food, ornaments, and other objects are imbued with souls. Animism is, then, the minimum definition of religion and the basis upon which "higher" religions are founded.

Tylor's theory was widely accepted in his time, though few anthropologists would accept it today. The theory is essentially intellectualistic; that is, it claims that religion came into being through a process of reasoning, as a means of explaining otherwise unexplainable phenomena. Modern interpretations generally put the case the other way around: people tend to rationalize their beliefs only after they already hold them. Further, Tylor derives all spirits and gods from extensions of human personality, when actually many supernatural beings are not thought to resemble men. Thus it is not animism, but the more general **supernaturalism,** which is the minimum definition of religion. Criticism has also been directed against Tylor's theory of the evolution of modern monotheism in a series of stages from early animism. Such a sequence incorporates most of the evolutionary fallacies of Tylor's time: the idea that technologically primitive cultures are primitive in all other areas; the unawareness of hundreds of examples that may not fit the evolutionary scheme; the lack of fieldwork; and so forth. Yet, despite such valid criticism of Tylor's work, it remains undeniably true that animism is characteristic of hunter-gatherers, and therefore may well have been the first form of man's religion.

Animatism

One of the problems with Tylor's theory was that the concept of animism involves a personal soul, yet there are many cases where supernatural power is considered impersonal. The Melanesians, for example, think of *mana* as a force inherent in all objects. It is not in itself physical, but it can reveal itself physically. A warrior's success in fighting is not attributed to his own strength but to the *mana* contained in an amulet which hangs around his neck. Similarly, a farmer may know a great deal about agriculture, soil conditioning, and the correct time for sowing and reaping, but he nevertheless depends upon *mana* for a successful crop, often building a simple altar to this power at the end of his field. If the crop is good, it is a sign that he has in some way appropriated the *mana*. Far from being a personalized force, *mana* is abstract in the extreme, a power lying always just beyond reach of the senses. As R. H. Codrington described it:

> Virtue, prestige, authority, good fortune, influence, sanctity, luck are all words which, under certain conditions, give something near the meaning. . . . *mana* sometimes means a more than natural virtue or power attaching to some person or thing. . . .[6]

This concept of impersonal power was also widespread among American Indians. The Iroquois called it *orenda;* to the Sioux it was *wakonda;* to the Algonkins, *manitu.* However, though found on every continent, the concept is not necessarily universal.

R. R. Marett called this concept of impersonal power **animatism.** The two concepts, animism and animatism, are not mutually exclusive. They are often found in the same culture, as, for example, in Melanesia, and also in the Indian societies mentioned above.

Magic and religion

Among the most fascinating manifestations of religion is the belief that powers—whether forces, gods, demons, ghosts, spirits or other imagined forces—can be compelled to act in certain ways for good or evil purposes. This is a classical anthropological notion of magic. Many societies have magical rituals to ensure good crops, the replenishment of game and the fertility of domestic animals, the avoidance or cure of illness in humans. Although Western man, in seeking to objectify and demythologize his world, has largely suppressed (but not abolished) the existence of these fantastic notions in his own consciousness, they continue to hold him nevertheless—nowadays in novels about demonic possession or witchcraft that he half-guiltily devours and discusses. Non-Western man, on the other hand, quite freely endows his world with psychic properties; an African jungle dweller, for instance, sees a nocturnal creature by daylight and knows it is a medicine man who has temporarily taken its shape. A tree may have its own soul and voice. Some South American Indians *know* that they are a kind of parrot, though they are aware they lack feathers, wings, and beaks.

Sir James George Frazer made a strong distinction between religion and magic. Religion is "a propitiation or conciliation of powers superior to man which are believed to direct and control the course of nature and human life."[7] Magic, on the other hand, is an attempt to manipulate certain perceived "laws" of nature. The magician never doubts that the same causes will always produce the same effects. Thus Frazer saw magic as a sort of pseudo-science, differing from modern Western science only in its misconception of the nature of the particular laws which govern the succession of events.

Frazer differentiated between two fundamental principles of magic. The first principle, that "like produces like," he called the **law of similarity** or **sympathetic magic.** In Burma, for example, a rejected lover might engage a sorcerer to make an image of his scornful love. If this image was tossed in water, to the accompaniment of certain charms, the hapless girl would go mad. Thus the girl would suffer a fate similar to that of her image.

Frazer's second principle was the **law of contagion**—the concept that things or persons which have once been in contact can afterward influence one another. The most common example of contagious magic is the permanent relationship between an individual and any part of his body,

---

[6] As quoted by Godfrey Leinhardt in "Religion" in Harvey Shapiro, ed., *Man, Culture, and Society* (London: Oxford University Press, 1971), p. 368.

[7] Sir James G. Frazer, "Magic and Religion" in Calverton, *op. cit.*, p. 693.

Figure 13-4. New ways do not necessarily displace the old; the two may coexist. The man at right is a Nigerian trained as a psychiatrist; helping him treat his patient is the local witch doctor, who has considerable skill in dealing with severe emotional upsets. He has been incorporated into the staff of the clinic under the title "native therapist."

such as his hair, fingernails, or teeth. Frazer cites the Basutos, a tribe in South Africa, who were careful to conceal their extracted teeth, because these might fall into the hands of certain mythical beings who could harm the owner of the tooth by working magic on it.

The functions of religion

If early anthropological theories were dominated by evolutionary perspectives and assumptions, the twentieth century saw an increasing tendency to study religions not in terms of origins or sequential stages, but rather in terms of their psychological and social functions. What psychological, biological, and social needs does religion satisfy? In what ways does religion maintain the fabric of society? What is the relation between religion and other social institutions?

The twentieth century has also seen a growing rejection of vast generalizations and of attempts to reduce all religious phenomena to one "ism" or another, such as animism or animatism. Another significant feature of the more recent research is the emphasis on fieldwork; modern theorists are expected to have extensive first-hand knowledge of one or more non-Western cultures. Equally important, anthropologists tend not to see religion as having originated from attempts to explain the world through individual introspection, as Tylor and Frazer had suggested.

Society as "God"

Even the early anthropologists were led by their research to a realization of the social functions of religion. The study of totemism points up this tendency. Totemism is based on the division of the whole world into those things which are profane, or have no spiritual value for the clan or tribe, and those which are sacred. Not only gods and spirits are sacred; indeed, according to sociologist Émile Durkheim, "a rock, a tree, a spring, a pebble, a piece of wood, a house, in a word, anything can be sacred."[8] Among the tribes that practice totemism, such as the Australian aborigines, each clan is distinguished by its own totem—a particular animal, plant, or object which the clan is named after and which is considered extremely sacred. The clan's emblem is a pictorial representation of the totem. Plant and animal totems can be eaten only under rigidly prescribed conditions, and totemic objects must be approached only with the proper religious ritual. Each clan identifies with one totem, but this is merely the center of an ever-widening circle of specified sacred things. Blackwood trees, dogs, fire, and frost are assigned to the Pelican clan. The stars and the moon are classed as in the realm of the Black Cockatoo clan. In this way all of nature is classified and organized into one Great Tribe.

Durkheim, who believed totemism to be the basis from which all religions have developed, attempted to create a general theory of religion through a detailed analysis of the religion of the Australian Arunta. Like Tylor and Frazer, he was interested in the origins and evolution of religion, but unlike his precursors he did not find the answer in the individual. According to Durkheim, the individual is totally dependent on his society. Society holds such an awesome power over the individual's whole being that it is literally sacred to him. However, the clan itself is too complex and too abstract to be the recipient of this tremendous respect and awe, so these feelings are projected onto the totem, which stands for society. In turn, the organization and classification of nature is made to mirror the organization of the clan and tribe. In short, man deifies his own society, which becomes virtually God. Religion, then, is a vast symbolic system encompassing every aspect of society, and at the same time stabilizing and maintaining the continuity of society by constantly reinforcing its traditions and values.

Claude Lévi-Strauss has argued that totemism is not a valid concept, since it incorporates under a single term a great number of phenomena that are not really alike. Another criticism of Durkheim's thesis is that many of the most profoundly religious experiences, whether among Arunta tribesmen or Western Christians, arise out of solitude. Although society may be the source of many religious beliefs and rituals, most theorists would agree that at least some religious phenomena directly arise from individual needs and emotions. Yet the Durkheim theory that saw society rather than the individual as central to explaining religious phenomena has held an integral place in anthropology.

Social function of religious customs

Looking at religious practices in terms of their functions for society enables us to make sense of seemingly bizarre customs. For example, one of the more gruesome (from our point of view) parts of the funerary rites of the Melanesians was the eating of the flesh of the dead person. This ritual cannibalism, witnessed by anthropologist Bronislaw Malinowski, was performed with "extreme repugnance and dread and usually followed by a violent vomiting fit. At the same time it is felt to be a supreme act of reverence, love and devotion."[9] This custom, and the emotions accompanying it, clearly reveal the ambiguous attitude of many people towards death: on the one hand, one longs to hold onto the dead person, and on the other hand, one feels disgust and fear at the transformation wrought by death. According to Malinowski, funeral ceremonies provide an approved collective means of expressing these individual feelings, while at the same time maintaining social cohesiveness and preventing disruption of society. Thus Malinowski attempted to reveal both the psychological and social functions of religious behavior.

Malinowski held that nontechnological people do not live in some prelogical dream world; rather they are extremely pragmatic and have a firm grasp of the workings of nature and of the practi-

[8] Émile Durkheim, *The Elementary Forms of the Religious Life* (New York: The Free Press, 1965), p. 52.

[9] Malinowski, *op, cit.,* p. 50.

cal aspects of survival. Religion and magic arise out of a need to reach beyond this practical knowledge in order to make the world acceptable and manageable. Religion and magic, then, can be viewed as the very foundations of culture and the basic integrative forces of society. Though Malinowski rejected Durkheim's theories almost totally, he shared with that great French sociologist the view that religion must be studied in terms of its functions.

A. R. Radcliffe-Brown went even farther than Durkheim in rejecting individual psychological interpretations of religion. He saw social phenomena as systems of adaptation, and society itself as a dynamic network of functionally interdependent elements. The function of religion is to celebrate and maintain the norms on which society depends. However, the need for social solidarity is not sufficient explanation for all religious phenomena. Deeper analysis, he believed, could show that objects selected for veneration are utilitarian; they either have practical social value or they have ritual value, the ability to fuse the natural and social orders. Thus, within any social system, those elements critical to social functioning will be made sacred.

Psychology and religion

Psychologists have generally followed Tylor and Frazer in tracing the source of religion to the needs and propensities of the individual. William James, for example, saw religion as developing, at least partly, from an intuitive individual awareness of a "More" just beyond consciousness. He claims "that our normal waking consciousness, rational consciousness as we call it, is but one special type of consciousness, whilst all about it, parted from it by the filmiest of screens, there lie potential forms of consciousness entirely different."[10] Although this postulates nothing about the objective truth of religion, it does suggest a subjective truth, namely the mystical experience.

[10] William James, *The Varieties of Religious Experience* (New York: Collier Books, 1961), p. 305.

Some later psychologists saw religion as the projection of the individual unconscious into the outer world. Chief among these were Sigmund Freud and Carl Jung. Although their theories of religion are accepted by very few anthropologists—and probably by only a minority of psychologists—they have had a subtle and far-reaching influence on the ways we view religion.

Religion as neurosis. As we saw in Chapter 5, Sigmund Freud believed that all culture originated in a sort of universal Oedipus complex. The primal father was killed by his sons, who ate him, because he was monopolizing their sisters and daughters. Expanding on this basic theory, Freud claims that sacrifice and feast were ritually practiced in order to assuage the sense of guilt over the murder of the father. God is simply the father projected into the heavens. According to Freud:

> The ordinary man cannot imagine this Providence in any other form but that of a greatly exalted father, for only such a one could understand the needs of the sons of men, or be softened by their prayers and placated by the signs of their remorse. The whole thing is so patently infantile, so incongruous with reality, that to one whose attitude to humanity is friendly, it is painful to think that the great majority of mortals will never be able to rise above this view of life.[11]

Classical psychoanalytic theory, then, sees religion as a system of defense mechanisms to relieve man of his burden of anxiety and guilt. Though Freud's evolutionary hypotheses are replete with logical and factual fallacies, many anthropologists have been influenced by his emphasis on anxiety-reduction as a primary function of religion and ritual. In many instances, religion seems to relieve the anxiety of the unknown by explaining it, or making it known.

Religion as therapy. Joseph Campbell notes that dawn and awakening from the world of

[11] Sigmund Freud, *Civilization and its Discontents* (Garden City, N.Y.: Anchor Books), p. 13.

dreams must always have been associated with the sun and sunrise. The night fears and charms are dispelled by light, which has always been experienced as coming from above and furnishing guidance and orientation. Darkness, weight, the pull of gravity, the dark interior of the earth, the jungle, the deep sea, must for untold ages have constituted a distinct and poignant area of human experience in contrast to the world of day. Thus a polarity of light and dark, above and below, guidance and the loss of bearings, confidence and fear may have arisen as a basic principle of human thought.

Part of the function of religion has been to dispel the fears of darkness. "In the morning, when the sun comes, we go out of the huts, spit into our hands, and hold them up to the sun." So was Carl Jung told of a simple ritual, performed almost unconsciously, by a native of Africa. However, though morning and day were celebrated, "From sunset on, it was a different world—the dark world of *ayik*, of evil, danger, fear." Jung, too, was impressed by the splendor of the African sunrise, and the brooding darkness of the African night. "It is the psychic primal night which is the same today as it has been for countless million years," he speculated. "The longing for light is the longing for consciousness."[12]

This interpretation of an African view of day and night epitomizes Jung's approach to religion. He believed that religion expresses the deepest truths of man's nature, that it draws these truths out of the dark night of man's unconscious and into the daylight of consciousness. For Jung, Freud's "subconscious" was merely the "personal unconscious," a concept of limited application. Beyond this lay the "collective unconscious"—a vast reservoir of inherited thought patterns called archetypes. These archetypes—abstract patterns which are universal to all mankind—are concretely projected into the outer world as symbols, such as the symbols of myth and religion.

For Jung, religion is not merely anxiety-reducing, but positively therapeutic. Religious

---

[12] Carl Jung, *Memories, Dreams, Reflections* (New York: Vintage Books, 1961), p. 266.

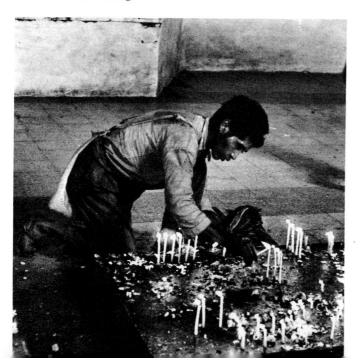

Figure 13-5. *Another example of the ability of religion to integrate both old and new customs can be seen in the festival held in Chichicastenango, Guatemala. Ceremonies combine the worship of Christian saints and Mayan gods, in a carnival atmosphere of quite boisterous drinking.*

behavior is instrumental in helping the individual toward greater integration and maturity. Religion is not, as Freud would have it, infantile; rather it is a means by which the person can transcend his infantile fixations. Thus Jung and his school of analytic psychology emphasize positively transformative rituals and myths, such as those involving rebirth into a new selfhood and the magical journey of the hero.

The practice of religion

Much of the psychological and social value of religion comes from the activities called for by its practice. Participation in religious ceremonies may bring a sense of personal transcendence, a wave of reassurance and security, or a feeling of closeness to fellow participants. Although the rituals and practices of religions vary considerably, even those rites that seem to us most bizarrely exotic can be shown to serve the same basic social and psychological functions.

Rituals and ceremonies

Religious ritual is the means through which persons relate to the sacred; it is religion made overt. Not only is ritual the means by which the social bonds of a group are reinforced and tensions relieved, it is also one way that many important events are celebrated and crises, such as death, are made less socially disruptive and less difficult for the individuals to bear. Anthropologists have classified several different types of ritual, among them **rites of passage,** which pertain to crises in the life of the individual, and **rites of intensification,** which take place during a crisis in the life of the group, serving to bind individuals together.

Rites of passage. In one of anthropology's classic works, Arnold Van Gennep analyzed the rites of passage which usher individuals through the crucial crises of their lives; such as birth, puberty, marriage, parenthood, advancement to a higher class, occupational specialization, and death. He found that ceremonies for all of these life-crises could be subdivided into three stages: rites of **separation;** rites of **transition;** and rites of **incorporation.** The individual would first be ritually removed from the society as a whole, then he would be isolated for a period, and finally he would be incorporated back into the tribe in his new status.

Van Gennep described the initiation rites of Australian aborigines. When the time for the initiation is decided by the elders, the boys are taken from the village, while the women cry and make a ritual show of resistance. At a place distant from the camp, groups of men from many villages gather. The elders sing and dance while the initiates act as though they are dead. The climax of this part of the ritual is a bodily operation, such as circumcision or the knocking out of a tooth. Anthropologist A. P. Elkin says, "This is partly a continuation of the drama of death. The tooth-knocking, circumcision or other symbolical act 'killed' the novice; after this he does not return to the general camp and normally may not be seen by any woman. He is dead to the ordinary life of the tribe."[13] The novice may be shown secret ceremonies and receive some instruction during this period, but the most significant element is his complete removal from society. In the course of these Australian puberty rites, the initiate must learn the tribal lore; he is given, in effect, a "cram course." The trauma of the occasion is a pedagogical technique which ensures that he will learn and remember everything; in a nonliterate society, effective teaching methods of this sort are necessary for both individual and group survival.

On his return to society, the novice is welcomed with ceremonies as though he had returned from the dead. This alerts the society at large that the individual has a new status—that they can expect him to act in certain ways and

[13] A. P. Elkin, *The Australian Aborigines* (Garden City, N.Y.: Anchor Books, 1964).

Figure 13-6. *In Chichicastenango, a Shaman pours an offering of firewater over an idol representing an ancient Mayan god. In the other photo, the king of Akure presides over a similar rite, in which a chicken is sacrificed to the tribal gods. The men performing the rites are tribal chiefs rather than specialized religious leaders.*

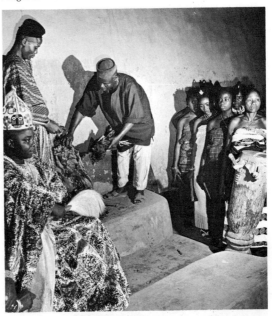

Social integration ● part **4**

in return must act in the appropriate ways toward him. The individual's new rights and duties are thus clearly defined. He is spared, for example the problems of "American Teenage," a time when an individual is neither adult nor child but a person whose status is ill defined.

Many societies engage in ritual sacrifice during rites of passage and intensification. Among the Nuer of Africa, when a boy is initiated his father gives him an ox. Through this ox, which represents oxen in general, the boy enters upon a new kind of relationship with god and with the ghosts of his ancestors. In effect, he identifies himself with his ox, which mediates between him and the supernatural world. When, as an adult, he sacrifices the ox, or a substitute animal, he is symbolically killing himself.

This custom is not so strange once we understand the nature of blood sacrifice. Sacrifice is a means of passing into the religious domain. Consecrated in death, the spirit of the sacrificial victim is released into the spiritual realm, and so far as the sacrificer himself is identified with the victim, he partakes of the sacred. Further, by eating the victim of the sacrifice, the participants in the ritual assimilate its sacred power.

One major reason for sacrifice is to avoid injury from supernatural forces by giving up something of value. For example, ritual "first-fruit" ceremonies, common among many agricultural peoples, are designed to protect the crops from the deity by appeasing him with the first vegetables or grains of harvest.

Rites of reversal. Another common kind of religious ritual is the rite of reversal, which involves an inversion of social rules or norms; it may take place during either rites of passage or of intensification. Among the Iatmul, a patrilineal society of New Guinea, the special relation between a man and his sister's son is expressed through a ritual called *naven.* The central feature of *naven,* which is performed to celebrate many of the important events in a boy's life, is the dressing of men in women's clothes and of

women in men's clothes. As described by Gregory Bateson, the maternal uncles of the boy put on "the most filthy old tousled skirts such as only the ugliest and most decrepit widows might wear" and hobble about the village. Much to the amusement and teasing of the village children, these grotesque "mothers" search for their "child," namely, their nephew, who hides in shame, knowing that if he is found he will be further humiliated by them. In those *navens* in which women participate, they dress not in rags as the men do, but in the smartest male attire.[14]

Another rite involving sexual inversion is the widespread practice of the *couvade;* following the birth of a baby, the husband takes on the symptoms of postnatal illness and disability of the mother, while she goes about her daily affairs as usual. During the installation rites of a chief among the Ndembu of Africa, a different type of role reversal is manifest; the chief must sit in silent humility while he is reviled in the most blunt and vulgar terms by anyone who feels so inclined.

Such practices are not always "religious," but like some religious rituals, they function to stabilize society by releasing tensions generated by oppositions between sexes, roles, and classes.

Religious practitioners

In societies large and complex enough to support occupational specialists, the role of administering the mythologies, ceremonies, and ethical systems that hold a society together belongs to the **priest.** He is the socially initiated, ceremonially inducted member of a recognized religious organization with a rank and function that belongs to him as the tenant of an office held by others before him. His source of power is the society and the institution in which he functions.

Even in societies that lack occupational specialization, there have always been individuals who have acquired religious power individually, usu-

[14] Gregory Bateson, *Naven* (Stanford: Stanford University Press, 1958).

ally in solitude and isolation, when the Great Spirit, the Power, the Great Mystery is revealed to them. Such a man becomes the recipient of certain special gifts, such as healing or divination; when he returns to society he is frequently given another kind of religious role, that of the **shaman.** Joseph Campbell describes the shaman as "master of his own initiation, the only valid expression of the initiation archetype for the entire tribal group to which he belongs."

Typicallly, one becomes a shaman by passing through stages common to many religious myths, often thought to involve torture and violent dismemberment of the body; scraping away of the flesh until the body is reduced to a skeleton; substitution of the viscera and renewal of the blood; a period spent in a nether region, such as Hell, during which the shaman is taught by the souls of the dead shamans and demons; and an ascent to heaven. Among the Crow Indians, for example, any man could become a shaman, since there was no ecclesiastical organization that handed down laws for the guidance of the religious consciousness. The search for shamanistic visions was pursued by most adult Crow males, who would engage in bodily deprivation, even self-torture. The majority of the seekers would not be granted a vision, but such failure carried no social stigma. While those who claimed supernatural vision would be expected to manifest some special power in battle or wealth, it was the sincerity of the seeker that carried the essential truth of the experience. Many of the elements of shamanism such as transvestitism, trance-states, and speaking in undecipherable languages can just as easily be regarded as abnormalities, and it has been frequently pointed out that those regarded as specially gifted in some societies would be outcasts or worse in others. The position of shaman provides a socially approved role for otherwise unstable personalities.

The shaman is essentially a religious entrepreneur. He acts for some human client, on whose behalf he intervenes to influence or impose his will on supernatural powers. He can be contrasted with the priest, whose "clients" are the

Figure 13-7a. *This sequence of photos shows some events in the life of Buddhist monks.*

Figure 13-7b. *Novices all eat together; their food is donated by local worshippers.*

Social integration ● part **4**

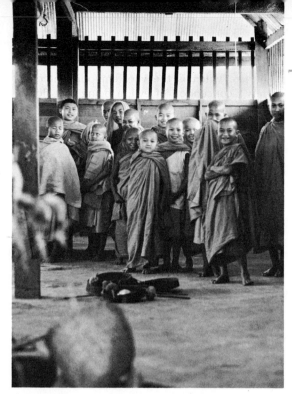

Figure 13-7c. *The monastery is one of the few sources of education for young boys.*

Figure 13-7d. *The higher status of the abbot is indicated by the decoration of his fan.*

Figure 13-7e. *A novice has his head shaved; all monks are shaved twice a month.*

Figure 13-7f. *A novice becomes a monk; his new name is written on the fan beside him.*

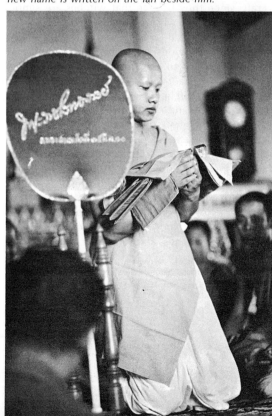

deities. The priest tells people what to do; the shaman tells supernaturals what to do. In return for his services, the shaman sometimes collects a fee—fresh meat, yams, a favorite possession. In some cases, the added prestige, authority, and social power attached to the status of shaman are reward enough.

Witchcraft

If blight seizes the groundnut crop it is witchcraft; if the bush is vainly scoured for game it is witchcraft; if termites do not rise when their swarming is due and a cold useless night is spent in waiting for their flight it is witchcraft; if a prince is cold and distant with his subjects it is witchcraft; if a magical rite fails to achieve its purpose it is witchcraft; if, in fact, any failure or misfortune falls upon anyone at any time and in relation to any of the manifold activities of his life it may be due to witchcraft.[15]

In this passage, E. E. Evans-Pritchard reveals the extent that witchcraft enters into the everyday life of the Azande, an African tribe. Although the Azande are not entirely typical in regard to witchcraft, since they believe that witches are simply ordinary persons who are born with a "substance" for witchcraft in their bodies, this list is an illustration of the widespread tendency on the part of some groups to explain many of the ordinary as well as extraordinary occurrences of life by reference to witchcraft.

The Azande and neighboring tribes distinguish between witchcraft or an inborn and often unconscious capacity to work evil, and sorcery, deliberate actions undertaken for the purpose of doing specific harm. Some anthropologists have attempted to generalize this distinction, but in many societies there is no division between the two types of evildoer. Perhaps a more practical classification is Lucy Mair's distinction between nightmare witches and everyday witches. The

---

[15] E. E. Evans-Pritchard, *Witchcraft, Oracles, and Magic Among the Azande* (London: Oxford University Press, 1950), pp. 63–66.

nightmare witch is the very embodiment of a society's conception of evil, a being that flouts the rules of sexual behavior and disregards every other standard of decency. Nightmare witches, being almost literally the product of dreams and repressed fantasies, have much in common wherever they appear: both the modern Navajo and the ancient Roman, for example, conceive of witches that can turn themselves into animals and gather to feast on corpses. Everyday witches are real people, often the social deviants of a group, those who are morose, who eat alone, who are arrogant and unfriendly. Such witches may be dangerous when offended and retaliate by causing sickness, death, crop failure, cattle disease, or any number of lesser ills; people thought to be witches are usually treated very courteously.

The functions of witchcraft

Why witchcraft? We might better ask, why not? As Mair aptly observed, in a world where there are few proven techniques for dealing with everyday crises, especially sickness, a belief in witches is not foolish, it is indispensable. No one wants to resign himself to illness, and if the malady is caused by a witch's hex, then magical countermeasures should cure it. Not only does the idea of personalized evil answer the problem of unmerited suffering, it also provides an explanation for many of those happenings for which no cause can be discovered. Witchcraft, then, cannot be refuted. Even if we could convince a person that his illness was due to natural causes, the victim would still ask, Why me? Why now? There is no room for pure chance in such a view; everything must be assigned a cause or meaning. Witchcraft provides the explanation, and in so doing, also provides both the basis and the means for taking counteraction. Moreover, the fact that certain kinds of antisocial behavior will result in an individual's being labelled a witch, and treated as such tends to deter people from such behavior. A belief in witchcraft thus serves a function of social control.

Figure 13-8. *In preparation for tribal religious rites, a Navajo man makes an elaborate sand painting of a god.*

Figure 13-9. *A witch doctor of the !Kung Bushmen chants a rite over his patient, whose leg was caught in a steel trap.*

Psychological functions of witchcraft among the Navajo.

Though widely known as one of the more peaceable of American Indian tribes, the Navajo possess a detailed concept of witchcraft. Several types of witchcraft are distinguished. **Witchery** encompasses the practices of witches, who are said to meet at night to practice cannibalism and kill people at a distance. **Sorcery** is distinguished from witchery only by the methods used by the sorcerer, who casts spells on individuals, using the victim's fingernails, hair, or discarded clothing. **Wizardry** is not distinguished so much by its effects as by its manner of working; wizards kill by injecting a cursed substance, such as a tooth from a corpse, into the victim's body.

Whether or not a particular illness results from witchcraft is determined by divination, as is the identity of the witch. Once a person is charged with witchcraft, he is publically interrogated and possibly tortured until he confesses. It is believed that the witch's own curse will turn against him once he confesses, so it is expected that he will die within a year. Some confessed witches have been allowed to live in exile.

According to Clyde Kluckhohn, Navajo witchcraft served to channel anxieties, tensions, and frustrations that were caused by the pressures from the white man. The rigid rules of decorum among the Navajo allow little means of expression of hostility, which is released in witchcraft accusations. Such accusations funnel pent-up negative emotions against individuals, without upsetting the wider society. Another function of accusations of witchcraft is that they permit the direct expression of hostile feelings against people to whom one would ordinarily be unable to express anger or enmity.

Social functions of witchcraft among the Ndembu.

Victor Turner described the use of sorcery in a struggle for political power in a small village of the Ndembu of Africa. Sandombu, a young man who had ambitions to the headmanship of Mukanza village, twice insulted the village headman, Kahali, in a challenge to his authority. This resulted in a fierce dispute, with each threatening the other with sorcery. Sandombu left for another village where a notorious sorcerer was supposed to live. A short time later, Kahali fell sick and died. There was no way to prove Sandombu's use of sorcery, but there was sufficient suspicion to prevent him from replacing Kahali as village headman. Instead, another man, not directly involved in the dispute, was chosen.

Turner shows that there is much more here than immediately meets the eye. Sandombu's insult to Kahali was a breach of the fundamental Ndembu principle that the older generation has authority over the younger. Further, Sandombu was of the same lineage as Kahali, and succession within the same lineage was looked upon with disfavor. Also, since Sandombu was sterile, and his sister barren, he had little basis for essential kin support. Though suspicion of sorcery was the ostensible cause of denying Sandombu headmanship, many other reasons lay beneath the surface.

This "social drama," as Turner calls it, shows how an accusation of sorcery was used to justify a political process and to effectively reaffirm such norms as the relationship between generations and the method of succession to authority. Belief in witchcraft, then, not only serves a number of psychological functions, it can also serve important social functions.

Religion and social change

In 1931, at Buka in the Solomon Islands, a native religious cult suddenly emerged, its prophets predicting that a deluge would soon engulf all whites. This would be followed by the arrival of a ship laden with European goods. The believers were to construct a storehouse for the goods, and to prepare themselves to repulse the colonial police. Because the ship would arrive only after the natives had used up all their own supplies, they ceased working in the fields. Although the leaders of the cult were arrested, the movement continued for some years.

This was not an isolated instance. Such "cargo

Figure 13-10. *Young New Guinea men parade with mock rifles made of bamboo in one of the rites of a cargo cult; note the letters USA on each man's chest. Many of the believers are also Christians, converted by missionaries; the people there see nothing contradictory in the two faiths.*

cults"—and many other movements which have promised the resurrection of the dead, the destruction or enslavement of Europeans, and the coming of utopian riches—have sporadically appeared ever since the beginning of the century throughout Melanesia. Since these cults are widely separated in space and time, their similarities may well be due to similarities in social conditions. In these areas, the traditional cultures of the natives have been uprooted. Europeans, or European influenced natives, hold all political and economic power. Natives are employed in unloading and distributing Western-made goods, but have no practical knowledge of how to attain these goods. When cold reality offers no hope from the daily frustrations of cultural deterioration and economic deprivation, religion offers the solution.

Revitalization movements

From the 1890 Ghost Dance of the American Indians to the Mau Mau of Africa to the cargo cults of Melanesia, extreme and sometimes violent religious reactions to European domination are so common that many anthropologists have sought to formulate their underlying causes and general characteristics. It has been suggested that all such religious innovations may be considered revitalization movements.

A revitalization movement is a deliberate effort by members of a society to construct a more satisfying culture. The emphasis in this definition is on the reformation not just of one sphere of activity such as the religious, but of the entire cultural system. Such a drastic solution arises when a group's anxiety and frustration have reached such a degree that the only way to reduce the stress is to overturn the entire social system and replace it with a new one.

Anthropologist Anthony Wallace has suggested that there is a sequence common to all expressions of the revitalization process. First is the normal state of society, in which stress is not too great and in which there are sufficient cultural means of satisfying needs. Under certain conditions, such as domination by a more powerful group, stress and frustration will be steadily amplified; this brings the second phase, or the period of increased individual stress. If there are no significant adaptive changes, the period of cultural distortion is ushered in, and stress becomes so chronic that the socially approved methods of releasing tension begin to break down. Steady deterioration of one culture may be checked at some point by a period of revitalization, during which a dynamic cult or religious movement grips a sizeable proportion of the population. Often the movement will be so out of touch with reality that it is doomed to failure from the beginning; this was the case with the Ghost Dance, which was supposed to make the participants impervious to the bullets of the white men's guns. More rarely, a movement may tap long dormant adaptive forces underlying a culture, and a longlasting religion may result. Wallace holds that all religions stem from revitalization movements.

Redemptive movements

Redemptive movements try to transform the individual, rather than the social order but in so doing, the social order may sometimes be changed. The Sun Dance of the Ute and Shoshone Indians of the Rocky Mountains is a true redemptive movement. In the early reservation period, around 1890, when misery and oppression were at their worst, the Sun Dance was introduced from the Great Plains tribes. The dance consists of a three-day, three-night ritual aimed at the acquisition of power. For the full period of the ritual, the dancers are forbidden food and water, and thus subject themselves to a long agony of hunger, thirst, and fatigue. With only brief rest periods during the long days, they charge and retreat from a pole in the center of a corral, concentrating intently on the power they are pursuing for their own health, for the health of their kin and of the whole community. Spectators, aware that the dancers are dancing for them, too, bring bundles of green plants to comfort and cool the dancers.

The Sun Dance flourished briefly after its introduction, then diminished, as the younger Indians drifted away from traditional ways of life and attempted more and more to identify with the white world. Then, in the 1960s, the Sun Dance sprang to vigorous life, to become again the religious center of Ute and Shoshone culture.

Why this resurgence of a tradition that one might reasonably have predicted would die out in the confrontation with modern technological culture? Joseph Jorgensen believes the Sun Dance of the Utes and Shoshones is a reaction to insoluble contradictions. The Indian is told that he must act like a white in order to be acceptable to whites, who hold economic and political power. But even when he does succeed in adopting white ways, he is still not acceptable. Since part of acting like a white means breaking tribal and kinship bonds and rejecting the values of Indian culture, he finds himself acceptable neither to whites nor to Indians. The Sun Dance offers a way out of this predicament. In reaffirming the Indian social ethic—as opposed to the individualistic and impersonal ethic of white culture—he regains his self-identity and esteem, a sense of belongingness, and brings an end to the impotence of trying to resolve a myriad of unresolvable contradictions. The Sun Dance provides both the subjective power and personal transformation of the religious experience, and the objective power of being a functional member of society.

Original study

THE SHAMAN

The stronghold of the shaman is among the reindeer herders and fishers of northeast Asia: the Yakuts and the Tungus, two widespread groups of tribes, and others living around the eastern shore of the Bering Sea: the Chuckchis, the Koryaks, the Gilyaks, and the Kamchadals of Kamchatka. Some of these live nomadically in felt tents and others in wooden villages, and in the long arctic nights of their bleak environment the comfort and entertainment that the shaman gives them is very well received. Typically it is believed that there are three realms of nature: an upper one, of light and of good spirits; a middle one, which is the world of men and of the spirits of the earth; and a lower one, for darkness and evil spirits. Men of the usual sort can move about the middle realm, and have some dealings with its spirits, but only a shaman can go above or below. A shaman also has the power of summoning spirits to come to him. Thus he can speak directly to spirits and ask what they want, which is his form of divining. Not only this, but a shaman deals with sickness in various ways through these same powers. If you have a disease spirit inside you, he can detect it and he knows how to send it off, perhaps by having a personal contest with it. Or you may have lost your soul—this explanation of illness turns up almost everywhere in the world—and the shaman gets it back. It has probably been enticed against its will by a stronger demon, and taken to the lower regions, and only the shaman can go after it, see, identify, and return it.

Both in Asia and America shamans, like witches, are generally believed to have familiar spirits, or animal souls, which are the things that gives them their peculiar qualities and powers. A Yakut shaman has two or three. One, called emekhet, is the shaman's own guardian angel, which is not only a sort of impersonal power like mana but also a definite spirit, usually that of a shaman already dead. This spirit hovers around its protégé, guiding and protecting him all the time, and comes at once when he calls for it, and gives him the advice he needs. Another spirit, the yekyua, has more character but is less accommodating. This one is an external soul, which belongs both to the shaman and to a living wild animal, which may be a stallion, a wolf, a dog, an eagle, a hairy bull, or some mythical creature, like a dragon. The yekyua is unruly and malevolent; it is dangerous and enables the shaman to do harm, rather like a witch, so that the people are in awe of him, but at the same time it has no consideration for the shaman himself and gives him continual trouble and anxiety, because his own fortunes are bound up with it. It is independent and lives far away, rather than upon the immediate tribal scene.

"Once a year, when the snow melts and the earth is black, the yekyua arise from their hiding places and begin to wander." When two of them meet, and fight, the human shamans to whom they are linked undergo the evil effects and feel badly. If such an animal dies or is killed, its shaman dies as well, so that a shaman whose yekyua is a bear or a bull can congratulate himself that his life expectancy is good. Of this phantasmal zoo the least desirable soul partners to have are carnivorous animals, especially dogs, because the shaman must keep them appeased, and if they go hungry they are not above taking advantage of their connection with the poor shaman to gnaw at his vitals to stay their appetites. When a person takes to shamanizing, the other shamans round about can tell whether a new yekyua has made its appearance far away, which will cause them to recognize the new shaman.

Siberian shamans all dress the part, as do so many shamans and medicine men of North America. The northeastern Asiatics wear clothing which is made of skin and tailored. A shaman has a cap and a mask, but it is his coat which distinguishes him like a collar turned around. It is a tunic made of hide—goat, elk, etc.—and usually comes down to his knees in front and to the ground behind, and is decorated to the point of being a textbook of shamanistic lore. On the front may be sewed metal plates which protect him from the blows of hostile spirits which he is always encountering. One of these plates represents his emekhet, and usually two others suggest a feminine appearance, since shamans have a hermaphroditic character, as we shall see. All over the tunic are embroidered or appliqued the figures of real and mythical animals, to represent those he must face on his travels in spirit realms, and from the back there hang numerous strips of skin falling clear to the ground, with small stuffed animals attached to some of them, all this alleged to be for attracting to the shaman any spiritual waifs of the vicinity, who might like to join his retinue. The whole getup would remind you of the unusual headdresses and paraphernalia in which medicine men are turned out among Indians of the Plains.

When a shaman goes into action the result is not a rite but a séance, which is full of drama and which the people enjoy immensely. A typical performance is a summoning of spirits, and is carried on in the dark (for the same reasons as among ourselves—i.e., to hide the shenanigans), in a house, a tent, or an Eskimo igloo. The people all gather, and the shaman says what he is going to do, after which he puts out the lamps and the fire, being sure that there is little or no light. Then he begins to sing. There may be a wait, and he beats his tambourine drum first of all, an immediate dramatic effect. The song starts softly. The sense of the song is of no consequence as far as the listeners are concerned; it is often incomprehensible, and may have no words at all. Jochelson knew a Tungus shaman who sang his songs in Koryak. He explained that his spirits were Koryak and said that he could not understand Koryak.

As the singing goes on, other sounds begin to make themselves heard, supposedly made by animal spirits and said to be remarkably good imitations. The shaman may announce to the audience that the spirits are approaching, but he is apt to be too absorbed or entranced himself to bother. Soon voices of all kinds are heard in the house, in the corners and up near the roof. The house now seems to have a number of independent spirits in it, all moving around, speaking in different voices, and all the time the drum is sounding, changing its tempo and its volume; the people are excited, and some of them who are old hands help the shaman out by making responses and shouting encouragement, and the shaman himself is usually possessed by a spirit or spirits, who are singing and beating the drum for him. The confusion of noises goes on increasing in intensity, with animal sounds and foreign tongues as well as understandable communications (among the Chuckchis, the wolf, the fox, and the raven can speak human language), until it finally dies down; the spirits give some message of farewell, the drumming ceases, and the lights are lit.

This is all a combination of expert showmanship and management and of autohypnosis, so that while the shaman knows perfectly well he is faking much of the performance he may at the same time work himself into a trance in which he does things he believes are beyond his merely human powers. He warns his audience strictly to keep their places and not try to touch the spirits, who would be angered and assault the offender, and perhaps even kill the shaman. When the show starts, the shaman produces his voices by moving around in the dark and by expert ventriloquism, getting the audience on his side and rapidly changing the nature and the force of the spirit sounds he is making.

A shaman need not perform only in the dark. He carries out some of his business in full view, especially when it is a matter of his going to the spirit world himself, rather than summoning the spirits to this world. The idea seems to be that he is in two places at once; i.e., his soul is traveling in spiritdom while he himself is going through the same actions before his watchers. He does a furious dramatic dance, rushing about, advancing and retreating, approaching the spirits, fighting them or wheedling them, all in a seeming trance. He may foam at the mouth and be so wild that he must be held for safety in leather thongs by some of the onlookers. After vivid adventures in the other realms, portrayed in his dance, he will accomplish his purpose, which may be to capture a wandering soul or to get some needed information from his spectral hosts. Then he becomes his normal self again.

After a death it is a regular thing for a Mongolian shaman to be called in to "purify" the yurt (felt hut) of the decreased's family, by getting rid of the soul of the dead, which of course cannot be allowed to hang around indefinitely. The mourners assemble late in the day, and at dusk the shaman himself comes, already drumming in the distance. He enters the yurt, still drumming, lowering the sound until it is only a murmur. Then he begins to converse with the soul of the newly departed, which pitifully implores to be allowed to stay in the yurt, because it cannot bear to leave the children or the scenes of its mortal days. The shaman, faithful to his trust, steels himself and pays no attention to this heartrending appeal. He goes for the soul and corners it by means of the power in his drum, until he can catch it between the drum itself and the drum stick. Then he starts off with it to the underworld, all in play acting. Here at the entrance he meets the soul of other dead members of the same family, to whom he announces the arrival of the new soul. They answer that they do not want it and refuse it admission. To multiply the difficulties, the homesick soul, which is slippery, generally makes its escape from the shaman as the two of them are on the way down, and comes rushing back to the yurt, with the shaman after it; he catches it all over again. It is lucky the people have a shaman! Back at the gate of the lower world he makes himself affable to the older souls and gives them vodka to drink, and in one way or another he manages to smuggle the new one in.

Source:
Excerpts from *The Heathens* by William Howells.
Copyright 1948 by William Howells.
Reprinted by permission of Doubleday and Company, Inc.

Summary

1.

Religion mediates between the profane, everyday world and the sacred world of supernatural powers and beings by means of values held in common by the group, and is made overt by ritual practices. Parsons postulates five components of every religion: sacred entities, expressive symbols, ritual activities, a sense of social solidarity in the group, and a relationship between the supernatural and the values, goals, and mores of the group.

2.

Early anthropologists sought an explanation for the origins of religion. Tylor explained the religious concepts of non-Western peoples by the concept of animism, in which humans, animals and even inanimate objects are thought to have a spirit or soul apart from their objective physical properties. Animatism as described by R. H. Codrington may be found with animism in the same culture. Animatism is a force or a power directed to a successful outcome which may make itself manifest in any object. Magic is a manipulation of natural laws. Frazer saw magic as a pseudo-science and found two principles of magic, "like produces like," or sympathetic magic, and the law of contagion.

3.

Durkheim introduced the idea of totemism and divided cultural life into the sacred and the profane. The totem is sacred and symbolic of the society and serves the function of stabilizing and binding the group together. On the other hand, Lévi-Strauss emphasizes the private and solitary functions of religion.

4.

The function of religion and magic for Malinowski was to allow the believer to have a sense of control over those areas of his experience which were beyond his practical knowledge. Radcliffe-Brown claimed that particular elements critical for social functioning were embued with religious significance and had adaptive value for the continuity of the social order.

5.

Individual needs as well as the capacity of the individual for mystical experience are psychological explanations of religion. Psychoanalysts like Jung and Freud explain religion in terms of man's unconscious. Freud sees religion as a system of defense mechanisms to relieve an individual of guilt. Jung went further and postulated a collective unconscious universal to mankind. These archetypes are projected onto the world as religious symbols and myths that have therapeutic value.

6.

Ritual is religion made manifest; through ritual social bonds are reinforced. Rites of passage are occasions for ritual. Van Gennep divided ceremonies for life-crises into rites of separation, transition, and incorporation. A ritual may consist of a sacrifice whose purpose is propitiation of the supernatural powers. A rite of reversal is a ritual in which there is a reversal of the normal values and customs. These may function as social safety valves.

7.

The priest is the religious expert and as part of the religious institution is a repository of the knowledge and practice of the religion. A shaman legitimates himself into the supernatural through a mystical experience and may practice healing or divination.

8.
Witchcraft functions much like science in offering an explanation for unwanted events. Sorcery is the practice of witchcraft for evil purposes and according to Kluckhohn serves as an expression of hostile emotions against individuals without disturbing the norms of the larger group.

9.
Domination by Western society has been the cause of certain religious manifestations in non-Western societies. In the islands of Melanesia the cargo cult has appeared spontaneously at different times since the beginning of the century. Wallace has interpreted certain religious reformations as revitalization movements in which an attempt is made, and sometimes successfully, to change the society. Redemptive movements, which try to change the individual, are a third method of coping with domination by a more powerful group by religious means. The "Sun Dance" of the Ute and Shoshone Indians is an example.

Suggested readings

Lessa, William A. and Evon Z. Vogt, eds. *Reader in Comparative Religion: An Anthropological Approach.* New York: Harper and Row, 1958.
The articles collected in the book discuss the universality of religion as it corresponds to deep and inescapable human needs. It discusses religion as a system of ethics, a response to the processes of nature, and an answer to the uncertainties of experience. The collection shows the relationship of religion to philosophy, theater, science, and ethics.

Malinowski, Bronislaw *Magic, Science and Religion, and Other Essays.* New York: Doubleday, 1954.
The articles collected here provide a discussion of a particular primitive people (the Trobriand Islanders) as illustration of conceptual and theoretical knowledge of mankind. The author covers such diversified topics as religion, life, death, character of primitive cults, magic, faith, and myth.

Norbeck, Edward *Religion in Human Life: Anthropological Views.* New York: Holt, Rinehart and Winston, 1974.
The author presents a comprehensive view of religion based on twin themes: the description of religious events, rituals, and states of mind and the nature of anthropological aims, views, procedures, and interpretations.

Wallace, Anthony F. C. *Religion, An Anthropological View.* New York: Random House, 1966.
This is a standard textbook treatment of religion by an anthropologist who has specialized in the study of revitalization movements.

The arts

Art is the product of a specialized kind of human behavior: the creative use of our imagination to help us interpret, understand, and enjoy life. Whether one is talking about a Chinese love song, a Navajo pot, a Balinese dance, or a Persian bracelet, it is clear that everyone involved in the activity we call art—the creator, the performer, the participant, the spectator—is making use of a uniquely human ability to use and comprehend symbols and to shape and interpret the physical world for something other than a practical or useful purpose.

What our other and perhaps "higher" purposes may be in what we call art will differ according to the specific kind of activity involved. Looking at a decorative wall-hanging will probably not serve precisely the same nonpractical purpose as singing a sea chanty or listening to a folktale. But the process in every case will require the same special combination of the symbolic representation of form and the expression of feeling that constitutes the creative imagination. Insofar as the creative use of the human ability to symbolize is universal and either expresses or is shaped by cultural values and concerns, it is properly and eminently an area of investigation for anthropology.

There appears to be no culture in the world without at least some kind of storytelling or a rudimentary kind of singing or dancing, if not a fully developed tradition of artistic expression. Reasoning backwards from effect to cause, some writers in recent times have consequently proposed the theory that humans may have an actual need or drive—either innate or acquired—to use their faculties of imagination. Just as we need food and shelter to survive, we may also need to nourish and exercise our active minds, which are not satisfied, except in times of crisis, with the mere business of solving the problems of daily existence. Without the free play of the imagination there is boredom, and boredom may lead to a lack of productivity, perhaps even in extreme cases to death. It is art that provides the means and the materials for our imaginative play and thus helps to sustain life. According to this way of thinking, art is therefore not a luxury to be afforded or appreciated by a minority of aesthetes or escapists, but a necessary kind of social behavior in which every normal and active human being participates.

As an activity or kind of behavior that contributes to well-being and helps give shape and significance to life, art must be at the same time related to and differentiated from religion. The dividing line between the two is not distinct: it is not easy to say, for example, precisely where art stops and religion begins in an elaborate tribal ceremony involving ornamentation, masks, costumes, songs, dances, effigies, and totems. Does religion inspire art, or is religion perhaps a higher kind of art in which the supernatural happens to be the central element?

This problem in semantics is not easy to solve, but it is often convenient to distinguish between secular and religious art, if not between art and religion. In what we call purely secular art, whether it is light or serious, it is clear that our imaginations are free to roam without any ulterior motives—creating and recreating patterns, plots, rhythms, and feelings at leisure and without any thought of consequence or aftermath. In religious art, on the other hand, the imagination is working still, but the whole activity is somehow aimed at assuring or establishing our past, present, or future through propitiation, celebration, and acknowledgment of forces beyond ourselves. Whether categorized as secular or religious, at any rate, art of all varieties can be expected to reflect the values and concerns of the people who create and enjoy it; the nature of the things reflected and expressed in art is the concern of the anthropologist.

In approaching art as a cultural phenomenon, the anthropologist has the pleasant task of cataloguing, photographing, recording, and describing all possible forms of imaginative activity in any particular culture. There is an enormous variety of forms and modes of artistic expression in the world. Because people everywhere continue to create and develop in new directions, there is no forseeable point of diminishing returns in the interesting process of collecting and describing the world's ornaments, body decorations, variations in clothing, blanket and rug designs, pottery and basket styles, architectural embellishments, monuments, ceremonial masks, legends, work songs, social dances, and other art forms. But the process of collecting must eventually lead to some kind of analysis, and then perhaps to some

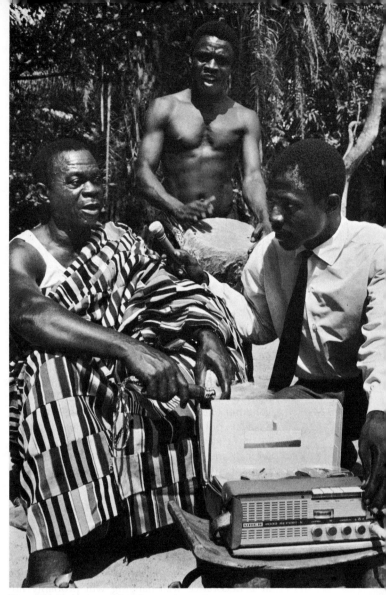

Figure 14-1. *A young historian at the new university on the Ivory Coast is taping many tribal legends; this story-teller is accompanied by a drummer.*

illuminating generalizations about relationships between art and culture.

Probably the best way to begin a study of this problem of the relationships between art and culture is to examine critically some of the generalizations that have already been made about specific arts. In order to do this, we will look carefully at some facts and interpretations of verbal arts, music, and sculpture in a number of cultures, chiefly in West Africa.

Verbal arts

The term **folklore** was coined in the nineteenth century to denote the unwritten stories, beliefs, and customs of the European peasant as opposed to the "sophisticated" traditions of the educated elite. The subsequent study of folklore, concentrating on folktales, has become a discipline allied to, but somewhat independent of, anthropology, working on cross-cultural comparisons of themes, motifs, and structures, generally more from a literary than an ethnological point of view. In general, both linguists and anthropologists prefer to speak of the oral traditions and verbal arts of a culture rather than its folklore and folktales, recognizing that creative verbal expression takes many forms and that the implied distinction between folk and sophisticated art is valid only in the context of civilization.

The verbal arts include narrative, drama, poetry, incantations, proverbs, riddles, word games, and even naming procedures, compliments, and insults, when these take elaborate and special forms. The narrative seems to be one of the easiest kinds of verbal art to record or collect. Perhaps because it is also the most publishable, with popular appeal in our own culture, it has received the most study and attention. Generally, narratives have been divided into three basic and recurring categories: myth, legend, and tale.

Myth

The **myth** is basically religious, in that its subject matter is the ultimates of human existence: where we and the things in our world came from, why we are here, and where we are going. Any aspect of these very large questions may be called a myth. The myth has an explanatory function; it depicts and describes an orderly universe, which sets the stage for orderly behavior.

Here is a typical etiological, or origin-explaining, myth traditional with the Fon of Dahomey in West Africa:

In the beginning the stars were visible both at night and in the daytime. The night stars were the children of the moon and the day stars were the children of the sun. One day the moon told the sun that their children were trying to outshine them. To prevent this they agreed to tie up the stars in sacks and throw them in the ocean. The sun went first and cleared the daytime sky of stars. The sly moon, however, did not keep her part of the bargain, but kept all of her children in the night sky. The sun's children became all of the brightly colored fish in the ocean, and from that time the sun has been the mortal enemy of the moon, pursuing her to try to get revenge for the loss of the stars to the sea. When there is an eclipse, the sun is trying to eat up the moon, and the people have to go out and beat on their drums to make the sun let her loose.

This myth may be encountered in a somewhat more elaborate form, with some more realistic and dramatic details, but the basic facts of the story will remain the same.

Such a myth, insofar as it is believed, accepted, and perpetuated in a culture, may be said to express a part of the **world view** of a people: the unexpressed but implicit conceptions of their place in nature and of the limits and workings of their world. The concepts of world view and science are intimately related, and it may be said that myth is the science of cultures which do not verify "truth" about nature by means of experiment. Extrapolating from the details of the Fon myth, for example, we might arrive at the conclusion that the Fon personify and respect the forces of nature, and that they believe they have both the ability and the duty to influence the behavior of these forces. In their protectiveness toward the moon in the myth, the Fon would seem to be approving either deceitfulness or cleverness. But other interpretations might be that the Fon simply accept a mixture of goodness and badness in the workings of nature, or that they fear any change in the balance of things already established. At any rate it is characteristic of an explanatory myth, such as this one, that the unknown will be simplified and explained in terms of the known. This myth accounts in human terms for the existence of fish and stars, for the movements of the sun and moon, and for the special phenomenon of the lunar eclipse. It is a product of creative imagination, and it is a work of art as well as a potentially religious statement.

The analysis and interpretation of myth have been carried to great lengths. The study of mythology has in fact become a science itself. It is certain that myth-making is an extremely important kind of human creativity, and the study of the myth-making process and its results can give some valuable clues to the way people perceive and think about their world. But the dangers and problems of interpretation are great. Several questions arise: Are the myths literally believed or perhaps accepted symbolically or emotionally as a different kind of truth? To what extent do myths actually determine or reflect human behavior? Can an outsider read into a myth the same meaning that it has in its culture? How do we account for contradictory myths in the same culture? New myths arise and old ones die: is it then the content or the structure of the myth that is important? All of these questions deserve, and are currently receiving, serious consideration.

Legend

Less problematical but perhaps more complex than myth is the legend. **Legends** are semihistorical narratives that account for the deeds of heroes, the movements of peoples, and the establishment of local customs, typically with a mixture of realism and the supernatural or extraordinary. As stories they are not necessarily believed or disbelieved, but they usually serve both to enter-

tain and to inspire or bolster pride in family, tribe, or nation.

The longer legends, sometimes in poetry or in rhythmic prose, are known as **epics.** In parts of West and Central Africa there are remarkably elaborate and formalized recitations of extremely long legends, lasting several hours, and even days. These long narratives have been described as veritable encyclopedias of the most diverse aspects of a culture, with direct and indirect statements about history, institutions, relationships, values, and ideas. Epics are typically found in nonliterate societies with a fairly complex form of state political organization; they serve to transmit and preserve a culture's legal and political precedents and practices. The Mwindo epic of the Nyanga people, the Lianja epic of the Mongo, and the Kambili epic of the Mande, for example, have been the subject of extensive and rewarding study by French, British, and American anthropologists in the last few years.

Legends may incorporate mythological details, especially when they make appeal to the supernatural, and are therefore not always clearly distinct from myth. The legend about Mwindo follows him through the earth, the atmosphere, the underworld, and the remote sky, and gives a complete picture of the Nyanga people's view of the organization and limits of the world. Legends may also incorporate proverbs and incidental tales, and thus be related to other forms of verbal art as well. A recitation of the legend of Kambili, for example, has been said to include as many as 150 proverbs.

For the anthropologist, the major significance of the secular and apparently realistic portions of legends, whether long or short, is probably in the clues they provide to what constitutes approved or model ethical behavior in a culture. The subject matter of legends is essentially problem-solving, and the content is likely to include combat, warfare, confrontations, and physical and psychological trials of many kinds. Certain questions may be answered explicitly or implicitly: Does the culture justify homicide? What kinds of behavior are considered to be brave or cowardly?

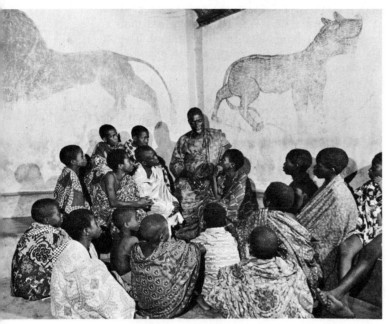

Figure 14-2. *A village elder of the Ivory Coast tells legends and tales to young boys of the tribe as part of their education.*

What is the etiquette of combat or warfare? Is there a concept of altruism or self-sacrifice? But here again there are pitfalls in the process of interpreting art in relation to life. It is always possible that certain kinds of behavior are acceptable or even admirable with the distance or objectivity afforded by art, but are not at all so approved in daily life. In our own culture, murderers, charlatans, and rakes have sometimes become popular "heroes" and the subjects of legends; we would object, however, to the inference of an outsider that we necessarily approved or wanted to emulate the morality of Billy the Kid or Jesse James.

Tale

The term **tale** is a nonspecific label for a third category of creative narratives, those which are purely secular, nonhistorical, and recognized as fiction for entertainment, though they sometimes draw a moral or teach a practical lesson. Here is a brief summary of a tale from Ghana, known as "Father, Son, and Donkey":

A father and his son farmed their corn, sold it, and spent part of the profit on a donkey. When the hot season came, they harvested their yams and prepared to take them to storage, using their donkey. The father mounted the donkey and they all three proceeded on their way until they met some people. "What? You lazy man!" the people said to the father. "You let your young son walk barefoot on this hot ground while you ride on a donkey? For shame!" The father yielded his place to the son, and they proceeded until they came to an old woman. "What? You useless boy!" said the old woman. "You ride on the donkey and let your poor father walk barefoot on this hot ground? For shame!" The son dismounted, and both father and son walked on the road, leading the donkey behind them until they came to an old man. "What? You foolish people!" said the old man. "You have a donkey and you walk barefoot on the hot ground instead of riding?" And so it goes. Listen: when you are doing something and other people come along, just keep on doing what you like.

This is precisely the kind of tale that is of special interest in traditional folklore studies. It is an internationally popular "numskull" tale; versions of it have been recorded in India, the Middle East, the Balkans, Italy, Spain, England, and the United States, as well as in West Africa. It is classified or catalogued as exhibiting a basic **motif** or story situation—father and son trying to please everyone—one of the many thousands that have been found to recur in world folktales. In spite of variations in detail, every version of the tale will be found to have about the same basic structure in the sequence of events, sometimes called the syntax of the tale; a peasant father and son work together, a beast of burden is purchased, the three set out on a short excursion, the father rides and is criticized, the son rides and is criticized, both walk and are criticized, and a conclusion is drawn.

Tales of this sort with an international distribution sometimes raise more problems than they solve: Which one is the original? What is the path of its migration? Could it be sheer coincidence that different cultures have come up with the same motif and syntax, or could it be a case of independent invention with similar tales developing in similar situations in responses to like causes? A surprisingly large number of motifs in European and African tales are traceable to ancient sources in India. Is this good evidence of a spread of culture from a "cradle" of civilization, or is it an example of diffusion of tales in contiguous areas? There are of course purely local tales, as well as tales with such a wide distribution. Within any particular culture, it will probably be found possible to categorize local types of tales: animal, human experience, trickster, dilemma, ghost, moral, scatological, nonsense, and so on. In West Africa there is a remarkable prevalence of animal stories, for example, with such creatures as the spider, the rabbit, and the hyena as the protagonists. Many were carried to the slave-holding areas of the New World; the Uncle Remus stories may be a survival of this tradition.

The significance of tales for the anthropologist rests partly in this matter of their distribution. They provide evidence for either cultural contacts or cultural isolation, and for limits of influence and cultural cohesion. It has been debated for decades now, for example, to what extent the culture of West Africa was transmitted to the Southern United States. So far as folktales are concerned, one school of folklorists has always found and insisted on European origins; another school, somewhat more recently, is pointing out African prototypes. But the anthropologist can be interested in more than these questions of distribution. Like the legends, tales very often illustrate local solutions to universal human ethical problems, and in some sense they state a moral philosophy. The anthropologist sees that whether the tale of the father, the son, and the donkey originated in West Africa or arrived there from Europe or the Middle East, the very fact that it has been accepted in West Africa suggests that it states something valid for that culture. The tale's lesson of a necessary degree of self-confidence in the face of arbitrary social criticism is therefore something that can be read into the culture's values and beliefs.

Other verbal arts

Myths, legends, and tales, prominent as they are in anthropological studies, turn out to be no more important than the other verbal arts in many cultures. In the Yoruba culture of Nigeria, for example, explanatory myths are now rare (the beliefs of Christianity and Islam have largely replaced them), but riddles, proverbs, figures of speech, poetry, and drama are all lively and active verbal arts that deserve and are beginning to receive more attention. Yoruba poetry, rich in both lyrical and dramatic elements, has only recently been studied and made available to the rest of the world, chiefly through the efforts of the new Nigerian institutes and local studies programs. Subjects of the poetry include alliances and conflicts with neighboring tribes; military and political triumphs and reverses; treaties, annexations, resettlements; the encroachment of the white man on the land of the Africans; and the undermining of the power of the chief by the missionary and the magistrate. Yoruba drama, previously not an especially popular verbal art, is being revived and cultivated and may be developing into a new and significant kind of creative activity.

In all cultures, the words for songs constitute a kind of poetry. Poetry and stories recited with gesture, movement, and props become drama. Drama combined with dance, music, and spectacle becomes a public celebration. The more we look at the individual arts, the clearer it becomes that that they are often interrelated and interdependent. The verbal arts are in fact simply differing manifestations of the same creative imagination that produces music and the plastic arts.

Figure 14-3. *A funeral is often an occasion for song and dance; men of the Mousgoum tribe blow horns and beat drums while relatives of the dead man dance.*

The art of music

The study of music in specific cultural settings, beginning in the nineteenth century with the collection of folksongs, has developed into a specialized field, called **ethnomusicology.** Like the study of folktales for its own sake, ethnomusicology is at the same time related to and somewhat independent of anthropology. Nevertheless, it is possible to sort out from the various concerns of the field several concepts that are of interest in general anthropology.

In order to talk intelligently about the verbal arts of a culture, it is of course desirable to know as much as possible about the language itself. In order to talk about the music of a culture, it is equally desirable to know the language of music— that is, its conventions. The way to approach a totally unfamiliar kind of musical expression is to learn first how it functions in respect to melody, rhythm, and form.

Elements of music

In general, human music is said to differ from natural music— the songs of birds, wolves, and whales, for example—in being almost everywhere perceived in terms of a repertory of tones at fixed or regular intervals from each other: in other words, a scale. We have made closed systems out of a formless range of possible sounds by dividing the distance between a tone and its first overtone or sympathetic vibration (which always has exactly twice as many vibrations as the basic tone) into a series of measured steps. In the Western or European system, the distance between the basic tone and the first overtone is called the octave; it consists of seven steps—five "whole" tones and two "semitones"—which are named with the letters A through G. The whole tones are further divided into semitones, for a total working scale of twelve tones. Westerners learn at an early age to recognize and imitate this arbitrary system and its conventions, and it comes to sound natural. Yet the overtone series, on which it is partially based, is the only part of it that can be considered a wholly natural phenomenon.

One of the most common alternatives to the semitonal system is the pentatonic system, which divides the octave into five nearly equidistant tones. In Japan there is a series of different pentatonic scales in which some semitones are employed. In Java there are scales of both five and seven equal steps, which have no relation to the intervals we hear as "natural" in our system. In Arabic and Persian music there are smaller units of a third of a tone (some of which we may accidentally produce on an out-of-tune piano) with scales of seventeen and twenty-four steps in the octave. There are even quarter-tone scales in India and subtleties of interval shading that are nearly indistinguishable to a Western ear. Small wonder, then, that even when we can hear what sounds like melody and rhythm in these systems, the total result may sound to us peculiar or out of tune. The anthropologist will need a very practiced ear to learn to appreciate—or perhaps even to tolerate—some of the music he hears, and only some of the most skilled folksong collectors have attempted to notate and analyze the music of nonsemitonal systems.

Scale systems and their modifications comprise what is known as **tonality** in music. Tonality determines the possibilities and limits of both melody and harmony. Not much less complex than tonality is the matter of rhythm. Rhythm, whether regular or irregular, is an organizing factor in music, sometimes more important than the me-

lodic line. Traditional European music is rather neatly measured into recurrent patterns of two, three, and four beats, with combinations of weak and strong beats to mark the divisions and form patterns. Non-European music is likely to move also in patterns of five, seven, or eleven, with complex arrangements of internal beats and sometimes polyrhythms: one instrument or singer going in a pattern of three beats, for example while another is in a pattern of five or seven. Polyrhythms are frequent in the drum music of West Africa, which shows remarkable precision in the overlapping of rhythmic lines. In addition to polyrhythms, non-European music may also contain shifting rhythms: a pattern of three, for example, followed by a pattern of two, or five, with little or no regular recurrence or repetition of any one pattern, though the patterns themselves are fixed and identifiable as units.

Although it is not necessarily the concern of the anthropologist to untangle all these complicated technical matters, he will no doubt want to know enough to be aware of the degree of skill or artistry involved in a performance and to have some measure of the extent to which people in a culture have learned to practice and respond to this often important creative activity. Moreover, as with folklore, myths, and legends, the distribution of musical forms and intruments can reveal much about cultural contact or isolation.

Functions of music

Even without concern for technical matters, the anthropologist can profitably investigate the function music has in a society. First of all, it is rare that a culture has been reported to be without any kind of music. Even the Tasadays of the Philippines, the recently described nearly Stone Age forest dwellers, have adopted, if not invented, a bamboo jaw harp called a *kubing*. Kenneth MacLeish translates in these words the comments of the Tasaday *kubing* player: "If I play my kubing, it is because someone is listening. I really know how to play the *kubing*." Interestingly, these simple words seem to express the value music—in fact, all art—has in far more complex cultures: it is an individual creative skill which one can cultivate and be proud of, whether from a sense of accomplishment or the sheer pleasure of performing; and it is a form of social behavior through which there is a communication or sharing of feelings and life experience with other humans.

The social function of music is perhaps most obvious in song. Songs very often express as much as tales the values and concerns of the group, but they do so with the increased formalism which results from the restrictions of closed systems of tonality, rhythm, and musical form. Early investigators of non-European song were struck by the apparent simplicity of pentatonic scales and a seemingly endless repetition of phrases. They often did not give sufficient credit to the formal function of repetition in such music, confusing repetition with repetitiveness or lack of invention. A great deal of non-European music was dismissed as "primitive" and formless, and typically treated as trivial.

Repetition is nevertheless a fact of music, even European music, and a basic formal principle. Consider this little song from Nigeria:

Ijangbon l'o ra,
Ijangbon l'o ra,
Eni r'asho Oshomalo,
Ijangbon l'o ra.
(He buys trouble,
He buys trouble,
He who buys Oshomalo cloth,
He buys trouble)

Several decades ago, the Oshomalo were cloth-sellers in Egba villages who sold on credit, then harassed, intimidated, and even beat their customers to make them pay before the appointed day. The message of the song is simple, and both words and music are the same for three lines out of four; the whole song may be repeated many times at will. What is it that produces this kind of artistic expression and makes it more than primitive trivia? A single Egba undoubtedly im-

provised the song first, reacting to a personal experience or observation, lingering on one of its elements by repeating it. The repetition gives the observation not emphasis but symbolic form, and therefore a kind of concreteness or permanence. In this concrete form, made memorable and attractive with melody and rhythm, the song was taken up by other Egba, perhaps with some musical refinements or embellishments from more creative members of the group, including clapping or drumming to mark the rhythm. Thus a bit of social commentary was crystalized and preserved even after the situation had passed into history.

Whether the content of songs is didactic, satirical, inspirational, religious, political, or purely emotional, the important thing is that the formless has been given form and feelings are communicated in a symbolic and memorable way that can be repeated and shared. The group is consequently united and probably has the sense that their experience whatever it may be, has shape and meaning.

Musical instruments

The human voice, used in song, is of course the basic, universal musical instrument for melody; and the human body—stamping with the heels and toes, hitting the fleshy or bony parts with the hands—is the basic instrument for rhythm. Although it is quite possible to make music without artificial instruments, it is rare that a culture does so. Musical instruments are the artifacts of music, and the study of instruments is another adjunct of anthropology that can reveal a great deal about culture.

Rattle.   Musical instruments are thought to have developed historically from experimentation with the augmentation of human sounds, perhaps first just for the sake of making audible our expressive body movements. The rattle, probably the simplest musical instrument, is a means of making audible the expressive body movement of shaking, suggesting fear, excitement, or perhaps anger. The simplest rattle is the strung rattle: a series of small hard objects such as shells or teeth strung on cords or tied in bunches and agitated vigorously in some regular rhythm. Because the objects used may be considered to have magical or supernatural value in some cultures, some anthropologists and musicologists have proposed a strong connection between magic or religion and music at this level of imaginative creativity. Nevertheless, it seems quite possible that the rattle could also have a secular origin.

Figure 14-4. *Kenyan dancers celebrate the independence of the nation. Their costumes and face paintings constitute another kind of expressive art. Note the modern addition of a flashlight for night-time dancing.*

The gourd rattle (a calabash filled usually with pebbles) is perhaps a higher refinement of the strung rattle. Countries where calabashes are not available have substituted wicker, clay, wood, and metal, achieving the same result. It has been observed that the rattle is often a woman's instrument; in East African cultures there are ceremonies or celebrations at which hundreds of women participate on the fringes of the action, all vigorously producing a rhythmic background with rattles. In our own culture the rather fanciful theory has been advanced that, as a woman's instrument,

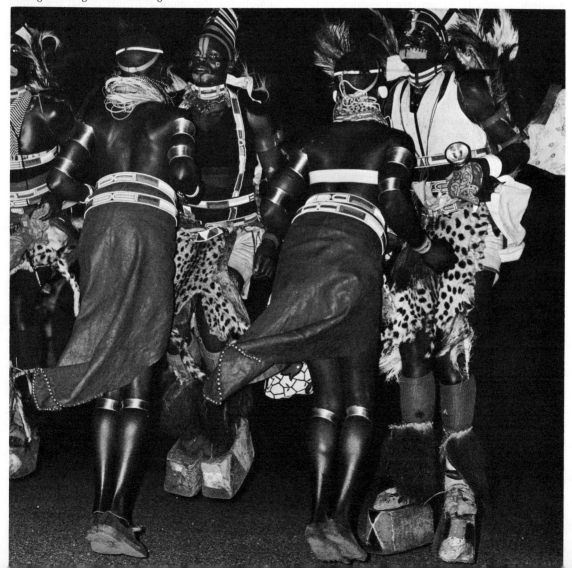

the rattle has been preserved and introduced into the woman's part of the household, namely the nursery.

Stamper. The rattle makes audible an inaudible expressive movement of the body. Probably the simplest type of augmentation of an already audible expressive human movement, that of stamping, is through the use of the stamper. Especially as it is found in the South Pacific, this may take the form of a pit dug in the ground and covered with a rough lid of bark or curved board. The resounding cavity produces a dull, hollow sound when the cover is stamped on—again often by women—and it serves as a drumlike accompaniment for dancing. The term stamper is sometimes also applied to hand-stamping augmentations, such as sticks on gourds, bamboo tubes on mats, and pestles on mortars. It is almost impossible not to see a sexual symbolism in the process, and anthropologists have long proposed a connection between fertility and marriage rites and ceremonies, and the development of this kind of artistic expression. Again, however, it is not clear whether the cultural activity may have inspired the use of the instrument or the instrument may simply have found its way into ritual, with appropriate interpretations coming after the fact.

Drum. Stampers of more sophisticated types begin to show development in the augmentation of expressive movement in two directions: first there is the substitution of an artificial striking surface for a natural one, and second there is the use of an artifical striking device instead of the hands. The next stage of development seems to be the drum—the most versatile and varied of the percussion or rhythm instruments.

The drum represents various degrees in the perfection of the artificial striking surface. Technically a drum is any instrument in which the sound is produced by striking a stretched membrane covering the opening over any kind of frame or hollow body. The degree of technical perfection in a drum will be judged by the effective choice of a membrane, the skillful application of membrane to frame, and the invention or discovery of appropriate shapes and qualities in the resonating body. The various possibilities are numerous, and there are literally hundreds of different kinds of drums in the world.

The two main categories of drums are the cut wooden drums and the molded clay drums. Since woodworking usually antedates pottery making, the wooden drums are believed to be the older.

But clay drums are generally single-headed, and the double-headed wooden drum, with membranes on both ends of a cylinder, appears to be a more recent development of the wooden variety, postdating the earliest clay drums. Stick-drumming is likewise thought to be later than hand-drumming, but combinations of the two are not rare.

What is especially interesting about the drum for the anthropologist is perhaps not so much its functions and capabilities as a purely musical instrument, which are considerable, as its ritual value and even sacredness in many cultures. In East Africa, for example, the drum is so sacred that even criminals find sanctuary when they run to the safety of a drum-yard. Among the Wahinda, to see a drum by daylight is fatal; men must carry them by night only. Unlike rattles and stampers, drums often seem to be man's instruments. In Oceania a new drum is rendered useless if a woman sees it before it is completely finished.

As an augmentation of audible human expressive movements, the drum appears to go a step further than the stamper. It has been argued that in using rattles and stampers, people still have the feeling that they are wholly responsible for the sounds they are producing. But the drum, with its musical, mysterious, variable, and responsive sounds, requiring coaxing and heating and shrinking and pampering very much as a living creature, seems to have a voice of its own, perhaps from some strange force living inside it. Whatever the explanation, it is a fact that in many cultures drums are considered to have souls or to be the voices of spirits. This is particularly evident in animistic cultures in West Africa, the places of origin for the voodoo (properly *vodoun*) drums of the Caribbean. The mother drum, the father drum, and the baby drum have their respective voices and their individually appropriate roles in calling to or speaking for the spirits. Drummers may work themselves into a trance, during which the drum takes over and speaks in its own voice. Drums are also an important part of the shaman's equipment.

Friction instruments. Friction drums, found for example with the Ewe in Togo, produce sounds with rubbing rather than beating. The humming and squeaking noises that result are easily imaginable as superhuman sounds or voices. Friction instruments in general, the last major category of percussive or rhythmic musical instruments, are perhaps the least pleasant-sounding of all. The principle type is known generally as the scraper. Scrapers are resonating boxes or notched bones or sticks, scraped rapidly with a rigid object to produce a whirring or grumbling sound, perhaps like a mysterious voice or an animal. It is reported that among Cheyenne Indians, bone-scraping accompanying a dance was once considered to inspire love and to encourage marriage. Scrapers nevertheless also have a purely rhythmic function in some parts of the world, and interpretations involving too close a connection between rite and instrument may not always be wise or even possible.

Wind and string instruments. Wind and string instruments ordinarily carry melody more than they mark rhythm, and consequently they may be considered as providing an extension or modification of the human voice. This is particularly clear for the wind instruments—the flute and trumpet for example—in which the breath of the performer actually passes through the instrument and is transformed into a voice unlike his own. The new voice may be more beautiful or more powerful, or again it may be likened to a voice from the supernatural. Of curiously wide distribution throughout the world is a variety of instrument known as the nose flute, actually played by blowing through the nose. In Polynesia, where nose flutes are especially widely used, it appears that breath from the nose is supposed to contain the soul (a notion that is by no means limited to Polynesia) and that it has more magical power than breath from the mouth. Therefore the curious method of playing this flute, probably an unacceptable one in our culture, would seem to have a reasonable explanation on cultural if not aesthetic grounds.

The enumeration and description of musical instruments as the artifacts of musical creativity and extensions of the basic human instrument, an intriguing and rewarding pursuit, can obviously be continued at considerable length; observations can lead to interesting theories and explanations, some of which can be supported with extramusical details in various cultures. Art of all kinds is again seen to be demonstrably related to human sensibilities, and it should not suprise us to find also even more relationships between the arts themselves. Musical instruments, in their more complex, decorative, and symbolic shapes, bring us quite close to the third major kind of artistic activity to be considered here, namely sculpture.

The art of sculpture

In the broadest sense, sculpture is art in the round. Any three-dimensional product of the creative imagination may be called a piece of sculpture: a ceremonial knife, a decorative pot, a hand-crafted lute, an ornamental gate, a funerary monument, or a public building displays the same essential artistic process as a statue, a mask, or a figurine. All of these human creations represent an imaginative organization of materials in space. The artist has given tangible shape to his feelings and perceptions, creating or recreating symbolically meaningful form out of formlessness. In a narrower sense, sculpture means only those artifacts that serve no immediate utilitarian purpose and are fashioned from hard or semipermanent materials. But it is difficult to state unequivocally what may or may not qualify as a piece of sculpture, even with this limitation. Are the beautiful and highly imaginative tiny brass figurines of Ghana, for example, formerly used as weights for measuring out quantities of gold, not to be considered sculpture, even though the somewhat larger brass figurines of comparable design in Dahomey, which have never had a practical use, are obviously to be so considered? Or should we perhaps now call the Ghana figurines sculpture because they are no longer put to use?

Art and craft

Our use of the word sculpture in English seems to impose a distinction between types of creative activity where none may in fact exist. One solution is to substitute the more modern term plastic art, but the phenomenon remains the same. Objects that are obviously skillfully made but still do not quite qualify as sculpture by virtue of being somewhat trivial, low in symbolic content, or impermanent—by the standards of the culture—are generally known and considered as the products of craft (or, in modern times, industry). An automobile, for example, however beautifully it may be designed, however lovingly it may be displayed in front of the house as an object for admiration, and however cleverly we may interpret its parts and its functions as symbolic in our culture, is for us above all a mass-produced consumable, and to treat it as sculpture would be misrepresenting its *usual* value in our society. Furthermore, we must also consider the intention of the creator. What we call sculpture or plastic art is not ordinarily artistic by accident or through after-the-fact interpretation, but by design. Detroit does not intentionally produce sculpture.

As a type of symbolic expression, sculpture may be representational, imitating closely the forms of nature, or abstract, drawing from natural forms but representing only their basic patterns or arrangements. Representational sculpture is partly abstract to the extent that it generalizes from nature and abstracts patterns of ideal beauty, ugliness, or typical expressions of emotion. Michelangelo's "David" is representational sculpture, clearly depicting a human being; it is also abstract insofar as it generalizes an ideal of masculine beauty, quiet strength, and emotional calm, therefore functioning symbolically. Henry Moore's gigantic women with holes through their midsections are abstractions, using nature but exaggerating and deliberately transforming some of its shapes for the purpose of expressing a particular feeling toward them.

West African sculpture

West African sculpture, only comparatively recently studied and described in adequate detail, is an especially rich non-European tradition that may help illustrate some of the anthropological aspects of representational and abstract sculpture, its subjects, materials, and meanings.

Ancestor worship and reverence of royalty have found expression in a realistic or portrait-style sculpture throughout the region of the Niger and Congo River basins. Probably the most dramatically realistic are the so-called Benin bronzes: hundreds of finely detailed heads of ancestors, royalty, and important persons produced at the ancient Benin capital of Ife (in present-day Nigeria) around the beginning of the fifteenth century. Most of these heads were carried off to England at the end of the nineteenth century, and they have served as a forcible reminder to Europeans that the Mediterranean region is not the only source of fine realistic sculpture.

In addition to the Benin bronzes, the royal statues of the Bakuba kings in the Congo River region, the ancestor figures of the Guro in the Ivory Coast, the secular and satirical representations of Europeans by the Yoruba in Nigeria, and the small brasses depicting the royalty and animals of the Fon in Dahomey are also naturalistic in detail, and are obviously often intended to represent real persons or animals in characteristic moods or poses. Features and proportions may be somewhat stylized according to regional conventions of what is appropriate or possible in sculpture: heads may be disproportionately large, necks may be elongated, and sexual parts either exaggerated or minimized. It is interesting to note that most of these sculptures come from cultures in which subsistence techniques were efficient enough to produce a surplus, which was used to support a variety of occupational specialists. The artist was one such specialist; much of his work was commissioned by other specialists, such as priests and government officials.

The majority of West African sculpture is abstract or expressionistic—giving form to human feelings and attitudes toward gods, spirits, other humans, and animals. Generalizations about the nonrepresentational styles and purposes for the region are, however, almost impossible. Every West African culture that produces or has produced sculpture has its own identifiable styles, and this artistic cohesion undoubtedly reinforces the social unity of the group. A Fon recognizes a Yoruba mask, and disassociates himself from whatever symbolic significance it has for the Yoruba. Materials as well as styles differ in neighboring cultures. The most common material is wood, but there is also regional use of brass, iron, terra cotta, mud, and raffia. Sculpture may be rubbed with ash, smoked in banana leaves, oiled, waxed, painted, and adorned with cowrie shells, teeth, iron or brass nails, strips of metal, or cloth.

Symbolic content. The anthropologist is interested in exactly what is abstracted from nature, and why, in all these varieties of sculpture, whatever their style and material. He is also interested in the extent to which traditions are perpetuated, and what meanings may be developing or changing. It appears that any single piece of sculpture in West Africa may be interpreted in terms of its symbolic significance for the group, and that generally such significance is well known by the people who make and look at the sculpture. Consequently the anthropologist has only to ask.

A small wooden figure of a person, with a head, rudimentary limbs, and a large trunk purposely riddled with holes may be found among the Balega of the northeast Congo region. The figure is known as a *katanda,* meaning the scattering of red ants when attacked; it is interpreted as symbolizing the bad effect of internal fighting on the unity of local descent groups. The *kanaga* mask of the Dogon in Upper Volta is an elongated head with triangular eyes, long pointed ears and nose, and a cap surmounted with an enormous crest, four or five times the size of the head, in the form of a double-armed cross; for young initiates the cross symbolizes a bird with out-stretched wings, the beginning of active flight into life, and for older initiates of high rank its structure symbo-

Figure 14-5. *This Nigerian house is decorated by a relief carved in wet cement; a bicycle and a car are prominent features.*

Social integration ● part **4**

lizes a synthesis of contradictory or competing life forces. The *akua'ba* dolls of Ashanti in Ghana, flat disc-headed figures on a long, narrow, legless body with a simple cross-piece for arms, are said to symbolize an Ashanti ideal of beauty in the high, wide forehead; the dolls are tucked into the waist-cloths of young girls, who carry them like real babies, perhaps as talismans to assure their own physical development or that of their children.

Ritual masks. The widest variety of expression in African sculpture is certainly to be found in

Figure 14-6. *These tombs of Nigerian farmers are topped by statues showing them as whites dressed in European garb.*

the ritual mask. Styles range from the relatively realistic and serene faces made by the Baule in the Ivory Coast to the frightening, violent, and extroverted faces with protruding eyes produced by the neighboring Ngere of Liberia. Theories about the symbolism of the masks have arisen beside the explanations of local informants, particularly in cases where certain masks are no longer produced or known. One of the more interesting is the notion that the unnatural features of some of the masks representing spirits or the dead are made systematically unnatural in order to suggest that the other world, or the spirit world, is somehow an opposite of this one: noses are long instead of short, ears are large rather than small, eye cavities are hollow rather than filled, and so on. The mask, as well as other sculpture, therefore becomes as much as the myth an expression of world view. The sculptor again gives shape and meaning to that which is unknown.

As in musical expression, sculpture also crystalizes feeling in a form that can be shared and perpetuated. African sculpture is impermanent because of the impermanent nature of its materials (fifty years has been suggested as an average lifetime for a wooden figure exposed to weather), but it is generally considered a great shame when a mask or piece of sculpture disintegrates. An important piece of sculpture may be replaced by imitation, copied and perpetuated so that the traditions and beliefs may be preserved. There is often a ritual in mask-making, with great care taken to preserve and copy exactly the traditional specifications. Similarly, there is still in some places a special reverence in the process of sculpting in general, and the soul of the wood must be respected with attendant rituals and beliefs similar to what we have seen in relation to the drum. Traditional West African sculpture is currently in decline, but it is not by any means everywhere dead. An excursion beyond the major urban centers reveals continuing activity in this important kind of symbolic creativity.

Summary

1.

The creative use of our imagination to help us interpret, understand, and enjoy life produces art. Art makes use of a uniquely human ability to use and comprehend symbols and to shape and interpret the physical world for something besides a practical or useful purpose. The creative use of our ability to symbolize either expresses or is shaped by cultural values and concerns. Anthropologists are interested in these values reflected by art.

2.

The verbal arts include narrative, drama, poetry, incantations, proverbs, riddles, and word games. Folklore denotes the unwritten stories, beliefs, and customs of the European peasant. The myth is basically religious; its subject matter includes where we and the things in our world came from, why we are here, and where we are going. A myth may be said to express part of a people's world view.

3.

Legends are semihistorical narratives relating the deeds of heroes, the movements of peoples, and the establishment of local customs. The longer legends, sometimes in poetry or in rhythmic prose, are called epics. Legends provide clues as to what constitutes ethical behavior in a culture. These clues give legends their major anthropological significance. Tales are purely secular, nonhistorical narratives. Although they are recognized as fiction for entertainment, tales sometimes draw morals or teach practical lessons.

4.

The study of music has developed into the field of ethnomusicology. Human music is almost everywhere perceived in terms of a scale. Scale systems and their modifications comprise tonality in music. Tonality determines the possibilities and limits of melody and harmony. Rhythm is an organizing factor in music. Traditional European music is measured into recurrent patterns of two, three, and four beats.

5.

The social function of music is most obvious in song. Songs often express a group's values and concerns as much as tales do. The closed systems of tonality, rhythm, and musical form place restrictions on songs, making their expression more formal. Musical instruments are thought to have developed historically from experimentation with the augmentation of human sounds. The development of the musical instrument has advanced in stages through instruments such as the rattle, stamper, drum, and scraper. Music enables people to communicate and share their feelings in a symbolic and memorable way.

6.

Sculpture is any three-dimensional product of the creative imagination. Sculpted objects, such as a ceremonial knife, or an ornamental gate, represent an imaginative organization of materials in space. A more modern term for sculpture is plastic art. Certain objects, although skillfully made, do not qualify as sculpture. This may be because they are somewhat trivial, low in symbolic content, or impermanent. Sculpture may be representational or abstract. Representational sculpture closely imitates the forms of nature; abstract sculpture draws from natural forms, but represents only their basic patterns. The anthropologist is interested in what is extracted from nature, and why.

Suggested readings

Boas, Franz. *Primitive Art.* New York: Dover, 1955.
 The book gives an analytical description of the basic traits of primitive art. Its treatment is based on two principles: the fundamental sameness of mental processes in all races and cultural forms of the present day, and the consideration of every cultural phenomenon in a historical context. It covers formal elements in art, symbolism, and style and has sections on primitive literature, music, and dance.

Fraser, Douglas. *Primitive Art.* Garden City, New York: Doubleday, 1962.
 The book presents a systematic survey of primitive art, aiming to place each style studied in relation to both its local setting and to other styles near and far away. The author covers the three main geographical areas of Africa, Asia-Oceania, and America. Good color illustrations.

Kurath, Gertrude Probosch. "Panorama of Dance Ethnology" in *Current Anthropology,* May 1960, Vol. 1.
 The article is a detailed survey of dance ethnomethodology, describing and analyzing dance throughout the world. It includes problems of choreography, form, relation to other fields, and recording of dances. It also discusses technological aids, and the training of ethnologists.

Nettl, Bruno. *Music in Primitive Culture.* Cambridge: Harvard University Press, 1956.
 The book is designed as an introduction to primitive music, and attempts to show the kinds of phenomena that characterize it. It provides examples of types of primitive music, shows how they have been studied, and provides general conclusions which have been drawn from them.

Thompson, Stith. *The Folktale.* New York: Holt, Rinehart and Winston, 1960.
 The book serves as a guide to the study of the folktale, in both written and oral form. It includes an account of well-known Western folktales and their history, and a section on the classical folktale as reconstructed from literary remains. North American Indian tales serve as examples of primitive culture tales. The final section provides some analysis of theory and methods in the field.

Wingert, Paul. *Primitive Art: It's Traditions and Styles.* London: Oxford University Press, 1962. World, 1965.
 The book serves as an introduction to primitive art, defining that term and examining various prevailing attitudes and approaches toward it. The method of approach places art in a cultural context, and analyzes objects from Africa, Oceania, and North America.

portfolio five

Ancient art

Although there are numerous examples of pictorial art created before man settled in cities ("civilized" himself), the great proliferation of art begins with our earliest civilizations—Sumer, Egypt, China, India, Middle America. Perhaps even the cave painters of Lascaux and Altamira and the carvers of the "Venus" figures of Willendorf and Lespugue were specialists in their craft, but in the hunter-gatherer society, art is often a propitiatory act performed by many hunters and not necessarily the work of a full time "artist." But there can be no doubt that the extraordinary bull's-head harp on the opposite page was created by someone with special skills, long training, a knowledge of another art—music and its requirements—and the ability to render the intricate legends of his time in inlaid ivory, wood and metal. The city of Ur, where the harp was found and presumably made, was one of the first cities on earth, but not so far from its prehistoric ancestors that its mythology was not filled with animals, a characteristic also of the Egyptian art that flourished at roughly the same time. The Sumerian genius included the invention of the wheel, glass, writing, bronze, the calendar, and indeed, even the city itself. On the pages following are shown a ram's head made of bronze and a tablet bearing the cuneiform, or wedge-shaped writing, with which Sumerians documented their daily business, mathematical calculations, and astronomical observations. Among Sumerian words that persist in English are alcohol, gypsum, and saffron.

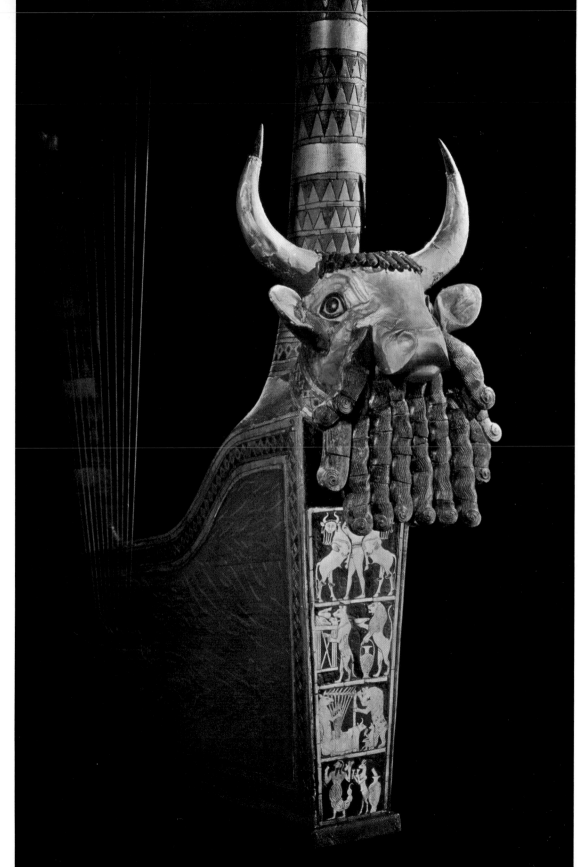

Harp, early Third
Millenium B.C.
From the
niversity Museum,
Philadelphia.

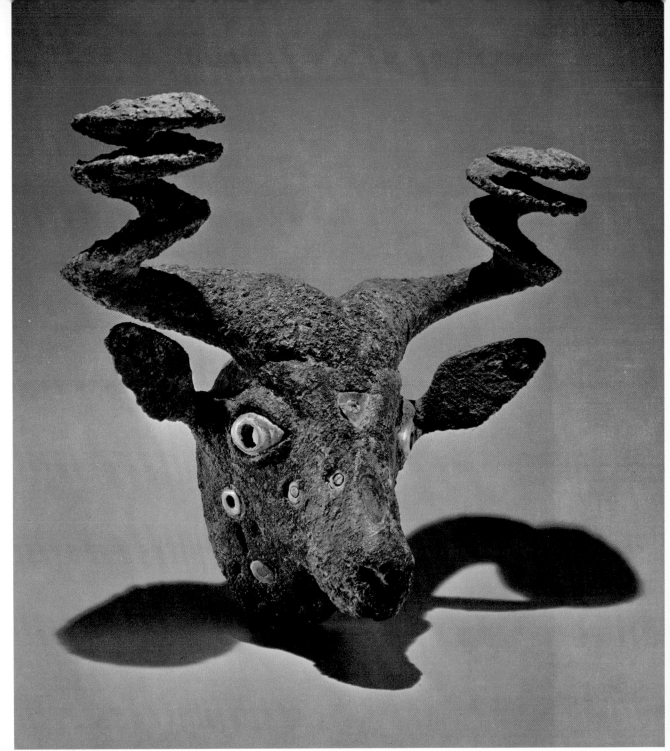

Ram's Head, Sumerian.
From the University Museum, Philadelphia.

Cuneiform Tablet, Sumerian.
From the University Museum, Philadelphia.

Statuette of Imhotep, Early Ptolomaic.
From the Metropolitan Museum of Art, New York.

Bracelet, Egyptian.

Miniature gold mummy-case of King Tutankhamen.

Egyptian Cat.
From the Metropolitan Museum of Art, New York.

Cycladic Idols.
Courtesy Andre Emmerich Gallery, New York.

Snake Goddess,
Palace of Knossos
Crete.
From the
Boston Museum
of Fine Arts.

Following the pages of Sumerian art are two devoted
to Egypt, whose concurrent civilization is perhaps even
more spectacularly represented by art objects. In addition,
of course, since the Egyptians had access to large quantities
of stone and the Mesopotamians did not, there remain
architectural antiquities which reveal much about the life
of the times. Indeed, much of early Egyptian art has been
found in tombs as imposing as the great pyramids. The
Egyptian art shown here includes a gold and inlaid bracelet,
a bronze cat with a gold earring, a bronze statue of a scribe
(probably a wealthy landowner or nobleman, since only the
rich could write) and one of the miniature gold coffins in
the canopic chest of King Tutankhamen.

On the third double-page of illustrations are four
remarkable marble idols from the Cyclades, the Aegean islands
near the Greek mainland. The story of these islands is almost
totally unknown since little is left but some modest tombs
built of stone. Among Cycladic artifacts are a great number
of such idols, almost all nude females with arms folded across
their chest. These are presumably mother or fertility
goddesses; they resemble not only those of the Ancient Near
East and Asia Minor, but earlier objects dating back some
20,000 years to the cave-sites of Europe. Cycladic idols
were carved in an enormous range of sizes, up to life
size—the oldest life-sized nude female figures known.
Not until about the fourth century in Greece does a full-
scale female figure appear again—the nude Aphrodite, mother
of so much subsequent Western art.

Finally, in this portfolio, on the page opposite is
an example of the extraordinary art of Minoan Crete whose
rise and fall within the span of years from about 3000 B.C.
to 1100 B.C. remains an archeological mystery. The ivory
and gold goddess shown here is from the Palace of Knossos,
also known as the Palace of Minos, a structure so large and
complex that it came down in Greek legend as the Labyrinth
of the Minotaur.

Although its beauty is self-evident, much must be guessed
about the art of all the periods shown here and its creators.
It was not until Greece flourished that men began to record the
lives of their artists with regularity; it was then that the
artist truly came to be valued as a special individual.

Photographs by Lee Boltin

THE ANTELOPE BOY OF SHONGOPOVI: A HOPI LEGEND

It was a time not at the beginning and not at the end, when the villages were standing there just as they are now. And in those days, it is remembered, there lived in Shongopovi a man and his wife and one daughter. The girl was old enough to marry, but she did not want it. She met with a certain young man of the village sometimes, but mostly she kept to herself. Her parents wondered about it. They said to each other sometimes, "She is really a young woman now. Why is she always alone? Does she want to live forever without a husband?"

One day the village crier went through Shongopovi announcing that there would be a rabbit hunt the next morning . . .

Early the following morning the young people began to gather at the edge of the village, and the girl's mother said to her, "Well, now, all the others are going out there to have a good time together, and you are staying behind like an old woman. This is not the way it should be."

The girl replied, "All right, I will go then." . . .

They arrived at the valley below. They began hunting. Whenever a boy saw a rabbit he chased it and tried to knock it down with his stick. If he found a rabbit hole he wet an end of his stick, poked it into the hole and twisted it to catch in the rabbit's fur. Each time a boy caught a rabbit he held it up by its hind legs, and the girls raced to see who could get there first. The boy gave the rabbit to the first girl to arrive, and she would give him somiviki [a corn meal paste] in exchange.

The girl who had been reluctant to participate in the rabbit hunt had won two rabbits and given away most of her somiviki. But she was not feeling well and was going along slowly. She fell behind the others. She could hear their voices in the distance but she could not see them. She stopped to rest. She felt pains in her stomach. She found a secluded place among the rocks and lay down. And while she was lying there she gave birth to a baby. She worried greatly. She thought, "I cannot take this baby home. My parents will be angry with me." And so, after staying there for a time, she arose, wrapped the infant in a piece of her clothing, and placed it in an abandoned badger hole. Then she returned to the village.

Now, after all the young people had finished with their hunting, a female coyote came out of hiding and began to look for food. Because she was old she could not run fast enough to catch game. She had watched the hunters, thinking that they might overlook some wounded rabbits and leave them behind. And so she went here and there where she had seen them using their sticks. She did not find any food. But she heard a sound coming from a badger hole. She approached the hole and looked inside. She saw the baby there and drew it out gently with her teeth. She thought, "This young one is hungry. If I were younger I would nurse it, but now I am dried up. I have no milk." She thought about the Antelope People living some distance north of Shongopovi. She thought, "Yes, I will bring it to them. They will take care of it."

Holding the baby carefully by its cloth wrapping, the old coyote went to the north. She came to the kiva of the Antelope People and set the baby down by the entrance. As was the custom, she stamped on the ground above the kiva, calling out, "I am here. Is there someone below?"

An antelope person called back, "Yes, we are here."

The old coyote said, "Come up. I have brought something."

So the antelope person went up the ladder to where the coyote was waiting. The coyote said to him, "Here is a male child I found out there in a badger hole. He is hungry, but I have no milk to give him. So I have brought him to you. One of your young women can feed him."

. . . Because the baby drank antelope milk it grew as rapidly as an antelope. In four days he could walk a little. When he was four weeks old he was allowed to go out of the kiva to run with the antelope children. At first he was slow, but in time he could run as fast as the others. And thereafter he went out with the antelopes every day and did whatever they did. In the kiva the Antelope People resembled humans. But when it was time to go out they took their antelope skins from the wall, put them on and became antelopes. At night when they returned they removed their skins and hung them on the wall again. While the boy was an adopted son of the Antelope People he was not an antelope. He did not have a skin to put on when they went out together. He ran along on two legs.

A man of Shongopovi went out one morning to search for game. He went to the north. He saw antelopes grazing there. He approached them silently. He saw the older antelopes. He saw the young antelopes running together, and with them a young boy running as though he too were an antelope. The hunter did not hunt anymore, but returned to Shongopovi to tell what he had seen. He entered the kiva where other men were sitting and discussing things. He said, "Out there in the north, I was hunting. I came upon a herd of antelopes. The young ones were running together and among them was a human child."

The others answered in doubt, saying, "This is hard to believe. A human child running with the antelopes? The antelopes are swift. No human, large or small, could run with the antelopes."

The hunter said, "What I have told you is the truth. I was there and I saw it."

The next day another man went to the north to see if a boy was there with the antelopes. He came to where the antelopes were grazing. He saw the boy with the young antelopes. He saw them run together. He returned to the village to report what he had seen. He said, "It is true. There is a boy among them, and he runs as swiftly as the others."

. . . In the kivas the people discussed what to do. Some said, "Do nothing. If the boy chooses to live with the antelope, surely he has a reason." Others said, "No, it is not right for a boy to live among the antelopes. We must capture him and bring him to the village." So a hunt was organized to capture the antelope boy.

. . . The chief of the antelopes was the boy's ceremonial uncle because he had taught him the knowledge and secrets of the antelope kiva. That morning, while the villagers were taking their positions for the hunt, the antelope chief said, "Wait, let us not go out yet. Something is happening today and there is something that must be done." He called the boy to sit with him in the kiva.

The chief said, "My nephew. Today the villagers are having a great antelope hunt. But it is you they are looking for. They say it is not right for a boy to be living with the antelope. They mean to capture you and take you back with them. It is true, they are your people. Therefore you must return with them. Whoever captures you will take you as his own. So it is important for you to know who among them are your parents. When we go out today do not run with the young antelopes. Stay close to me. I will tell you who is your father and who is your mother. When the time comes I will let you know what to do."

The boy said, "My uncle, I do not want to go back to the village to live. The antelopes are my people."

The antelope chief said, "It is true, you are like one of our own. If things do not go well for you in the village, if they treat you badly, you can come back to us. But as for now, today you will have to go with your parents."

Then the Antelope People prepared the boy. They washed his hair and cut it above his eyes in the Hopi fashion. They put a fluffy white eagle feather in his hair. They powdered his face with white cornmeal and painted his legs yellow. Around his waist they wrapped a white kilt, and around his ankles they fastened ankle bands. When this was done the Antelope People took their antelope forms and set out to their usual grazing place.

The people of the villages were waiting. They surrounded the antelopes. They moved in closer, making the circle smaller. The antelopes sought to escape. But if they went one way, there were people there. If they went another way, there were people there also. So they kept going around in a circle, and as the people came closer the circle became smaller and smaller. And at last the antelopes were confined in a very small space.

The antelope chief said to the boy, "Look carefully. That young woman standing over there is your mother. And over there, that man by the rocks, he is your father. Do you see them?"

The boy said, "Yes, I see them."

The antelope chief said, "The next time we pass this way, go quickly to your mother. Otherwise someone else may take you."

. . . The boy left his place among the antelopes. He ran swiftly to his mother. He put his arms around her, saying, "My mother." People gathered around. He said again, "My mother."

At first the young woman said nothing. She was thinking, "How can this be? He is mistaken." But remembering at last how she had put her baby in the badger hole, she placed her arms around the boy, saying, "My son."

The young woman's uncle who had been standing nearby said to her, "Is it true? Is this boy your son?"

She answered, "Yes, he is my son."

Her uncle asked, "Where is the boy's father?"

The boy went to where his father was standing. He took his hand. He said, "My father."

His father replied, "My son."

The young woman's uncle was angry. He said, "Why have you deceived us?"

The young woman said, "I was afraid. I tied my belt tight so that no one would notice. I went on a rabbit hunt and the baby was born there. I was afraid to bring him home, so I wrapped him in some of my clothing and left him in a badger hole."

Her uncle said, "It was a bad thing you did. If the antelopes had not taken care of your son he would have died." He came forward. He pulled down the hair whorls from each side of her head. He straightened her hair and and tied it in a knot the way it is worn by married women. He said, "Take the boy home. His father will join you there."

She returned to her parents' house, taking the boy with her. After a while the boy's father came and lived with them there, as is the custom. They went on living. The mother loved the boy. The father loved him also, but he felt restless about the way things had happened. He scolded the boy and spoke to him sharply. He loved him but he could not manage to speak to him except in hard words. He neglected him as well. He did not provide him with moccasins like other boys had. He did not make a bow for him and teach him how to hunt.

The boy was unhappy. And one day after his father scolded him sharply he went out of the village and travelled north until he came again to the place of the Antelope People. He entered the kiva. He said to the antelope chief, "My uncle."

The chief said, "My nephew."

The boy said, "As you told me to do, I went to Shongopovi. But I cannot live there anymore. My father is angry with me. He does not want me. Therefore I have come back. You are my people. I will live here.

His antelope uncle said, "Yes, live here. From now on you are one of us."

The Antelope People washed his hair and fixed it in the antelope style. They dressed him in the antelope manner. His uncle gave him an antelope skin, and a name. He named him Yuteu. The boy became an antelope.

Back in Shongopovi they missed the boy and searched everywhere. His parents went to Shipaulovi and Mishongnovi to see if he was there. They looked in the fields on all sides of Shongopovi.

His mother said at last, "There is no use looking for him any more. He has returned to the Antelope People who were kind to him."

. . . The boy's father was filled with remorse. He wanted his boy. He went north to the antelope country. He watched the antelopes, hoping to catch sight of his son. But he did not see him. Day after day he went to watch the antelopes, forgetting to take care of his fields. But there was no boy there, only the antelopes, nothing more.

Source:
Harold Courlander, "The Antelope Boy of Shangopovi" in *The Fourth World of the Hopis.* Copyright 1971 by Harold Courlander.
Reprinted by permission of Crown Publishers.

5

Change
and the future

Culture
change

Culture is the medium through which the human species adapts to its physical and social environment. Various cultural institutions, such as kinship and marriage, political and economic organization, and religion, mesh together to form one fully integrated cultural system. Because this system is adaptive, it is fairly stable and remains so unless the conditions to which it is adapted change. Archaeological studies have revealed how elements of a culture may persist for long periods of time. For example, the calendar used a thousand years ago by the Pre-Columbian Maya of Central America is still used in some modern Maya communities. Similarly, today's Maya live in houses resembling those built by their forbears during the height of Maya civilization (250 to 870 A.D.).

Although the most striking feature of most cultures is stability, cultural change does take place—we need only look at the incredible diversity of cultures today, all ultimately derived, in less than two million years, from a hunting-gathering base. Even more amazing is the fact that all nonhunting-gathering cultures have developed in the past 10,000 years. The causes of change are various. One common cause is change in the environment, which must be followed by an adaptive change in culture; another is individual variation in the way people within a culture perceive its characteristics, which may lead to a change in the way society in general interprets the norms and values of its culture. A third source of change is contact with other groups, which introduces new ideas and ways of doing things, eventually producing change in the traditional values and behavior.

Change is characteristic of all cultures, but the rate and direction of change vary considerably. Among the factors that influence the way change will occur within a given culture are: the degree to which a culture encourages and approves flexibility; the particular needs of the culture at a specific time; and, perhaps most important of all, the degree of "fit" between the new trait and the existing cultural matrix.

Even when cultural changes are most beneficial and adaptive they may well be difficult for individuals within the culture to accept. Thus cultural change is considered a social problem even though it is part of the necessary process of adaptation. New ways of doing things not only feel wrong, they also require relearning. An example of this can be seen in the problems of Americans who move to England, where cars are driven on the left-hand side of the road rather than the right. In this case the individual's very body has become adjusted to certain patterns of behavior that bypass his presumed "openness" to change.

Mechanisms of change

Cultural change may be slow, occurring over long periods of time, or it may be rapid, occurring over relatively brief periods of time. The processes or mechanisms which determine cultural change are diffusion, invention, devolution, and acculturation. Diffusion is generally associated with slow rates of cultural change, while invention and acculturation are associated with rapid change. Devolution, or loss of a culture trait without replacement, may be either a slow or rapid change.

Invention

The term **invention** refers to the formation, by a single individual, of a new habit, tool, or principle that eventually gains the acceptance of others and thus becomes socially shared. It may be passed along through imitation by all members of society or by a subculture or subgroup such as an age-grade, status, or kinship group. The prestige of the inventor and imitating groups may influence the degree of social acceptance, while the invention's acceptance depends on how much better it is than the thing or idea it replaces.

The term "invention" can be further broken down into "primary" and "secondary" inventions. Primary inventions are the chance discoveries of new principles; secondary inventions are the improvements made by applying known principles. The bow may be considered the primary invention from which not only the bow and arrow but also the musical bow and the bow drill emerged; the latter, because it contained the principle of the shaft, gave rise ultimately to the potter's wheel and the wheel and axle. Another primary invention, the cooking oven, led to the

Figure 15-1. *Technological innovations require a leap forward in the imagination not only of the inventor but also of the beholder, as these pictures (the top is of the Wright Brothers' flight) show.*

pottery kiln, harder pottery, the discovery of ore smelting, and finally to the forced-draft furnace.

Primary inventions may set off rapid cultural change and stimulate other inventions. Indeed, cultural values and goals can themselves lead to inventions. There are many instances of an invention that had more than one discoverer: the theory of evolution, for example, was proposed by Wallace as well as Darwin; three men separately produced the telescope; and the steamboat had no less than four inventors—all of whom worked before Fulton's time. On the other hand, an invention's chance of acceptance is limited if it fails to fit into a society's pattern of established needs, values, and goals. Galileo's discovery of the rotation of the planets and Mendel's contribution to genetics are instances of genuine creative insights out of step with the needs of their times. In fact, Mendel's work remained obscure until 16 years after his death when it was "rediscovered" by three scientists working independently in 1900. Mendel's discovery thus is an example of an idea whose time had not yet come.

Diffusion

In cultural borrowing, or **diffusion,** the "inventor" is the introducer of a new cultural element from another society. Murdock[1] cites the colonial European-Americans, who borrowed not just the use of corn, squash, and beans but the entire Indian way of producing them. Borrowing is so common that Malinowski,[2] for instance, regarded it as being just as creative as other forms of cultural innovation, and Linton[3] suggested that borrowing accounts for 90 percent of any culture's content. People never borrow all available innovations but exercise a high degree of selectivity, limiting their selections to those compatible with the existing culture. The Hopi, for example, have accepted the tin roofs, stoves, and glass of the white man but have resisted tractors and modern farm equipment. The Hopi religion, it seems, has certain rites essential to planting and harvesting with which machinery would interfere. Adoption would require far-reaching changes in Hopi religious practices.[4] On the whole, some areas, like technology, are highly prone to borrowing, and others, like social organization, far less likely to be borrowed. In all cases, the borrowed innovation must satisfy needs quicker and better than what has previously existed.

While the tendency toward borrowing is so great as to lead Robert Lowie to comment, "Culture is a thing of shreds and patches," the borrowed traits usually undergo sufficient modifications to make this wry comment more colorful than critical. Moreover, the borrowed trait may modify existing cultural traits. An awareness of the extent of borrowing can be eye-opening. Beals, for instance, points out the numerous things we have borrowed from the American Indians. Plants domesticated by the Indians—"Irish" potatoes, corn, beans, squash, and sweet potatoes—furnish nearly half the world's food supply. Among drugs and stimulants, tobacco is the best known, but others include coca in cocaine, ephedra in ephedrine, datura in pain relievers, and cascara in laxatives. Native American varieties of cotton cultivated by Indians supply much of the world's clothing needs, while the woolen poncho, the parka, and moccasins are universally familiar items. Not only has American literature been permanently shaped by such works as Longfellow's *Hiawatha* and James Fenimore Cooper's *Leather-Stocking Tales,* but American Indian music has contributed such ultramodern devices as unusual intervals, arbitrary scales, conflicting rhythms, and hypnotic monotony to world music. These borrowings are so well integrated into our culture that few people are aware of their source.

[1]George P. Murdock, "How Culture Changes," in *Man, Culture and Society,* Harry L. Shapiro, ed. (Chicago: University of Chicago Press, 1956).
[2]Bronislaw Malinowski, *The Dynamics of Culture Change* (New Haven: Yale University Press, 1945).
[3]Ralph Linton, *The Study of Man* (New York: Appleton-Century-Crofts, 1940).

[4]Alan R. Beals *et al., Culture in Process,* 2nd edition (New York: Holt, Rinehart and Winston, 1973) p. 298.

Devolution

Most often, we tend to think of change as an accumulation of innovations; new things being added to those already there. We do so because this seems so much a part of the way we live. A little reflection, however, leads to the realization that frequently the acceptance of a new innovation leads to the loss of an older one. This sort of replacement is not just a feature of Western civilization. For example, at one time the Indians of northeastern North America learned the art of making pottery, which then came into widespread use in the region. By the time Europeans arrived on the scene, this seemingly useful trait had been lost, and containers were made of basketry and birch bark instead. Actually, pottery is heavier and more breakable than baskets and birch bark containers, a serious drawback for peoples who move about from one campsite to another and must carry their belongings themselves. Basketry and birch bark were better adapted to their way of life than pottery.

Often overlooked is another facet of the loss of apparently useful traits: loss without replacement. This phenomenon we may call devolution, and it constitutes change just as surely as does the acceptance of a new innovation.

An example of devolution is the abandonment of an admittedly important ceremony by the Itza, a group of Indians living in the community of Soccotz, British Honduras (Belize). The ceremony, known as primicias, was a public ritual expression of gratitude to the deities. It was sponsored by an extended family in times of illness, with the object of overwhelming the deities by the quantity of offerings and the emotional intensity. For this, the utmost solemnity and propriety were mandatory for 24 hours. Moderation in all things, sexual restrictions, and achievement of a uniform feeling were essential. In short, a kind of mental paralysis through concentration was necessary to the success of the whole venture. The deities would tolerate no error, and the result of carelessness was death.

In 1942, the Itza became convinced that pri-micias presented an impossible task for human beings to accomplish, and so they abandoned it. This was the result of death apparently resulting from carelessness; the right attitudes were not maintained without exception for the 24-hour period. For example, in one case the wife of an ill person complained she was not rich enough. Following this, their food soured, the man died, and his wife followed soon afterwards. Shortly after that, a son died, and then the Ah-men who had conducted the ceremony died. As a result of this and other cases, public primicias are no longer given. As far as the Itza are concerned, it is better to have a sick man die than risk a wider calamity.

Acculturation

The process of **acculturation** demands special attention from anthropologists. Acculturation results when groups of individuals having different cultures come into intensive firsthand contact, with subsequent major changes in the original culture patterns of one or both groups. Its numerous variables include degree of cultural difference; circumstances, intensity, frequency, and amiability of contact; relative status of the agents of contact; who is dominant and who is submissive; and whether the nature of the flow is reciprocal or nonreciprocal.

Anthropologists use the following terms to describe what may happen during acculturation:

1) **Substitution,** in which a pre-existing trait or complex may be replaced by one that fills its function, involving minimal structural change;

2) **Syncretism,** in which old traits blend to form a new system, possibly resulting in considerable cultural change;

3) **Addition,** in which new traits or complexes may be added, and structural change may or may not occur;

4) **Deculturation,** in which part of a culture may be lost;

5) **Origination** of new traits to meet the needs of the changing situation;

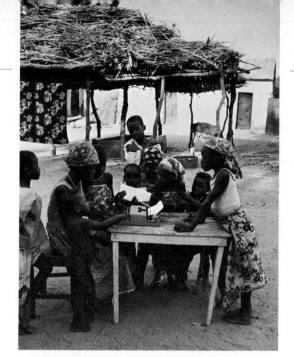

Figure 15-2a. *A Tahitian woman cuts her grass with a gasoline-powered lawnmower.*

Figure 15-2c. *A Camerounian schoolgirl does her homework on a typewriter.*

Figure 15-2b. *A Kenya television station broadcasts an American-style game show.*

Figure 15-2d. *Mexican boys carry a portable radio styled to resemble a television set.*

6) **Rejection,** in which changes may be so rapid that a large number of persons cannot accept them, resulting in either total rejection, rebellion, or revitalization movements.

As a result of one or a number of these processes, acculturation may then develop along several lines. Merger or assimilation occurs when two cultures lose their separate identities and form a single culture. Incorporation takes place when one culture loses autonomy but retains its identity as a subculture, such as a caste, class, or ethnic group; this is typical of conquest or slavery situations. Extinction is the phenomenon in which one culture loses its individual members until it can no longer function, and members either die out or join other cultures. In adaptation, a new structure may develop in dynamic equilibrium. In this last instance change may continue, but in the slow, "melting pot" form.

It should be emphasized that acculturation and diffusion are totally disparate terms; one culture can borrow from another without being in the least acculturated.

Forcible change

Quite logically, instances of the acceptance of change are highest when the element of change results from a need within the society. This may represent a simple society's striving to economically adapt to the worldwide technological revolution, even though the ramifications of the change may be felt throughout the society. The changing roles of women in Africa, or, for that matter, right here, may be considered an example of such a change. However, changes are often imposed from outside a culture, usually by colonialism and conquest. We have examined in Chapter 13 two examples of societies attempting to deal with such intrusions: the cargo cults of Melanesia and the Ghost Dance of the American Indian. Here we will look at some of the anthropological theories that attempt to explain the dynamics of changes that are forcibly imposed.

Colonialism and conquest

One positive aspect of colonialism is the growth of applied anthropology and the use of anthropological techniques in helping a society improve itself in accordance with the goals it—and the anthropologists, too—sets up. British anthropology, for the most part, has often been considered the "handmaiden" of that country's intensive colonial policy. American applied anthropology began with World War II, and the first efforts at colonial administration, especially in the Pacific, were made by officers trained in anthropology. The rapid recovery of Japan was due in no small measure to the influence of anthropologists in structuring the American occupation. Other American experiments aimed at a full understanding of native culture so the colonial culture could fit into a native structure with the least possible disturbance also bore fruit. Although many of these studies were admittedly for purposes of military intelligence, they proved useful also in postwar programs.

On the other side of the coin, however, and reflected especially in the early literature of contact between Europeans or Americans with indigenous groups, is a complete lack of anthropological understanding, and often of humaneness. Such contacts frequently brought to many areas the decimation, misery, and community degeneration that is known colloquially as "culture crash." Severe disruption of the traditional community life, with indications of social chaos or discord and personal or individual malaise, often followed in the wake of colonial occupation. This by no means implies that traditional societies were frictionless before contact with "civilization" but rather that existing conflicts could be handled through established cultural institutions without prolonged disruptions of daily life. In these early cases, degeneration occurred because traditional institutions designed to deal with traditional stress or conflict could not cope with new and rapid change that did not fit into the context of the traditional system. Too rapid change in a value system, for example, leaves other parts of the

Figure 15-3. *These Indians are listening to a recorded speech made to them by President Wilson.*

culture to catch up. Beals points out the rather striking change brought to the Manus of the Admiralty Islands as studied by Margaret Mead:

> The anthropologist had left an isolated, nonliterate people twenty-five years earlier. She returned to find them moving rapidly and purposefully into the stream of modern world culture. She found them searching for education that would permit them and their children to participate more fully in the modern world. And this occurred in one lifetime![5]

Whereas most anthropologists had thought that rapid change was disruptive, Dr. Mead suggested the opposite: if change is desired by an entire group and if it affects all the culture and its parts simultaneously, there may be less social disorganization and personal maladjustment than if changes occur segmentally over a long period of time. The great danger, Beals observes, is that the Manus believed that by modelling themselves in the image of American society they could participate in a world dominated by the Western way of doing things and benefit from this participation. If they should find out, as many other peoples have discovered, that this is not necessarily the case, they too will become discouraged and demoralized. One way that the Manus manifested their faith in the American way of life was through the cargo cults.

The most extreme cases of acculturation usually occur as a result of military conquest and displacement of traditional political authority by the conquerors who know nothing about the culture they control. The indigenous people, unable to resist imposed changes and restricted in their traditional social, religious, and economic activities, may be forced into new activities that tend to isolate individuals and tear apart social integration. Slavery in the early years of the United States, possibly the best-known example to us, provides many explanations for racial problems once shrugged off as inferiority. It should be pointed out that slavery in early America was not confined to the United States. As part of the

[5] *Ibid.,* pp. 305-7.

prevailing economic system (known as "the plantation system") slavery was characteristic of the Caribbean Islands and coastal South America. The racial problems the United States inherited from the slavery era are shared by other areas in the Americas where slavery was practiced.

Rebellion and revolt

When the scale of forced acculturation reaches a certain level, the possibilities for rebellion and revolt—such as the Cuban Revolution or the Red Revolution on Mainland China—are high.

The question of why revolutions come into being, as well as why they frequently fail to live up to the expectations of the people initiating them, is a problem. It is clear, however, that the colonial policies of countries such as England, France, Spain, Portugal, and the United States during the nineteenth and early twentieth centuries have created a worldwide situation in which revolution has become nearly inevitable. In numerous technologically undeveloped lands which have been exploited by more powerful countries for their natural resources and cheap labor, a deep resentment of the foreign ruling classes prevails. Lack of responsiveness to this feeling makes revolution or rebellion in some emerging nations the only alternative. One historian who has examined four revolutions of the past—English, American, French, and Bolshevik—offers the following conditions that may precipitate rebellion and revolt:

1) Loss of prestige of established authority, often as a result of the failure of foreign policy, financial difficulties, dismissals of popular ministers, or alteration of popular policies.

2) Threat to recent economic improvement. In France and Russia, those sections of the population (professional classes and urban workers) whose economic fortunes had previously taken an upward swing, were "radicalized" by unexpected setbacks such as steeply rising food prices and unemployment.

3) Indecisiveness of government, as exempli-

fied by lack of consistent policy; such governments appear to be controlled by, rather than in control of, events.

4) Loss of support of the intellectual class. Such a loss deprived the prerevolutionary governments of France and Russia of philosophical support, thus leading to their lack of popularity with the literate public.

5) A leader or group of leaders with charisma enough to mobilize a substantial part of the population against the establishment.

Apart from resistance to internal authority, such as in the English, French, and Russian Revolutions, many revolutions in modern times have been struggles against an externally imposed authority. Such resistance usually takes the form of independence movements that wage campaigns of armed defiance against colonial powers. The Algerian struggle for independence from France and the American Revolution are typical examples.

Revolts are not without their own problems. Hoebel quotes Max Gluckman writing of rebellion to oust the incumbents of offices without attempting to alter the nature of these offices. According to Gluckman, rebellions:

'throw the rascals out' and substitute another set, but there is no attempt to alter either the cultural ideology or the form of the social structure. In political revolution, attempts are made to seize the offices of power in order to change social structure, belief systems, and their symbolic representations. Political revolutions are usually turbulent, violent, and not long-lasting. A successful revolution soon moves to re-establish a stable, though changed, social structure; yet it has far-reaching political, social, and sometimes economic and cultural consequences.[6]

It should be pointed out, however, that revolution is a relatively recent phenomenon, occurring only during the last 5000 years. The reason for this is the fact that political rebellion requires a centralized political authority (or state) to rebel

[6] E. Adamson Hoebel, *Anthropology: The Study of Man*, 4th edition (New York: McGraw-Hill, 1972) p. 667.

against; the state has been in existence for only 5000 years. Obviously, then, in "primitive" societies, typified by tribes and bands and in other nonindustrial societies lacking central authority, there could not have been rebellion or political revolution.

Hoebel characterizes as benign the cultural revolutions that move technologies and societies in a significant, though hardly discernible, direction while they are in progress. Through this kind of revolution alone can the quality of life be fundamentally and irrevocably altered. He cites as examples the development of Paleolithic culture when man developed toolmaking, the use of fire, speech, and symbolic systems; the Neolithic Revolution, which saw the development of food production; the Urban Revolution, during which cities and civilization emerged; and today's urbanization, that continues with the assimilation of the last of the earth's small-scale peoples within the cultural network of civilization.

Revitalization movements. One important aspect of rebellion and revolt as modes of forcible change is the revitalization process. Revitalization may be defined as a deliberate attempt by some members of a society to construct a more satisfactory culture by the rapid acceptance of a pattern of multiple innovations.[7] Once primary ties of culture, social relationships, and activities are broken, and meaningless activity imposed by force, individuals and groups characteristically react with fantasy, withdrawal, and escape.

Perhaps the most dramatic example of the revitalization theory is found in our own country, where today's youth turn to drugs in their attempt to deal with the imposed values of the American dream. Thus, many American youths have adopted lifestyles completely different from those of the preceding generation. Revolting against an overwhelming technology, they call for a return to the earth and simpler ways of living. Their revolt is expressed in their use of drugs, outlandish or "freaky" clothes, hair styles, music, speech,

[7] Anthony Wallace, *Culture and Personality* (New York: Random House, 1961).

and in their behavior toward authority and authority figures.

Investigators have pointed out that American youth is reacting not against the American dream, but against the fact that reality as they perceive it does not reflect the dream. These scholars believe that whenever the ideal and the real cultures are too disparate, revitalization movements are inevitable.

Clearly, when value systems get out of step with existing realities, a condition of cultural crisis is likely to build up that may breed some form of reactive movement. Not all suppressed, conquered, or colonialized people eventually rebel against established authority, although why they do not is still a debated issue. When they do, however, resistance may take one of the following forms, all of which are varieties of revitalization movements. A culture may seek to speed up the acculturation process in order to share more fully in the supposed benefits of the dominant cultures, as the cargo cults, in which case it is called **transitional.** It may attempt to resurrect a suppressed pariah group that has long suffered in an inferior social standing and that has its own special subcultural ideology, and is then referred to as **millenarism;** the most familiar examples of this are prophetic Judaism and early Christianity. If a movement tries to reconstitute a destroyed but not forgotten way of life, as did the Ghost Dance of the Plains Indians, it is known as **nativistic** or **revivalistic.** If the aim of the movement is directed primarily to the ideological system and the attendant social structure of a cultural system from within, it is then called **revolutionary.**

Modernization

Two of the most frequently used terms in describing social change as it occurs today through any of the aforementioned processes are urbanization and modernization. Urbanization implies the influence of western technology but need not be so limited. Modernization is a more general term that includes the less disruptive types of change.

One aspect of modernization, the technological explosion, has made it possible to transport human beings and ideas from one place to another with astounding speed and in great numbers. Formerly independent cultural systems have been brought into contact with others. Cultural systems that once served a multipolitical function have come to serve relatively few functions. Vast increases in population have multiplied the number of existing cultural systems. The cultural differences between New York and Pukapuka are declining, while the differences between fishermen and physicists are increasing. No one knows whether this implies a net gain or net loss in cultural diversity, but the worldwide spread of anything, whether it is DDT or a new idea, should be viewed with at least caution. That human beings as human cultural systems are different is the most exciting thing about them, yet the destruction of diversity is implicit in the worldwide spread of rock and roll, communism, capitalism, or anything else. When a song is forgotten or a ceremony ceases to be performed, a part of the human heritage is destroyed forever.

An examination of several small-scale cultures which have felt the impact of modernization or other cultural changes will be examined to pinpoint some of the problems these cultures have met. The cultures are the Pueblo Indians of the American Southwest, the Tanala of Madagascar, the Blackfeet Indians of Montana, and African tribal society in general.

The modern Pueblo Indians

An interesting example of an entire culture that has continuously undergone change in the last century are the Pueblo Indians of the American Southwest. The Pueblo, traditionally an agricultural people with a population of about 200,000, have been studied by Edward Dozier, himself a Tewa Indian, and others. Despite the influence of the Spanish and American conquest, basic Pueblo culture and society have endured. Dozier has

Figure 15-4. Many European countries have sent technological "missionaries" to teach people in other countries new ways of doing old tasks.

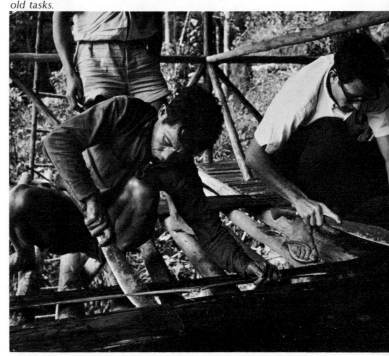

attributed this to the retention of the large extended family and the community as primary units of socialization and the persistence of indigenous languages. The traditional network of kin and community relations has not been disturbed. Thus, these factors have formed the same personality types over the years and have continued to reproduce individuals faithful to Pueblo beliefs. Pueblo social structure has remained virtually intact because the Indians have been able to retain their basic ethical and moral concepts.

However, outside influences, primarily those of the materialistic and technological American culture, have forced a number of cultural changes among the Pueblo. Not surprisingly, many of these changes have arisen as a result of modifications in the Pueblo's traditional agrarian economy.

As a result of their exposure to, and domination by, Americans, the Indians have abandoned their subsistence farming economy and have adopted the western credit system and cash economy. Thus, many facets of Pueblo life have changed. For example, the Pueblo village, or pueblo, has changed many of its communal characteristics. Isolated family adobe homes are replacing the traditional apartmentlike dwellings. Some of the more Americanized villages boast single-family dwellings similar to American houses, complete with garage, lawn, trees, yard, and shrubbery. Many villages also have electricity, running water, and inside plumbing.

Family possessions also reveal the increased economic status of many of the Pueblos: the furnishings found in a modern Pueblo home are quite similar to those found in many contemporary American homes. In the Santa Clara pueblo of New Mexico, television antennas are as numerous as in any small American town. Indeed, for many Pueblos, the television set has replaced the traditional gathering of the bilateral kin group to listen to Pueblo stories and legends. The formerly all-important corn-grinding equipment—*metates* and *manos*—is gone. Manufactured chairs and couches rest side by side with the trunk containing the ceremonial and dance paraphernalia. In nearly all pueblos, the long pole suspended from the ceiling to hold the family's clothing and possessions has disappeared. While the Pueblos still wear their brightly colored dresses and shawls, they purchase these items from stores rather than manufacture them themselves as in the past. Refrigerators and pantries have taken the place of the small back room where melons were stored and corn was stacked. The busy activities of the annual harvest time have been replaced by weekend shopping trips to the local supermarket.

In most pueblos, automobiles and pickup trucks furnish the transport once provided by horses and wagons. Working for wages in nearby towns and cities is the new way of Pueblo life, and it does not seem probable that farming will ever return as the primary economic occupation. This is because Pueblo thinking remains communal and small scale; those Pueblos who still practice farming are no match for their profit-minded American counterparts. The Indians think only in terms of planting small plots of corn and garden crops rather than multi-acre cash crops. Similarly, investment in land, livestock, and machinery are beyond the Pueblo way of thinking.

In spite of all the outward materialistic and economic changes, the Pueblo remain a communal people, chiefly because of their social organization. Disagreements, which are common in every pueblo, are seen as family quarrels and have rarely broken up a village. In fact, most Pueblo communities occupy the same sites they have lived on for centuries before the Spanish came. One reason for the long life of the Pueblo community is found in the ways they deal with criminals: discipline is harsh, and eviction from the community is not a rare punishment for a persistent wrongdoer. Another more important reason for the survival of the Pueblo is the integration found in Pueblo lifestyles. Kroeber has described the integration of the Zuni; his description is just as applicable to the other Pueblos:

Four or five different planes of systemization crosscut each other and thus preserve for the whole society an integrity that would speedily be lost if the planes merged and thereby inclined to encourage segregation and fission. The clans (among the Tanoans, extended families and moieties), the fraternities, the priesthoods, the kivas, in a measure the gaming parties, are all dividing agencies. If they coincided, the rifts in the social structure would be deep; by countering each other they cause segmentations which produce an almost marvelous complexity, but can never break the national entity apart.[8]

Just as the central core of Pueblo life remains, so do their religion and ceremonials, despite the fact that the farming life around which they were built no longer exists. Pueblo religion still provides its members with recreational outlets and a strengthening of communal living and identity. Dozier theorizes that this may be sufficient to keep the religion alive and to maintain the positions required for the rich ceremonial and religious life. In the face of the American economic influence, it is surprising that among many Pueblos there appears to be a religious upsurge, and many ceremonies which have long been in disuse have been resurrected and reenacted in a number of pueblos. This may be due to a revitalistic movement among the Indians, or it may have something to do with the Pueblo agricultural background. Edward Spicer has observed that religion developed in an agricultural ethos may survive in other settings. For example, the Yaquis, who like the Pueblos work for wages in the city, still believe and practice the ancient ceremonies of their religion. The same holds true for the Pueblo; while many of them work in neighboring cities, they continue to practice their age-old ceremonies.

The Tanala of Madagascar

Despite the effects of modernization, the Pueblos have been able to maintain their own special cultural identity. What happens to a culture when

[8] Alfred L. Kroeber, quoted in Edward Dozier, *The Pueblo Indians of North America* (New York: Holt, Rinehart and Winston, 1970) p. 19.

it adopts a new method of food production because of a change in the natural environment? One such people, the Tanala of Madagascar, were forced to adapt to a new kind of environment. When dwindling land resources pressured the Tanala to change from dry rice cultivation to the newer technique of wet rice cultivation, an entirely new social system evolved. Under the traditional system, the Tanala moved their villages from one area to another as land was depleted. When they adopted the new cultivation technique, the Tanala were transformed from an individualistic, democratic society to a class-society with a king, a system of warfare, settled villages, and a less permissive family life.

The new cultivation techniques made available large tracts of land that previously had been unusable and hence undesirable. As a result, a new class of landowners emerged with a concomitant breakdown in the traditional Tanala extended family structure. The unity of the family was destroyed because the new cultivation technique required only a single family to tend it and not, as in the past, the cooperation of large numbers of people.

The new rice fields became the center of a permanent settlement because the new technique did not deplete the land. Some families, caught in a land squeeze as the permanent sites became occupied, had to move further and further into the jungle, thus becoming separated and isolated from the rest of the village. Each village was surrounded by a group of irrigation fields under private ownership and a constellation of "branch" or offshoot villages with a similar social organization.

Methods of warfare also changed because permanent settlements required permanent upkeep and defense. Extensive defensive systems requiring big investments had to be initiated and maintained to assure each village of adequate protection.

Religion, as practiced by the extended family, did not lose its importance in the culture of the Tanalans. Even after the households of the extended family had been dispersed, its members would come together on ceremonial occasions to venerate common ancestors. Intermarriage between different permanent villages occurred, and thus Tanala society moved from independent villages to tribal organization. Tribal organization gave rise to kingship. However, the kingdom ended before any adequate machinery of government could be brought into play.

The Blackfeet Indians of North America

Unlike the tightly-knit and communally-organized Pueblo Indians who resisted modernization, the Blackfeet Indians of Montana have uniquely adjusted to modernization. Among the Blackfeet, a bicultural community has evolved: the white-oriented group is organized around such values as work, individuality, acquisitiveness, and pursuit of future goals. The Indian-oriented group, on the other hand, attempts to retain its ethnic and cultural identity, staving off full economic integration with the encroaching American culture.

Anthropologist Malcolm McFee has described how this bicultural community functions in his study, *Modern Blackfeet Montanans on a Reservation*. According to McFee,

> The past events have not resulted in tribal disorganization, but in a reorganization that accommodates the simultaneous persistence of many traditional social and cultural characteristics from both interacting societies. A large part of the tribe has adopted the culture of the dominant (American) society and aspires to assimilate. A smaller number, for reasons already mentioned, retains more from the Blackfeet past and resists further change. The reservation social structure has changed to accommodate these contrasting points of view. The structure of a nonreservation community tends to be unilinear, with one general set of values, and one status hierarchy. But the physical and social boundaries of the reservation and the tribe incorporate two societies, and make possible a bilinear structure that offers a choice

of alternative limitations and possibilities for adaptation. An individual, consciously or otherwise, can choose, and possibly choose again, which pattern he wishes to follow. His choice, and his acceptance and class assignment, depend upon what he brings to the situation in the way of aspirations, experiences, and capabilities.[9]

Changing tribal Africa

Colin Turnbull's concluding observations of his study of Africa in transition embody many of the essential features of the entire changing world: the removal of economic activities from the family-community setting; the altered structure of the family in the face of the changing labor market; the increased reliance of young children on parents for affection instead of on the extended family; the decline of general paternal authority; schools replacing the family as the primary educational unit; the discovery of the generation gap; and many others.

Among Turnbull's observations are many that reinforce some of the ideas that we have thus far discussed. For example:

> The Africa we have been looking at has been tribal Africa. The tribe still exists, and tribal ways still flourish in many parts of the continent. But change has come to other parts, and change is sweeping through everywhere. No tribes are untouched. Even when change comes, however, it cannot destroy everything it finds. It has to build on something. So the African tribal past is very important if we are to understand what is happening in Africa today. . . .
>
> Africa has seen many invasions from outside, just as it has seen continuous movement and invasions within. Greeks, Romans, Arabs, Southeast Asians, and Chinese have all at one time or another come to Africa and left their mark. Most recently of course came the Euro-

[9]Malcolm McFee, *Modern Blackfeet Montanans on a Reservation* (New York: Holt, Rinehart and Winston, 1972).

pean colonial powers, bringing change more drastic than anything that had been seen until then. These colonial powers brought with them a new and total way of life. They did not just bring change by being there, they did everything they could to force change. There was a conscious effort. They tried to bring change not to just one aspect of African life, but to the whole tribal way of life. . . The European colonial powers felt that the ideal would be for Africans to live and behave just like Europeans. Wherever schools were set up they were designed to bring this kind of change. It really amounted to an all-out attack on tribal life. On top of this, with the changes that colonialization brought in the way countries were governed, more and more Africans found that they were forced to abandon much of their traditional life. The tragedy is that it all happened so suddenly that there was no time for tribal society to adapt itself gradually, as it had always done in the past. It was as though the whole foundation had suddenly been swept away from beneath it. Yet tribal society is still far from dead, and in some ways it seems to be asserting itself again. . . .

As [the modern African child] grows up the change continues. Horizons begin to widen but again in a pattern quite unfamiliar in the tribe. Rather than learning about life by watching and being with parents and older relatives all the time, children are separated from their parents more and more, and spend their time at school. It is in school that they learn things that will help them in their future life. The break with their parents has already begun. Not only are they spending more time away from home, but they are learning things that will make them different from their parents. A boy whose father is a road worker may be learning to be an engineer. A boy whose father is a farmer may be learning to be a lawyer. No longer do children follow in the ways of their fathers, let alone their ancestors. . .[10]

[10]Colin M. Turnbull, *Tradition and Change in African Tribal Life* (New York: World Publishing Company, 1966).

Figure 15-5. *Slow change is coming to the Masai, a tribe of herdsmen. Young girls of the tribe are being taught agriculture, a skill needed for the adjustment to a settled way of life. The men of the tribe are being taught scientific methods of animal husbandry, such as vaccination against disease.*

Modernization: Must it always be painful?

Although most anthropologists see the traditional acculturation process among "primitive" peoples caught up in the modern technological world as an ordeal, some scholars, like sociologist Alex Inkeles, see emerging from the process of modernization a new kind of man.[11] This man is kind of a prototype who, whether he comes from an African tribe, a South American village, or an American city, will be open to accept and benefit from the changes in the modern world. The first element in his definition of the modern man is a readiness for new experience and an openness to innovation and change. Here he is talking of a "state of mind, a psychological disposition, an inner readiness," rather than of specific techniques and skills a man or group may possess because of an attained level of technology. In this sense, therefore, a man working with a wooden plow may be more modern in spirit than someone in another part of the world who drives a tractor.

Secondly, a man is more "modern" if he "has a disposition to form or hold opinions over a large number of the problems and issues that arise not only in his immediate environment but also outside of it . . ." This man shows more awareness of the diversity of attitude and opinion around him rather than closing himself off in the belief that everyone thinks alike and, indeed, just like him. He is able to acknowledge differences of opinion without needing to deny differences out of fear that they will upset his own view of the world; he is also less likely to approach opinion in a strictly autocratic or hierarchical way.

Adaptation to cultural change. In the past mankind has survived periods of explosive cultural change similar to ours. Ten thousand years ago the invention of agriculture brought a period of rapidly increasing population, energy con-

[11] Alex Inkeles, "The Modernization of Man" in *Modernization: The Dynamics of Growth*, Myron Weiner, ed. (New York: Basic Books) pp. 141-44.

sumption, and invention. Self-limiting as this revolution proved once the potentials inherent in agriculture were worked out, it nevertheless witnessed environmental destruction and decline in population among numerous peoples in its wake. If civilizations such as these could destroy their own limited world, our worldwide civilization is certainly capable of far more destructive acts.

Whether or not the current cultural explosion proves to be self-limiting, however, certain scholars foresee that the systems caught up in it must adapt within the next few generations to a totally different and unprecedented set of environmental circumstances. If this adaptation is to be planned and systematic, it must, they say, make use of the experience and wisdom preserved in the existing variety of human cultural systems. The problem of unlimited population growth may perhaps be solved through the development of new techniques of contraception and abortion; but it also needs to be solved culturally through the introduction of new traditions, new forms of marriage, and new social arrangements.

The population explosion too can be regarded as a reflection of the rapid development of new ideas and ways of doing things. It would hardly have been possible without great increase in the production of food and other requirements for human existence. The numerous developments in technology have inevitably led to an explosive increase in man's capacity to exterminate himself or to alter the face of the earth. The threats of atomic warfare, bacteriological warfare, or chemical warfare are obvious and visible. Less visible are those threats posed by the introduction of new chemicals or by slow but massive changes in the seas, land masses, and atmosphere of earth, problems for physicists or marine biologists but also for human cultural traditions and human social arrangements.

Change in basic cultural units and the growing bureaucracy. As cultural traditions and cultural systems have become larger and more all-encompassing, the little traditions of neighborhood, community, and tribe have lost their uniqueness and their coherence. One hundred years ago most of the population of the earth lived in small communities, and in intimate relationship to their neighbors. Because the small community has been so general and pervasive for so many years, anthropologists have often drawn the conclusion that communities are essential to the preservation of human identity and well-being. In the modern world, it almost seems as if the small group and the small community have been declared enemies of the state. It is believed to be more efficient to have one large university with ten thousand students than ten small universities. The same principle holds true for factories and farms and all the other contexts within which people work, play, or live.

Modernization has also affected another basic cultural entity, the family. For example, Neil Smelser observes modernization's tendency to encourage "the development of a family unit that is formed on emotional attraction and built on a limited sexual-emotional basis." The family, he adds, removed from other major social spheres except for the segmental external ties of individual family members, impinges less on other social spheres, making nepotism an illegitimate basis for recruitment into roles and making the family a one-dimensional institution.[12]

In many modern societies, the life of the individual is governed not by small cultural units such as the family, or neighbors, or religious organization, but by faceless bureaucracies. In modern states and cities, such bureaucracies contend against each other for resources and seek to increase their size and influence. Whether seeking to grow or to control their clients, bureaucracies formulate new rules and employ more persons to enforce them. The individual is governed now, not by the cultural traditions of his community, but by the countless and inexplicable rules of the innumerable bureaucracies with which he must deal in order to survive. On the other hand, with the evolution of larger and larger cultural systems, and the increasing inclusion of mankind within a single world order, perhaps all of this is necessary, but perhaps it is time to consider what has been sacrificed upon the altars of modernity and efficiency.

Understanding cultural change. Since we cannot reverse the tide of this phenomenon for which we are at least in part responsible, the next best thing may be to continue our efforts to understand just where and how to apply our technological, sociological, psychological, and, above all, anthropolitical discoveries. For change will always be with us. In the words of Murdock:

> change is always uncomfortable and often painful, and people frequently get discouraged with its slowness or even despair of achieving any genuine improvement. Neither history nor anthropology, however, gives cause for pessimism. However halting or harsh it may appear to participants, cultural change is always adaptive and usually progressive. It is also inevitable and will endure as long as the earth can support human life. Nothing—not even an atomic war—can destroy civilization.[13]

As soon as such a statement goes into print it is challenged. Whether or not it is true, it is undeniably true that since this statement was issued the world as we know it has changed, in some areas beyond recognition, and in the face of numerous threats to civilization, we are still here.

---

[12]Neil J. Smelser, "The Modernization of Social Relations" in Weiner, *op. cit.,* p. 119.

[13]Murdock, *op. cit.,* p. 260.

Original study

THE MODERNIZATION OF JAPAN

And what has happened since the end of the Tokugawa era to the family and other kin groups, the common-interest associations, the structure of Japanese society in general? Some of the major trends may be summarized as a decline in the size and functional importance of the family and other kin groups, a weakening of the bonds of kinlike personal ties with unrelated persons, a change in patterns of authority within the family and elsewhere, and the emergence or increased growth of many impersonal institutions that provide economic and social security. Social classes have taken form following occupational lines, and all indications point to the growth of a huge urban middle class.

The nuclear family is the prevailing form throughout the nation. At least until the young go out into the world as adults, however, ties between familial members remain intimate. When relatives beyond husband, wife, and their children live under one roof and form part of the familial unit, these are customarily the aged parents of the household head and the family is rural rather than urban. In the city a sentiment has grown against living with one's parent, parents-in-law, or mature children, and the idea is not a total stranger to rural residents. Father's voice has lost a good deal of authority and mother's has gained. Younger sons are often at no disadvantage as compared with the eldest son, and sisters and new brides have lost some of their meekness. To prepare them for an adult life that is likely to take them away from farming, younger sons and even daughters of rural families may receive more formal education than eldest sons, who are ordinarily expected to remain on the farm. The mother-in-law who attempts to dominate her son's bride is in danger of being branded as "feudal," a demeaning word. A common postwar saying is that two things have grown in strength since the war, stockings—now of tough nylon—and women.

The relationship between man and wife is both more nearly equal and more intimate than in former times. This trend of change is part of a group of alterations in familial relations, some of which represent complementary emphases and de-emphases. As other social devices have taken over various of the former roles of kinship, the familial continuity through the generations is both less important and more difficult to maintain. The status of the eldest son thus holds less eminence, and its loss of importance has been accompanied by a rise in the position of wife and mother. At the same time, the strict supervision of marriage has become less important. Conventions of former times discouraged intense bonds between men and women, for these endangered the position of preeminence of the eldest son. Relations of intimacy and equality between man and wife endangered familial continuity by detracting from the father-son relationship and by placing authority in the hands of women. The new bride was ideally the lowest member of the household. In her youth a woman was traditionally under the domination of her husband and in her old age under the authority of her eldest son. In their roles as bearers and rearers of children, women were necessary mechanical appurtenances to a scheme of social structure which had provisions for continuity that involved many people and which was made to seem far more important than the relations between any two individuals. Proper men did not admit to romantic love for their wives; instead they spoke of them and to them as lowly creatures. Many other customs insured that women did not endanger the operations of the social machine.

Under the conditions of Tokugawa times, a low social position for females was congruous, and romantic love could find no approval either as a mode of selecting mates or as a desirable relationship between man and wife. It was only among people of lowest social classes, those lacking property and confined to egalitarian association with others of bottommost station, that men and women ordinarily married for love. Modern conditions of life provide increasing encouragement to romantic love and to lifelong attachments between spouses. The wife who walks some distance behind her husband on streets and roads has become a curiosity.

One of the many additional indications of the diminished importance of kinship is provided by present customs of using kin terms. Today they find less frequent use, especially for distant relatives and unrelated persons, and the use of personal names has grown. Kin terms long ago ceased to be appellations of respect and honor. The modern woman is often none too anxious to be called "aunt" or "grandmother," and it is of course possible deliberately to insult by choice of a kin term suggesting that the addressee has lost the premium of youth. In this matter, too, it seems reasonable to think that the changed culture of Japan offers an explanation. Where romantic love between husband and wife finds encouragement, a desire on the part of men and, especially, of women to appear attractively young seems congruous. The modern Japanese wife gives growing attention to her personal appearance, and the commercial beauty industry of Japan has become a vast network of establishments providing cosmetics and services that reaches down to the smallest community.

Fictive kinship has had an interesting career. In the earlier stages of the industrialization of Japan, the *oyabun-kobun* flourished as a social device transitional between the peasant and the industrial society. Young men and women migrating to cities entered this relationship with their employers or supervisors, and labor was often recruited on this basis. Today the *oyabun-kobun* relationship in its old form is common only at the fringes of society, in the world of professional criminals and prostitutes, where the economic innovations connected with legal employment have not penetrated. In the world of law-abiding citizens, the formal *oyabun-kobun* has generally been transmuted into milder forms of paternalism and these permeate Japanese society.

As compared with circumstances in the United States, Japanese society continues to give much importance to kinship and to personalized ties with unrelated people. Industrial and commercial concerns are heavily paternalistic, looking into and after the welfare of their personnel in ways that go far beyond the demand of coldly rational business. Small family enterprises remain very common and even the smallest shops and business concerns may provide living quarters for unrelated employees, especially the young and unmarried. Thus the firms take on many of the aspects of family enterprises. Large industrial firms frequently maintain apartments for married employees as well as dormitories for single people, and also often provide recreational facilities for their personnel. Labor unions are most frequently company unions. Nepotism in practices of employment is standard and often thoroughly approved. In the religious world priestly posts are customarily inherited. University professors are often still masters, and the students who become associated with them are their disciples. Leaders of gangs of criminals are also masters, who look after the welfare of their followers. No segment of Japanese society may be described as entirely free of familism, but even here continued trends of change are evident. The "progressive" inveigh publicly against paternalism, and the primary qualification for important positions in the worlds of industry and finance is personal ability. Commercial concerns have grown larger, rendering personalized relations more and more difficult to maintain, and the growth of the large business enterprises has been accompanied by the bankruptcy of many small concerns, which form the greatest strongholds of familism. The emphasis in employment shifts increasingly toward the recognition of talent and toward impersonality in employer-employee relations.

The functional substitutes for kinship that have emerged—institutions of social welfare, banks, labor unions, schools, courts of law, common-interest associations, and many other social and economic devices—continue to grow in importance. Among these, common-interest associations loom importantly in both city and county, and certain of them have assumed positions of vital importance to the rural resident. Any farming community of the nation includes among its residents members of twenty-five or more associations concerned with economic matters, community affairs, religion, and recreation. Of these, the agricultural cooperatives, in their postwar form, are the most important. These are the agency through which the farmer obtains machinery, tools, fertilizer, education in new techniques of agronomy, loans of money for farm improvement, insurance on crops and livestock, and much else. The cooperative is the farmer's bank for savings accounts as well as loans, the normal agency for sale of crops, and its social activities may provide much of the recreation available to the rural family. Under the circumstances of modern urban life—for the country as well as the city has become urbanized—common-interest associations offer a number of advantages. Their growth in Japan, as elsewhere, has marked a transition from strong reliance upon kinship and personal ties. Associations are highly elastic; kin groups are not. Associations may be formed, changed, or dissolved to meet altered circumstances, and their presence or absence does not disrupt family or community membership in any consequential way.

Various of the modern associations of Japan are modeled after American counterparts and bear English or English-derived names. The Parent-Teachers' Association (Pee-chee-eh) and 4-H (Yon-eichi) are examples introduced during the military occupation after World War II. Fraternal organizations stemming from the West that have high prestige in Japanese cities are the Rotary International and the Lions Club. Many other associations that have goals of social reform or humanitarian aims also resemble organizations of the Western world, especially of the United States, and have doubtless often been inspired by the foreign organizations. But here caution must be used. Common-interest associations are ancient in Japan as well as in the West, and they are a world-wide feature of human society, when circumstances encourage or allow their formation. When governmental control during the preceding century allowed the people of Japan to do so, they showed no reluctance to form their own common-interest associations, many of which had aims of social reform. Associations that appear to be entirely Japanese have sprung up thickly since the end of World War II, and their growth should not be interpreted as a mere copying of foreign social features. As an indication of the rising position of women, it is noteworthy that one of these is a large national organization called the Housewives' League (Shufuren) that seeks with considerable success to improve conditions of daily life and to combat social evils.

Source:
From *Changing Japan* by Edward Norbeck. Copyright © 1965 by Holt, Rinehart and Winston, Inc. Reprinted by permission of Holt, Rinehart and Winston, Inc.

Summary

1.
Because cultures are adapted to their environment, they are remarkably stable. And yet the diversity of the cultures in existence today attests to the amount of change that has actually taken place. Only 10,000 years ago all cultures were based on hunting and gathering. No culture escapes change altogether, not even those still based on hunting and gathering, but the rate and direction of change vary considerably. Individuals within a culture usually find change difficult to accept, beneficial though it may be.

2.
Cultural change by means of invention is originated by an individual within the culture who invents a new habit, tool, or principle. Other individuals adopt the invention and it becomes socially shared. Diffusion is the borrowing by one society of a cultural element from another. Acculturation is more than just borrowing. It stems from intensive first-hand contact of groups with different cultures and produces major changes in the culture patterns of one or both groups. Devolution is the loss of an important trait without replacement.

3.
Colonial administration guided by an understanding of the native culture can avoid causing serious disruption of the native culture. In many cases, however, colonialism has resulted in "culture crash": decimation, misery, and community degeneration. A struggle against externally imposed authority may be a rebellion, in which the aim is simply to oust the incumbents of offices, or it may be a revolution, in which attempts are made to change not only the incumbents but the nature of the offices, and to change belief systems and the social structure as well.

4.
When value systems diverge too widely from the realities in a culture, a condition of cultural crisis may develop and revitalization movements may appear. In a transitional revitalization movement, the culture tries to speed up the acculturation process in order to get more of the benefits it expects from the dominant culture. In millenarism it attempts to resurrect a pariah group with a subcultural ideology. Nativistic or revivalistic movements aim to reconstitute a destroyed but not forgotten way of life. Revolutionary movements try to reform the cultural system from within.

5.
An example of modernization is found in the Pueblo Indians, who have retained their extended families and indigenous languages but adopted the American economy and consumer goods. The Tanala of Madagascar have fared differently under modernization. Forced to adopt a new rice-growing technique that employs single families, the Tanala have suffered a breakdown of the extended family. The Blackfeet Indians have responded in yet another way. They have evolved a bicultural community with a white-oriented group and an Indian-oriented group.

6.
Modernization everywhere has tended to reduce the influence that the community and the family have over the individual. The trend is for the individual to be governed less by these small units and more by larger systems such as bureaucracies.

Six centuries of culture change

Among the most fascinating of early man's urge to build greatly are the megaliths of Europe. Begun as early as 4000 B.C. (long before the time of the pyramids in Egypt), they include five types of structure whose remains are mainly stone, but which may have originally included wood: menhirs, huge, single standing stones; tombs, mainly composed of several standing stones topped by a large capstone; alignments of standing stones, sometimes in long rows; circles of large stones, often connected at their top by stone lintels; and apsidal temples, found principally in Malta. Examples of some of these structures are shown here.

Probably the best known megalithic monument is Stonehenge, which stands majestically on Salisbury Plain in Wiltshire, England. Since written history began, Stonehenge has captured the imagination of many who have wondered about its origins. The story of the monument presents an interesting study in culture change over a 600 year period. Most archeologists think an early Bronze Age culture, known as the Beaker folk after their unique pottery drinking cups, began the monument around 2000 B.C., roughly the same time as the Minoan culture was flourishing in Crete, and about the same time as the construction of the great pyramids.

The Beaker folk were a highly organized, warlike people who migrated to England from Spain. They completely overran the existing Neolithic hunters and small farmers, absorbing them into their culture. The Beakers were a society of agriculturists and pastoralists who lived in small villages, each dominated by a petty prince. Their society was stratified into a farmer class, skilled

Stonehenge, Wiltshire, England.

A trilithon at Stonehenge.

Passage grave, County Sligo, Eire.

Carronmore, megalithic tomb, County Sligo, Eire.

Stone circle, Scotland.

Pentre Ifan dolmen, Wales.

Stone circle, Isle of Lewis, Hebrides, Scotland.

Callanish stone circle, Isle of Lewis, Hebrides, Scotland.

craftsmen, an aristocratic class of warriors, a merchant class, and possibly a class of priests.

The Beakers started the first important building stage of Stonehenge, transporting huge bluestones (80 or more weighing up to five tons each) from Wales—some 240 miles by sea and land from Salisbury Plain. Investigators have speculated that the monument served as a burial ground and ritual gathering place, and possibly even an astronomical observatory.

Around 1600 B.C., the Beakers were conquered and assimilated by another invading culture, the Wessex folk, who are thought to have originated in Brittany. The society of the conquerors differed little from that of the conquered, save for the fact that the Wessex lords, grown wealthy from the increased agricultural yields, were able to make the peasants who worked their lands more and more dependent upon them for security and for economic reasons. Thus, at this early stage of history, the seeds of feudalism were sown. Later, feudalism diffused throughout England, profoundly changing the cultural organization of all it touched.

The Wessex people completed the final building stage of Stonehenge between 1600 and 1500 B.C., transporting the large sarsen stones from 20 miles away, and arranging them with the existing bluestones into their familiar pattern that exists today. It has been estimated that some 1.5 million man days of labor went into the building of Stonehenge over this 400 year period.

Around 1400 B.C., Wessex domination of England ceased; like the Beakers, the Wessex folk were assimilated into more powerful cultures that migrated from other parts of the British Isles. This process of cultural change—successive migration, conquest, and assimilation—continued in England until the Norman Conquest in the 11th Century A.D. when feudalism emerged as a unifying cultural force on the Islands.

As successive cultures were syncretized into one another, social and religious beliefs changed to the extent that the stone monuments shown here—Stonehenge, the dolmens of Ireland and Wales, and the circles of Scotland—lost their religious import. Today, they stand as signs of early man's connection with the earth, with the force of nature which he needed to comprehend. That force of intimacy communicates itself over the millenia.

Photographs by Paul Caponigro

Suggested readings

Arensberg, Conrod and Arthur H. Nieloff, *Introducing Social Change: A Manual for Americans Overseas* (Aldine, 1964).
This is an excellent "eye opener," showing the westerners that what appears to be bad or inefficient ways of doing things have purpose and meaning in the matrix of the particular culture, and that failure to understand such customs can lead to disaster when programs of change, no matter how well meaning, are introduced.

Barnett, Homer G. *Innovation: The Basis of Cultural Change* (McGraw-Hill, 1953).
This is the standard work on the subject, widely quoted by virtually everyone who writes about change.

Dalton, George (ed.) *Economic Development and Social Change: The Modernization of Village Communities* (Nat. Hist. Press, 1971).
The phenomenon known as modernization (it might almost be called westernization) is the subject of much anthropological attention these days, and this selection of writings is a good introduction to the subject.

A. L. Kroeber, *Anthropology* (see Suggested readings for Chapter 13 for complete reference). Several chapters of this work are given over to excellent discussions of innovation and diffusion. Particularly good are sections dealing with the histories of specific inventions.

Redfield, Robert; Ralph Linton, and Melville J. Herskovits Memorandum of the Study of Acculturation. *American Anthropologist* (38:149-152) (1936).
This article was the result of the growing interest of anthropologists in the effect of massive contact with western cultures on more traditional cultures. It was the first major attempt to specify what the phenomenon of acculturation was.

Tax, Sol, ed., The Fox Project. *Human Organization* (17:17-19) (1955).
A statement on a recent attempt by anthropologists to facilitate the kinds of changes desired by those who are to be affected by those changes.

The future

Anthropology is sometimes described as a backward-looking discipline. The work that we typically associate with anthropologists is the interpretation of the past and the description of the present. Yet anthropologists also have a special concern with the future and the changes it may bring. Like all residents of an industrialized culture, they wonder what the postindustrial society now being predicted will hold. More pressingly, they also wonder what changes the coming years will bring to non-Western cultures. As we saw in the preceding chapter, when non-Western pastoralists and hunter-gatherers are thrown into contact with Western industrialized peoples their culture is rapidly changed, often for the worse—it becomes both less supportive and less adaptive. How, then, can these threatened cultures adapt to the future?

The cultural future of man

Whatever man's biological future, culture remains his primary mode of adaptation. Yet some anthropologists have noted with concern what they interpret as a trend toward loss of adaptability in our culture. What can anthropologists tell us about the culture of the future?

One-world culture

Some anthropologists believe that the future world will be homogenized into a single culture. The concept that man is moving toward a "one-world culture" springs from the rapid developments in communication, transportation, and trade that link the great majority of today's people; the seeming Westernization of other countries (Japan, for example) exemplifies this trend. There can be little doubt that such a one-world culture would be a superculture, an outgrowth of modern industrial society where computers, cybernetics, and communications—in effect, technology—reign supreme. If this culture does develop, an American travelling in the year 2100 to Tierra del Fuego, Peking, or New Guinea will find that the inhabitants of these areas live in a manner identical or similar to him. They will eat the same kinds of food, read the same newspapers, go to the same kinds of churches, have the same kind of government.

Such a culture, many anthropologists believe, would be bland, lacking the richness and variety found in cultural diversity. They also believe that a standardized culture would lead to a loss of adaptability, should some future crisis arise. For example, suppose that the earth's supply of fossil fuels were to be totally exhausted by the start of the twenty-first century. What would happen to the people living in northern climates if they could no longer heat their homes artificially or buy gasoline for their piston-engine vehicles? If such a calamity were to occur today, while true cultural diversity still exists, it is highly probable that Eskimos, Lapps, Siberians, and other peoples accustomed to a frigid, harsh environment would survive; these marginal cultures have the social organization and technology necessary to live, perhaps even to thrive, in this kind of ecosystem. Such cultures, being the only survivors of the human species in the north, would proliferate and carry on the human race. From these, other cultures would gradually develop and civilization would again emerge.

If the Eskimos had been assimilated into the single culture, they would all have traded in their dog sleds for snowmobiles, and their kayaks and umiaks for stainless steel boats powered by outboard motors. Thus their traditional techniques for survival would be lost and forgotten; the Eskimos would perish with everyone else, making *Homo sapiens* a species no longer found in northern climates. Thus, some anthropologists believe that fully developed cultures of great diversity, such as still exist in many parts of today's world, will be necessary in the future to provide options for human survival in the event of a global emergency.

Other anthropologists suggest that perhaps a generalized culture would be more desirable in the future, because certain fully developed cultures of today may be too specialized to survive in a changed environment. Examples of this situation abound in modern anthropology. When a traditional culture well adapted to a specific environment, such as the Indians of Brazil who are beautifully adapted to a life in a tropical rain forest, meets European-derived culture and the social environment changes suddenly and drastically, the traditional culture often collapses, because its traditions and its political and social organizations are not at all adapted to the new lifestyle. Usually, such societies adopt many of the cultural features of the Western societies to which they have been exposed. The apparently limited adaptability of non-Western cultures may be compared to some early hominid populations, such as *Australopithecus robustus,* who was physically less able to adapt to changing environmental conditions than were some other hominids, and so became extinct. The more generalized *Australopithecus africanus,* on the other hand, had the capacity to survive in the available environment; this group survived and evolved into what today is *Homo sapiens.*

Cultural pluralism

A second possibility for man's future may be the rise of cultural pluralism, in which more than one culture exists in a given society. Cultural pluralism is the social and political interaction within the same society of people with different ways of living and thinking. Ideally, cultural pluralism implies the rejection of bigotry, bias, and racism in favor of respect for the cultural traditions of other peoples. In reality, it has not always worked out that way.

An example of one form of cultural pluralism may be found in New York City where the Puerto Ricans, who have their own cultural traditions and values, exist side by side with other New Yorkers. The Puerto Ricans have their own language, music, religion, food; some live in their own *barrio* or neighborhood. This particular pluralism, however, is probably of a temporary nature, a stage in the process of integration into standard American culture. Thus, the Puerto Ricans, in four or five generations, like the Italians, Irish and Jews before them, may also become Americanized to the point where their lifestyle will be indistinguishable from others around them.

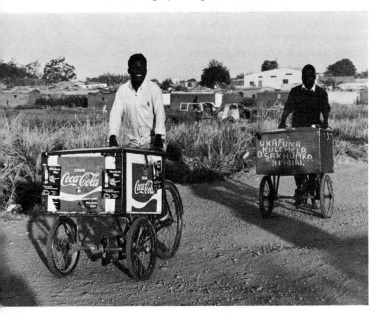

Figure 16-1. *Signs of the growing trend toward worldwide homogenization of culture include this supermarket in Mexico City that carries Bayer aspirin, Ritz crackers, and Nescafé, and these Zambian boys who earn their living by selling Coca-Cola.*

The United States, then, does not have a truly culturally pluralistic society where distinct cultures flourish. Rather, it has been a "melting pot" society where many cultures have been absorbed into the mainstream of American culture. There are, however, signs that a true pluralism may be emerging. Blacks, American Indians, Chicanos, and Puerto Ricans are proclaiming their intentions of retaining identifiable cultural characteristics. This could be the beginning of a trend away from the melting pot philosophy and toward real pluralism.

Other examples of cultural pluralism may be found in Switzerland where the Italian, German and French cultures exist side by side; in Belgium where the French Walloons and the Flemish each have different cultural heritages; and in Canada, where French and English-speaking Canadians live in a pluralistic society. An excellent example of a recently formed (1960) culturally pluralistic society is that of the Federal Republic of Nigeria, in West Africa.

Nigerian cultural pluralism. Nigeria, with a population in excess of 58 million, is very heterogeneous; it has a variety of culture groups and languages, nearly 100 of which have been recorded. The three chief languages are spoken by the country's three principal entities—the Ibo, Yoruba, and Hausa—each of which has its own customs, religion, and political organization.

For example, the Ibo, who live in southeast Nigeria, represent a combination of village groups related by a common language and culture. Their social organization is based on kinship groups, most of which practice ancestor worship and live on land containing spirit shrines. Ibo political organization is a form of democracy whose center is the village. Their religion is a combination of ancestor worship and belief in natural forces, but most Ibo have recently converted to Christianity.

Across Nigeria, the Yoruba live in southwestern Nigeria on the Guinea Coast, predominantly in large urban centers. These cities are basically communities of farmers and groups of people joined by kinship. Their political organization is stronger than that of the Ibo: they have powerful state governments, each with a king and bureaucracy. Traditional Yoruba religion had an elaborate pantheon; however, Christianity and Islam have made considerable inroads into the traditional beliefs.

In northern Nigeria live the Hausa and the pastoral Fulani peoples. The Hausa developed principles of kinship, chieftanship, and office in centralized emirates. A strong element of Islamic religion and social forms is found in Hausa society, and its members pride themselves on their unique tradition of literacy in Arabic.

In the last century, the pastoral Fulani settled in Hausaland and unseated the Hausas as the source of power in northern Nigeria. In Hausaland, many Fulani have given up their all-important cattle culture and have become assimilated into the Hausa by marriage. Unlike the Hausa, the Fulani have an egalitarian form of political organization. The Fulani are Moslems; as pastoralist nomads, they have been largely responsible for the spread of Islam in West Africa.

Thus, in Nigeria, a number of ancient, fully integrated, fully developed separate cultures are trying to exist side by side, united politically and economically into a modern republic. Although, as the recent civil war has shown, such efforts are not always acceptable to all minorities, the policy of cultural pluralism is endorsed by many of the nation's diverse peoples. Similar pluralistic arrangements, some anthropologists say, will exist around the world in the future. They see cultural pluralism as the only true feasible instrument for global equilibrium and peace.

Ethnocentrism.   An adjunct of cultural pluralism is the concept of ethnocentrism, or the belief that one's own culture is better than all others. In its natural form, ethnocentrism identifies the positive way an individual feels about his own culture; it serves to strengthen the individual's ego and his social ties to his own group. In many societies, this concept is important because it provides the individual with a world outlook and eases his social integration and adjustment as well. Ethnocentrism is stronger than patriotism or loyalty, because it assumes that every aspect of a culture—art, science, religion, politics, economics—is superior to all aspects of other cultures.

In its virulent form, ethnocentrism is a form of cultural evangelism that is often characterized by militaristic or aggressive tendencies on the part of one culture, as it tries to spread its beliefs to other cultures. Among large industrialized nations, ethnocentrism is often stretched to the point that the society may be blinded by its belief in its own "rightness." It is rationalized and made the basis for programs often detrimental to the wellbeing of other societies being influenced. This, of course, gives rise to social problems such as unrest, hostility, and even war.

Melville Herskovits believes that any culture that institutionalizes ethnocentrism is, in the end, basing its policy on a psychocultural unreality. No culture, he believes, is a commodity for export. No society can, by conquest or persuasion, influence another society to change its entire lifestyle. When such a practice is attempted, it must fail because the original culture is rarely entirely lost; some aspects of it always appear in some form.

Virulent ethnocentrism has been practiced by European countries, such as England, France, and Spain, in their colonial policies toward India, America, and Africa. The United States has also been guilty of a form of economic ethnocentrism. Interpreting through its own culture the Biblical injuction to help fellow man, the United States, convinced that its way of life is best, has attempted to spread democracy to certain so-called backward nations, by extending to them economic aid. In many cases, such aid led to the total destruction of the country's traditional cultures, resulting in power struggles and bloodshed, and the loss of economic and social welfare.

Perhaps the most memorable example of this form of ethnocentrism in recent history can be found in Nazi Germany. The Germans under Hitler thought themselves to be the master race who wished to rule the world. They wished to inflict their entire culture—art, politics, technol-

Problems of the future

It seems that a currently popular amusement is the writing and reading of apocalyptic visions of the future. We have heard how the world will end with a bang, thanks to a nuclear holocaust; and how it will end with a whimper, from the effects of too many people and too much pollution. Biologists and sociologists have predicted many changes in man's physical and social environment; what can anthropologists tell us about the way that culture can help man adapt to these changes?

Population, urbanization, and crowding

One of the most critical problems facing mankind in the future is the so-called "population explosion." We are not sure yet whether urbanization and crowding themselves are serious problems, but there can be no doubt about the urgency of the crises which accompany rapid population increase, such as famine, poverty, social unrest, and psychological stress.

Because of such factors as increased longevity, improved agricultural techniques, and advances in medicine, population has grown at a dramatically increasing rate throughout recent history. For example, in 1974, world population reached four billion, thus doubling the two billion population of 1930.

Intricately connected with this astounding proliferation of human beings is the trend toward urbanization: each year, more and more people are crowding into the world's cities, causing a crisis certain to have far reaching consequences in the future. However, urbanization is only partly the effect of population growth; even more, it is the direct result of technology and the centralization of industry. Urbanization typically accompanies a shift from an agrarian to an industrial economy. As population increases, production demand also increases, making industrial jobs

Figure 16-2. All large American cities contain pockets of immigrant cultures, such as this Spanish market in New York City.

ogy, language, religion—on the countries they conquered. Their ethnocentrism resulted in a devastating world war in which millions of people perished. Today, various degrees of institutionalized ethnocentrism can be seen in Russia, China, and other communist societies, as well as in some countries in Africa, the near east and mideast.

Although some anthropologists believe that traditional ethnocentrism may be replaced by one-world culture and cultural pluralism in the future, there can be little doubt that in the present, at least, ethnocentrism presents many problems that must be solved if mankind is to avoid further conflicts on an international scale.

more plentiful. Simultaneously, automation in agriculture reduces the need for manpower. The result is a large-scale migration from rural to urban areas, as workers seek industrial jobs.

Our minds may suffer from overpopulation and urbanization long before our stomachs do. Such consequences of overcrowding as the loss of personal space and a surfeit of face-to-face encounters can give rise to a number of negative behavioral and physiological responses.

The effects of overcrowding on animals have been extensively studied by social and natural scientists. At the very least, overcrowding among animals results in the disturbance of normal social interactions, such as courtship, mating, and maternal behavior. Usual dominant-submissive relationships cease to function, with the result that a stable group organization can no longer be maintained. At the worst, the prolonged stress of overcrowding can stimulate extreme tension and hyperactivity, culminating in death.

Konrad Lorenz has suggested in his book, *Civilized Man's Eight Mortal Sins*,[1] that the earth may become so overpopulated that man will give vent to uncontrolled aggression, much like rats do when faced with overcrowding. But unlike rats, who always leave a few members alive for future breeding, man may destroy himself totally. Of course, men are not rats; their culture conditions them to accept a variety of personal space differences. But rats in crowded conditions behave very much like people in overpopulated human communities.

On the other hand, although man may react aggressively in an overcrowded environment, the flexibility of his cultural adaption has certainly extended his tolerance for human congestion. Stanley Milgram in a study entitled, "The Experience of Living in Cities,"[2] has observed the way

[1] Konrad Lorenz *Civilized Man's Eight Mortal Sins* (Munich: Pieper Verlag, 1974).
[2] Stanley Milgram, "The Experience of Living in Cities," in *Science*, 167:141–68.

Figure 16-3a. *The European idea that objects of daily use can be regarded as art has spread to Africa; this pottery museum is one result.*

Figure 16-3b. *The Nigerian government has instituted a program of conservation of its cultural heritage.*

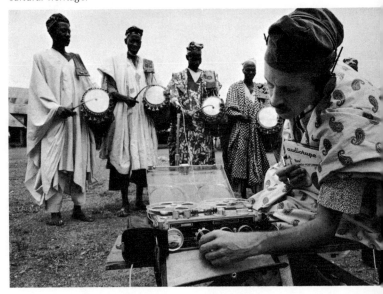

New Yorkers have adapted to their overcrowded environment. Milgram believes overcrowding, or in his word, "overload," deforms urban life on several levels: it affects role performance, the evolution of social norms, cognitive functioning, and the use of facilities. This deformation leads to a number of adaptive mechanisms which create the distinct tone of the city life.

The first of these adaptive responses to overcrowding is a cutback in the amount of time spent with each acquaintance; this enables urbanites to conserve some of their psychic energy to perform necessary daily tasks. Second, the New Yorker invests his time and energy only with a few carefully selected friends and acquaintances. Thus, although he will go out of his way to keep a lunch date with an important business associate, he casually ignores a drunk lying sick in the street. Third, overcrowding causes a shift in function in some business exchanges and social transactions. For example bus drivers used to make change for passengers. Now, however, harried bus drivers are no longer able to do so, and this function must be assumed by the passenger. Fourth, there is a loss of receptivity on the part of New Yorkers to unannounced visitors. In some small towns, any citizen can drop into the Mayor's office unannounced for a chat. In New York, some people maintain unlisted phone numbers, others keep their phones off the hook to prevent incoming calls. Another manifestation of this "superprivacy" syndrome occurs when a New Yorker assumes an unfriendly face to discourage strangers from making contact.

The fifth adaptive mechanism ensures that relationships with friends remain on an entirely superficial level and never get very intimate. Sixth, specialized institutions are created to handle situations that would swamp the individual urbanite. For example, the welfare system prevents an army of beggars from roving the city besieging individuals for alms.

Can the problem of overpopulation and crowding be solved by disbanding the city and spreading the population more evenly throughout the country, as some have suggested? Probably not,

Figure 16-4. *The fight against disease, carried on by such groups as the World Health Organization, has led to great increases in world population; this picture of a middle-class suburb in Nigeria typifies the problems of population growth and rising expectations.*

because it is not population density by itself that creates problems. Sociological studies in New York, Chicago, and Los Angeles indicate that it is not population density that causes antisocial behavior, social breakdown, or breakdown of production. These are organizational and economic problems, deriving from society's chronic inability to provide optimal services; this inability is exacerbated in densely populated areas. Such problems result from overpopulation in general, not population density. Many of the troubles of the cities are found in equal proportion in rural areas. In the cities, they are amplified, because more people are involved. Moreover, spreading the population more sparsely would necessitate the use of more valuable agricultural land for housing and commercial purposes, thus causing serious problems of food production.

Food shortage

The foremost question deriving from the burgeoning world population is simply, "How can we feed so many people?" On a worldwide scale, many think man is faced with the prospect of possible exhaustion of his traditional food resources.

Most futurologists acknowledge that man has the technological capability to increase food production. The big question is: will he be able to do so? There have been major advances in agriculture and livestock breeding: powerful fertilizers, improved irrigation, genetical advances to yield bigger and better crops and animals, along with sea-harvesting techniques and even the chemical production of artificial foods. All of these developments augur the probability that man will be able to produce more food in the future. Some problems do exist. More intensive agriculture relies on one-crop cultivation; this increases the possibility that insects or diseases can decimate the crop. Moreover, the increased use of pesticides is producing genetically resistant species, larger and hardier. It remains debatable whether or not food supplies can be increased

fast enough to keep up with population growth.

All his technological advances will be useless if man cannot change his cultural preferences for certain kinds of food. It is, and will continue to be, difficult to change the eating habits of people. For example, in America, one of the world's largest producers of soybeans, most people refuse to eat soybeans and prefer beef instead. Soybeans are just as nutritional as beef; they are better for the health in that they contain less fats and cholestoral; they are much less expensive; and they are easier to grow. Further, an acre of land can feed many more people—about 50 times as many—if it is planted with soybeans rather than being used to graze cattle. In many East African societies, where cattle are considered a form of wealth rather than food, people live off such nutritional foods as ant larvae, insect grubs and locusts. Most Americans would find this type of food repulsive; nevertheless, like soybeans, such food is readily available in America.

On the other hand, many societies think that any food that comes from a can is unfit for human consumption. Totemic and religious taboos also affect the kinds of food people will eat. Beef is disgusting to Hindus, and pork is sinful to Mohammedans and Jews. If an individual of certain non-Western societies unwittingly eats his totemic animal, psychological vomiting may result when he discovers what he has done.

Another example of the difficulty of changing eating habits can be seen in the experiences of some American aid programs to countries with severe food shortages. The United States sent wheat to several countries—notably India—with severe food shortages. Wheat, especially American wheat, is very high in protein, higher than the poor grade of rice these people had subsisted on. But the people, who were accustomed to eating rice for centuries, had no idea how to prepare wheat and did not like its taste. Many Indians died of starvation because they were unable to switch to wheat as a substitute for rice.

This example also points to the importance of anthropology in helping solve some of the world's problems. If members of the American

Figure 16-5. *Technological advances, such as the development of harvesting machines, allow increased crop yield.*

foreign aid program had consulted qualified anthropologists, such an error would not have occurred; anthropologists would have been familiar with the eating habits of the people who were receiving the food and would have recommended another kind of food, or perhaps a program that taught Indians how to cook and eat wheat. Although it raises serious ethical problems, future anthropologists may be faced with the task of trying to change peoples' cultural tastes and customs to enable their survival. In this country, for example, anthropologists may have the exceedingly difficult task of advising the government about how to convince consumers that synthetic foods developed from single-cell organisms cultured on petroleum are nourishing.

Birth control

The primary method of meeting the population problem and the food crisis is to reduce the birth rate. The development of effective birth control methods has made this possible as never before; but whether or not these methods will be utilized on a vast enough scale depends on availability and cultural acceptance. Zero population growth goals have been adopted in many countries, and programs for dissemination of birth control information have been developed.

However, in many societies, the chief problem is to convince individuals to use birth control devices and techniques. Many of the world's peoples adhere to cultural customs and beliefs which are totally antipathetic to the idea of birth control. For example, among the Kipsigis, a cattle-breeding people of East Africa, one of the primary duties of the young warrior is to enrich the tribe by begetting many children. In some societies, the number of children an individual has is a sign of prestige; if a man does not produce many children, he is looked down upon and thought a weakling. In other societies, particularly in the mideast, motherhood and fatherhood are respected and desirable institutions. A male is not thought of as a man nor a female a woman unless they bear a large number of children. Moreover, it is extremely difficult to convince a farmer to limit the size of his family when large families have been traditionally necessary to help with the great amount of manual labor agriculture requires. The problem is compounded by the fact that minorities often view birth control programs as subtle plots by the majority to diminish their numbers.

Perhaps the solution to the problem of birth control will be brought about indirectly with the application of some other technological advance. For example, in parts of India, the introduction of electricity into some rural areas has been a more effective means of birth control than any of the devices and information offered by the government agencies. Apparently lighting gave the inhabitants of these areas other leisure time activities to engage in after dark. This connection is strengthened by the case of the events in New York City in 1965, when a power failure that crippled the city overnight caused an upsurge in births nine months later.

Pollution

Only recently has man come to realize the potentially disastrous consequences of overpopulation and unchecked industrialization on the environment for which humanity is completely dependent for life. Pollution has become a direct threat to human health—in the air we breathe, in the water we drink, in the food we eat. Less direct, but potentially as dangerous, are those pollutants, such as chemical pesticides and inorganic nitrogen fertilizers, that may upset the earth's fragile ecosystems.

Modern man knows the causes of pollution, and he realizes it is a danger to his future survival. Why then, can he not control this evil by which he fouls his own nest? The answer lies perhaps in his philosophical and theological traditions. As we saw in Chapter 12, Western industrialized so-

Figure 16-6. *Man continues to look for cultural adaptations that will permit him to extend his range and live in new environments. The National Aeronautics and Space Administration sponsored this research project in which small teams lived underwater for extended periods; it was designed to test man's ability to adapt to an environment of high stress. The technological problems of such a life are easier to solve than the social and emotional ones.*

Change and the future ● part **5**

cieties, using the Bible as a guide, believe that they have dominion over all the creatures of the earth and all that grows and lives on it. This exploitative world view characteristic of civilization extends to all natural resources. Only when it has been of any advantage to him has Western man protected or replaced what his greed and acquisitiveness have prompted him to take from his environment. In recent years, recognizing the seriousness of the environmental crisis man was creating for himself, authorities have been forced to pass laws against such activities as hunting whales out of existence, dumping toxic wastes into streams and rivers, and poisoning the air with carbon monoxide fumes.

Members of many other societies see their environment in more symbiotic terms. They feel that the land and the forests are full of gods and ghosts who hold great power over them. Such people believe there is a special totemic relationship between themselves and their environment, including animals, plants, and natural forces. This kind of world view is particularly characteristic of hunter-gatherers. Hunters, for example, regard their game with respect, since their welfare depends on the animals. One avoids offending the animals, especially when their strength or cleverness make them dangerous. Among the Tupians and other South American tribes, the concept of the "Lord of the Game Animals" is common. After the hunt, the Gaboon Pygmies implore the slain "Father Elephant" not to avenge himself on his killers, and many tribes in the woodlands address the bear politely and apologetically before attacking him. The Ainu of Japan capture bear cubs and raise them for a year or two; they then kill and eat the animals during a special ceremony. They hope that the bear soul will return loaded with gifts to his master, the "Old Man of the Mountains" and convey to him man's wishes.

Among some agricultural people, plants are at the center of many totemic beliefs. For example, the Lamet, a tribe in Indochina, believe the soul of the rice is a kind of fluid that gradually collects at harvest time in a specific, consecrated part of the field; the crops harvested on that spot are used for sowing the following spring. The plant soul is also frequently visualized in animal or human form. Thus, the Indians in Peru believe in a Maize Mother and a Potato Mother. Similarly, in Indonesia, a Rice Mother is venerated, while the Grain Mother is likewise honored in parts of Europe.

Moreover, many non-Western societies stand in awe of natural forces, bestowing on them a special place in their religious system. For example, many people believe that rushing rapids, storms, the mountains and the jungles possess awful powers. This is also true of fire, which warms and destroys. For farmers, the sun, rain and thunder are important to their existence and are therefore often considered divine. Such world views prohibit the kind of environmental manipulation that causes severe pollution.

Figure 16-7. *In an effort to check the rapid rise in the population growth rate, many governments are sponsoring birth control programs; the Indian woman holds an IUD.*

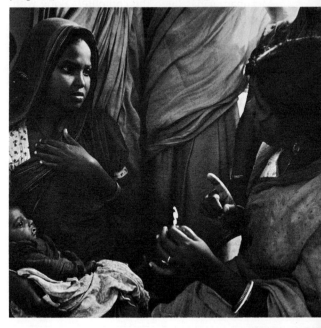

Scientific and technological expansion

If the future looks singularly bleak from the point of view of the social scientist, many physical scientists and medical researchers are relatively optimistic. Emmanuel Mesthene, director of the Harvard Program in Science and Technology, has summarized the reasons for this optimism:

> We have now, or know how to acquire, the technical capacity to do very nearly everything we want. Can we transplant human hearts, control personality, order the weather that suits us, travel to Mars or Venus? Of course we can. If not now or in five or ten years, then certainly in 25 or 50 or 100.

As knowledge in all areas grows, and technological society becomes increasingly complex, societies come more and more to rely on computers. According to futurologist Marshall McLuhan, it has been the computer, along with television, that has been responsible for what he calls "the Electronic Age" in which we now live. McLuhan's basic belief is that the form of communication drastically affects what is being communicated; similarly, the sensory apparatus alters the information it receives. Hence, McLuhan says, "the medium is the message."

Formerly, before the invention of typography and printing, man lived in a collective "tribal" world where his oral and aural orientation enabled him to perceive and experience many things at one time. In his small tightly-knit world, there was no written word, and man depended heavily on his ears to receive information about the world around him. His whole world of knowledge was contained in the "tribal encyclopedia"—a body of myths, religious tenets, moral and civil laws that was passed on by word of mouth by each generation. With the invention of printing, which is characterized by uniformity, continuity, and lineality, man was forced into a

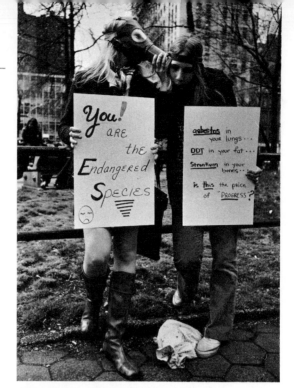

Figure 16-8. *Two girls dramatize the problems of pollution. Yet many experts point out that pollution is only a resource in the wrong place; there may be constructive uses, such as the use of garbage for landfill.*

visual, sequentially logical way of perceiving and thinking. In his tribal state, man was accustomed to perceiving groups or patterns of sounds rather than one sound at a time. Unlike the man in the tribal society who heard and experienced many things simultaneously, visual man, accustomed to focussing his attention on specialized segments (letters and words), saw and perceived only one thing at a time. Such a way of organizing reality resulted in isolated individualism and contributed to the mechanical or industrial age where the environment (machines) was arranged in a series of lineally connected fragments, each following the other in orderly fashion like words on the printed page. Mechanization, then, was the fragmentation of a product or entity, followed by putting forth each of these fragments in a series. Thus the symbols of the mechanical age are the nut, bolt, wheel, gear and assembly line.

According to McLuhan, with the advent of the computer and television, man entered the electronic age and became tribal once more. Tribal man perceived patterns or groups of sounds as part of the entire whole or sentence. Now electronic technology has created an entirely new environment in which the old linear method of fragmentation and classification have yielded to computer methods where pattern recognition, or seeing relationships as part of an entire whole are once again important. With television, man becomes involved in the entire world and experiences more than one thing at a time. In effect, he is tribalized again; the electronic speed of computers and television causes everything to happen simultaneously, by compressing space and time. Man can experience a battle in the jungle of Vietnam, an election in Paris, a baseball game in Chicago, a strike in Tokyo, or a landing on the moon as soon as it happens via television. Television also provides the high involvement the tribe used to provide; it brings together men so they share experience collectively, not individually. The world has become, in McLuhan's words, "a global village," in which electronic speed brings all political and social functions together, impelling commitment and participation.

The work of the future

There can be no doubt that the role of the anthropologist is changing. The time is long past when the anthropologist could go out and describe small tribal groups, in out of the way places, which had not been "contaminated" by contact with Westerners. There are few such groups in the world today. Indeed, many classic ethnographies dealt with societies more affected by contact with Westerners than previously thought.

The disappearing past

At the same time that societies with which anthropologists have been traditionally concerned are fast disappearing, the need for information about them has become steadily more apparent. If we are ever to have a realistic understanding of that elusive thing called "human nature," we need lots of good data on all humans. We are confronted, then, with an urgent job of salvage. In spite of the fact that the societies traditionally studied by anthropologists are rapidly disappearing, anthropologists will continue to be concerned with them, gathering whatever data can still be obtained.

The need for salvage applies to archeological, as well as ethnological, data. Here, we are not confronted with societies which are rapidly being Westernized; rather, we are dealing with the remains of societies which are being drowned in reservoirs, covered by parking lots for shopping centers, or just plain bulldozed into oblivion. Archeological sites are being lost at an alarming rate, and this is a critical problem for two reasons. First, they are nonrenewable; second, they provide the essential data needed by anthropologists to understand the process of change over extended periods of time.

The archeological problem is not one of earthmoving alone. The last decade has seen the spectacular rise of an illicit international traffic in antiquities. So it is, for example, that ancient Maya monuments in the forests of Guatemala are broken up, smuggled out of the country, and reassembled to be purchased by art dealers and museums. Not only have prize pieces of Maya sculpture been destroyed, there has also been at least one murder connected with these operations. Although a number of museums and governments have acted to discourage such purchases, not nearly enough has been done to stem the flow of the illegal antiquities traffic.

Important though archeological and ethnological salvage work may be, anthropologists, as they must, are concerning themselves with the longer range future and are opening up new fields of research. More and more anthropologists are turning their attentions to studies of modernization, the process by which traditional, non-Western societies adopt such features as state governments, nationalism, and integration into industrial economies. This is a logical outcome of the traditional anthropological concern with the non-Western world, and it obviously involves anthropologists with problems of immediate concern. Some of these are: How should the so-called underdeveloped nations develop? What will be the effect of development on traditional ways? What traditional ways are worth preserving? How can this be done? How can a desired change be introduced into a traditional community with some chance of success?

Anthropologists are also becoming more concerned with the study of minority groups in their own countries. In part, this stems from the civil rights and related movements which became prominent in the United States in the 1960s. These created a new awareness of the problems of ethnic and other minorities. To a degree, such studies have brought anthropologists into an area of research which previously was the domain of sociologists. This opens up a new fruitful area for cooperation between the two fields, for the ethnographic techniques of the anthropologists offer a valuable supplement to the more traditional sociological techniques of census taking and administration of questionnaires.

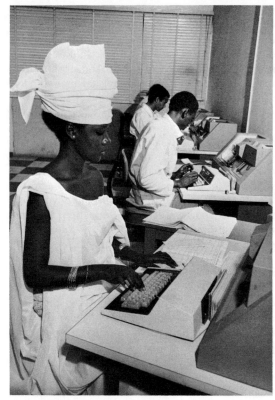

Figure 16-9. *Many suspect that the widespread use of the computer will change not just man's technology but also his world view. These users work for Senegal's Ministry of Finance.*

Questions of ethics

The kinds of research outlined above raise a number of important questions concerning the ethics of scientific research. Who will make use of the findings of anthropologists, and for what purposes? In the case of a militant minority, for example, will others use anthropological data to suppress that minority? And what of traditional communities around the world—who is to decide what changes should, or should not, be introduced for community "betterment"? By whose definition is it "betterment," the community's or

Change and the future ● part **5**

that of a remote national government? Not surprisingly, because of these and other questions, there has been a hot debate among anthropologists over the past decade on the subject of ethics. In 1967, the American Anthropological Association adopted a statement on problems of anthropological research and ethics. Among other things, this expressed concern about conditions that might threaten the ability of anthropology to contribute to the general interests of human welfare. What concerned the anthropologists was that their research findings might be used as a basis for policy formation, and that this policy might be to the detriment of the group from which those findings came.

This question has not always been a primary worry for anthropologists, although the anthropologists of the nineteenth and early twentieth centuries in the United States almost all felt a personal obligation to the people whom they studied. This sometimes involved them in fighting court battles on behalf of their informants, often at their personal expense.

In World War II, anthropologists were in great demand by the United States government, largely because of their familiarity with foreign cultures and the places where war operations were taking place. The anthropologists responded by preparing manuals for the troops, interpreting cultures for various agencies, and formulating policies for occupied areas. Perhaps the best-known by-product of these wartime activities was Ruth Benedict's *The Chrysanthemum and the Sword* (1946), an analysis of Japanese national character based on second-hand sources. Similar studies were made by Geoffrey Gorer and Weston LaBarre. Many of the conclusions of these studies have not stood up in the face of closer scrutiny based on first-hand observation.

Some of this wartime anthropological work was amazingly sound, but was not always listened to. A case in point is the work of the Foreign Morale Analysis Division of the Office of War Information. Headed up by an anthropologist-psychiatrist, it included several other anthropologists as well as psychiatrists and sociologists. This group correctly analyzed the deteriorating morale of Japanese soldiers and civilians as early as late 1944. Because it conflicted with the prevailing military view, it was largely ignored. In early 1945 the Division predicted a major blowup in Japan and, by spring, predicted a Japanese surrender between July and September 1945. Again they were ignored, but later it was learned that the Japanese, in May, 1945, before the atomic bombs were dropped, made a decision to surrender before November.

The current issue that has made anthropologists reexamine the ethics of their ties to the government was Project Camelot. This was a vast research project planned by the Department of Defense to find out the causes of social unrest leading to armed insurgency. From this data, ways of averting or suppressing armed rebellions could be found. Social scientists would thus be involved in the intervention of the United States government in the internal affairs of other nations. Project Camelot was cancelled while still in the planning stages. Anthropologists had reacted vigorously, both because other nations might react by refusing to allow United States anthropologists to conduct any research within their borders, and because of the larger ethical issues involved. The traditional concern of the anthropologist for the welfare of the people he studies, as *they* see it, has been reawakened.

☐

CULTURE AND ADAPTATION

The intense crisis that threatens the world we live in seems to have come upon us so suddenly that it is understandable that we frantically search for immoralists to blame or scapegoats to sacrifice. When we were children and when some of us were young adults, we saw a disturbed world before us, but at that time the malady was focused so that it seemed to be the result of human error—we could still blame individuals, specific leaders, specific peoples. There was little to indicate to us, in our innocence, that civilization itself was threatened—that we were witness not merely to human moral weakness and error, but to an overwhelming evolutionary process. Yet today we know that civilization is threatened—threatened by itself.

But which civilization? We must repeatedly ask what civilization itself is. Not just our civilization, but civilization as a process: what it provides for us and what its future may be. To examine the crises of civilization one must go back to the idea of culture, and man's use of culture as his device for adapting to the world he lives in. Culture is the technical term, coined by anthropologists in the nineteenth century, to refer to the "artificial" extensions of the human being that allow him greater control over his own environment, over his social system, and ultimately, over himself. Culture is, to make an analogy, what the medical men call a prosthesis—an extension of the animal that makes it possible for him to do things he could not otherwise do. Artificial limbs, false teeth, and eyeglasses are common prostheses in the modern world. But by analogy all of culture can be seen as the prosthesis of the human being—an animal who specialized in brain and central nervous system and developed, through their use, extensions of himself that allowed him to remain an otherwise non-specialized animal, without built-in fighting equipment such as claws or horns or canine teeth; protective devices such as fur, natural camouflage, or fleetness; indeed, without any other form of physical specialization to give him any great advantages toward survival.

Culture, in other words, comprises all the things and devices—including the nonmaterial, such as myths and beliefs and stories—that human beings create to enhance, protect, or express themselves. Culture has, in the course of evolution, become the peculiar (but not unique) property of human beings, and human specialization in culture (like the specialization of tigers in saber teeth or of giraffes in long necks) has been the means by which man has survived and aggrandized himself on the planet. By it he must survive or perish.

Today we know that culture is a two-edged sword. The very while that it allows us to express ourselves more fully, to explore social organization more broadly, and to master our environment more thoroughly, it creates situations of alienation, tyranny, and ecological imbalance. It seems an irony when we realize that only by cultural means can man overcome the evil effects of culture and yet retain the good effects. Once he has started on this road man must learn more about how to get from himself the best and most enjoyable of lives; he must learn more about human social organization and how to control it without what we see as immoralities, even when we do them; and he must learn more about the physical world in which he lives so that his accomplishments will not so alter the earth as to make it uninhabitable.

Man, through several million years of evolution, is committed to living as a cultural being. Only in the last few decades have we realized that culture must be controlled by man himself, and his evolution altered to special kinds of cultural activities, if he is not to become extinct from overspecialization—from blind overspecialization in culture. There is, at this stage of the game, literally no answer except to treat the blindness, to have the courage to see.

The source of the human (and hence cultural) problem is an irony—man is born an *individual, social* animal. In that contradiction lies the basis of our neuroses, our social problems, our moralities. Since intelligence is brought to the survival of both the individual organism and the species, it is possible for the individual to act in what seem to be his own interests at the very time he is acting against the interests of the species. It is this irony that every society must, with one degree or another of success, organize itself to deal with.

But even the organization is ironic, for no two intelligences see it quite the same way. Since man is a social animal and has opted for a cultural mode of self-preservation, all human social groups consist of parties (sometimes individuals, sometimes small groups) interacting in terms of the available culture. Each social group—from the family to the nation, indeed, from the marriage or the mother-child relationship to the United Nations—has a cultural tradition. That tradition changes as new cultural items are invented by members of the group, or as members of the group come into contact with other people whose repertoires of cultural items are different from their own. Therefore, culture is not only handed on from generation to generation, it is also handed "sideways" from one social group to the next. In today's world, we live in a culturally privileged time because items from so many different cultural traditions are available to large numbers of people—indeed, prosperity can in one sense be gauged by the kind and amount of human culture available to a group. But so, obviously, can the potential for disaster. Culture grows as the group flourishes, and the group grows in size as culture flourishes. And then, suddenly—at least it always seems sudden—there is a vast disparity between the capacities of the available culture and the group it serves. The culture that was adequate for yesterday is inadequate for today and disastrous for tomorrow. If there is a law of culture, that is it.

And so it has always been. But today our ironic harvest seems particularly bitter because there is so much *good* culture, judged by our own inward awareness of what is good for us. And, worse, the bad culture is an epiphenomenon, or so its seems. Slowly we must realize that the problem of evil is with us again. In Roy Rappaport's words, it takes the form of the "evolution of maladaptation."

Actually, of course, the problem of evil was never absent, but for a while evil seemed to be attached to individuals, to institutions. And now, again, we see it as the other side of our natures—all our natures. In spite of villains, I too have an evil dimension. Existing culturally creates evil. Culture is, indeed, as the Genesis myth puts it, the knowledge of good and evil. We were thrown out of the garden we wish had once existed into a hell we wish did not.

For the dynamics of culture work in ways that are beyond the purposes of men, whatever they may be. Culture becomes something in itself, something beyond man. Ultimately, it becomes, in the inspired phrase of Jules Henry, culture against man. One's own prostheses turn on one's very self. That is the price one must always pay for prostheses, medicines, drugs, or even love.

When a small group of human beings adapts and successfully adjusts to its environment, the group survives. If its adaptation is unsuccessful, the group perishes: to survive, its members change and adapt in different groups, or they too will perish. If the cultural adaptation is successful, then the group is safe, its members perhaps comfortable. In response to the animality in us and to thousands of millions of years of evolution, the group, in its comfort, grows larger. As the group grows larger the available culture is "stretched"—it is like putting water in the soup to feed unexpected guests. Such diluted culture does not serve as it once did; the situation is no longer that for which it was designed and in accordance with which it evolved.

Three things can happen when culture is stretched too far: the population growth can be checked, either by a natural disaster of some sort or by a population policy; the group can break into two or more groups that separate, and each of them can begin again the process of achieving first optimum, then maximum, and finally destructive growth; the third choice is to invent new culture—new ways of coping with the environment, new ways of dealing with each other, of experiencing the human animalness of us.

Obviously, only those groups that choose the last way survive in the long run. Breaking into several groups, cell-fashion, works only so long as the ecological carrying capacity of the world is not seriously affected.

Thus the real problem arises because man is clever and can devise ways and means of beating the system—for short periods of time. The use of fire, the use of metals, the use of more complex hierarchies to achieve larger social organizations, all of these cultural discoveries and many others have allowed larger populations to survive and multiply, outgrowing the culture that spawned them, and in a sort of cultural Malthusianism, creating worse problems than they solved. Worse because so many more people are involved, and because they are more helpless the further they are removed from a simple ecological position in nature: man as a hunter and gatherer was just another animal.

Source:
Paul Bohannan, "Beyond Civilization,"
Natural History Special Supplement, February, 1971.

Summary

1.

Some anthropologists believe that the future world will be homogenized into a single culture. Rapid developments in communication, transportation, and trade link the great majority of today's people. These developments gave rise to the idea of a "one-world culture." Many anthropologists believe a "one-world culture" would lack richness, variety, and the adaptability to handle a future crisis. Other anthropologists believe that certain cultures may be too specialized to survive in the future. Therefore, they find a generalized culture preferable to diverse cultures.

2.

Cultural pluralism is another possibility for man's future. Cultural pluralism is the social and political interaction within the same society of people with different ways of living and thinking. In its purest form, cultural pluralism rejects bigotry, bias, and racism and recognizes the cultural traditions of other people. Ethnocentrism, an adjunct of cultural pluralism, is the belief that one's own race or culture is better than all others. In its natural form, ethnocentrism identifies the positive way an individual feels about his culture. In its virulent form, it can lead to militaristic or aggressive behavior during attempts of one culture to spread its beliefs to other cultures.

3.

In the future, the "population explosion" will be one of man's most critical problems. A declining death rate, improved agricultural techniques, and advances in medicine have spurred rapid population growth. Urbanization has accompanied this growth. Urbanization is the direct result of tecnology and the centralization of industry. As population increases, production demand increases, making industrial jobs more plentiful; agricultural automation reduces the demand for farm workers. The result is large-scale migration from rural to urban areas.

4.

Overcrowding and food shortages have also accompanied population growth. Overcrowding causes a loss of personal space and too many face-to-face encounters. Such conditions can give rise to negative behavioral and physiological responses. Most futurologists believe that man has the technological capability to meet the nutritional needs of the future. This capability will prove useless unless man changes the cultural preferences of the world's peoples. A people's eating habits often exclude food that is plentiful and demand that which is scarce.

5.

The primary method of meeting the population problem is to reduce the birthrate. Effective birth control methods are now available. Whether or not these methods are used on a vast enough scale depends on their availability and acceptance. Many of the world's peoples adhere to cultural customs and beliefs that reject the idea of birth control.

6.

Pollution has become a direct threat to human health. Western man has protected his environment only when it was immediately advantageous to do so; he has felt no responsibilities toward the earth or its resources. Western man could learn much from non-Western societies which recognize themselves as integral parts of the earth.

7.

Marshall McLuhan believes that computers and television are making modern man tribal like early man. The electronic speed of computers and television compresses time and space, causing everything to happen simultaneously. All political and social functions are brought together, impelling participation. Modern man sees relationships as part of a whole and becomes highly involved just as early man did.

8.

The changing role of the anthropologist brings with it the need for careful ethical evaluation of any proposed project. A major concern is the welfare of the people who are subjects of anthropological studies.

Suggested readings

Alland, Alexander, Jr. *Human Diversity*. New York: Columbia University Press, 1971.
Chapter 5 of this book, "Of Mice and Men: Behavioral Genetics and Human Variation" traces the implications of certain kinds of cultural change for man's biological future. Working from the supposition that man is relatively free of behavioral programming, the author examines one way this freedom has enabled man to cope with diverse environments and how these environments in turn have shaped him both culturally and biologically.

Kahn, Herman and Anthony J. Wiener *The Year 2000*. New York: The Macmillan Company, 1967.
To an anthropologist, the most interesting chapter of this book is Chapter 6, "Some Canonical Variations from the Standard World." It projects a number of possible cultural futures, including both a world of greater integration and one of greater disarray. Although there is much emphasis on technological factors throughout the book, this chapter focuses squarely on cultural alternatives.

McHale, John *The Future of the Future*. New York: George Braziller, Inc., 1969.
McHale's thesis is that the future of the future is in the present. Therefore much of his book is devoted to an analysis of present conditions, with a special emphasis on technological aspects of modern industrial culture. From this analysis, McHale then selects certain aspects that seem to foreshadow the future.

Photo Credits

Chapter one

Chapter two

Chapter fourteen

Chapter fifteen

Chapter sixteen

Glossary

acculturation – the process that occurs when members of one society are brought into prolonged contact with another society and one group acquires cultural elements of the other group.

adaptation – the possession of anatomical, physiological, and behavioral characteristics that permit organisms to survive in the special environmental conditions in which they are generally found.

age category – a generalized role disposition determined by age.

age-class – a collection of people occupying an age-grade.

age-grade – category of persons who fall within a particular, culturally distinguished, age range.

age-set – a group of persons initiated into an age-grade together who move through life's stages together.

akua´ba – dolls made by the Ashanti of Ghana.

allomorphs – two varieties of the same morpheme occurring in different contexts but with no difference in meaning; a term in linguistics.

allophones – in linguistics, two different pronunciations of a sound having the same meaning.

animatism – a religious concept of impersonal power.

animism – a term used by Edward Tylor to describe a religious belief in personal spirits which are thought to animate nature.

anthropoids – higher primates; monkeys, apes, and man.

anthropology – the systematic study of man and his works, past and present.

apartheid – a policy of segregation and discrimination against non-European groups in South Africa.

archeology – the study of extinct cultures through the recovery of their material remains.

Australopithecus – a fossil with a mixture of simian and hominid characteristics; two species: *A. robustus* and *A. africanus*. A true hominid.

balanced reciprocity – refers to an exchange in which the giving and the receiving is specific as to goods and time.

band – a small group of related people occupying a single region.

berdache – an institutional arrangement among the Plains Indians in which a man may assume women's attire, perform women's work, and even marry another man.

bilateral descent – a system in which a person relates to close relatives on both the mother's and the father's side.

bilocal residence – a pattern in which a married couple have the choice of living with either the relatives of the wife or the husband.

bound morpheme – a sound which can only occur in a language in combination with other sounds, as *s* in English to signify the plural.

capital – any resource that is not used up in the process of producing goods.

Cargo cult – a religious belief in Melanesia that a deluge will engulf all the whites, following which a ship will arrive laden with European goods.

caste – a special form of social class in which membership is determined by birth and remains fixed; the group is ranked in a hierarchy of groups in the system.

chiefdom – a ranked society in which every member has a position in the hierarchy.

clan – a noncorporate descent group with each member claiming descent from a common ancestor without actually being able to trace descent genealogically through known links.

class – a division of a society into groups which are ranked and have an unequal share of power, prestige, and worldly goods.

cognatic descent – a system of descent in which the individual has the option of affiliating with either the mother's or the father's side.

consanguine family – a family consisting of a woman and her brothers and the offspring of the woman.

conspicuous consumption – a term coined by Thorstein Veblen to describe a display of wealth for social prestige.

couvade – religious ritual in which the husband, following the birth of a baby, takes on the symptoms of postnatal illness and disability, while the wife goes about her usual daily routine.

Cro-Magnons – the first modern men.

cultural anthropology – the study of man as the animal of culture.

cultural ecology – the interaction of specific cultures with their environment.

cultural focus – an emphasis on a particular area of cultural activity.

cultural materialism – an approach to anthropology which studies the manner in which a culture adapts to its environment.

cultural preadaptations – characteristics within a culture that allow the group to survive in a different environment.

cultural relativism – the thesis that a culture be evaluated according to its own standards and values.

culture area – a geographic region where a number of different societies follow a similar pattern of life.

culture type – a relationship of a particular cultural technology to the environment exploited by that technology.

deep structure – in the theoretical linguistics of Noam Chomsky, a term based on the habits, conventions, and social adaptations of a culture on which a language is based.

descriptive linguistics – a study of language concerned with registering and explaining all the features of a language at one point in history.

diffusion – a process by which culture traits or elements are borrowed from another culture as the result of contact, for example, trade.

diffusionism – the thesis that all cultures share a common origin.

divination – a process of trying to contact the supernatural to foretell future events.

double descent – descent established matrilineally for some purposes and patrilineally for others.

ecology – the study of the relationships between organisms and their environment.

ecosystem – an ecologists' term referring to a system composed of both the physical environment and the organisms living within it.

egalitarian society – one in which as many positions for prestige exist as there are persons capable of filling them.

enculturation – the process by which culture is transmitted from one generation to another in a society.

endogamy – the practice of marriage within a group of related individuals.

epics – long legends in oral tradition, sometimes in poetry or rhythmic prose that may last for several hours or even days.

erosi – a guardian spirit with political power among the Afkibo of Nigeria.

ethnocentrism – the belief that one's own culture is best.

ethnology – the study of contemporary cultures.

ethnomusicology – the study of music in a specific cultural setting.

ethnosemantics – an approach to anthropology which seeks to arrive at a description of a culture as a member of that culture sees it.

exogamy – the practice of marriage outside the group.

extended family – a collection of nuclear families, related by ties of blood, which live together

field linguistics – collecting raw data from speakers of a language, analyzing and describing it; primarily a descriptive process.

folklore – a nineteenth century term first used to refer to the oral traditions of the European peasant, later extended to those of all rural peoples.

formalism – a school of thought which holds that the principles of economics are general enough to be applied usefully to all societies.

form classes – in linguistics, the parts of speech or categories of words that work the same way in all sentences.

fossil – the preserved remains of plants and animals that lived in the past.

free morpheme – in linguistics, a sound which has meaning and can occur unattached to another sound.

functionalism – a theory which explains culture and traits on the basis of their role in maintaining the integrity of the society.

generalized exchange – sharing without the expectation of a direct return.

generalized reciprocity – an exchange in which neither the value of the gift is calculated nor the time of repayment specified.

generative transformational grammar – Noam Chomsky's theory of linguistics.

glottochronology – a method of dating divergence in branches of language families in linguistics.

grammar – in linguistics, the rules by which sounds are combined in a language to make meaningful statements.

historical linguistics – the study of language which investigates relationships between earlier and later forms of the same language.

historical particularism – the thesis that each culture is unique and that similarities between cultures are best explained by cultural exchange.

hominid – belonging to the family of man.

Homo erectus – earliest known members of the genus *Homo,* in the direct line of descent of *Homo sapiens.*

Homo sapiens – modern man.

horticulture – plant cultivation carried out with relatively simple tools.

hunter-gatherers – peoples who subsist on the collection of plants and animals which occur in nature.

hypothesis – a tentative assumption of the relationship between certain phenomena.

ideational order – pertains to the symbols of a culture.

incest taboo – the prohibition of sexual relations between parent and child, or siblings.

independent invention – a process whereby cultures develop similar features without cultural exchange.

informant – a member of a society being studied with whom the anthropologist can communicate in a common language to learn the language and culture of the society.

integration – the tendency for all aspects of a culture to function as an interrelated whole.

kanaga – a variety of mask fashioned by the Dogon of Africa.

katanda – a small wooden sculpture found among the Balega in Africa.

kindred – a circle of the maternal and paternal relatives of a specific individual.

Kula ring – a trading system among the Trobriand Islanders first described by Malinowski.

kulturkreise school – a German school of anthropology which held that culture originated in several culture circles.

legends – semihistorical narratives that account for the deeds of heroes, the movements of peoples, and the establishment of local customs.

levirate – the custom that a widow marry one of the brothers of her dead husband.

lineage – a corporate group who claim descent from a common ancestor and can trace genealogy through known links to that ancestor.

linguistics – the study of language.

magic – an attempt to manipulate certain perceived laws of nature.

mana – a powerful force among the Melanesians, inherent in all objects.

matrilineal descent – descent traced through the female line for purposes of group membership.

matrilocal residence – a pattern in which a man lives in the locality associated with his wife's relatives.

Mesolithic – the Middle Stone Age, occurring about 12,000 years ago.

moiety – a group which results from a division of a society into two halves on the basis of descent.

monogamy – the taking of a single spouse in marriage.

morphemes – in linguistics, the smallest units of sounds that have a meaning.

myth – a religious narrative which explains ultimate questions of human existence.

natural selection – the evolutionary process through which factors in the environment exert a pressure that favors some individuals over others to reproduce the next generation.

Neanderthal man – early representative of *Homo sapiens;* a true man.

negative reciprocity – a form of gift giving in which the giver tries to get the better of the exchange.

neo-evolutionism – an anthropological school of thought which seeks a revival of the search for universal laws of culture and cultural development.

Neolithic – the New Stone Age; marked the transition from hunting-gathering to a food-producing economy.

neolocal residence – a pattern in which a married couple form a household in an independent location.

nomadism – having no fixed place of residence.

norm – a cultural value governing behavior.

nuclear family – a family unit consisting of a mother, father, and dependent children.

Paleolithic – the Old Stone Age, characterized by chipped stone tools.

parallel evolution – the development of similar adaptations to similar ecological conditions.

pastoralism – a subsistence pattern in which food production is based largely upon the maintenance of herds of animals.

patrilineal descent – descent traced through the male line for purposes of group membership.

patrilocal residence – a pattern in which the woman goes to live with her husband in the locality associated with his father's relatives.

phenomenal order – that which can be actually observed by the anthropologist.

phonemes – in linguistics, the sounds that make a difference in meaning.

phratry – a unilineal descent group composed of two or more clans which claim to be related by kinship. If there are only two such groups, each is a moiety.

physical anthropology – the study of man as a biological organism.

plural society – a society in which there exists a diversity of cultural patterns and social frameworks.

polyandry – the marriage custom of a woman having several husbands; a form of polygamy.

polygamy – marriage to more than one spouse simultaneously.

polygyny – the marriage custom of a man having several wives; a form of polygamy.

rank society – a society which limits its positions of prestige without affecting the access of the other members to the basic resources of life.

reciprocity – a transaction between groups within a community in the form of gifts and counter gifts prescribed by ritual and ceremony.

redemptive movements – religious movements with the purpose of transforming the individual.

redistribution – a form of exchange in which goods flow into a central place, such as a market, and are distributed again.

revitalization movements – social movements of a religious nature with the purpose of a total reformation of the society.

rites of passage – religious ceremonies which mark important changes in the status of individuals, such as birth, marriage, and death.

segmentary lineage system – a form of political organization in which a larger group is broken up into clans, which are segmented into lineages.

serial marriage – a form in which a man or a woman marries or lives with a series of partners in succession.

shaman – a person who has special religious power acquired through his own initiative and perhaps possesses certain special gifts such as healing or divination.

sib – see clan.

sign – a sound or gesture which has a natural or biological meaning.

silent trade – a form of barter in which no verbal communication takes place.

social organization – same as social structure. The relationships that bind individuals together in a society.

social stratification – the ranking of people by socioeconomic class.

social structure – the relationships which hold a society together.

society – a group of people occupying the same territory, speaking the same language, and sharing the same cultural traditions.

sociolinguistics – a discipline concerned with the structure and use of language as it relates to society, culture, and human behavior.

sorcery – deliberate actions undertaken for the purpose of doing specific harm.

sororate – the custom that a widower marry the sister of his dead wife.

status – position in a society. May be ranked or unranked.

stratified society – a society in which members do not have equal access to the basic resources which support life nor to social prestige.

structuralism – a theory of culture as an expression of the underlying structure of the mind.

subculture – a group sharing different standards within a larger culture.

symbol – any sound or gesture which stands for a meaning among a group of people.

syntax – in linguistics, parts of grammar which establish the rules or principles of phrase or sentence making.

tale – a creative narrative recognized as fiction for entertainment.

technology – objects made by men and the means of making them.

theoretical linguistics – the study of language which makes a framework and a system for describing what happens in the whole encoding and sentence-making process for all languages.

theory – a system of validated hypotheses which explain phenomena systematically.

totem – a symbol, usually an animal but sometimes a plant, natural force or object, used by a clan as a means of identification, with religious significance.

totemism – a form of religion in which people are thought to be descended from animals, plants, or natural objects.

trade – a form of exchange between communities in which scarce items from one group are exchanged for desirable items from another group.

tribe – a group of bands which speak a common language, share a common culture, and occupy a specific region. The tribe may or may not be a unified political entity.

unilinear descent – establishes group membership exclusively through either the mother's or the father's line.

witchcraft – see *sorcery*. It is often seen as an inborn and unconscious capacity to work evil.

world view – the unexpressed but implicit conceptions of a society or an individual of the limits and workings of their world.

Bibliography

Aberle, David (1961) "Culture and Socialization" F. Hsu, ed. *Psychological Anthropology: Approaches to Culture and Personality.* Homewood, Ill.: Dorsey Press: 381–99.

Aberle, David F., Urie Bronfenbrenner, Eckhard H. Hess, Daniel R. Miller, David H. Schneider and James N. Spuhler (1963) "The Incest Taboo and the Mating Patterns of Animals" *American Anthropologist,* 65:253–65.

Adams, Robert McC. (1966) *The Evolution of Urban Society.* Chicago: Aldine.

Al-Issa, Ihsan and Wayne Dennis, eds. (1970) *Cross-Cultural Studies of Behavior.* New York: Holt, Rinehart and Winston.

Alland, Alexander (1970) *Adaptation in Cultural Evolution: An Approach to Medical Anthropology.* New York: Columbia University Press.

Anderson, Robert T. (1972) *Anthropology: A Perspective on Man.* Belmont, California: Wadsworth Publishing Co.

Ardrey, Robert (1971) *The Social Contract.* New York: Dell.

Arensberg, Conrad (1961) "The Community as Object and Sample" *American Anthropologist,* 63:241–64.

Arensberg, Conrad M. and Arthur H. Niehoff (1964) *Introducing Social Change: A Manual for Americans Overseas.* Chicago: Aldine.

Bagby, P. (1953) "Culture and the Causes of Culture" *American Anthropologist,* 55:535–54.

Balandier, Georges (1971) *Political Anthropology.* New York: Pantheon.

Banton, Michael (1968) "Voluntary Association: Anthropological Aspects" *International Encyclopedia of the Social Sciences,* 16:357–62.

Barber, Bernard (1957) *Social Stratification.* New York: Harcourt Brace Jovanovich.

Barnett, H. G. (1953) *Innovation: The Basis of Cultural Change.* New York: McGraw-Hill.

Barnouw, Victor (1963) *Culture and Personality.* Homewood, Ill.: Dorsey Press.

Barth, Fredrick (1961) *Nomads of South Persia: The Basseri Tribe of the Khamseh Confederacy.* Boston: Little, Brown (Series in Anthropology).

Bascom, William (1965) "The Forms of Folklore-Prose Narratives" *Journal of American Folklore,* 78:3–20.

Bateson, Gregory (1958) *Naven.* Stanford, Calif.: Stanford University Press.

Beals, Ralph and Harry Hoijer (1971) *An Introduction to Anthropology.* New York: Macmillan (4th edition).

Beals, Alan R. with G. and L. Spindler (1973) *Culture in Process.* New York: Holt, Rinehart and Winston (2nd edition).

Beidelman, T. O., ed. (1971) *The Translation of Culture: Essays to E. E. Evans-Pritchard.* London: Tavistock.

Belshaw, Cyril S. (1958) "The Significance of Modern Cults in Melanesian Development" William Lessa and Evon Z. Vogt, eds., *Reader in Comparative Religion: An Anthropological Approach.* New York: Harper and Row.

Benedict, Ruth (1932) "Configurations of Culture in North America" *American Anthropologist,* 34:1–27.

Benedict, Ruth (1959) *Patterns of Culture.* New York: New American Library.

Bennett, John W. (1964) "Myth, Theory and Value in Cultural Anthropology" E. W. Caint and G. T. Bowles, eds., *Fact and Theory in Social Science.* Syracuse: Syracuse University Press.

Bernstein, Basin (1961) "Social Structure, Language and Learning" *Educational Research,* 3:163–76.

Berreman, Gerald D. (1962) *Behind Many Masks: Ethnography and Impression Management in a Himalayan Village.* Ithaca: Society for Applied Anthropology (Monograph No. 4).

Berreman, Gerald D. (1968) "Caste: The Concept of Caste" *International Encyclopedia of the Social Sciences,* 2:333–38.

Bidney, David (1953) *Theoretical Anthropology.* New York: Columbia University Press.

Birdwhistle, Ray L. (1970) *Kinesics and Content: Essays on Body Motion and Communication.* Philadelphia: University of Pennsylvania Press.

Bloch, Marc (1961) *Feudal Society.* Chicago: University of Chicago Press.

Boas, Franz, ed. (1938) *General Anthropology.* New York: Heath.

Boas, Franz (1965) *The Mind of Primitive Man,* revised ed. New York: Free Press.

Boas, Franz (1962) *Primitive Art.* Gloucester, Mass.: Peter Smith.

Boas, Franz (1966) *Race, Language and Culture.* New York: Free Press.

Bock, Philip K. (1970) *Culture Shock: A Reader in Modern Cultural Anthropology.* New York: Random House-Alfred A. Knopf.

Bohannan, Paul (1966) *Social Anthropology.* New York: Holt, Rinehart and Winston.

Bohannan, Paul and George Dalton, eds. (1962) *Markets in Africa.* Evanston, Ill.: Northwestern University Press.

Bohannan, Paul and John Middleton, eds. (1968) *Kinship and Social Organization.* Garden City: Natural History Press (American Museum Source Books in Anthropology).

Bohannan, Paul and John Middleton, eds. (1968) *Marriage, Family, and Residence.* Garden City: Natural History Press (American Museum Source Books in Anthropology).

Bolinger, Dwight (1968) *Aspects of Language.* New York: Harcourt Brace Jovanovich.

Brace, C. Loring (1967) *The Stages of Human Evolution: Human and Cultural Origins.* Englewood Cliffs, N.J.: Prentice-Hall (Foundations of Modern Anthropology).

Braidwood, Robert J. (1960) "The Agricultural Revolution" *Scientific American,* 203:130–41.

Braidwood, Robert J. and Gordon R. Willey (1962) *Courses Toward Urban Life: Archeological Consideration of Some Cultural Alternatives.* Chicago: Aldine (Publications in Anthropology Series, no. 32).

Brew, John O. (1968) *One Hundred Years of Anthropology.* Cambridge, Mass.: Harvard University Press.

Brinton, Crane (1953) *The Shaping of the Modern Mind.* New York: Mentor Books.

Bruner, Edward M. (1970) "Medan: The Role of Kinship in an Indonesian City" William Mangin, ed., *Peasants in Cities: Readings in the Anthropology of Urbanization.*

Burling, Robbins (1970) *Man's Many Voices.* New York: Holt, Rinehart and Winston.

Burling, Robbins (1969) "Linguistics and Ethnographic Description" *American Anthropologist,* 71:817–27.

Butzer, K. W. (1971) *Environment and Anthropology: An Ecological Approach to Prehistory.* 2nd ed. Chicago: Aldine-Atherton.

Calverton, V. F., ed. (1931) *The Making of Man: An Outline of Anthropology.* Westport, Conn.: Greenwood.

Carneiro, Robert L. (1961) "Slash and Burn Cultivation among the Kuikuru and its Implications for Cultural Development in the Amazon Basin" J. Wilbert, ed. *The Evolution of Horticultural Systems in Native South America: Causes and Consequences.* Caracas: Sociedad de Ciencias Naturales La Salle: 47–68.

Carneiro, Robert L. (1970) "A Theory of the Origin of the State" *Science,* 169:733–38.

Chapple, Eliot D. (1970) *Culture and Biological Man: Explorations in Behavioral Anthropology.* New York: Holt, Rinehart and Winston.

Chomsky, Noam (1968) *Language and Mind.* New York: Harcourt Brace Jovanovich.

Clifton, James A., ed. (1970) *Applied Anthropology: Readings in the Uses of the Science of Man.* Boston: Houghton Mifflin (Resources for the Study of Anthropology).

Codere, Helen (1950) *Fighting With Property.* Seattle: University of Washington Press (American Ethnological Society Monograph, 18).

Cohen, Myron L. (1968) "A Case Study of Chinese Family Economy and Development" *Journal of Asian and African Studies,* 3:161–80.

Cohen, Myron L. (1967) "Variations in Complexity Among Chinese Family Groups: The Impact of Modernization" *Transactions of the New York Academy of Sciences,* 29,5:638–47.

Cohen, Yehudi (1968) *Man in Adaptation: The Cultural Present.* Chicago: Aldine.

Cottrell, Fred (1965) *Energy and Society. The Relation Between Energy, Social Change, and Economic Development.* New York: McGraw-Hill.

Cox, Oliver Cromwell (1959) *Caste, Class and Race: A Study in Dynamics.* New York: Monthly Review Press.

Dalton, George (1971) *Economic Anthropology and Development: Essays on Tribal and Peasant Economics.* New York: Basic Books.

Dalton, George, ed. (1967) *Tribal and Peasant Economies: Readings in Economic Anthropology.* Garden City: Natural History Press.

Davenport, W. (1959) "Linear Descent and Descent Groups" *American Anthropologist,* 61:557–73.

Deevy, Edward S., Jr. (1960) "The Human Population" *Scientific American,* 203:194–204.

Despres, Leo A. (1968) "Cultural Pluralism and the Study of Complex Societies" *Current Anthropology,* 9:3–26.

Dobyns, Henry F., Paul L. Doughty and Harold D. Lasswell, eds. (1971) *Peasants, Power, and Applied Social Change.* London: Sage.

Douglas, Mary (1958) "Raffia Cloth Distribution in the Lele Economy" *Africa,* 28:109–22.

Driver, Harold (1964) *Indians of North America.* Chicago: University of Chicago Press.

Dubos, Rene (1968) *So Human an Animal.* New York: Charles Scribner's Sons.

Durkheim, Emile (1965) *The Elementary Forms of the Religious Life.* New York: The Free Press.

Edmonson, Munro S. (1971) *Lore: An Introduction to the Science of Folklore.* New York: Holt, Rinehart and Winston.

Eggan, Fred (1954) "Social Anthropology and the Method of Controlled Comparison" *American Anthropologist,* 56:743–63.

Bibliography

Elkin, A. P. (1964) *The Australian Aborigines.* Garden City: Anchor Books.

Ember, Melvin and Carol R. Ember (1971) "The Conditions Favoring Matrilocal vs. Patrilocal Residence" *American Anthropologist,* 73:571–94.

Erasmus, C. J. (1950) "Patolli, Pachisi, and the Limitation of Possibilities" *Southwestern Journal of Anthropology,* 6:369–81.

Erasmus, C. and W. Smith (1967) "Cultural Anthropology in the United States since 1900" *Southwestern Journal of Anthropology,* 23:11–40.

Ervin-Tripp, Susan M. (1973) *Language Acquisition and Communicative Choice.* Stanford: Stanford University Press.

Evans-Pritchard, Edward E. (1968) *The Nuer: A Description of the Modes of Livelihood and Political Institutions of a Nilotic People.* Oxford: Oxford University Press.

Evans-Pritchard, E. E. (1950) *Witchcraft, Oracles and Magic Among the Azande.* Oxford: Oxford University Press.

Farsoun Samih K. (1970) "Family Structure and Society in Modern Lebanon" Louise E. Sweet, ed., *Peoples and Cultures of the Middle East.* New York: Natural History Press, Vol. 2.

Firth, Raymond (1952) *Elements of Social Organization.* London: C. A. Watts and Company.

Firth, Raymond (1957) *Man and Culture: An Evaluation of Bronislaw Malinowski.* London: Routledge and Kegan Paul.

Firth, Raymond, ed. (1967) *Themes in Economic Anthropology.* London: Tavistock Publications.

Forde, Daryll (1968) "Double Descent Among the Yako" Paul Bohannan and J. Middleton eds., *Marriage, Family and Residence.* Garden City: Natural History Press: 179–92.

Forde, C. Daryll (1963) *Habitat, Economy and Society.* New York: Dutton.

Forde, C. Daryll (1955) "The Nupe" Daryll Forde, ed. *Peoples of the Niger-Benue Confluence.* London: International African Institute (Ethnographic Survey of Africa. Western Africa, part 10): 17–52.

Fortes, Meyer (1969) *Kinship and the Social Order: The Legacy of Lewis Henry Morgan.* Chicago: Aldine.

Fortes, Meyer and E. E. Evans-Pritchard, eds (1940) *African Political Systems.* Oxford: Oxford University Press.

Foster, G. M. (1955) "Peasant Society and the Image of the Limited Good" *American Anthropologist,* 67:293–315.

Fraser, Douglas, ed. (1966) *The Many Faces of Primitive Art: A Critical Anthology.* Englewood Cliffs, N.J.: Prentice-Hall.

Frazer, Sir James George (1931) "Magic and Religion" V. F. Calverton, ed. *The Making of Man: An Outline of Anthropology.* Westport, Conn.: Greenwood: 693–713.

Frazer, Sir James George (1961 reissue) *The New Golden Bough.* Garden City: Anchor Books.

Freud, Sigmund (n.d.) *Civilization and its Discontents.* Garden City: Anchor Books.

Fried, Morton (1960) "On the Evolution of Social Stratification and the State" S. Diamond, ed., *Culture in History: Essays in Honor of Paul Radin.* New York: Columbia University Press: 713–31.

Fried, Morton (1967) *The Evolution of Political Society: An Essay in Political Anthropology.* New York: Random House.

Fried, Morton (1972) *The Study of Anthropology.* New York: Thomas Y. Crowell.

Fried, Morton H., ed. (1968) *Readings in Anthropology.* 2nd ed. New York: Thomas Y. Crowell.

Geertz, Clifford (1963) *Agricultural Involution: The Process of Ecological Change in Indonesia.* Berkeley: University of California Press.

Geertz, Clifford (1965) "The Impact of the Concept of Culture on the Concept of Man" John R. Platt, ed., *New Views of Man.* Chicago: University of Chicago Press.

Geertz, Clifford (1968) "Religion: Anthropological Study" *International Encyclopedia of the Social Sciences,* 13. New York: Macmillan.

Gellner, Ernest (1969) *Saints of the Atlas.* Chicago: University of Chicago Press (The Nature of Human Society Series).

Gibbs, James L., Jr. (1965) "The Kpelle of Liberia" James L. Gibbs, ed., *Peoples of Africa.* New York: Holt, Rinehart & Winston.

Godlier, Maurice (1971) "Salt Currency and the Circulation of Commodities Among the Baruya of New Guinea" George Dalton, ed., *Studies in Economic Anthropology.* Washington, D.C.: American Anthropological Association (Anthropological Studies No. 7).

Goldschmidt, Walter (1971) *Exploring the Ways of Mankind.* New York: Holt, Rinehart and Winston, 2nd ed.

Goode, William J. (1963) *World Revolution and Family Patterns.* New York: Free Press.

Goodenough, Ward (1961) "Comment on Cultural Evolution" *Daedalus,* 90:521-28.

Goodenough, Ward (1956) "Componential Analysis and the Study of Meaning" *Language,* 32:195-216.

Goodenough, Ward (1970) *Description and Comparison in Cultural Anthropology.* Chicago: Aldine (Lewis H. Morgan Lecture Series).

Goodenough, Ward, ed. (1964) *Explorations in Cultural Anthropology: Essays in Honor of George Murdock,* New York: McGraw-Hill.

Goodenough, Ward (1956a) "Residence Rules" *Southwestern Journal of Anthropology,* 12:22-37.

Goodenough, Ward (1965) "Rethinking Status" and "Role: Toward a General Model of the Cultural Organization of Social Relationships" Michael Benton, ed., *The Relevance of Models for Social Anthropology, ASA Monographs 1.* New York: Praeger.

Goodfellow, D. M. (1973) *Principles of Economic Sociology: The Economics of Primitive Life As Illustrated from the Bantu Peoples of South and East Africa.* Westport, Conn.: Negro Universities Press (Reprint of 1939 edition).

Goodman, Mary Ellen (1967) *The Individual and Culture.* Homewood, Ill.: Dorsey Press.

Goody, Jack, ed. (1972) *Developmental Cycle in Domestic Groups.* New York: Cambridge University Press (Papers in Social Anthropology, No. 1).

Gough, E. Kathleen (1968) "The Nayars and the Definition of Marriage" Paul Bohannan and J. Middleton, eds., *Marriage, Family and Residence.* New York: Natural History Press: 49-71.

Graburn, Nelson H. (1971) *Readings in Kinship and Social Structure.* New York: Harper and Row.

Greenberg, Joseph H. (1968) *Anthropological Linguistics: An Introduction.* New York: Random House.

Gulliver, P. (1968) "Age Differentiation" *International Encyclopedia of the Social Sciences,* 1:157-62.

Hallowell, A. Irving (1955) *Culture and Experience.* Philadelphia: University of Pennsylvania Press.

Hammond, Peter B. (1971) *An Introduction to Cultural and Social Anthropology.* New York: Macmillan.

Harris, Marvin (1965) "The Cultural Ecology of India's Sacred Cattle" *Current Anthropology,* 7:51-66.

Harris, Marvin (1971) *Culture, Man, and Nature: An Introduction to General Anthropology.* New York: Thomas Y. Crowell Company.

Harris, Marvin (1968) *The Rise of Anthropological Theory.* New York: Thomas Y. Crowell.

Haviland, W. A. (1970) "Tikal, Guatemala and Mesomerican Urbanism" *World Archaeology,* 2:186–198.

Haviland, W. A. (1974) "Farming, Seafaring and Bilocal Residence on the Coast of Maine" *Man in the Northeast* 6:31–44.

Hawkins, Gerald S. (1965) *Stonehenge Decoded.* Garden City: Doubleday.

Hays, H. R. (1965) *From Ape to Angel: An Informal History of Social Anthropology.* New York: Alfred A. Knopf.

Helm, Hune (1962) "The Ecological Approach in Anthropology" *American Journal of Sociology,* 67:630–49.

Herskovits, Melville (1952) *Economic Anthropology,* New York: Alfred A. Knopf.

Hjelmslev, Louis (1970) *Language: An Introduction.* Francis J. Whitfield, trans., Madison: University of Wisconsin Press.

Hodgen Margaret (1964) *Early Anthropology in the Sixteenth and Seventeenth Centuries.* Philadelphia: University of Pennsylvania Press.

Hoebel, E. Adamson (1966) *Anthropology: The Study of Man.* New York: McGraw-Hill (3rd ed.).

Hoebel, E. Adamson (1954) *The Law of Primitive Man: A Study in Comparative Legal Dynamics.* Cambridge: Harvard University Press.

Honigmann, J. (1954) *Culture and Personality.* New York: Harper and Row.

Hsu, Francis (1961) *Psychological Anthropology: Approaches to Culture and Personality.* Homewood, Ill.: Dorsey Press.

Hubert, Henri and Marcel Mauss (1964) *Sacrifice.* Chicago: University of Chicago Press.

Hymes, Dell (1964) *Language in Culture and Society: A Reader in Linguistics and Anthropology.* New York: Harper and Row.

Hymes, Dell, ed. (1972) *Reinventing Anthropology.* New York: Pantheon.

Inkeles, A. and D. J. Levinson (1954) "National Character: The Study of Modal Personality and Socio-Cultural Systems" in G. Lindzey (ed.) *Handbook of Social Psychology.* Cambridge: Addison-Wesley: 977–1020.

Jopling, Carol F. (1971) *Art and Aesthetics in Primitive Societies: A Critical Anthology.* New York: E. P. Dutton.

Jorgensen, Joseph (1972) *The Sun Dance Religion.* Chicago: University of Chicago Press.

Jung, Carl (1961) *Memories, Dreams, Reflections.* New York: Vintage Books.

Kaplan, David (1972) *Culture Theory.* Englewood Cliffs, N.J.: Prentice-Hall (Foundations of Modern Anthropology).

Kaplan, David (1968) "The Superorganic: Science or Metaphysics" Robert Manners and David Kaplan, eds. *Theory in Anthropology: A Sourcebook.* Chicago: Aldine-Atherton.

Kardiner, Abram and Edward Preble (1961) *They Studied Men.* New York: Mentor.

Keesing, R. M. and F. M. Keesing (1971) *New Perspectives in Cultural Anthropology.* New York: Holt, Rinehart and Winston.

Kluckhohn, Clyde (1949)*Mirror For Man.* New York: McGraw-Hill.

Krader, Lawrence (1965) *Formation of the State.* Englewood Cliffs, N.J.: Prentice-Hall (Foundations of Modern Anthropology).

Kroeber, A. L. and Clyde Kluckhohn (1952) *Culture: A Critical Review of Concepts and*

Definitions. Harvard University (Papers of the Peabody Museum of American Archaeology and Ethnology, 47).

Kroeber, A. L. (1939) "Cultural and Natural Areas of Native North America." Berkeley, Calif.: University of California Pub. in *American Archaeology and Ethnology,* vol. 38.

Kroeber, Alfred (1958) "Totem and Taboo: An Ethnologic Psychoanalysis" William Lessa and Evon Z. Vogt, eds., *Reader in Comparative Religion: An Anthropological Approach.* New York: Harper and Row.

Kuhn, Thomas S. (1968) *The Structure of Scientific Revolutions.* Chicago: University of Chicago Press (International Encyclopedia of Unified Science, vol. 2, no. 2)

Kummer, Hans (1971) *Primate Societies: Group Techniques of Ecological Adaptation.* Chicago: Aldine.

Kuper, Hilda (1965) "The Swazi of Swaziland" James L. Gibbs, ed. *Peoples of Africa.* New York: Holt, Rinehart and Winston: 479–511.

Kushner, Gilibert (1969) *Anthropology of Complex Societies.* Stanford: Stanford University Press.

Laguna, Grace A. de (1966) *On Existence and the Human World.* New Haven: Yale University Press

Lanning, Edward P. (1967) *Peru Before the Incas.* Englewood Cliffs, N.J.: Prentice-Hall.

Lanternari, Vittorio (1963) *The Religions of the Oppressed.* New York: Mentor.

Leach, Edmund (1962) "On Certain Unconsidered Aspects of Double Descent Systems" *Man,* 214:13–34.

Leach, Edmund (1962) "The Determinants of Differential Cross-Cousin Marriage" *Man,* 62:238.

Leach, Edmund (1963) "The Determinants of Differential Cross-Cousin Marriage" *Man,* 63:87.

Leach, Edmund (1965) *Political Systems of Highland Burma.* Boston: Beacon Press.

Leach, Edmund (1961) *Rethinking Anthropology.* London: Athione Press.

LeClair, Edward and Harold K. Schneider, eds. (1968) *Economic Anthropology: Readings in Theory and Analysis.* New York: Holt, Rinehart and Winston.

Lee, Richard B. (1969) "Kung Bushman Subsistence: An Input-Output Analysis" Andrew P. Vayda, ed., *Environment and Cultural Behavior.* Garden City: Natural History Press: 47–49.

Lee, Richard B. and Irven DeVore, eds. (1968) *Man the Hunter.* Chicago: Aldine.

Ledds, Anthony and Andrew P. Vayda, eds. (1965) *Man, Culture and Animals: The Role of Animals in Human Ecological Adjustments.* Washington, D.C.: American Association for the Advancement of Science.

Lenski, Garhard (1966) *Power and Privilege: A Theory of Social Stratification.* New York: McGraw-Hill.

Lessa, William A. and Evon Z. Vogt, eds. (1972) *Reader in Comparative Religion: An Anthropological Approach.* New York: Harper and Row.

LeVine, Robert A. (1973) *Culture, Behavior and Personality.* Chicago: Aldine.

Lévi-Strauss, Claude (1969) *The Elementary Structures of Kinship.* Boston: Beacon Press.

Lévi-Strauss, Claude (1971) "The Family" Harry L. Shapiro, ed., *Man, Culture and Society.* London: Oxford University Press: 333–57.

Lévi-Strauss, Claude (1963) *Structural Anthropology.* New York: Basic Books.

Lévi-Strauss, Claude (1963) *Totemism.* Boston: Beacon Press.

Lewis, I. M. (1965) "Problems in the Comparative Study of Unilineal Descent" Michael Banton, ed., *The Relevance of Models for Social Organization* (A.S.A. Monograph No.1).

Lienhardt, Godfrey (1971) "Religion" Harry Shapiro, ed., *Man, Culture and Society.* London: Oxford University Press: 382–401.

Leinhardt, Godfrey (1964) *Social Anthropology.* London: Oxford University Press.

Linton, Ralph (1936) *The Study of Man.* New York: Appleton-Century Crofts.

Lounsbury, F. (1964a) "The Structural Analysis of Kinship Semantics" Horace G. Lunt, ed., *Proceedings of the Ninth International Congress of Linguists.* The Hague: Mouton: 1073–93.

Lowie, Robert (1966) *Culture and Ethnology.* New York: Basic Books.

Lyons, John (1970) *Noam Chomsky,* New York, Viking Press.

Mair, Lucy (1971) *Marriage,* Baltimore: Penguin.

Mair, Lucy (1969) *Witchcraft.* New York: McGraw-Hill.

Malefijt, Annemarie de Waal (1969) *Religion and Culture: An Introduction to Anthropology of Religion.* London: Macmillan.

Malinowski, Bronislaw (1922) *Argonauts of the Western Pacific.* New York: Dutton.

Maybury-Lewis, David (1960) "Parallel Descent and the Apinaye Anomaly" *Southwestern Journal of Anthropology,* 16:191–216.

Mead, Margaret (1928) *Coming of Age in Samoa.* New York: Morrow.

Mead, Margaret (1970) *Culture and Commitment,* Garden City: Natural History Press.

Middleton, John, ed. (1970) *From Child to Adult: Studies in the Anthropology of Education.* Garden City: Natural History Press (American Museum Source Books in Anthropology).

Montagu, Ashley (1964) *The Concept of Race.* London: Free Press of Glencoe, Collier-Macmillan.

Montagu, Ashley (1964) *Man's Most Dangerous Myth: The Fallacy of Race:* New York: The World Publishing Company, (4th ed.).

Murdock, George Peter (1965) *Social Structure.* New York: Free Press.

Murphy, Robert (1971) *The Dialectics of Social Life: Alarms and Excursions in Anthropological Theory.* New York: Basic Books.

Murphy, Robert and Leonard Kasdan (1959) "The Structure of Parallel Cousin Marriage" *American Anthropologist,* 61:17–29.

Nash, Manning (1966) *Primitive and Peasant Economic Systems.* San Francisco: Chandler Publishing Co.

Needham, Rodney (1973) *Belief, Language and Experience.* Chicago: University of Chicago Press.

Nimkoff, M. F. and Russell Middleton (1960–61) "Types of Family and Types of Economy" *The American Journal of Sociology,* 66,3:215–26.

Ortiz, Alfonso (1969) *The Tewa World.* Chicago: University of Chicago Press.

Oswalt, Wendell H. (1970) *Understanding Our Culture.* New York: Holt, Rinehart and Winston.

Oswalt, Wendell H. (1972) *Other Peoples Other Customs. World Ethnography and Its History.* New York: Holt, Rinehart and Winston.

Otten, Charlotte N. (1971) *Anthropology and Art: Reading in Cross-Cultural Aesthetics.* Garden City: Natural History Press (American Museum Sourcebooks in Anthropology).

Ottenberg, Phoebe (1965) "The Afikpo Ibo of Eastern Nigeria" James L. Gibbs, ed., *Peoples of Africa.* New York: Holt, Rinehart and Winston.

Ottenbein, Keith F. (1971) *The Evolution of War.* New Haven: HRAF Press.

Parsons, Talcott (1958) "Religious Perspectives in Sociology and Social Psychology" William Lessa and Evon Z. Vogt, eds., *Reader in Comparative Religion:* An Anthropological Approach. New York: Harper and Row.

Pelto, Tertti J. (1966) *The Nature of Anthropology.* Columbus: Charles E. Merrill (Social Science Perspectives).

Penniman, T. K. (1965) *A Hundred Years of Anthropology.* London: Duckworth.

Piddocke, Stuart (1965) "The Potlatch System of the Southern Kwakiutl: A New Perspective" *Southwestern Journal of Anthropology,* 21:244-64.

Pospisil, Leopold (1971) *Anthropology of Law: A Comparative Theory.* New York: Harper and Row.

Powdermaker, Hortense (1966) *Stranger and Friend: The Way of An Anthropologist.* New York: Norton.

Price-Williams, D. R., ed. (1970) *Cross-Cultural Studies: Selected Readings.* Baltimore: Penguin (Penguin Modern Psychology Readings).

Pumpelly, R. (1908) *Explorations in Turkestan: Expedition of 1904: Prehistoric Civilization of Anau.* Washington, D.C.: Publications of the Carnegie Institute, #73, Vol. 1.

Rodman, Hyman (1968) "Class Culture" *International Encyclopedia of the Social Sciences,* 15:332-37.

Sahlins, Marshall (1968) *Tribesmen.* Englewood Cliffs, N.J.: Prentice-Hall (Foundations of Modern Anthropology).

Sapir, E. (1924) "Culture, Genuine or Spurious?" *American Journal of Sociology,* 29:401-29.

Sapir, E. (1917) "Do We Need a Superorganic?" *American Anthropologist,* 19:441-47.

Sapir, E. (1921) *Language.* New York: Harcourt, Brace.

Sapir, E. (1916) *Time Perspective in Aboriginal American Culture: A Study in Method.* Ottawa: Geological Society of Canada (Memoir 90, Anthropological Series, no. 13).

Schaller, George B. (1963) *The Mountain Gorilla.* Chicago: Chicago University Press.

Service, Elman R. (1966) *The Hunters.* Englewood Cliffs, N.J.: Prentice-Hall (Foundations of Modern Anthropology)

Service, Elman R. (1971) *Primitive Social Organization: An Evolutionary Perspective.* New York: Random House (2nd ed.).

Shapiro, Harry, ed. (1960) *Man, Culture and Society.* New York: Oxford University Press.

Shinnie, Margaret (1970) *Ancient African Kingdoms.* New York: New American Library (Mentor).

Slobin, Dan I. (1971) *Psycholinguistics.* Glenview, Ill.: Scott, Foresman.

Smith, Raymond (1970) "Social Stratification in the Caribbean" Leonard Plotnicov and Arthur Tudin, ed., *Essays in Comparative Social Stratification.* Pittsburgh: University of Pittsburgh Press.

Speck, Frank G. (1920) "Penobscot Shamanism" *Memoirs of the American Anthropology Association.* VI:239-88.

Spiro, Melford E. (1954) "Is the Family Universal?" *American Anthropologist,* 56:839-46.

Spiro, Melford E. (1966) "Religion: Problems of Definition and Explanation" Michael Banton, ed., *Anthropological Approaches to the Study of Religion,* ASA Monograph #s. London: Tavistock Publications.

Stanner, W. E. H. (1968) "Radcliffe-Brown, A. R." *International Encyclopedia of the Social Sciences,* 13. New York: Macmillan.

Stephens, William N. (1963) *The Family in Cross-Cultural Perspective.* New York: Holt, Rinehart and Winston.

Steward, Julian H. (1972) *Theory of Culture Change: The Methodology of Multilinear Evolution.* Urbana, Ill.: University of Illinois Press.

Tax, Sol, ed. (1962) *Anthropology Today: Selections.* Chicago: University of Chicago Press.

Thomas, W. L., ed. (1956) *Man's Role in Changing the Face of the Earth.* Chicago: University of Chicago Press.

Tumin, Melvin M. (1967) *Social Stratification: The Forms and Functions of Inequality.* Englewood Cliffs, N.J.: Prentice-Hall (Foundations of Modern Sociology).

Turnbull, Colin (1961) *The Forest People.* New York: Simon & Schuster.

Turner, V. W. (1969) *The Ritual Process.* Chicago: Aldine.

Turner, V. W. (1957) *Schism and Continuity in an African Society.* Manchester: The University Press.

Tylor, Sir Edward B. (1931) "Animism" V. F. Calverton, ed., *The Making of Man: An Outline of Anthropology.* New York: The Modern Library.

Tylor, Edward Burnett (1971) *Primitive Culture: Researches Into the Development of Mythology, Philosophy, Religion, Language, Art and Customs.* London: J. Murray.

Valentine, Charles A. (1968) *Culture and Poverty.* Chicago: University of Chicago Press.

Van Gennep, Arnold (1960) *The Rites of Passage.* Chicago: University of Chicago Press.

Vansina, Jan (1965) *Oral Tradition: A Study in Historical Methodology,* translated by H. M. Wright. Chicago: Aldine.

Vayda, Andrew P. (1961) "A Re-Examination of Northwest Coast Economic Systems" *Transactions of the New York Academy of Sciences,* 2nd series, 23:618–24.

Vayda, Andrew P. (1961) "Expansion and Warfare Among Swidden Agriculturalists" *American Anthropologist,* 63:346–58.

Voget, F. W. (1960) "Man and Culture: An Essay in Changing Anthropological Interpretation" *American Anthropologist,* 62:943–65.

Wagner, Philip L. (1960) *The Human Use of the Earth.* Glencoe, Ill.: Free Press.

Wallace, Anthony F. C. (1970) *Culture and Personality.* New York: Random House (2nd ed.)

Wallace, Anthony F. C. (1965) "The Problem of the Psychological Validity of Componential Analysis" *American Anthropologist, Special Publication,* 67, no. 5, part 2:229–48.

Wallace, Anthony F. C. (1956) "Revitalization Movements" *American Anthropologist,* 58:264–81.

Wardhaugh, Ronald (1972) *Introduction to Linguistics.* New York: McGraw-Hill.

Westermarck, Edward A. (1926) *A Short History of Marriage.* New York: Macmillan.

White, Leslie (1959) *The Evolution of Culture: The Development of Civilization to the Fall of Rome.* New York: McGraw-Hill.

White, Leslie (1949) *The Science of Culture: A Study of Man and Civilization.* New York: Farrar and Strauss.

White, Leslie (1940) "The Symbol: The Origin and Basis of Human Behavior" *Philosophy of Science,* 7:451–63.

Whiting, Beatrice B., ed. (1963) *Six Cultures: Studies of Child Rearing.* New York: Wiley.

Whiting, J. and J. Child (1953) *Child Training and Personality: A Cross-Cultural Study:* New York: McGraw-Hill.

Wolf, Eric (1966) *Peasants.* Englewood Cliffs, N.J.: Prentice-Hall (Foundations of Modern Anthropology).

Wolf, Eric (1959) *Sons of the Shaking Earth.* Chicago: University of Chicago Press.

INDEX

Levirate, definition of, 173
Lévi-Strauss, Claude
  and exogamy, 173
  and symbolic polarities, 40
  and technology, 244
  and totemism, 314
Lineage, definition of, 198–199
Linguistics, 88–89, 91, 94–96
Linton, Ralph
  and diffusion, 365
  and the individual in society, 13–14
Lorenz, Konrad, and overpopulation, 396
Lowie, Robert
  and associations, 220
  and diffusion, 365
  and reciprocity among Crow Indians, 246
Lyell, Charles, 30

McFee, Malcolm, and modernization of Blackfeet
  Indians, 375
McLuhan, Marshall, and the future, 401–402
Magic, and religion, 312–313
    See also Witchcraft
Mair, Lucy, and witchcraft, 322
Malinowski, Bronislaw
  definition of law, 291–292
  and diffusion, 365
  and Kula trading system, 247–248
  and levels of needs, 39
  and personality, 114–115
  and religion, 308
  and social order in Trobriand Islands, 286
Marriage
  and choice of mate, 173–174
  in matrilineal descent group, 195
  and sexual access, 170
Marx, Karl, 30
  and social class system, 223–224
Masai, and age-grouping, 215
Matrilineal descent, description of, 193–195
Matrilocal residence, 179–180
Maya
  loss of data on, 403
Mbuti pygmies (Congolese Ituri), 141, 144
  and crime, 294
  hunting style of, 143
  and social control, 295, 297
Mead, Margaret, 173
  and individual personality, 114–115
  and Manus and cultural change, 379

and Samoan adolescents, 112–113
  and sexual roles, 181–183
Melanesian big man, 269, 271, 459
Melanesians and mana, 311
Mendel, Gregor, 365
Mesolithic
  cultivation and domestication during, 70–71
  cultures during, 71
Milgram, Stanley, and overcrowding, 396
Modal personality
  definition of, 116
  of Russians, 119
Modern Blackfeet Montanans (McFee), 375
Modernization, and culture change, 371–382
Moiety, definition of, 199
Monogamy, 173
Montagu, Ashley
  definition of family, 175
Morgan, Lewis
  and descent groups, 201
  and social evolution 33
Morphemes, definition of, 95
Murdock, George
  and cultural change, 378
  and descent groups, 201
  and diffusion, 365
Music, 344–346, 534
  diffusion of, 365
  elements of, 341–342
  functions of, 342–343
Musical instruments, 343–345, 531–533
Myth
  description of, 337–338
  among Penobscot Indians, 287

Nambikwara, family line of, 184–186
Natchez Indians, social class system of, 223–224
National character, 117, 119
  studies on, 120
Navajo Indians
  fusion of, 34
  political organization of, 266
  study of, 8–10
  and witchcraft, 323
Nayar (India), consanguine family of, 177
Neanderthal man, 66–68
  as hunter, 67
  physical traits of, 67
Neo-evolutionism
  cultural advances during, 72–73